The Slave State

ALBERT SPEER

The Slave State

Heinrich Himmler's Masterplan for SS Supremacy

Translation by Joachim Neugroschel

WEIDENFELD AND NICOLSON

London

Contents

Himmler's state within the state, assisted by Hitler. Nazi leaders with limited intellectual quality. Hitler's successes with the help of the intelligentsia of the Weimar Republic. Industrial failures of the SS because of mediocre SS leaders. Hitler's war aim: extermination of the Jews. Problems of habituation. The human being as a production factor. General manager of the industry of a continent. Departmental thinking with no moral component. The consequences of a totalitarian state.

Himmler's plans (December 1941) for exploiting the manpower of Jews. Counterforces. Concentration camps for Pohl. Joint industrialization plans. Test case Buchenwald. Himmler's industrial aims. 46,000 prisoners slated. Hitler's counterdecision: prisoners in private industry.

SS leaders circumvent Hitler's decision and promote concentration camp armaments empire. Character description of Himmler. Himmler threatens and Buchenwald commandant is blackmailed. Concentration camp factories as alien bodies in the armaments structure. Himmler tries to have armaments people sent to concentration camps. Himmler's figures: one-third of fighter planes, one-third of rifle barrels. A devastating comparison of performances.

Prisoners as investments. Considerate treatment not for sentimental reasons. Corruption and concealment. Visit to Mauthausen. A false front. Was Himmler deceived too? Primitive construction methods. Catastrophic conditions at Auschwitz; other camps evaluated positively. Immediate delivery of plumbing material. Do new barracks for concentration camps make sense? Epidemics due to overcrowding. Two sets of statistics for mortality. Half of all deaths concealed. Himmler plans mass kidnapping in Germany.

Kaltenbrunner and Ohlendorf go after my department chief Schieber. Himmler involved. No loss of prestige possible in the system. Gauleiter Hanke mounts a massive attack. Schieber's high treason. Bormann supports intrigue. Hitler trivializes and adds fuel. Kaltenbrunner's information. Himmler and Bormann do not transmit the truth. Hitler orders Schieber's dismissal. Berger: Speer's position very weak now. Schieber's achievements. Bormann gets two other department heads dismissed.

SS state within the state. Himmler's agents in the ministries. Kranefuss regards himself as Himmler's deputy in the Ministry cf Economy. Ohlendorf attacks the "self-responsibility" of industry. Himmler rejects the capitalist system. Kranefuss dismissed by Himmler. Hitler confirms his trust in the "self-responsibility" of industry. Himmler confers with Funk and Landfried. Funk's life-style. My expansionist policies fail. Ohlendorf's power. Ohlendorf's intentions as a secretary-general of industrial management with Hayler as state secretary of a mammoth ministry. An end to Ohlendorf's plans.

National Socialist industrial ideology before 1933. Ohlendorf against the efficiency principle. My counterspeech in Essen. Ohlendorf: Instead of the optimal factory, work in small plants. Against late capitalism and bolshevism. Quality versus quantity. Ideas stronger than production figures. Cultural values versus "civilization." Rubber wall of ideological miscalculations. Emotional worlds.

Industry in the protectorate an SS domain. The SS pushed back. Hitler's praise for Skoda's armaments contributions. SS resistance to Hernekamp's authority. Request to Lammers to maintain Reich authority. SD assignments. The reason for excesses is the force of events. Prague SD versus Speer's ministry. SD demands for regional control versus Speer's demand for direct control. Speer's champion in Prague stripped of power. Attempt to woo people away.

SD reports are superficial nonsense. SD on the bureaucratization of armaments controls. The SD industrial information service threatened by Gestapo competition. Bormann's letter against the SD. Ohlendorf offers himself and the SD to the Allies in 1945. Hitler's directive for the protection of the armaments industry. Agreement with the Gestapo, a question of power position. Director General Winter of Opel seeks protection. After the 20th of July, 1944, a purge demanded in industry. Attacks against Lüschen of Siemens and against Telefunken are refuted. Kaltenbrunner against the shipyard industry. Proceeding against Purucker. Telephones tapped by the Gestapo.

Petitions against members of my ministry. Pleiger versus Rohland. Disagreement regarded as sabotage. Industry converts to peacetime production. Meinberg accuses Sohl of crimes against the state. Denunciation of poor leadership in air armaments. Frontal attack by SS headquarters. Accusation of sabotage. Himmler to have decision-making power in air armaments. A turning point in war expected with Himmler's execution authorization. Sauckel too: Heads must roll. Letter to Hitler about distrust in the Party. System of coercion rejected.

An Untersturmführer forces Field Marshal Milch to manufacture a utopian remote firing weapon. One year later, Himmler's project of a rapid U-boat. Naval staff pretends agreement. Failure of SS pistol. Independent high-frequency research of SS in concentration camps. Electrical remote influence by atmosphere. Chimney emissions as source of alcohol. Oil from geraniums. Fuel from fir tree roots. Ohlendorf complains about atomic research.

Pohl tries to gain control of the German stone industry. General Ziegler's assignment and Frank's Commission for Simplification of Administration. Highest-level fight over 18 employees. Accusation of squandering of manpower by the Armaments Ministry. Himmler would like to appropriate data bank. He is dismissed as commander in chief of army armaments by Hitler.

Hitler approves control of the SS armaments factories. Himmler on his plans for an industrial concern. Himmler takes over the Weiss concern as the nucleus of his armaments empire. Light-metal foundry rejected. Production of wndow frames. Porsche's secret weapon. Jüttner to manufacture generators. Pohl to found peatworks. Himmler promises but does not come through.

Himmler confiscates quartz deposits. Interest in gold, diamonds, and copper in an African colonial empire. Dandelions for rubber production. 800 kilograms per acre planned. 15 kilograms per acre achieved. Keppler offers new process for lead-zinc foundries. Manganese expedition of the SS in Poland. Armaments factories, blast furnaces, and steelworks in Poland. Himmler's interests in brown-coal mines. Pleiger ordered to hunt oil as a joint project with the SS. Himmler takes over a chemical factory that produces the poison gas sarin.

Filling gaps. SS infiltration in Peenemünde. Hitler's A-4 assignment with German manpower. Hitler's A-4 counterassignment with concentration camp prisoners. Himmler gives orders within my jurisdiction. Scandalous conditions in the Central Works. Inspections, help. Edicts and counteredicts on distribution of labor for the A-4 project. The production attained.

My negative standpoint. Himmler assigns cave research. Kammler's success in the construction of the Central Works. Himmler's underwater factories. Underground fuel manufacturing. Six concrete bunkers by Dorsch. Hitler's successor. Bizarre events. Rheumatism instead of infarct. Koch's suspicion. The political doctor. Himmler forces a conference. Hitler goes back on his word.

The Fighter Plane Staff and Kammler. His unusual powers. Höss in trouble. 425,000 square meters of cave space. Kammler's utopian authorizations. Bizarre implementation in a vacuum. Plenipotentiary of the plenipotentiary. Sold-out.

No mercy in the Jewish question. Goebbels's demand in September 1941 for the evacuation of all Berlin Jews. Bormann's circular on the protection of Jews in the armaments industry. Hitler's directive to remove all Jews from the German armaments industry. Goebbels attacks intellectual protectors of Jews. The Berlin evacuation. 4,000 Jews not to be found. Dr. Ehrlich and other Jews obtain ministry passes. Jews protected by Germans. Goebbels's triumph. The bridges are burned.

Heydrich on the fate of the Jews. Himmler's drastic order to remove all Jews from Polish factories. Army departments versus SS departments. Attempts to protect Jews. Compromise for Warsaw. Two days later, all Jews shipped to concentration camps. Keitel more drastic than Himmler. Keitel's order impracticable. Hitler to Sauckel: Polish Jews remain. Himmler: But only in concentration camp factories. Frank complains about Himmler's actions. Warsaw uprising.

Himmler's series of speeches on the murder of the Jews. Official speeches require Hitler's approval. Himmler promises the Gauleiters to kill all Jews by the end of 1943, but continues using them for his industrial purposes. Annihilation of an industrial concentration camp. Maurer not oriented about Auschwitz. The Jewish reservoir in Poland exhausted. Labor report lists 1,400,000 able-bodied Jews in the Generalgouvernement in 1942. Hence, Hilberg's figure of 3 million Polish Jews killed must be correct.

Uncertainty about the fate of the Jews in the armaments industry in Upper Silesia. Lodz Ghetto is not evacuated. Greiser wires Himmler that Speer is about to interfere in regard to Jews. 100,000 Hungarian Jews to build bunkers. Jews for the armaments industry in the Reich. Only 50,000 able to work. Sauckel is opposed. Prisoner statistics. The goal is the annihilation of the prisoners. Himmler and Kaltenbrunner pay a visit.

Epilogue: The Somber Final Victory

Active lower echelons in the SS. The SS peacetime program of 1941. SS confiscation of factories in East European territories. Himmler's program to have prisoners do construction work. Kammler's SS brigades are organized. Governmental or concentration camp factories? 4 million concentration camp inmates slated by Kammler for East European program. Himmler's construction estimates of 9.4 billion marks annually require 14.5 million prisoners. The icy resoluteness of Hitler and Himmler.

Foreword

My ORIGINAL PLAN was to write a book about German armaments in the Second World War. I thought it best to begin with the most difficult chapter, that of the role of the SS in the armaments industry and in the war economy. While preparing this chapter, I stumbled upon the writings of the SS Reichsführer in the Federal Archives at Koblenz. To my surprise I found, neatly arranged, all the documents that I had sensed existed in those times: the protocols of Himmler's attempts to man the war economy with his own people and to build up his own industrial empire. The material was so rich that it soon exceeded the scope of a chapter; hence I resolved to devote my book to the failure of SS industrial efforts.

I had always seen these events from the perspective of my ministry, the Führer's headquarters, and my proximity to Hitler. Now as I read Himmler's correspondence I realized more than ever before that I had been a part of—not the center of—the events. Reluctantly I forced myself back into that world. I cannot say that it was a painful process, for my relationship to these documents had been greatly depersonalized during the past thirty years. I also felt that it might be helpful to make use of this material in some form.

As a witness, I may be accused of allowing my subjectivity to interfere and of not always evaluating the material as objectively as a scholar might have done. Involuntary memories emerged; personal likes and dislikes of the people involved were reflected.

Often I was aware of having repressed things in order to shield myself against guilt feelings. Now, confronted with these documents, I tried to face the events in which I had been entangled.

A scholar of the postwar generation, especially one unfamiliar with the seductions and dangers of any position of power, would have a difficult time feeling his way into the atmosphere of the Third Reich—an atmosphere that the documents themselves can evoke only imperfectly. The results of his research in this area would certainly have to be different from my presentation.

I have attempted to break down the subject, even though the mass of material appears confused and chaotic, not only in the jumble of documents but also in the tangle of reality. The disorderliness of Himmler's empire and the unsystematic nature of the material reflect the character of the events and not an inability on my part to put things in order. In short, the seeming disarray of the material in this book arises from the disorder inherent in that empire. The closest to a unifying element that can be found is the bizarre way that Himmler tried to intercede in areas of which he did not have the least understanding. These attempts caused him to chase after fantastic notions—for instance, his *idée fixe* of making gasoline from the roots of fir trees.

ALBERT SPEER

August 15, 1980

Acknowledgments

I WOULD LIKE TO EXPRESS my gratitude to the head of Deutsche Verlags-anstalt, Ulrich Frank-Planitz, and to Wolf Jobst Siedler, my friend of many years and the editor of my first two books, as well as to Dr. Ernst Ludwig Ehrlich, Ulrich Volz, and Adelbert Reif. I would also like to express my hearty thanks to Dr. Alfred Wagner, director of archives, and to Frau Hedwig Singer of the German Federal Archives, as well as to my sister-in-law Paula Speer for her patience in typing the handwritten manuscript.

PART ONE

The SS and the Self-Responsibility of Industry

Chapter 1

Background

IN THE SPRING of 1944 Hitler approved of Himmler's proposal to build an SS-owned industrial concern in order to make the SS permanently independent of the state budget. Hitler cited similar reasons when he asked me to support Himmler's project. Thus Himmler achieved something he had been aspiring to for years. Furthermore, Hitler's consent made it clear that he was not aiming at any rigid state authority even for peacetime. Since 1933 he had been undermining the state apparatus by emphasizing the Party as the element determining policies, politics, and administration. However, we had always suspected that his goal was the primacy of the Party over the state and that he would not permit anything that might weaken the Party. But now it turned out that he wanted to secure a position for the SS that would keep it independent of the state *and* the Party. In case a successor should try to use the state budget as an instrument to curtail the power of the SS and the Gestapo, Hitler wanted to create a financial source to provide the SS with its own budget. Such reflections were in keeping with the overall organization of the Reich. Even the notion of an SS independent down to its own budget originated in Hitler's tendency always to promote oppositions in order to create conflicting forces in domestic politics. These conflicting forces would then be bound to struggle against one another in the distant future as well. The system was tried and tested; the creation of states within the state had long since been introduced into the political structure of the Reich. The minister of food, for instance, was confronted with an organization of farmers acting independently in the Party's Department of Agriculture. The German Labor Front formed a financially independent counterpart to the Ministry of Labor as well as to the state wielders of educational policies. And since 1942 the leading industrialists had taken over administrative predominance of the state in the area of production.

It was not only Himmler's hunger for power that stood behind the building of this new state within the state. Bizarre political considerations were also involved, as well as those theories of self-sufficient power that actually negate the state. However, Himmler's attempt to construct his own economic empire never reached its goal. His methods were too brutal and at the same time too amateurish.

I remember the times before 1933 when I was active in the lowest echelons of the Party. I was already surprised at the paltry intellectual level and the lack of intellectual members. At times, in those days, the Party struck me as an organized troop that was easy to lead precisely because the lower-level leaders had no leadership qualities. If these mediocre leaders had taken over the economy after the Nazi rise to power, they would have accomplished as little as Himmler did when he tried to build industrial complexes in the concentration camps. With his Party comrades alone, Hitler could never have ruled. His triumphs, which astonished the world for a time, could not be traced to the strata of functionaries who began in the Party and forged ahead into the administrations of the Reich and the regional governments. Quite the reverse. These "veterans" were so hidebound that they slowed down development in many areas. The economic upswings after 1933 were due chiefly to the cooperation of those echelons that derived from the days of the Kaiser and the Weimar Republic and that now continued whether under coercion or from a sense of duty. An excellent officialdom and outstanding technocrats in the widest sense of the word offered their services in 1933. And in many respects they were behind Hitler's economic and administrative successes. A good example was the autobahn. The highway system was planned and carried out by construction agencies of the German Railroad when Hitler ordered the project as a way of eliminating unemployment. It was only this cadre of engineers, not the veteran Party members, who were capable of carrying out such a vast enterprise so impeccably.

A decade later, my own successes were possible because I made use of a staff of industrial specialists who had already excelled before 1933 or who stood out after 1933 in a relatively free selection in individual factories. But there was one decisive change after the Weimar Republic. Hitler offered these experts and the German Railroad and the industrial sector all the financial, organizational, and—most important—political possibilities of realizing their talents.

The SS took the opposite path. For leaders in the industrialization of the concentration camps, the SS used the cadres that had joined it before 1933 or soon after. It was unable to construct major industrial complexes precisely because it failed to gain capable industrial people to run its enterprises. A good example was Oswald Pohl, flushed up from the mass of the veteran Party members and utterly unsuitable for building an economic empire. The example of Buchenwald clearly shows the inability of the concentration camp bureaucracy. When the manufacture of carbines was to be launched in Buchenwald, even this industrially simple task could not be realized because the men assigned to the production process turned out to be totally unfit—for instance, the commandant of the camp, who was suddenly asked to run a factory.

SS industry did not fail, as Himmler sometimes apologetically maintained, because German industry was against it (although the industrial sector was quite content to see its political competition founder). No amount of opposition from the armaments industry would ever have hindered the industrial goals of the SS, which was far too powerful. Its ineffectiveness was due rather to the inability of SS leaders to analyze industrial processes and to translate their findings into organization. Hence, despite its huge power, the SS remained peripheral to armaments and wartime production.

This fiasco of one major arm shows how Hitler himself would have failed if the politically lukewarm intellectuals had not made themselves available to him. In that case, Hitler would have called upon the mediocrities who had been brought together in his party before 1933 for other purposes (fighting the Weimar Republic and other parties, even by violent means). And he would have used these mediocrities to build up the economy, the army, the state. The incompetence of the National Socialist party functionaries would have led to catastrophically poor performances in industry.

In late 1941 Himmler intended to construct his industrial empire with the aid of Jewish manpower and other concentration camp inmates. But Hitler foiled his plans. During the second phase of the war, Hitler had two military goals. He wanted to conquer Russia and he wanted to wipe out the Jews, or, to use his standard word, "exterminate" them. The latter goal obstructed the first one. For the "extermination" of the Jews necessarily interfered with both Himmler's plans and the continuation of the war. The millions of Jews who were lost for the armaments industry, plus the hundreds of thousands of Soviet prisoners of war who died in German camps, could have solved our most urgent problem—labor. Furthermore, because of their intelligence, Jews could have been used more easily at the lathes than Russian women, with whom the Germans could not even communicate because of language problems.

At a Gauleiter conference in Posen in October 1943, Heinrich Himmler promised the top leadership of the Party that by the end of that year all Jews would be destroyed down to the last man. And he polemicized against people who wanted to make exceptions for a wide variety of reasons. Yet it was he who, several weeks later, sent tens of thousands of Jewish laborers to the SS factories in the East European territories. The dichotomy in this man, who was in charge of total mass murder and yet who constantly opposed extermination policies, leads me to suspect that he was not the driving force in the murder of the Jews. I would point instead to Hitler, Joseph Goebbels, and that hate-filled mover Martin Bormann.

Himmler, as his diaries reveal, must have felt intimidated in his youth. But a few years later, under Hitler's influence, Himmler's irresolute character developed energy and decisiveness. Virtually overnight he became the cuttingly icy fanatic who fought unswervingly for the Führer and his cause. He is a fine example of what Hitler could achieve as a catalyst. This hesitant, nay, irresolute agricultural student suddenly saw as his single task the perfect fulfillment of Hitler's policies. This task also brought out a pedantic tendency in him. From then on, Hitler's orders were for him above any humane considerations, which had long since died out anyway through the years of National Socialism and its countless slogans— for instance, the slogan that anything is good if it serves the people.

Hitler so thoroughly embodied his politics, and all his helpers had so utterly lost their own willpower, that Hitler's person, rather than political considerations, counted for everything. In regard to anti-Semitism, Hitler could have safely taken a radical about-face without his followers' rebelling. For example, there was unprotesting acceptance of his pact with the Soviet Union, which directly contradicted his doctrines of many years. Such denial of all the principles with which he had waged his struggle for power was accepted unthinkingly. His will alone determined destiny.

On July 18 and August 25, 1956, my Spandau diary shows me occupied with the problem of familiarization.[1] When a new guard arrived in Spandau, I wrote, he was at first deeply impressed by our world of suffering, while we, because of some hardening of feeling, could scarcely understand or perceive his sympathy or his emotional reaction. Yet this petrifaction was what made life bearable for us during decades of imprisonment. Soon, however, my diary goes on, the new guard grew accustomed to us and hence indifferent as he adjusted to our random group of guards and inmates. "The daily schedule, the rotation, are not viewed as anything special by guards and prisoners. We five prisoners have likewise long since grown accustomed to our useless activities and wretched appearance. This process is one of mutual fortification. Yet we do not even realize this. None of us stands up to point out this immorality. On the contrary, each group fortifies the other in feeling that bad things are not at all bad but actually good in the best sense. For instance, the fact that the guards keep us from any harmful contact with the outer world. All this shows the low morale of our 'inmate-and-guard group.' "

These Spandau observations can also, to a crass extent, be applied to Hitler's regime. The well-meaning guard no longer perceived how deeply involved he was in his prison work. The high Party functionary could not leave his system, he was so imprisoned in it. He was no longer aware of his moral deformation, caused by the seemingly orderly, legally anchored prison structure of the Reich. In the face of the seeming lawfulness of the regime, he was unable to make himself aware of the totally unlawful events around him. The moral sensitivity of the individual had gradually atrophied. Often, at Spandau, I felt as if nothing whatsoever had changed, as if I were still rooted in the same world. Except that I had once been a guard, and now I was a prisoner.

C. S. Forester, in *The General*, his novel about World War I, depicts a British division's headquarters, where military issues are discussed matter-of-factly and orders for engaging units are given. Then the author switches to the place where these matter-of-fact orders are carried out, where soldiers are wounded, suffer, and die. The army staff must act coolly and dismiss any thoughts of the cruel consequences of its decisions. Otherwise it could not do its job properly. So a general staff decides upon the sufferings and deaths of thousands of people—detached from reality, abstracted as strategic problems.

Hitler's decisions in strategic discussions from 1942 to 1945 were obviously so wrong that any properly trained General Staff officer ought to have perceived the mistakes. No doubt, after years of belonging to this topmost level of the military apparatus, the officers taking part in these discussions were so far removed from the reality of the war that they were no longer willing or able to project the consequences of this irrationality onto the level of the mass murders. Thousands of soldiers were perishing every day. But we coldly spoke of "losses"—one of the innumerable words that suppressed reality—to avoid confronting the truth. One of the terrifying developments in a war is the anonymity with which, say, an officers' discussion establishes that "so-and-so many divisions have been ground down" or that "it is better to let the divisions bleed to death and form new ones at home."

In my area, armaments, man had also been devalued, into a production factor. He was as countable as the production figures for tanks, steel, or munitions. Today, moral sensibilities are being suppressed everywhere and the human factor is being ubiquitously degraded by technology. But in the totalitarian state, man was reduced to a commodity or a number in an extreme fashion. The fates of all men, whether Jews or non-Jews, were decided at desks in the interest of armaments and defense.

Such ethical hardening still exists today, beyond any ideology, regardless of any specific regime, in both bureaucracy and technocracy. Obsessed with performance goals, devoured by personal ambition, people still tend to see human events in the technocratic terms of efficiency. This fundamental problem exists unchanged in our achievement society. Except that the situation of war and dictatorship intensified the phenomenon to the extreme.

German cities were being bombed. Thousands of women and children burned to death or suffocated in the ruins. One of my tasks was to contact the directors of bombed factories right after the attacks and discuss the measures to be taken for a speedy resumption of production. These experiences hardened us more and more to reality. And vice versa: when the Allies received the first reports about the crimes in German concentration camps, they dismissed any moral qualms about bombing German cities. Thus, feelings hardened on both sides. Today, after thirty-five years of peace, one can barely understand that wartime decisions were bound to be different from peacetime considerations. People became more and more accustomed to cruelties because of the emergency situation of a war being waged inhumanely on all sides.

We generally refrain from using statements or actions of the other side, say by Churchill or Roosevelt or their colleagues, in order to justify ourselves. But when I read such documents today, I get the impression that there, too, the same technocratic indifference repressed humanitarian considerations. In the Henry Morgenthau diaries,[2] letters and telephone conversations offer insight into the coldblooded way that people could speak about the possible starvation of millions of Germans—as if it were the most normal thing in the world. I would certainly not wish to make it sound as if the two worlds were comparable. I would only like to fathom how such inhumane thinking was possible.

Hitler's system gave the able man a chance. Ability could work in any direction, in the bureaucracy of evil as well as in architecture. Anything was possible if—mostly by chance—a man was discovered with extraordinary capabilities. Not that such men were actually sought. Anyone who had entered the Party at an early date had his pick of a wide variety of jobs. Hitler had actually found me more or less by chance.

It was he who, against my proclivities, made me manager of all the industry of almost an entire continent—and at the age of thirty-seven to boot. A momentary inspiration of Hitler's called me to a task for which I was in no way prepared. I was instantly obsessed with performance and was also driven by personal ambition, which may have been strengthened by the fact that I was young. Last but not least, I was ruled by the constant fear of losing the Führer's goodwill and hence also the task he had assigned to me. Hitler—our personal relationship was based on this—had charged me with a responsibility that was an enormous challenge, thereby giving me incredible satisfaction. In such a position, everyone working with Hitler put up with a great deal of hardship, even humiliation, in order not to lose his job.

Certainly it was possible—albeit within a limited framework—to act independently and responsibly in the Third Reich. While the mechanics of its command system required that orders indeed had to be carried out, they often permitted the individual a certain freedom to interfere by exaggerating or softening the orders. Even an Adolf Eichmann, in his subordinate position, could have shown less persistence in some things, because the command apparatus of the SS had not created any effective controls, especially on low and middle levels. Hence, according to the individual's personality, certain things could be made better or worse. Typical of this possibility are the improvements made at the Auschwitz labor camp when Rudolf Franz Höss was replaced by Arthur Liebenhenschel. Once Höss took over again, the catastrophic conditions were soon restored.[3] Of course, it is still a moot point whether Himmler called Höss back just because Liebenhenschel ran the camp more leniently.

Naturally, now, at seventy-five, decades after the events, I am still haunted by the thought that I could have made decisions in a minute that would have improved the situation of the unfortunate inmates. By simple means, I could probably have increased the survival chances for countless numbers of people. For instance, during factory inspections I saw concentration camp prisoners working in our plants among German workers. They were not on the verge of collapse, but they were not in good condition, either. I could have done a lot merely by telling the director accompanying me to help them. Encouraging him to do so would not have spelled any danger for me. But I hid my conscience behind the countless problems that I had to settle at such times. Furthermore, I was always in a hurry. I barely had five or ten minutes to hold a conversation in peace and quiet. One decision after another had to be made.

I was friendly with Hans Joachim Riecke, the state secretary in the Food Ministry, and perhaps I could have gotten him to increase the food rations in the concentration camps. When transportation was breaking down toward the end of the war, I was empowered to direct the transportation system; and perhaps I could have used my authority to send enough food and medication to the concentration camps to help prevent starvation and epidemics. Perhaps I might even have been able to influence some army leader to take strategic or tactical measures in order to hinder the clearing of the camps when the Allied armies approached. This would have prevented the long death marches.

The entanglement was ruthless and indissoluble. Humanitarian considerations?

Why did I forfeit the possibility of doing good? Why did it never even occur to me that I was acting heedlessly when I failed to think about a higher responsibility and used my ministerial work as an excuse? Since I was absorbed in company—and departmental—thinking and never considered the department of humanity, I never took the small step that separated me from proper realization. When I rejected the moral responsibility for the forced laborers, it was the final confirmation of a petrifaction that had long since gotten hold of me.

I certainly could have helped at times, for instance in Lodz, when Greiser wanted to liquidate the ghetto. Perhaps I might even say that my considerations were not merely rational when I did a few things to enable the victims to survive. But I cannot claim that humane considerations stood above the interests of wartime economy. If I was able to help, I had a feeling of satisfaction. If I was unable to help, I turned my back on the misery insofar as I perceived it. My motivation had gotten "out of plumb"; for me the question of efficiency was decisive. Even if it had been possible occasionally to secure better treatment, the fact remains that those people were ruthlessly exploited. Today we recognize that even simple relative humanity is far from adequate. We are dealing with a fundamental question that, back then, I generally viewed in terms of efficiency. Exploitation was in the foreground. We did not do what we might and should have done to keep those people alive!

The inhumanity of slave labor in the concentration camps is not the object of my study here. But nevertheless, as a background to the events, it must not be concealed. Nor should certain efforts to keep able-bodied laborers alive deceive us as to the fact that, at the same time, millions of people were being systematically murdered in the death camps.

The aim of this book is not to defend my own work by saying: We were not so bad; the SS was the villain. After all, this was *one* system, and we all belonged to it. From the standpoint of responsibility, it makes no difference whether the individuals in power disliked one another. Hence, it would be wrong to present the SS as the sole embodiment of evil.

Certainly, I was one of those co-workers of Hitler's who are called "technocrats" today. These armaments technocrats can also include "Wehrmacht specialists," for instance Field Marshal Fritz Erich von Manstein, who was probably the most important strategist of World War II.[4] He had no interest whatsoever in areas beyond the pure military. This society of technocrats also included the Luftwaffe leaders, particularly Field Marshal Erhard Milch.

Of course there was the other side, the group of people who were not morally infected. Indeed, the army offers countless examples of moral integrity. These include Gen. Carl Ludwig von Gienanth, the German military commander in the Generalgouvernement [Polish territory under German rule.] Because of his active resistance to Hitler's Jewish policies, Gienandt was dismissed by Field Marshal Wilhelm Keitel. Likewise, Col. Wilhelm Freter, who opposed Himmler's aims and during the Warsaw uprising in 1944 was court-martialed by Commandant Jürgen Stroop. Or the commandant of Przemysl, who had serious conflicts with local SS agencies because of the military protection he gave to Jews. We would also have to mention Oskar Schindler, who, with the help of armaments bureaus and Wehrmacht agencies, managed to evacuate several thousand Polish Jews to Czechoslovakia.

Protest also arose from the group of officers connected with the conspiracy of July 20, 1944. Through additions permitted by latitude for independent action, they toned down the execution orders issued by the supreme command of the Wehrmacht. However, they were unable to keep these orders from being transmitted.

Thus, there is sufficient evidence to say that it was possible not to let one's conscience be deadened under the pretext of technocratic coercion. For instance, ethics and morals of the men of July 20 must have been protected from decay by a strong faith in the laws of humanity. I knew most of them, and we had mutual esteem for one another, as is revealed in the document that points out that, without even consulting me, they planned to have me as a member of their government. But the extent of their moral strength was concealed from me.

Today I still wonder how interchangeable we were—we who were under the influence not only of Hitler but also of the technicalized fascination of the mass media, whose slogans we had created ourselves. Where would the maelstrom have taken me if Hitler's favor had placed me further in front? Would inhibitions have hindered me at the barriers that I would have been forced to cross? What would have happened if Hitler had asked me to make decisions that required the utmost hardness, and that I could not have evaded because Hitler would have insisted that they were necessary for Germany? How far would I have gone? I can no more answer this question than so many others concerning my life under Hitler.

I think of how far the seeming force of events brought Wilhelm Keitel and Alfred Jodl and all the other generals who were of the same middle-class background as myself and who, even at the start of the war, would not have thought it possible that they might lose completely their moral equanimity and their conscience despite their background.

I am thinking especially of Keitel, who in the final years of the war seemed totally at Hitler's mercy and gave an impression of complete physical exhaustion. Retrospectively, Keitel appears cold and ruthless. Yet I see him before me, friendly and kindhearted, often trying to do his best for others.

Or Hans Kammler. I knew him when he was running the construction division in the Ministry of Air Transport. An inconspicuous, sociable, and very hardworking official. Nobody would have dreamed that some day he would be one of Himmler's most brutal and most ruthless henchmen. It was simply inconceivable, and yet that was what happened.

And Heinrich Himmler himself. He gave a friendly, reticent impression, had good manners, and in his personal dealings avoided the strong words he used in his speeches, especially about the annihilation of the Jews. The more I study Himmler, the more I sense that neither his background nor his upbringing predestined him to enter history as one of the greatest of mass murderers. Was he a born criminal? I feel that his murderous activity came from a corrupt, perverted morality; perhaps not even from an ideology. I actually believe that Himmler could have unhesitatingly followed an ideology contrary to Hitler's, whereas with Goebbels or Bormann, I had the impression that their notions coincided with Hitler's. The transformation of Himmler from the well-bred offspring of a prominent middle-class family into the murderer of millions of Jews is a psychological enigma to me—not only with regard to Himmler personally, but with regard to the functioning of the Nazi system. And yet it is no enigma if one observed the enormous impact that Hitler's will, together with his system, had upon Party leaders.

I should not be cowardly and evasive. The question remains: If I had occupied a different position, to what extent would I have ordered atrocities if Hitler had told me to do so?

When I look back today, the image of a romantic and also cruel and ruthless world rises before me—romanticism in its unruliness and wildness, not in its pleasant Biedermeier *Gemütlichkeit*. I am reminded of the religious siege of Münster during the time of the Anabaptists. In both eras, I see a blend of romantic notions of salvation, cruelty, religious selflessness taken to bizarre and peculiar extremes, self-sacrifice and brutality, excessive obedience and enthusiastic dilettantism. This blend produced a society that drove a sixteenth-century Westphalian town to the verge of ruin and plunged the twentieth-century world into chaos.

Chapter 2

Euphoric Notions

O N JANUARY 26, 1942, exactly two weeks before I began my work as armaments minister and six days before the Wannsee Conference, Himmler informed SS Brigade Commander Richard Glücks, head of inspection of all concentration camps, that "since Russian prisoners of war are not expected in the near future,"[1] he [Himmler] would take "a large number of the Jews and Jewesses who are being emigrated [sic] from Germany and send them to the camps. . . . During the next few weeks, prepare to receive 100,000 male Jews and up to 50,000 Jewesses in the concentration camps. Large-scale tasks and assignments will come to the concentration camps in the next few weeks. SS Squad Commander Pohl will instruct you in detail."[2] Fourteen days earlier, Hitler had rather belatedly drawn the proper conclusions from the German defeat at Moscow and had restored the priority of army armaments over air armaments. At the same time, he demanded maximum production efforts.[3]

Himmler was always ready with words; he also tended toward long-winded fantasies. But this time, he appeared to see the realization of his plans for an extensive industrial concern as tangibly near. Höss, in his autobiography, reports that Himmler had visited the Auschwitz concentration camp almost one year earlier, in March 1941. During his inspection, he had said that he wanted to turn the camp into an armaments labor center with one hundred thousand prisoners.[4] In this connection, Höss states: "I always treated this issue [the murder of inmates] in my reports, but I could do nothing against the pressure from Himmler, who kept wanting more and more

[14]

prisoners for the armaments industry."[5] "The special prisoners [Höss means Jews] who were under Himmler's jurisdiction had to be treated with consideration. We could not do without the major source of manpower, especially in the armaments industry."[6] Words have a relative value. What Höss means by "consideration" can be evaluated in relation to reality only in connection with the technical annihilation apparatus at Auschwitz, which Höss commanded and which killed two and one-half million people.

This contrast between Himmler's goals and an unnamed power cannot be clarified. One guesses that the Reich Security Main Office demanded the murder of all Jews and that this goal was supported by Bormann on behalf of Hitler.

Himmler's intention of profiting from the military emergency and constructing an SS industrial concern was reflected several weeks later in a fundamental change in the SS organizational structure. On March 16, when various main agencies were combined, the SS put Oswald Pohl in charge of all economic and administrative matters.[7] Pohl, as the verdict against him establishes,[8] was not responsible for committing or releasing prisoners or for the executions. His "legal authority began with the arrival of the prisoners at the gates of the concentration camps." However, he and the SS Economic Administrative Main Office, which was directed by him, were in charge of "the ultimate details of remuneration, production, and employment of prisoners. He was also in charge of supplying food and clothing for prisoners, and this obligation went all the way down to the lowest level of distribution, [to] the actual responsibility for having prisoners receive the necessary rations."[9]

Exaggerating Pohl's role, probably for tactical reasons, the court stated "that he was an experienced, active, and ruling leader of one of the largest branches of the German war machine."[10] Elsewhere, the court went so far as to speak of the "great genius Pohl":[11] "In the planning and building of the housing of the Economic Administrative Main Office, no mistakes were made. It was skillfully planned and expertly built. It was a good building, but it harbored criminal things. The building was put to bad use. A noble cathedral can be the meeting place of thieves, kidnappers, and counterfeiters."[12]

My judgment of Pohl's abilities was more negative. As I stated in July 1945, during the first few months of my captivity, I had always regarded him as a man of little intelligence.[13] Indeed, under Pohl's leadership, the SS had not managed to construct a well-organized economic apparatus.

From the time I took over, Dr. Walter Schieber, a chemist and one of my nine office heads, was responsible for the punctual delivery of impor-

tant components like ball bearings and castings, as well as chemical products, including explosives.

It was only after my release from twenty years of prison that I learned
that Schieber was in effect Himmler's confidential agent in my ministry.
Thus, on June 17, 1941, Schieber sent him a carbon copy of his report—
prepared for Dr. Fritz Todt—on his six-day trip to Moscow and Rostov
on the Don. During this period of German entente with the Soviet Union,
he had been invited by the Soviet government to visit industrial plants.[14]
On July 24, 1941, a few weeks after the start of the Russian campaign,
Schieber sent Himmler a further report about a trip to Italy. Himmler felt
the account was so important that he ordered a copy sent to the head of the
security police and the SD [the SS Security Service], SS Squad Commander
Reinhard Heydrich.[15] Furthermore, on October 8, 1941, Pohl was asked
by SS Squad Commander Hans Kammler, head of the construction office,
to advocate Schieber's promotion. Approving this request, Pohl transmitted it to SS Obergruppenführer Karl Wolff, the head of Himmler's
personal staff, with this remark: "I myself greatly esteem Schieber. He is
also probably well regarded by the SS Reichsführer."[16]

On March 16, 1942, Pohl was authorized to act for the SS in all economic and administrative matters, and he was also responsible for the
industrial employment of concentration camp inmates. On the day of his
appointment, Pohl appeared at the office of Karl Saur, the most important
agency head in my ministry. He was in charge of the actual armaments production, which at that time, however, was still limited to the army. The
responsibility for naval armaments was added in July 1943, and that for
aerial armaments in June 1944.

In this meeting with my agency head and my other staffers, Himmler's
request for armaments production in concentration camps was instantly
approved. "The trustee firms must transfer their production to the area
of the concentration camp, occasionally making engineers and specialists
available to train the inmates. [This] manufacture transfer to the concentration camps [should] be overseen by the firm involved, not only in terms
of the production itself, but also economically." The necessary machines
were to be obtained by the armaments ministry. "The overall task of
employing the concentration camps for armaments has been taken over by
Herr State Councillor Dr. Schieber. He will attempt two tests as quickly
as possible—namely, first the Buchenwald camp, near Weimar, and
Neuengamme near Hamburg."

The plan was to employ 25,000 prisoners in five concentration camp factories: Buchenwald, Sachsenhausen, Neuengamme, Auschwitz, and Ravensbrück.[17]

One day later, on March 17, 1942, Schieber, on the basis of his assignment to transfer production to the concentration camps, ordered the Gustloff Works, a huge armaments factory under Fritz Sauckel, Gauleiter of Thuringia, to transfer the monthly output of 15,000 carbines and 2,000 defense sporting rifles (for the premilitary training of the Hitler Youth) to Buchenwald. Responsibility for producing the guns was to be assumed by the company itself. "The transfer is to commence immediately and be completed in about three or, at most, four months."[18] I found this ministerial order from my agency head in the files of Himmler's personal staff. Thus, Schieber had unhesitatingly transmitted an internal concern to the SS leaders. According to administrative procedure, my ministerial bureau should certainly have been involved.

That same day, Himmler discussed as point 10 of his meeting with Hitler, "Work with Speer. Carbines."[19]—a sign of how quickly he was informed of this news. Two days later, in an armaments discussion covering 52 items, I informed Hitler: "Reported to the Führer about armaments production in the concentration camps." Hitler approved of the plan to begin in Buchenwald. He "consented to the planned production of carbines" and ordered that "the given numbers of workers, a total of 25,000 prisoners for now, [was] to be absolutely maintained."[20]

Schieber was promptly rewarded for his zeal. On October 9, 1941, after five months of waiting, Pohl's request for Schieber's promotion was approved.

SS Obergruppenführer Wolff congratulated "comrade Schieber heartily on his well-deserved promotion to SS Oberführer."[21] Just a few weeks later, on April 22, Obergruppenführer Gottlob Berger, Himmler's confidant and head of the SS Main Office, sent a handwritten letter to Himmler, saying that Schieber was willing "to work with us in every way" and that he "requests a brief appointment with the SS Reichsführer at his convenience" for this purpose. Furthermore, Berger suggested that Himmler "soon promote Schieber to the personal staff of the SS Reichsführer."[22]

This time it did not take five months. Just six days later, Himmler expressed his willingness to meet with Schieber and take him into his personal staff.[23] "Member of the personal staff" signified nothing less than that Schieber was now a kind of subordinate of Himmler's, without, of course, my knowing about it. This episode strikes me as important, because it shows that Himmler knew not only how to arouse personal ambition by simple means, but also how to attract officials holding key positions in other agencies.

On June 21 Schieber was honored anew. Only three months after his last promotion, he was appointed SS brigade commander. This time it was Pohl who, on June 5, had encouraged the honor. And so the head of the SS Main Personnel Office informed Pohl of the promotion so that he could break the news personally to Schieber.[24]

The considerations may have been similar when Himmler, in the spring of 1942, offered me the honorary rank of SS Oberstgruppenführer through the head of his personal staff, Obergruppenführer Wolff. This would not only have put me into an unofficial vassalage to Himmler. Accepting the honor would also have sharply disrupted my confidential relations with the command posts of the army. Therefore I rejected his offer amiably. Just four years later, during the Nuremberg Trial, I mused that such an honorary title would have destroyed any chance of my survival.

Two "tests" were to be made in the manufacture of the carbines: in Buchenwald and in Neuengamme. Schieber had announced that monthly production of 15,000 carbines should be launched at Buchenwald within three or, at most, four months.[25] This was not an exaggerated goal, just a simple test case; the production of carbines requires little manufacturing expertise. In any case, the machines and the technical knowledge were to be supplied by the Gustloff Works.

The course of this first experiment in producing weapons in concentration camps can be followed through an extensive correspondence. The four-month deadline was already past when Pohl informed Himmler on July 11, 1942, that all *preparations* for the "construction of the gun factory on the terrain of the concentration camp of Weimar-Buchenwald" had been completed and that construction would begin on Monday, July 13, 1942. The letter goes on: "In regard to making prisoners available for production, you will receive under separate cover an agreement between the SS Economic Administrative Main Office and the Gustloff Works."[26] It is obvious from this remark that the Gustloff Works were viewed as the entrepreneur of the gun factory by the SS.

A few days later Himmler, who liked making boastful claims, sent Sauckel a letter expressing his delight that "the plant in Weimar-Buchenwald began operations on July 13, 1942." He deliberately ignored the fact that "operations" generally refers to the start of *production* and not to the imminent start of the construction of factory wings. Moreover, disclaiming his plans to build up an industrial concern, he assured Sauckel that "in peacetime the plant will in no event compete with the Gustloff Works. I have no intention of being active in this area in peacetime, since it is utterly peripheral to my tasks and interests."[27]

With the four-month deadline past, Buchenwald, which had not yet produced a single carbine, could hardly be viewed as a success. But Himmler was already demanding the takeover of further armaments production. "I had occasion today to speak with SS Brigade Commander Dr. Schieber. He was very satisfied with the overall development in our concentration camps," said Himmler in a letter of July 7, 1942, to Pohl. A pure fabrication, for Schieber must have known that on that date, not even the construction work for Buchenwald had as yet begun. Despite all his undeniable successes as agency head, Schieber had a weak character. He tended to view things euphorically, and he was certainly careful not to disappoint Himmler.

Himmler promptly worked out an agreement with Schieber. Paralleling the imminent manufacture of carbines in Buchenwald, the following goals were set. At the concentration camp of Neuengamme, .08 pistols were to be produced. The 3.7 cm antiaircraft gun was to be manufactured on a large scale at Auschwitz. Mass production of communications devices was to be set up at Ravensbrück. And also in Buchenwald, a factory for producing 55,000, instead of the slated 12,000, carbines was to be constructed and start operations as soon as possible. Himmler pointed out to Schieber that "I am very interested in the truck factory of the Opel Firm. . . . The factory should be set up near Katowice, Upper Silesia. . . . It is important to me that this factory be erected and run by us."[28] None of these programs was ever carried out.

For months Himmler had been keen on taking over the manufacture of trucks, because since the start of the Russian campaign there had been a shortage of trucks for motorized divisions. He had already broached this theme with Hitler in May. In Himmler's conference notes, there is a laconic entry under point 5: "Opel Factory. Speer."[29] Two days later Himmler could inform me via Obergruppenführer Wolff that Hitler had agreed to his plan. At the same time, he transmitted Hitler's decision to SS Group Leader Hans Jüttner, who was in charge of arming the SS divisions.[30]

However, nothing happened for two years. Only in early July 1944 did Hitler and I establish once again: "In order to guarantee the production increase of 2,000 trucks [a month] demanded by Hitler, the SS Reichsführer has promised the 12,000 necessary workers. For this purpose, one or several truck-producing factories must quickly be transferred to concentration camp plants."[31] I stated pretty much the same thing to the Gauleiters on August 3, 1944: We "could easily produce ten or eleven thousand trucks a month [instead of roughly 7,300 in July 1944] if a few basic premises [are created] which have meanwhile been introduced through the helpfulness of Party Comrade Himmler."[32]

In reality, however, as of October annihilatory air raids on the German transportation network were causing serious breaches in production. They were felt first in the highly technological manufacture of automobiles. Instead of increasing, the output went down. Thus, the truck project was also wrecked once and for all.

When Himmler made his proposals to me on September 9, 1944,[33] I willingly agreed to consign large-scale armaments orders to the SS. Himmler instantly recorded this good news in a letter to Pohl.[34] A few days later, on September 15, 1942, I chaired a conference that seemed to bring the problem of employing concentration camp inmates to a definitive solution. The SS was represented at this meeting by Pohl and Kammler, while my side was represented by Schieber, Saur, and two men from the construction sector, ministerial councillors Steffens and Briese.

The ministry chronicle remarks as follows about this session: "It was agreed with SS Obergruppenführer Pohl and Dr. Kammler that concentration camp inmates are to be made available as workers for the armaments plants."[35]

Pohl reported the matter to Himmler in greater detail. Naturally, this internal elaboration was not made available to me. Pohl confirmed triumphantly that in the future, huge armaments plants would be set up that could be run with 10,000 or 15,000 prisoners away from the cities. Or else understaffed armaments plants would be operated with prisoners. The German workers thus freed could be employed in other, similar factories.

According to this agreement, 50,000 Jews would soon be occupied in existing factories. Their lodgings, according to the agreement, were guaranteed. "The able-bodied Jews destined for eastward migration must therefore interrupt their journey and do armaments labor,"[36] wrote Pohl, avoiding the words *annihilation* and *extermination*, in a letter to Himmler. One may thus assume that Pohl left even the conference participants in the dark about the fate of the Jews.

Three days later Saur wrote to Pohl, indicating—as agreed—three factories that would employ Jews and be taken over as SS armaments factories by the SS, in the manner discussed:

1. the 3.7 cm antiaircraft artillery factory in Riga, which will be getting under way again, with a final work force of 6,000 men;
2. the already operating heavy antiaircraft factory . . . near Katowice with a final work force of 5,000 men;

3. the new gear-transmission factory, now under construction, of the Z. F. Friedrichshafen firm in Passau, with a final work force of 3,000–4,000 men.

To guarantee the most intense production, said Saur, he had "taken a survey in the other relevant German manufacturing plants of the same branch and located specialists who are SS men and SS Unterführers [noncommissioned officers]."[37]

So the promise was now made: the Buchenwald carbine factory with some 5,000 inmates; .08 pistol production in Neuengamme with 2,000 inmates; 3.7 cm antiaircraft artillery in Auschwitz with 6,000 inmates; communications devices in Ravensbrück with 6,000 female inmates; truck production near Katowice with 12,000 inmates; a 3.7 cm antiaircraft factory in Riga with 6,000 inmates; an 8.8 cm antiaircraft plant near Katowice with a work force of 5,000 men; the gear-transmission plant in Passau with 3,000 to 4,000 inmates. In September 1942, these 46,000 prisoners could be contrasted with 110,000 mostly sick or feeble prisoners, of whom 39,700 died of undernourishment that very same month.[38]

In September 1942, representatives of industry had heard about the plan to transform entire plants into concentration camp factories and to give SS leaders considerable influence in running them. Those representatives begged me, the newcomer in the armaments ministry, to abandon such plans.[39] Six months later I stressed to Himmler: "You yourself know the position of industry, which would not like to see the SS developing as a competitor."[40]

Likewise, Colonel General Friedrich Fromm, chief of the home army and thus in charge of military armaments, called upon me with General Wilhelm von Leeb, head of the Army Ordnance Office, on September 18, when the iron allotments for the next quarter were to be discussed.[41] Fromm remonstrated with me about the consequences of having SS armaments factories. He had always, he said, supplied the SS divisions with weapons in a fair manner on the Führer's behalf. Hitler, Fromm argued, would make sure anyway that the SS divisions got first crack at the most modern tanks and weapons. But in shipments from the concentration camps, parts of the products meant for the army might, without proper supervision, be siphoned off for SS units, and the army divisions could thus be at a disadvantage. For how could he check on what was being produced in the SS factories? In the existing system, the delivered weapons could be inspected and approved in the factories under the supervision of the Army Ordnance Office. Indeed, the system offered a flawless overview.

Saur, too, opposed SS-owned production, although for different reasons.

He feared interference from the SS leaders, who might disturb our undisputed hegemony in industry. After the basic conference of September 16, Pohl had pointed out to Himmler that his plan to take over "large-format armaments tasks" had failed. This, Pohl told him, was due to a resistance "that, much to my surprise, I discovered in Reich Minister Professor Speer himself. But I will tell you about this in person at the proper occasion. The name Saur plays a strange part here."[42]

Any promise made in Hitler's Reich was valid only so long as Hitler did not utter an opposing opinion. Thus, I fully entered the scheme of things when, without notifying Himmler, I drove to headquarters two days later. There, eagerly supported by Saur, I got Hitler to make a decision that turned all previous agreements topsy-turvy.

Our powerful troop consisted of representatives from the Army Ordnance Office, leaders of various main committees, and members of my ministry. Also present was Gauleiter Sauckel, in charge of forced labor. We had brought along plans and statistics concerning the construction of self-propelled assault guns as well as the new tank program. In fact, matters involving tank production were in the foreground of this discussion. In all, 49 items were treated in three days, September 20 to 22, 1942.

At the end of one of the meetings, I informed Hitler that I had to discuss a thorny problem, and that I wanted only Saur and Sauckel present. Hitler amiably dismissed the other participants and then turned to Saur and me. I had asked Saur to take the floor first. As a long-time expert of Dr. Todt's, he enjoyed higher prestige with Hitler than I, who had nothing more than seven months' apprenticeship.

In such cases it was expedient to admit openly the real issue. For it was certain that Bormann would soon inform Himmler, who would then try to present his own arguments. Therefore, we explained frankly to Hitler that an agreement with Pohl had pushed us in a direction that we considered inappropriate. Naturally, we avoided any mention of the qualms voiced by industrialists and by Fromm. Such qualms would only have annoyed Hitler. And once his mood was set, it was hard steering him where you wanted him to go. Also, we knew that Himmler had already convinced Hitler to employ the vast potential manpower of concentration camp inmates in new armaments factories, which would be put up in the immediate vicinity of the camps for expedience. After all, said Himmler—and his argument had not failed to have its effect on Hitler—new factories had to be erected anyway. It would therefore be expedient, he said, to build them right near a huge supply of unused manpower.

Saur reported on the failures so far. Appealing to Hitler's hatred of bureaucracy, Saur spoke about all the red tape that we had been unable to cut through during the test production at Buchenwald and Neuengamme. In Buchenwald, he said, they had not even managed to start building the factory. From Neuengamme there had still been no reports, nor any demands for machine tools. In this connection Saur emphasized the swift and uncomplicated work methods of industry, which could have achieved the planned increases if it had had the necessary labor force at its disposal. I added a few sentences about the inadequacy of the SS business leaders. Before the war they had promised Hitler that they would quickly supply bricks and granite for his buildings. But only the tiniest portion of this promise had been kept, I said.

To our surprise, Hitler's reaction was one of good cheer. Laughing, he said that prisoners should really produce felt slippers and bags. However, he went on, the problem of labor had been settled by Sauckel in the best way. We had not anticipated having Sauckel as an ally in this matter. For profit reasons connected with internal Gau matters, he did not approve of siphoning any production from the Gustloff Works to Buchenwald. Sauckel therefore assured Hitler that he would supply any necessary manpower. We could easily forgo Himmler's offer, he said.

But this was not in line with our aims. Saur spoke again. He plausibly assured Hitler that concentration camp prisoners could be of valuable assistance in the factories already existing in the industrial sector. These factories would merely have to be expanded by means of more buildings and additional machines. An experienced stock of specialists and engineers was already available in them, he said. This argument for private business instantly won Hitler over.

In order to forestall future arguments, I said that Himmler could be given a work force for additional weapons. Surely, Himmler was hoping to siphon a few weapons for his SS from the output of armaments plants under his control. "You can rely on that," Hitler interjected, in a very good mood. "For Himmler is capable of anything, even deception, for the sake of better equipment for his SS divisions."

Now Sauckel assured Hitler that he could rely on the success of Sauckel's actions. However, he required a sharp order from Hitler to the often sluggish agencies of the Reich administration and of the military administrations in the occupied territories. On this premise, he guaranteed the supply of all manpower demanded. It would then not be at all necessary to go along with Himmler's plan for employing 50,000 Jews within the Reich. "Sauckel," Hitler interrupted, "naturally I'll sign any authorization you need. Give [Reich Minister Hans] Lammers a strongly worded order for me to sign, and do it tonight. You know how important the missing manpower is for the additional armaments programs."[43] To be sure, Hitler added, he too considered it quite impossible to employ 50,000 Jews within the Reich "now that we have gotten rid of the Jews. On the contrary, make sure that the Jews now working in Berlin are replaced as fast as possible. Goebbels has vehemently protested this scandal to me several times."[44] And indeed, Joseph Goebbels, the agile propaganda minister and Gauleiter of Berlin, was fanatically agitating against the presence of the Berlin Jews. He would not let up. On May 12, 1942, his diary speaks of the unbearable circumstance that tens of thousands of Jews were still occupied in the Berlin armaments industry.[45]

Seven months later, in his report of April 15, 1943, Sauckel could inform Hitler that during 1942 he had brought 3,638,056 men and women to Germany, of whom 1,568,801 were employed in armaments. While my colleagues viewed these figures as exaggerated, the numbers do show the vast scope of the undertaking. In contrast, Himmler's offer to employ 50,000 Jews in armaments was not very weighty, even from a production point of view.

Thus all of Himmler's plans to employ Jews within the Reich had come to naught. At the same time, his ambitious plans to construct an SS-owned armaments concern also failed. Under point 36 of this session, it was tersely recorded that I had "pointed out to the Führer that—beyond a small amount of work—it will not be possible to set up armaments manufacture in the concentration camps for lack of: (1) the necessary machine tools; (2) the necessary buildings; whereas in the armaments industry both were available through the use of a second shift." Hitler agreed with my suggestions that factories that had to be put up outside cities for protection against air raids should give up their work force in the cities to the second shift in other factories. In exchange, they would receive "the necessary manpower from the concentration camps, likewise for two shifts." In this connection, I had pointed out to Hitler that Himmler would want to exert a decisive influence on these factories. According to the minutes, Hitler, too, "did not consider such an influence necessary."

In order to offer Himmler some small recompense, I proposed that we give him "a percentage of the working hours of his prisoners through an additional supply of war matériel. [There was] talk of a three to five percent participation," and Hitler declared his willingness "to order this additional allocation of weapons to the SS."[46]

This conversation, which was to determine the fate of countless unfortunates through the next two and a half years, took place in a matter-of-fact, technocratic manner detached from any human considerations. It is hard to reconstruct from memory whether the participants had any sense that they were talking not just about production figures but also about human destinies. (See Appendix 1.)

Had Himmler lost a match? I would have been underestimating him had I not assumed that from then on he would pursue his goals all the more stubbornly. But I would have been overestimating his arbitrary nature had I assumed that he would not respect Hitler's decision so long as it was not gone and forgotten. Himmler did go along with Hitler's decision, which foiled his own plans. He did not try to thwart it.[47] And yet, as we shall learn, he took part only with extreme reluctance in the measures ordered by Hitler in September 1942. Himmler very seldom expanded his responsibilities through protracted jurisdictional fighting. Instead he would patiently lie in wait, and then suddenly spring into action when he saw his chance. He soon hit on a way of obtaining further SS-owned armaments factories.

Chapter 3
Threats Instead of Production

HITLER'S SEPTEMBER 1942 DECISION on armaments manufacture in private industry had thus not changed Himmler's goals. Undaunted, he pursued his project of a concentration camp armaments empire. The fact that Hitler's decision went unheeded emerged from a single figure that Schieber apprised me of on May 7, 1944. "The number of hours worked by concentration camp inmates has not yet [reached] eight million, so certainly no more than some 32,000 men and women in concentration camps are employed in our armaments factories. This number is constantly decreasing."

Schieber said that he had spoken once again with Pohl's deputy, SS Obersturmbannführer Hermann Maurer, and had pointed out to him that "with a decentralized distribution of the concentration camp labor force, a technically more expedient use of their manpower, along with better nourishment and more sensible lodging, would be possible. With the food that our factory directors continue to supply to their labor force in spite of all impediments, and with the generally decent and humane treatment . . . both the Jewesses and the concentration camp inmates work well and will do anything to keep from being sent back to the concentration camp. These facts clearly make it imperative that we transfer even more concentration camp inmates to the armaments industry." In his letter, Schieber reported that Maurer argued against this:[1] "The SS cannot supply enough guards for a large-scale drain of many small labor divisions;

[Maurer also says] that we [the armaments ministry] are not delivering enough barbed wire to encircle the factory grounds, and that we must not underestimate the danger of secret sabotage in non-concentration-camp factories, given the less rigorous supervision and discipline there. . . . [He also says] that we must make experienced specialists and foremen available as managerial personnel in the SS-run" armaments industry.[2] Schieber replied to Maurer that "the requested supply and transfer of managerial personnel is out of the question. The only possibility is the previously planned, clearly agreed-on, and fairly successful alternative of transferring concentration camp inmates to the SS-run armaments industry."[3]

Himmler and his staff could afford to evade such objections by amiably ignoring them. The question of seniority was decisive. Whether a Reich minister or someone lower down, an early Party member like Himmler or Bormann was superior to a member who, like myself, had joined the Party in January 1931. For that reason alone, Himmler stood higher in the hierarchy than I. For instance, Himmler would never have condescended to confer with me in my offices, much less my home. *I* was always the one who had to visit him. In all our work together, we never achieved any personal relationship. Detachment was maintained at every instant. Besides, no one in the leadership apparatus of the Third Reich was keen on personal dealings.

Naturally, an unimportant man can become very important in an important position. Himmler was a cross between a sober realist who single-mindedly pursued his goals and a visionary of often grotesque proportions. I still find it inexplicable today that this inconspicuous man could achieve and know how to maintain such power. It will always be an enigma to me. Himmler strove to impress people with the importance of his title or with the flashy uniforms of the men surrounding him—or with the princes and counts that he attracted. Yet, oddly, he seemed like a philistine who had suddenly been catapulted to the top, an utterly insignificant personality who, in some inexplicable manner, had risen to a high position.

Himmler had no doubt shown talent in his choice of close staffers. Intellectually, his managerial personnel were the most capable in Hitler's Reich. I believe that the SS ambition to create a junior staff of leaders even for the ministries went back a long way. But they were all at loggerheads with one another. In July 1945, shortly after my capture, I wrote in my discussion "Political Connections" that the SS was "the mirror image of the leadership of the Reich, in which nearly every minister had to fight with the others. Kammler fought against Pohl and Jüttner, and vice versa. And

Sepp Dietrich had rows with all three of them. But Himmler's personality was so strong that, despite everything, he always held the steering wheel firmly in his hands."[4] (See Appendix 2.)

Himmler's colleagues seemed mere machine parts to him. He employed them in a mechanism of instruments, levers, and bars that was inexplicable to an outsider. However, he always took time when making decisions and he apparently mulled them over very thoroughly.

Himmler's prestige was represented solely by the power concentrated in him. If he had been deprived of his control over life and death, over spying by the Gestapo and the Security Service, then he would have been deprived of power overnight, as the surviving SA [Storm Troopers] leaders were on June 20, 1934. No one would have paid any more attention to his remaining power in other areas than, say, to that of a Wilhelm Frick or a Bernhard Rust, who both seemed as colorless as Himmler.

He was as dependent on Hitler as all his colleagues were. Felix Kersten correctly writes in his journal that Himmler "was sometimes frightened when summoned to the Führer. Not because he had to fear criticism; it was an automatic, groundless, nervous fear. Hence, when receiving praise from Hitler, he was as delighted as though he had passed an examination."[5] The same applies to all of us who worked directly with Hitler.

How right we were about the qualms we presented to Hitler in September 1942. After an inspection of Buchenwald, Himmler sent an indignant letter to me on March 5, 1943, saying that my ministry had ordered the manufacture of automatic rather than plain carbines in that concentration camp. They could not reckon with the delivery of machines for such production before early January 1944, he said. I could see by this, Himmler complained, "what a hard time I have being merely a subordinate firm within a larger firm—in this case, the Gustloff Works. . . . The Gustloff Works are my spokesman, and they obviously have no great interest in the success of these manufacturing sites. I cannot even tell whether the information presented to me is correct." He told me to "think about it and check whether it would not be better if the firms delivered their experts to us and we worked as self-responsible people at the rate we are used to." Himmler's goal was thus the same as before: autonomous manufacturing plants under the management of the SS. His letter went on with arguments that struck me as dangerous, given Hitler's unpredictable character. In any event, they could undermine my standing with Hitler. "The Führer expects me to manufacture. I am convinced that in the near future he will ask me how great the output is. . . . I believe that you, Party

Comrade Speer, understand perfectly well that I do not like to attach my name to any commission regarding the Führer if I cannot put it into practice, and that in this case I do not wish to disappoint the Führer's expectations in any way. May I therefore ask you to help me."

Himmler added that he could not help feeling "that this factory [in Buchenwald] is now somehow a thorn in the side of the Wilhelm-Gustloff Works, creating the highly foolish fear that this manufacturing plant might eventually compete with the Gustloff Works. I explained to the gentlemen once again that in peacetime I will have absolutely different ambitions than competing in this area. As you know, I see the peacetime mission of the SS in the area of settlement and wherever I can encourage the establishment of families with many children and their healthy life."[6]

In my reply to Himmler, I ignored both his protestations and Hitler's decision merely to have assembly plants in the concentration camps. As though it were the most natural thing in the world, I wrote him that "I consider it quite proper for the SS to maintain its own carbine manufacture in peacetime as well. . . . I would be glad to help put the Buchenwald camp entirely on its own feet. However, I would like to ask you to wait until production there has begun. I have no qualms whatsoever about a self-sufficient plant in the camp as soon as Buchenwald has familiarized itself with the operation. However, I consider it expedient to let the state of affairs, as planned so far, remain as is in order to prevent the start of operations from being afflicted by any unnecessary difficulties owing to resistance by the Gustloff Works, on whom I must depend for setting up the factory in the Buchenwald camp because of their *geographic proximity*."[7]

Himmler reacted a month later by telling Pohl to "strive for autonomy in our plant as soon as operations have gotten off to a good start." In the same terms, he told me how delighted he was that I was willing to assist him in the project.[8]

A few days after this exchange of letters, the SS must have realized that it lacked an important foundation for starting production—namely, the transporting of material to the camp. Himmler ordered the construction of a railroad line to Weimar. However, Sauckel, as a responsible Gauleiter, raised objections in telegrams on April 1.[9] He was known for his stubbornness and his concern about his prestige, and when he voiced qualms about the construction of this line, his resistance must have had an effect on Pister, the commandant of the camp. For on April 14, Himmler told Pister that he was to obey only his, Himmler's, orders. "The office of commandant of a concentration camp is a position in the Waffen-SS, which is under the command of the SS-Reichsführer alone." Himmler sent a copy of this order to Sauckel with the characteristic additional comment that he was quite amazed at Sauckel's conduct.[10]

Devoid of any technical knowledge, Himmler decided that the railroad connection between Weimar and Buchenwald would have to be completed by June 20 of the same year. Thirteen kilometers of track, covering three-hundred-meter differences in elevation, would have to be constructed within roughly two months.

The deadline was met. But in his book, Eugen Kogon points out that when the first locomotives were run, the substructures sagged. It was not until six months later that the railroad could actually begin operating.[11]

In order to counter Himmler's demands for the expensive construction of a factory in Buchenwald, I stated my objections in a meeting with Hitler on March 6, 1943. "Self-contained new carbine works" such as the SS was planning in Buchenwald "are out of the question at this time," I said, "since the necessary machinery cannot be made available. Hence, increased output must be striven for in presently existing factories, where a lower machine expenditure is possible. The SS facilities that have been made available should be used primarily as *assembly plants*."[12]

Basically, I was merely repeating Hitler's decision of September of the previous year. Hitler had felt that the lack of machine tools made it impossible to set up armaments manufacturing in the concentration camps. Himmler and I both talked about manufacturing and producing the K 98 carbine; but while he meant a complete factory, I was thinking of the assembly of component parts that would be supplied.

Hitler's decision was not sufficient to stem the urging of the SS. We had to supply both Buchenwald and Neuengamme with new machines, even though they were not necessary for production. For Himmler was aiming at production independent of suppliers. Assembly alone did not correspond with his notions. Pister, the commandant of Buchenwald, complained to Himmler that the machine tools had not yet arrived.[13] Three days later, however, he could state with satisfaction: "Evidently my repeated threat to appeal to the SS-Reichsführer was the reason for the sudden promise of two thousand machine tools confiscated in France."[14] (The two thousand machine tools that were siphoned off to Buchenwald against our better judgment could not be installed there usefully, and in addition their lack was felt elsewhere.)

One can hardly say that Commandant Pister was qualified to manage an industrial plant. But like a plant manager, not an official in charge, he conferred with Hornig, the director of the Gustloff Works, and picked his brain about internal plant matters. We can easily imagine the pressure brought on the technical leaders (whom Pister had summoned without further ado) when they were virtually interrogated by the feared commandant of the nearby concentration camp. Under these circumstances, we can understand why they blamed the delay on Schieber, the chairman of their company's board of directors.[15]

The very day after receiving this report of Pister's, Himmler, obviously excited, dictated the draft of an answer to be sent to me.[16] But the telegram was not dispatched. Himmler had evidently decided that it would be better to order Pohl to have the director of the Gustloff Works confirm the unfavorable information about Schieber "and then to summon SS Brigade Commander Schieber to his office."[17]

This blackmail of Himmler's and Pister's shows how hard it was to insert an SS factory into our system. My staffers always feared direct interference from Himmler.

The management of these concentration camp factories was necessarily at a considerable remove, and technicians were often restricted to the telephone when making arrangements and coping with problems that arose in Buchenwald. My colleagues were used to adjusting plans to fit a given program. Difficulties of this nature within the self-responsibility of industry were handled by a colleague in the special committee in charge. I would never have had to deal with such problems myself. But it was irritating to see how minor details were discussed on the highest level here and to note how much work was demanded by this carbine production, which was actually insignificant within the overall framework of armaments and war economy.

By the summer of 1943, only one thousand prisoners were employed in Buchenwald's assembly process, even though Himmler had announced in March 1942 that he would be able to occupy five thousand inmates within three to four months. Even after a year, one could not speak of success at Buchenwald. Himmler tried to blame the failure on my armaments agencies, and it may be true that my representatives did not develop any enthusiasm for setting up production for the SS.

Eugen Kogon traced this belated, and then only tentative, start of the assembly operations to sabotage by prisoners.[18] Such sabotage can certainly be assumed. But it is doubtful that it could continue for several years without the SS's finding ways and means of counteracting it. My ministry at the time had the impression that the poor results were due to lack of ability in the SS agencies. (See Appendix 3.)

On August 20, 1943, Himmler had managed to get Hitler to promise him responsibility for the manufacture of the V-2 rocket.[19] That same day,

Himmler reached an agreement with my representative Saur to transfer the production of parts of this rocket to Buchenwald. Exactly one year later, on August 24, 1944, 120 American Flying Fortresses raided Buchenwald. Within fifteen minutes, from 12:30 to 12:45 P.M., they dropped 400 one-ton bombs, 600 1,800-pound bombs, and 6,000 or 7,000 stick-type incendiary bombs. Ninety-six SS men and 110 prisoners were killed; 200 SS men and 300 prisoners were severely or lightly wounded.[20]

Regarding the course of carbine manufacture at Buchenwald after that, the minutes of a meeting with Hitler on October 12, 1944, are revealing. They contain a note saying that the production quota of carbines for December 1944 (270,000, including the automatic G 43 gun) is to be maintained *despite* the loss of output at Buchenwald.[21] Thus, by October 1944, the exact quantity of infantry weapons being assembled at Buchenwald can no longer be determined.

The second test case, involving assembly of the Pi 38 pistol in Neuengamme, was no less amateurish than the test case in Buchenwald. Himmler's files are silent about this factory until the autumn of 1943 —a sign that there were no remarkable triumphs to be registered. In the summer of 1943, Himmler tried, as he had done in Buchenwald, to replace the manufacture of this unimportant pistol with the manufacture of an automatic weapon, the self-loading G 43 gun.[22] For a long time, our troops had been urgently requesting a weapon equal to the automatic pistol that the Soviet soldiers carried. However, Hitler hesitated despite the insistence of the Army General Staff.

Meanwhile, at Neuengamme, Himmler had likewise managed to ignore Hitler's order to set up an assembly plant. On September 7, 1943, Pohl could inform Himmler that production of the self-loading G 43 was about to begin. A whole five months later, on February 26, 1944, Pohl had to write Schieber that production at Neuengamme could not commence after all. The factory buildings were ready for production, he said, except for the forging building; but in Berlin, "three firms that had machines ready for transportation have not yet dispatched them, and the roughly two hundred necessary machines beyond those have not yet been allocated by the Main Committee" of the Armaments Ministry. Pohl told Schieber "to allocate the missing machines as quickly as possible so that operations could finally begin." The letter ended rudely on a note of superior to subaltern. Pohl, the Obergruppenführer, ordered the brigade commander: "Please inform me about these vital measures."[23]

This showed how he was being constantly ignored by the Armaments Ministry, Pohl remarked to Himmler when sending him a copy of the letter.[24]

Himmler reacted with annoyance. "Dear Pohl: Who is the man responsible for neglecting to ship the machines that are ready at three Berlin firms? I intend to have him arrested for sabotage as soon as your report arrives," he wrote, by "telegram—rush."[25] At the same time, Himmler notified Lieutenant Colonel Suchanek, who was on his staff, that the "SS Reichsführer wants [a blank space for the name to be filled in later] to be arrested for sabotage."[26] Naturally, Himmler was hoping to apprehend one of my men; who else could he hold responsible for this failure?

Nine days later Himmler warned Pohl's adjutant: "My wire of 3/7/44 requested the name of the man who neglected to send the machines to Neuengamme, and the SS Reichsführer has still not received any answer."[27] Pohl now had to admit that his accusations had been groundless. The delay was caused by other circumstances. He notified Himmler the next day that a number of the machine tools destined for Neuengamme had been destroyed in an air raid.[28]

Nevertheless, upon receiving this information, Himmler dispatched an urgent telegram to Schieber: "I am dismayed that the manufacture of self-loading guns can still not begin at Neuengamme. Our preparations were completed apart from a few details." He generously failed to mention that the necessary forging plant had not been built. "The Main Committee has, regrettably, not yet allocated the necessary machines. May I ask you to get the committee to do so as soon as possible. The rate so far is shameful—to avoid sharper words. May I also inform you that I had intended to arrest for sabotage the man responsible for neglecting to ship the machines now ready at three firms in Berlin. I will stand by and watch for only a short time more. I have asked SS Obergruppenführer Pohl to wire the delivery dates of each machine."[29]

Schieber replied instantly that the plants, including Neuengamme, under the jurisdiction of the Main Committee for Weapons were under Saur's aegis. All the machines provided with contingents had already been delivered; and he was not aware of any complaints.[30]

Ten months after his first letter, which had spoken optimistically about speedy manufacture of the G 43, Pohl was now blaming his failure on the low priority of the project. Yet industrial plants on the same low priority level were expanding parallel production and carrying out their assigned programs.[31] While Pohl was making promises for the future, the industrial output of the G 43 rose from 15,013 units in January to 33,010 in July 1944. In other words, it doubled.[32]

Naturally, Himmler refused to admit his failures. On some occasions he showered his listeners with reports of the SS's enormous triumphs in armaments. Himmler was frivolously playing with figures when he informed Hitler in April 1943: "Labor in the concentration camps: 140,000 workers."[33] At that time, according to Pohl's statistics, the work force there numbered 171,000 prisoners,[34] but 22 percent were "not able-bodied (sick, quarantined),"[35] and 10 percent were used in "running sixteen camps." Hence, subtracting 63,000 inmates, there remained 107,000.

In his speech to the Reichsleiters and Gauleiters in Posen on October 6, 1943, Himmler boasted that "50,000 to 60,000 political and criminal felons, together with roughly 150,000 others, including a small number of Jews," i.e., an overall total of 200,000, were working for the armaments industry.[36] In his next sentence, Himmler went ad absurdum when he bragged that the prisoners worked "a monthly total of some fifteen million hours."[37] According to Schieber, who had reported an average work time of 250 hours per prisoner,[38] there were 60,000 prisoners, not three and a half times that number.

Even when discussing his armaments performance, Himmler reveled in columns of figures that had nothing to do with reality. On June 21, 1944, in his Sonthofen speech to the generals, he reported: "First of all, I would like to let very sober figures speak for themselves. Today, in the concentration camps, in this year of the war, forty million hours are worked every month for armaments. In the concentration camps, one-third of the German fighter planes are being manufactured by the mostly—i.e., nine-tenths—non-German inmates and criminals. There, one-third of Germany's gun barrels are being manufactured today, with one German foreman to every ninety prisoners. Countless other things are also being produced, from the finest optical instruments to munitions and gigantic quantities of trench mortars and 3.7 cm antiaircraft guns."[39]

One can hardly assume that Himmler produced the barrels for one-third, i.e., 71,866 guns, of the 215,690 K 98 carbine barrels manufactured in May 1944. If for no other reason, this was impossible because he did not have the proper factories. Nor could it be even remotely correct that the concentration camps produced 457 of the 1,372 fighter planes completed in May 1944.[40] The basis of this claim might have been Pohl's letter written to Himmler one week earlier, on June 14, 1944: "Reich Marshal Goering has sent a telegram (of which a copy is enclosed) to the management, the staff, and the representatives of the Messerschmitt Works in

Regensburg. This telegram acknowledges the outstanding performance of this company, and Linder, the director of the Messerschmitt Works in Regensburg, has informed me that about 35 percent of that is due to the operations under my jurisdiction: at Flossenbürg and Mauthausen." Himmler, overjoyed, wrote on the margin in big letters: "Very good."[41]

The Messerschmitt Works in Regensburg were producing only one part of the frames for the fighter planes. Besides, a plane has an engine as well as electrical and mechanical equipment. In June 1944, air armaments employed 2,330,000 workers.[42] Since the fighter planes amounted to 53.7 percent of the overall production,[43] we may estimate that over a million people were involved in their output. Himmler's claim that he was not only contributing greatly to military armaments but also producing one-third of the fighter planes was thus so absurd that I could never understand how a man as distrustful as Hitler could accept such figures without checking them.

One further comparison demonstrates the invalidity of Himmler's claim. As agreed upon with Himmler in September 1942, the SS was to receive 5 percent of its production share in additional weapons.[44] In the Führer's Protocol of May 1, 1943, point 10, this portion was stipulated at 17,000 carbines for the period from September 1942 to the beginning of May 1943. This 5 percent figure would thus imply that 100 percent equaled 340,000 carbines.

In October 1943, some 60,000 prisoners were committed to armaments production. Since the number was still small in the spring of 1943 and increasing only gradually from month to month, we can estimate that an average of 30,000 prisoners were working in armaments during the seven months on which the calculation is based. These 30,000 prisoners produced a total of 340,000 carbines. During World War II, an American defense plant in Springfield, Illinois, had 14,000 men and women producing 1,800,000 carbines a year, or 1,050,000 in seven months. If I substitute 14,000 for 30,000 employees, that would give me an output of 2,250,000 carbines as opposed to the fictitious number of 340,000 in the concentration camps. Thus, the performance in the camps amounted to a bit more than one-seventh that in Springfield.

A similar result can be calculated in a different estimate. A memorandum of November 1942 on the machine production of the K 98 indicates an average work time of 25 hours per carbine. Assuming 250 hours of work every month, a laborer must therefore have produced 10 carbines in the time outlined. For the manufacture of 340,000 carbines in seven months, a private factory like Mauser employed a monthly average of

4,857 people. Hence, according to this comparison, each of the 30,000 prisoners did one-sixth of what a normal worker did[45]: a performance comparison that is devastating for the concentration camp bureaucracy.

The Army Ordnance Office paid 75 marks for a K 98 carbine in 1942.[46] This amounts to 25.5 million marks for the labor of an estimated 30,000 prisoners in those seven months. During the same seven months, Germany produced armaments with a total value of 13.2 billion marks.[47] When I compare this total sum of our production to the SS performance, it is easy to see how minimal their overall contribution to armaments was. In this period of seven months, the SS did not contribute more than two-thousandths of a percent to the overall armaments output.[48] This share may have gone up as of May 1943 with the increased use of prisoners. But never did the armaments production of the SS reach the scope attributed to it by Himmler's imagination.

Furthermore, the SS factories in concentration camps were extremely unprofitable because of the cost of guards and barracks. According to a statistic of January 1945, an average of 74 guards were used for 1,000 male prisoners.[49] Thus, it took 12,664 soldiers to guard 171,000 prisoners (the figure for April 1943). One guard cost an average of 1,500 marks annually if we recall that, while the soldiers' salaries were not high, the payments to their families were generous, and officers received a great deal more. Hence, 12,664 soldiers and officers meant a yearly burden of 18 million marks just for guard duty.

With 300 prisoners per barrack, 556 barracks were needed for 170,000 prisoners in the fall of 1943. Each of the barracks cost 41,000 marks, including the preparation of the terrain. Thus, it cost 23.5 million marks to house all the prisoners. Given an estimated ten years' longevity for barracks, the annual burden went up to some 20.3 million marks, not counting the expenses incurred for the camp bureaucracy of the SS and for maintaining the prisoners. The resulting production amounted to 43.7 million marks, almost half of which was devoured by overhead.

The SS could have achieved greater profits if it had hired out the able-bodied prisoners at an average daily rate of 4.70 marks.[50] In the fall of 1943, according to Pohl's figures, 107,730 of the 171,000 prisoners were able-bodied.[51] The daily income would thus have been 506,000 marks, i.e., 184 million marks a year. But Himmler's plans for building up an industrial empire obstructed such rational considerations.

Chapter 4
Fantasy and Reality,
Production and Mortality Rates

THE PRISONERS BROUGHT CASH incomes or opened prospects for SS-run factories. Like machines and tools, they had become investment goods. It would have been only too natural of Himmler to be personally concerned about improving the situation of the prisoners.

In the area of nourishment, a series of edicts shows that strenuous efforts were made to increase the work capacity of the prisoners.[1] Thus, on March 23, 1942, Himmler had already asked Pohl "to gradually develop a diet which, like that of Roman soldiers or Egyptian slaves, contains all the vitamins and is simple and cheap. Naturally, our climate here is to be taken into account."[2] To be sure, such historicist orders lacked any humanitarian concern, as shown by an almost simultaneous order of Pohl's on April 30, 1942: "The operation must be exhausting in the true sense of the word in order to achieve maximum performance. The work time is not limited. Its length depends on the structure of the camp. . . . Circumstances that can shorten work time, like meals, roll calls, etc., are therefore to be restricted to an irreducible minimum . . . time-consuming lunches are prohibited."[3]

A short time later, Himmler came back to his pet theme of healthy nutrition through vitamins. On December 12, 1942, writing of food for prisoners in 1943, Himmler suggested to Pohl that he "acquire large quantities of raw vegetables and onions," hand out large amounts of carrots, kohlrabi, and turnips, and store up "a sufficient amount for the prisoners for this winter . . . so that the prisoners can get an adequate measure of them every day. I believe that we will thereby greatly raise the state of health."[4]

In late October 1943, Pohl once again reminded the commandants of the concentration camps that the manpower was now important. The prisoners had to be treated with care, "not out of false sentimentality, but because we need them with their arms and legs, since they must contribute to the German people's winning a great victory."[5]

The rations established by the Reich Ministry of Food for all prisoners in concentration camps were already at a minimum. However, according to Hans Marsalek, a longtime inmate of Mauthausen:

> [The] prisoners *never*, not even for a week, received any meal in which anything like the food listed in the tables was cooked or distributed. . . . First, the SS commanders, then the SS junior commanders, finally the ordinary SS organs took whatever they felt like from the storehouses, the kitchen, etc. Then the prisoners working in the storehouses, transportation squads, and kitchens "liberated" food. The block personnel then stole while handing out marmalade, cottage cheese, bread, and even turnip stew, picking out potatoes and pieces of meat from the caldron. Hundreds of members of the SS squadron as well as the families of the staff of the SS commandant—and this meant more than a thousand people!—stretched their food rations with lard, meat, sugar, cereals, and potatoes from the supplies meant for the prisoners.[6]

Why was it not possible for the leaders of the SS, the German organization responsible for combating all corruption, to abolish these abuses, especially since they endangered Himmler's economic goals? Administratively, everything was regulated. In Office V of the Reich Criminal Investigation Department there was a section for "economic crime," and its unit Wi 4 was supposed to deal with "corruption in the army, the SS, the police, and the armaments industry."[7]

But in reality the true state of affairs was a knot that could not be untangled. It was mortally dangerous to attempt an exposure of irregularities and scandals in the concentration camps. We must bear in mind the difficulties encountered by SS Obersturmführer Dr. Konrad Morgen when he investigated the embezzling committed by Karl Koch, the commandant of Buchenwald—and Morgen met with these obstacles while acting in an official capacity as a leading member of the headquarters of the Reich Criminal Investigation Department. On August 17, 1944, Morgen brought charges at the SS and Police Court, stating that Koch "murdered the prisoners Fredemann and May because they had been subpoenaed as witnesses in a pending legal proceeding."

How could an investigating commission of the Gestapo expect prisoners in a concentration camp to testify against their guards? They valued their lives too highly to bear witness against SS functionaries. The latter remained in the camp and continued to rule them, could torment or kill them. Kogon confirms this problem in a different, but no less important, connection:

> There was little in the SS that was not kept secret. . . . The bizarre extremes of this system [of secrecy] can be seen from such things as the fact that not even Gestapo officials had the right to enter the camp without special permission from the Reich Security Main Office, Division IV, even though it was the Gestapo who sent thousands of people to the concentration camps. . . . Very few Gestapo officials, therefore, knew in detail what it looked like in the hell to which they condemned their victims. The questions they asked of released prisoners as to what it had been like were seldom meant to catch them; these were truly questions of curiosity![8]

It is certain that the pilfering of food meant for prisoners greatly contributed to undermining their health and ultimately causing their deaths. Lethargy and impotence can be inferred from Himmler's speech in Posen to the SS squad commanders on October 4, 1944:

> We have become a very corrupt people. But we must not and need not take this very profoundly or with weltschmerz tragedy. We shall not gain control of this plague known as corruption in our circles [of the SS] if we do not act against any outbreak of corruption in our circles, unconditionally and unrestrictedly with no ifs, ands, or buts, if we do not barbarically pursue it, degrade the corrupt man, remove him from office, and expose him before his subalterns. However, what actually deserves to be called corruption is not serious in our circles. Still, there are little things to which one does not give a second thought and for which one uses the expression "to liberate something."[9]

How vast was the gap between threat and reality! One notices over and over again that Himmler's threats of severe punishment were usually carried out no more than Hitler's were. If a threat is not carried out in one's own retinue, then it quickly loses its edge, no matter how harsh it may be. For instance, on March 28, 1945, Goebbels complained in his diary: "It would be desirable if the Führer not only had the proper insights" about penalties for high functionaries who have failed, "but if he also drew the correct conclusions therefrom. In my opinion, he differs greatly in this from Frederick II, who was so ruthless in his measures against the high and the low that he frequently aroused hatred and condemnation from his troops and his generals."[10]

Hitler held on to Goering, for instance, never dismissing him from his offices, which were important for the war effort even though he knew that Goering was corrupt and lazy and a drug addict. However, Hitler had always been lenient concerning the corruption of his high functionaries, always obstructing prosecution, even during the harsh war years, when Goebbels, for propaganda reasons, asked for their dismissal. Himmler himself had a reputation for being painfully precise in all personal and financial matters. Nevertheless, he was remarkably lax when speaking to his SS commanders about the corruption in Germany.

Himmler had ordered that the work strength of the prisoners be maintained. Yet the SS statistics reveal that they were no more capable of fulfilling this demand than of manufacturing primitive handguns in Buchenwald and Neuengamme.

Because of inadequate conditions, a total of 109,861 prisoners died from June to November 1942,[11] and the official figure may be far lower than the true number of deaths. In September 34 percent of new inmates died, which spelled an imminent draining of the camps. Only such an emergency can explain why Himmler categorically ordered in December 1942 that "the mortality must absolutely be reduced."[12] An SS brigade commander added: "With such a high mortality figure, the number of prisoners can never be brought to the level that the SS Reichsführer has ordered." Camp doctors, the edict continued, must "make sure with all the means at their disposal that the mortality rates in the individual camps go down greatly. The best physician in a concentration camp is not the one who believes that he must be conspicuous by inappropriate harshness, but rather the one who keeps work capacity as high as possible by staying on the alert and trading prisoners between the individual work sites. Camp physicians must watch over the nourishment of the prisoners more closely than before and submit suggestions for improvements in conjunction with the camp commandants. Such proposals, however, should not merely remain on paper; camp physicians should check into them regularly. Furthermore, camp physicians must see to it that working conditions at the individual sites are improved wherever possible. For this purpose, it is necessary for camp physicians to personally go and observe the working conditions in situ."[13] This edict was addressed to the same camp physicians who were busy with such measures as "selection," i.e., determining which new arrivals were to live or die, and "injections," i.e., killing prisoners by injecting air into the bloodstream.

In September 1943, nine months later, these evidently ongoing efforts were successful, if we are to believe Pohl's list of mortalities in the camps. Further, the result tends to agree with the statistics gathered by Langbein, secretary to the garrison physician at Auschwitz.[14] In a long report on September 30, 1943, Pohl pointed out to Himmler that the mortality rate had gone down to one-fifth from December 1942 to August 1943. He also cites the implementation of hygienic measures that had been demanded for a long time.[15]

At armaments meetings in Linz, I had found that the SS intended to build a vast harbor on the Danube, near the Mauthausen concentration camp, in order to ship cobblestones from the nearby stone quarry to Vienna after the war. This was a purely peacetime task, which I could in no way allow. I wanted to make sure that the prisoners intended for the project would be sent instead to the Linz Steelworks, called the Hermann Goering Works back then. My goal was to reduce the steel plant's manpower shortage, which lowered production. This plant was very important for manufacturing not only high-quality steel but also steel tank hulls and turrets.

For this reason, I visited the concentration camp at Mauthausen in late March 1943.[16] During my inspection I was surprised to see expensive granite retaining walls, on which barracks, likewise of natural stone, had been erected. I was shown the inside of the kitchen barrack, a washhouse barrack, and a living barrack. Everything was clean and orderly. The level of, say, an average antiaircraft barrack. The camp, or rather the small portion that I saw, made an almost romantic impression with its stone portal and medieval castle yards, its pseudohistorical walls and towers. I saw no emaciated inmates. They were probably at the infamous stone quarry at the time.[17]

The fact that prominent visitors at concentration camps were shown an illusion was stated by Franz Blaha, a witness for the prosecution at Nuremberg.[18] Marsalek, too, reports that "for camp inspections [at Mauthausen] only the second barrack, for 'functionary prisoners,' was visited, where meticulous order and cleanliness prevailed and where vases of flowers were placed on some tables. . . . Visitors were shown only selected, clean, well-dressed, physically strong prisoners who were employed by the SS commanders."[19]

Eugen Kogon, who spent many years in Buchenwald, had similar experiences. Even when there were numerous visits by SS functionaries, Kogon writes, the camp directors disguised the true situation. They revealed only special showpieces. Visitors were taken mainly to the infirmary, the library, the kitchen, the supply room, or the laundry. They were shown the movie theater and agricultural grounds. "If they ever came to an actual living block, it was usually one for the so-called 'commanded,' where barbers for the SS and other SS trusties lived, as well as specially privileged inmates; and such a block was therefore never overcrowded and was always clean."[20] These descriptions by Kogon and Marsalek show that when I visited Mauthausen, the concentration camp leaders were merely following normal routine.

Immediately after the war, a book entitled *Mordhausen*, by eyewitnesses, depicted a visit by Himmler and Commandant Ernst Kaltenbrunner in Mauthausen. "The half-starved and sick were herded like sheep and locked up in one block. A sign was placed on the door, saying: 'Caution—Typhus!' " Himmler was shown the block for the head inmates. These were the "prisoners who worked in the SS kitchen, the officers' quarters, the canteen, etc. They all had the opportunity of living somewhat better. With bared chests—the most powerful ones, of course—they stood at attention when Himmler entered the block. 'Well, prisoners, how are you? You all look good. Lots of good food, *nicht wahr*? Open up your lockers.' The lockers contained a three-pound loaf of bread for each man and a pound of sausage for every three. 'And what's for lunch?' he asked in the kitchen, telling them to open the caldrons. 'Peas with bacon! Yes, the heavy labor in the quarry.' They handed Himmler a bowl of pea soup. 'This tastes wonderful!' One did not have to be very observant to read the play of features between Himmler and the camp commandant, who understood each other perfectly.

"No sooner had Himmler left the camp than the rubber clubs whizzed through the air. 'C'mon!' the SS men shouted. 'Get the bread and the sausage back to the SS kitchen on the double!' "[21]

This story sounds incredible. But Höss reports that prior to Himmler's visit to Auschwitz on March 1, 1942, Glücks showed up to make sure that a rosy picture would be painted "when the big shots arrive from Berlin."[22]

Was Himmler willingly deceived? We can hardly imagine that he did not see through this masquerade if it was put on so blatantly. At headquarters he would speak with the face of an upright man when telling Hitler's Round Table how good conditions were in the concentration camps. Occasionally he would illustrate this with stories of soccer matches or musical soirées or other pleasures. Never was mistreatment or executions mentioned; not even were the high death rates ever brought up. In 1941 a jocular Himmler did tell Hitler that he much preferred using criminals as guards for the prisoners. And Hitler agreed. That was an extremely good idea, he said; they would be pitiless and make sure of order and discipline, if for no other reason than to avoid losing their jobs.

About a week after visiting Mauthausen, on April 5, 1943, I sent Himmler a letter that was drafted for me by my agency of the "plenipotentiary for the regulation of the building trade."

> While we lack not only iron and wood but also manpower to construct armaments works for the immediate needs of the front lines, I saw during my inspection of the concentration camp at Mauthausen that the SS is carrying out plans that strike me as more than generous given today's conditions. For the expansion of concentration camps, we must carry out any new planning with an eye to achieving the highest degree of effectiveness with the deployment of the least means and the achievement of the utmost success for the *momentary* armaments demands, that is, we must switch immediately to primitive construction methods.[23]

Mr. Erich Fried, in a letter to *The New York Times*, interpreted my demand as an order to have the prisoners dig their lodgings in the soil with their fingernails.[24] In reality, I was referring to an edict of mine issued in March 1943: ". . . all construction during the war must be of the simplest form possible. Permanent building methods must be widely replaced by temporary methods. Buildings meant only to outlast the war will be normally quite adequate. . . . Outer and inner walls are to be of light construction as far as practicable. We should generally forgo outer and inner adornment."[25]

Pohl evidently did not know of these regulations, for he wrote to Himmler that the letter of April 5, 1943, from Reich Minister Speer to the Reichsführer was "really a pretty strong number." But Pohl went on to say that he had forgotten how to feel amazement. He restricted himself to stating that it "would be completely wrong to shift to primitive construction in concentration camps immediately. Reich Minister Speer does not seem to know that we have over 160,000 prisoners now and are constantly fighting epidemics and a high mortality because the lodgings for the inmates, including the sanitary facilities, are totally inadequate." He "therefore had to point out now, in accordance with his duty, that the return to primitive construction methods will probably cause a so-far-undreamt-of mortality in the camps."[26]

In my letter of April 5 I had suggested to Himmler that one of my officials along with one of his staff members should check all concentration camps in situ. This inspection tour by Desch and Sandler from my staff and SS Brigade Commander Kammler, head of the SS Building Administration, took place a short time later. At Auschwitz they uncovered catastrophic sanitary conditions. As revealed in a handwritten addendum in Pohl's report to Himmler, I was told at the same time "that the inspection of the other concentration camps resulted in a highly positive picture."[27]

The finding of catastrophic sanitary conditions at Auschwitz indeed alarmed me. On May 30 I raised the iron allotment for concentration camps to 450 tons a month.[28] In addition, to end the emergency conditions in Auschwitz, I allocated "a special order of 1,000 tons of building iron; 1,000 tons of cast-iron pipes, for which the SS will make 300 tons of iron available from their overall allotment; some hundred tons of half-inch water pipes from the stocks of the plenipotentiary for building in Hamm; and the necessary quantity of hard round bar steel, 8–20 millimeters in diameter. The acquisition of rationing certificates for the 1,000 tons of cast-iron pipes as well as the dispatching of the water pipes has already been set into motion."[29] An extraordinary measure, for in general the contingent bearer had to order his commodity on the basis of the quota certificates issued to him—which normally meant a delivery period of many months.

I expressly emphasized on this occasion that these "construction iron supplies are to be used only for building up the concentration camps, especially Auschwitz. . . . Unfortunately, I cannot allocate any further quantities of construction iron for new divisions of the Waffen-SS."[30] I felt it was important to note this restriction on the use of the special allocation for fear that the SS leaders might yield to the urging of their generals who were assigned to create these divisions.

Pohl sent Himmler the draft of a letter to me (which was never dispatched) saying 2,400 more tons of iron were now available. That exceeded "by far the amount of iron that has so far been available every quarter for the entire SS." This, he wrote, was an unexpected result of the joint inspection.[31] The letter must have run to four pages. Himmler contented himself with five lines when he expressed his terse but hearty thanks on June 15. He was "confirmed in the conviction that there was still such a thing as justice," he ironically added.[32]

Just two weeks later Pohl could notify Himmler that "some of the promised iron quotas have already been distributed and applied to their designated purposes."[33] Considering the delivery problems in the summer of 1943, this matter had been taken care of extraordinarily quickly.

Nevertheless, the SS and the police department were given 76,800 tons of steel a year by Central Planning.[34] These iron allocations were mainly destined for the police force, which was under Himmler's command. The iron was to be used for fire trucks to fight the vast conflagrations caused by aerial attacks. Hence, a diversion of 70 tons a month and a special allocation of some 2,500 tons for correcting the sanitary abuses could have been possible for some time.

But even within my area, this increase in the SS quotas was a mere bagatelle when I recall that in May 1943 I distributed 2,520,000 tons of iron to the entire war economy.[35]

Retrospectively, I am astonished that Himmler did not use his great power to demand the necessary material directly from one of my staff members, who was in the SS. Yet oddly enough, until the end of the regime, individual areas of authority were maintained in an almost ludicrous way, to the extent that they did not overlap. For instance, as late as the spring of 1944, Goering sent me a request, bearing the letterhead "Reich Hunting Master," to make ammunition available to German hunters in order that this valuable additional source of food could be maintained. The amount was ridiculously tiny in comparison with the entire infantry's ammunition. His department could have seen to this matter at any time through one of my subalterns.[36]

None of this had anything to do with the death camps in Poland and Upper Silesia, for instance, Sobidor, Treblinka, and Auschwitz. There the "selected" prisoners were killed. In the camps where the survivors vegetated in order to work, there were economic reasons for keeping the inmates alive. Pohl, in his report of September 1943, listed these camps. Their very enumeration arouses memories of cruel details in us: Dachau with 17,300; Sachsenhausen with 26,500; Buchenwald with 17,600; Mauthausen/Gusen with 21,000; Flossenbürg with 4,800; Neuengamme with 9,800; Auschwitz with 48,000 men and 26,000 women; Gross-Rosen with 5,000; Natzweiler with 2,200; Bergen-Belsen with 3,300; Stutthof with 3,800 men and 500 women; Lublin with 11,500 men and 3,900 women; Ravensbrück with 3,100 men and 14,100 women; Riga with 3,000; Herzogenbusch with 2,500; hence, a total of 224,000 prisoners slated for labor.

Soon the quick delivery of the installation material had positive consequences. In December 1942, the mortality rate in the concentration camps amounted to 10 percent of the total number of prisoners. After that it went down steadily, sinking to 2.23 percent in July 1943 and 2.09 percent in August 1943.[37] In a letter to Himmler, Pohl confirmed that the lowering of the death rate in these camps was due mainly to the fact that "the hygienic measures that were requested long ago have now at least to a great extent been carried out." And in his reply of October 8, 1943, Himmler made this reference to the assistance from my ministry: "I am convinced that these final difficulties too will go down to the extent that a sewage system and better sanitary facilities become technically possible."[38]

The Auschwitz labor camp should not be confused with the Auschwitz death camp at Birkenau. In the labor camp the prisoners had escaped "selection" and were to be used on large industrial projects around Auschwitz, e.g., those of I. G. Farben. These prisoners, too, as Höss wrote, were to be treated with consideration in order that they might contribute to building Himmler's industrial concern. But all the more drastic are the figures of casualties resulting from the catastrophic sanitary conditions of this former army prison camp. These figures were considerably higher than the average at all other concentration camps. In March 1943, casualties there totaled 15.4 percent; in July, August, and September 1943, an average of 3.6 percent died in Auschwitz (despite the aid we gave) as against the overall Reich average of 2.4 percent. Nevertheless, the SS had succeeded in lowering the mortality at this camp to one-fourth.[39]

Should I have refused to allocate materials to concentration camps because I did not want to have anything to do with them? What would have happened if I had refused to support the construction of the camps? Would my conscience be calmer today? If I helped to abolish abuses, then I was actively participating in the SS system; if I had avoided any action on the basis of principles, then the situation in the camps would have gotten more catastrophic. Pohl was preparing to lie to me about the death rates when he sent Himmler the already mentioned draft of a letter on June 9, 1943. In this draft Pohl did not mention anything about the high mortality. He spoke only about "people not able to work—sick people, quarantine, etc.—22 percent."[40]

It is understandable that with the extortion to which my staff and I were exposed in regard to the Buchenwald and Neuengamme projects, we felt no desire to increase the number of prisoners working in the concentration camp factories; and all the less so when the results were utterly inconsistent with our industrial experience. But as early as September 1942, Pohl wanted to slate 13.7 million marks to expanding the Auschwitz camp.[41] This meant additional facilities for lodging 120,000 inmates. His demand was not met—as revealed by my ministry's itemization of the barracks construction approved for concentration camps in 1943. This statement is dated April 5, 1943, i.e., six months later. For Auschwitz, investments of only 3,081,000 marks were approved, or less than one-fourth.[42] In the same letter, I told Himmler that 7,151,000 marks would be allocated in 1943 for the expansion of all concentration camps in Germany and 5,985,000 marks for barracks in 1944. This corresponded to 157 barracks for 1943 and 131 barracks for 1944. Since each barrack was to house 400 prisoners, this building program would raise the capacity of the concentration camps by 115,200 by the end of 1944.[43]

At the same time, I had to question the possibility of carrying out this program. I warned Himmler: "As I see the development, you will not complete the implementation of the plans this year [1943], if for no other reason than because you will not receive the necessary supplies for the expansions in time, aside from the fact that the situation in the iron and wood sector will soon get much worse than previously. . . . You are thus burdening next year [1944] and also the year 1945 with building aims whose expedience cannot be calculated by anyone today for a longer period," i.e., for peacetime.[44] This was a clear-cut allusion to the difference in our attitudes. I doubted the sense of Himmler's concentration camps. Eleven days later, I sent Himmler a letter with almost the same content: "It has been established that the intended plans and expansions in the concentration camps cannot generally be carried out in the requisite scope. The causes lie not only in the generally difficult situation of materials acquisition, but also in supplying the required manpower for implementing these construction measures."[45]

In April 1943, when I warned Himmler not to overestimate the possibility of expanding the concentration camps, they housed 171,000 prisoners. The buildings that I then approved for all concentration camps signified an increase of 115,000 in their capacity, which made a total of 286,000 prisoners. Yet the statistics say that the overall number of prisoners by August 15, 1944, almost doubled that—523,286.[46] During the next five months, the number of prisoners went up by almost another 200,000. According to a statistic of January 15, 1945, there were 714,211 prisoners in the Reich territory.[47] According to a list of Marsalek's, there were 643,290.[48] Eugen Kogon confirms this terrible situation in his *The SS State*. He speaks of a fourfold overcrowding.[49]

This overcrowding of the barracks explains at least in part the rise of the monthly death rates after the fall of 1943. The danger of epidemics also increased; indeed, a spotted fever epidemic in the Auschwitz women's camp greatly contributed to the rapidly rising mortality.[50] (See Appendix 4.) In Poland the problem of the barracks shortage was solved in an especially cold-blooded way. As Simon Wiesenthal writes in his book *The Sunflower*, when new transports arrived, "the old prisoners were liquidated —by entire barracks—to make room for the new ones. We experienced this every two months."[51]

As armaments minister, I could be suspicious when statistical accounts veiled circumstances by means of unclear data. Thus, it is not possible to go through Pohl's report on the deaths in the labor concentration camps (September 30, 1943)[52] and explain the decrease from 110,000 people in September 1942 to 85,800 people in October 1942—given the official death rate of only 11,205 prisoners. Had the missing 12,995 prisoners been released?

This lacuna in SS statistics is explained by another set of figures (see Appendix 5, Table 3), which, unfortunately, permits comparisons only for July to November 1942. This comparison offers the inconsistencies that in six months 49,175 additional deaths were concealed as Pohl reported 48,703 deaths to Himmler for these five months.[53] According to this computation Himmler was informed of a 10.6 percent mortality for all concentration camp inmates in August 1942. Yet in fact, the death rate was actually more than twice that, namely, 25.6 percent. In September the report to Himmler spoke of 10.18 percent; but the death rate was actually over thrice that, namely, 36.2 percent. And in November 1942, when the death rate was 13.35 percent, Himmler was deceptively told it was 9.69 percent, or over one-third less. (See Appendix 5.) Obviously, the aim was to cover up.

Likewise, Dr. Richard Korherr, the SS statistician, demonstrated to Himmler that a Lebensborn report on infant mortality was false. Lebensborn had claimed that the death rate in its delivery home was 4 percent, as compared with the overall German average of 6 percent. In reality, however, as Korherr learned in his investigation, the death rate there was 8 percent.[54]

Why did the SS strive to make the mortality rate seem lower? Why were false data presented?

In his autobiographical *Commandant in Auschwitz*, Rudolf Höss must have been thinking of Himmler's efforts in the summer of 1942 when he recalled:

Himmler tells the armaments industry: Build [labor] camps and request manpower from me through the Ministry of Armaments; there's enough! He is already promising tens, nay, hundreds of thousands of prisoners from actions that have not even [begun] and whose final results cannot be estimated. Neither Pohl nor Kaltenbrunner dares to try and stop Himmler from promising more unknown [prisoner] contingents. Even though Himmler is accurately informed of the exact number of prisoners, [their] condition and labor employment, by highly detailed and lucidly depicted monthly reports on the concentration camps, he keeps driving and pushing: Armaments! Prisoners! Armaments! Even Pohl has been infected by Himmler's constant driving, and is now himself working on the commandants, or else the inspector of concentration camps and D II [Maurer], to devote all their strength exclusively to this most important task of using prisoners for the armament industry and to do everything to push this forward.[55]

In January 1944, Fritz Kranefuss wrote to Himmler's chief of staff that "SS Obergruppenführer Pohl has the best will to help, but I have the impression that he does not dispose of as many people as the Reichsführer may think."[56] Himmler wanted to remedy this lack in a large-scale action. The catastrophic death rates, Himmler's absurd promises, and his ambition to construct an industrial empire, which existed only in his fantasy, must have led to the arbitrary additional arrests of 30,000–40,000 people a month, of which Schieber informed me on May 7, 1944: "Of the high percentage of foreign, especially Russian, workers in our armaments factories, a no-longer-to-be-ignored portion is gradually passing over to the industrial factories of the SS and is thus being lost to us. You know that we are satisfied with the Russian workers, especially with the women, under sensible treatment. Many of them, who tend to fluctuate greatly for understandable reasons, are now being assigned to the SS plants by the police organs for some delinquency or other and are not returning to the old work site. This removal is due to a further expansion of the large-scale business concern of the SS." Therein lay a very serious peril for our entire armaments output, Schieber said in conclusion.[57]

At my next opportunity, in a meeting from June 3 to 5, 1944, I pointed out to Hitler that "every month 30,000–40,000 runaway workers or POWs from industry are being caught by the police and are then assigned as concentration camp inmates to the projects of the SS. This is not acceptable to me, since these are largely trained or specialized workers, who ought to be allowed to practice their original trade as soon as possible. I could not sustain a yearly loss of 500,000 workers; hence, the distribution of this manpower must be made by me or Sauckel. This is all the more valid since a large number of these workers have been trained with great difficulty." Hitler promised to decide in my favor after I had met with Himmler to discuss the matter.[58]

This meeting that Hitler demanded took place a few days later in Himmler's villa near Berchtesgaden. With an impenetrable expression on his face, Himmler promised to help me. I informed Hitler of this and asked him to speak to Himmler about the matter once again.[59] I could not oversee Himmler's agreement, but I had no reason to distrust him.[60] It was only when studying the Himmler files that I learned that he had already ordered such a dragnet action at the end of December 1942. (See Appendix 6.)

Chapter 5
Pattern of an Intrigue

W HILE HIMMLER WAS STILL WORKING closely with Schieber to build
up armaments plants for the SS, Otto Ohlendorf, an SS brigade commander
and head of the SD, was already planning Schieber's downfall. On August
26, 1942, he transmitted a negative report on Schieber to Himmler.[1]
Given the tight intertwinings within the SS leadership, it is not surprising
that on September 16, 1942, three weeks after Ohlendorf's accusations,
Dr. Kaltenbrunner supported his colleague in the SS by means of a massive
thrust. At that time, Kaltenbrunner, later head of the Gestapo, was still
leader of the Austrian SS Upper Department Danube. In this capacity he
addressed a report to SS Obergruppenführer Wolff, chief of the main
office of the personal staff of the SS Reichsführer.[2] According to this
report, Schieber was involved "in the serious food racketeering affair of the
Lenzinger Zellwolle Company, Upper Danube,[3] and seriously incriminated." Speer had managed, the report went on, to maintain Schieber in
his position as head manager of this plant despite the reservations of the
responsible Gauleiter Eigruber.[4] Schieber, Kaltenbrunner said, was "fully
out of place in my eyes." The Reich Main Security Office had a detailed
report on Schieber in its hands, this annihilating accusation concluded.[5]
Just a few days later, Wolff demanded this report for his own information.[6]
Over two years later, Himmler assured me that none of the accusations
against Schieber had turned out to be correct.

Kaltenbrunner's and Ohlendorf's reports spelled a massive interference
in my domain, and Himmler then went one step further. He did not turn

to me. Instead, on October 5, 1942, he ordered Ohlendorf to see to it "that Schieber removes all his relatives from his official jurisdiction and dismisses a Herr Pollack, former Party business manager of the Gau of Thuringia, from his responsible position in the Ministry of Armaments. For this man was expelled from the SS." This was necessary "for the sake of the high duties and tasks entrusted to him, for the sake of Reich Minister Speer, Gauleiter Sauckel, and all the many people who place their full confidence in him." Ohlendorf's letter was important enough for Himmler to send Bormann a copy,[7] but not me, Schieber's superior.

Walter Schieber was, no doubt, an unstable person, but extremely hard-working, and, as it later turned out, a devoted, loyal office head. A large man, he tended toward corpulence. He seemed timid and virtually struck by some hard fate, for two of his brothers were indeed good-for-nothings.

I, too, I would like to stress, had meanwhile become distrustful of Pollack and thus also of Schieber. The system, however, permitted no loss of prestige. Rivals lurked everywhere, ready to interpret any yielding as a first sign of weakness and, in my own case, as a waning of the many demonstrations of Hitler's favor. I had to deploy all means to prevent any invasion of my position. Other holders of high offices fared no better. The result was a freezing of personnel policies. It was practically impossible to drop a man without losing face oneself.

To counteract the assaults and to strengthen Pollack's, and thereby also Schieber's, position, I managed to get Hitler to agree a few months later, in early February 1943, to award "the War Merit Cross, First Class, to Chief Clerk Pollack, despite his [Hitler's] initial objection."[8] After all, compared with the cases of corruption tolerated by the Gauleiters all the way up to Goering, Himmler's charges against Schieber were quite trivial.

Schieber himself sensed that people were plotting against him. In order to support him, I took advantage of the next suitable opportunity, a report on activities on May 13, 1943, to make Hitler aware of the performance of the subcontracting industries under Schieber.[9] I pointed out that the output of pipe steel, bar steel, strip steel, and wire had gone up by 45 percent in one year, the output of steel castings by 48 percent, the output of malleable iron by 42 percent. Under Schieber's aegis, die forgings had risen by 55 percent, crankshafts by 30 percent, ball bearings by two-thirds. The production of pistons and piston joints, I said, was close to 100 percent higher and that of piston rings 67 percent higher than a year ago.

In September 1943, as an indirect consequence of my enumeration, Hitler awarded Schieber the highest decoration for service in the civilian sector: the Knight's Cross to the War Merit Cross. This honor restored

Schieber's prestige in the eyes of the Party. In fact, Himmler wired his brigade commander Schieber his "hearty congratulations on the high decoration" and told his staff to add this expression of his goodwill to the SS file on Schieber.[10] Thus, one would think, the intrigue launched behind my back had collapsed.

Willy Liebel, the head of my central office, had fallen sick, so in the autumn of 1943 I asked my old friend Karl Hanke, Gauleiter of Lower Silesia, to take over Liebel's work for a time. Hanke had assisted my first steps as architect of the Party, and I felt I had a reliable ally in him. However, he soon reproached me about the unreliability of my staff members in terms of the Party, which, he said, had neither enough influence nor the necessary control in my ministry. One day he voiced the grave suspicion that Schieber was guilty of treason, that he was using his negotiations with Swedish suppliers and Swiss industrialists[11] in order to make illicit contacts. Furthermore, he was opening foreign bank accounts and preparing to flee to a neutral country. I pointed out Schieber's energy and success and demanded evidence, which, however, did not come.

The good rapport between Hanke and me was not dimmed by his accusations. Thus, in a letter of June 21, 1944, I thanked him heartily for his now terminated work as temporary head of the central office.[12] I had no idea that my friend had long since begun plotting against me behind my back. Only recently, when reading the biography of the architect Hermann Giessler, could I ascertain that in March 1944 Hanke had asked this confidant of Hitler's to arrange a meeting between him (Hanke) and Hitler, whom he wanted to inform about a crucial matter. Hanke, Giessler reports, had "gained insight into his [Speer's] ministry. . . . He particularly distrusted two close colleagues of Speer's. Hanke named the names. I knew them both. They had high honorary positions in the SA and the SS respectively."[13] Schieber was a high-ranking SS commander, and Liebel had high honorary rank in the SA.

Evidently Giessler did not succeed in getting Hanke an appointment with Hitler. Hanke therefore went to Reichsleiter Bormann and informed him of his suspicion. On March 6, 1944, Bormann received a letter from Hanke. The letter contained a report from a Frau von Johnston,[14] who, incidentally, was having an affair with Hanke. Just twenty-four hours later, Bormann told Himmler: "The Führer, to whom I have presented the written document, is himself not yet clear about the further processing of the matter. The Führer is especially wondering in what manner, that is, by what route it can be demonstrated that State Councillor Schieber has committed this treason. . . . Through his work," Bormann went on in a later part of his letter, "Schieber knows about the most secret manufacturing processes, bottlenecks, raw-material situations, etc. Thus, the treason possibilities in Schieber's hand are simply enormous." According to the letter, Hitler told Bormann that he had "never much liked" Schieber. Gauleiter Sauckel, my rival, had supposedly told me about "the defects in Schieber's character shortly after Schieber had been taken over by Speer. . . . Herr Speer emphasized at that time that Schieber was professionally capable, and that was why he could not do without him."[15] This letter of Bormann's is a characteristic symptom of the seemingly twisted pettiness influencing government business on Hitler's behalf. It also shows how Bormann and Hitler conspired about a member of my staff (who was, after all, a deputy of mine), and even informed Himmler while I, as the responsible minister, was not apprised of these machinations. Nor is it even certain that Bormann rendered Hitler's opinion correctly rather than exaggerating, as was his wont, in order to get Himmler to take further steps.[16]

In late April 1944, I went to see Hitler about another matter. Hitler revealed to me that Schieber was suspected of preparing his escape abroad. Also, Liebel was likewise being watched distrustfully by high Party functionaries; and General Wäger, the head of the armaments office, was not considered reliable either. But Hitler at the same time minimized all charges against these three office heads of mine, whose dismissal I was already assuming after all the rumors reported to me. Hitler's casually offered information was probably meant to put my mind at ease. It was typical of Hitler to circumvent problems by leaving troublesome facts unclear in order to avoid any discussion. While concealing things from me, he told Bormann a few days later, on May 8, 1944, to request "a report on the present state of the [Schieber] matter" from Himmler.[17]

The previous day, May 7, 1944, Schieber had made me aware of Himmler's dark methods in obtaining manpower. Without too much beating about the bush, Schieber had hinted that they were arresting countless people in order to get workers for the concentration camps. He had also quite bluntly warned me about Himmler's plan to set up a huge SS business concern.[18] Himmler truly could no longer bank on his follower.

At almost the same time as Bormann's attack on Schieber, I received some news from Albert Hoffmann, the Gauleiter of Westphalia South. The letter included a memo from the Dortmund district attorney's office,[19] announcing the immediate arrest of Werner Schieber, the brother of my office head. My ministry's answer indicates that I advised against any arrest for the present, since Kehrl (then the Generalreferent in the Ministry of Economy) had begun an investigation. The results did not justify an immediate arrest. Walter Schieber, the reply went on, against whom these charges were indirectly addressed, had left the directorate a long time ago and no longer had anything to do with this work.[20]

Two months later, Schieber, seeking help, appealed directly to Himmler. "For months now, I have known that my industrial activity . . . as well as my personal life are being closely watched and checked by the Reich Main Security Office." His fellow worker Pollack had been arrested, and Frau Pollack, who worked on Schieber's financial matters, had been interrogated; the files and assets belonging to Schieber had been confiscated.

In this situation, Schieber asked that he, as an SS commander, be tried by a court of honor, since it was impossible for him to continue working as my deputy if he did not "possess [Himmler's] fullest confidence." This meant that for personnel policies in my own ministry, Himmler's opinion was more decisive than that of the minister in charge. Schieber's letter concludes: "I believe you understand that it is impossible for me to continue working at the head of industry and be responsible for very important things at such a serious time if the Reich Main Security Office is simultaneously induced to take investigatory measures without my ever being able to comment on the charges raised against me."[21] Schieber evidently did not know about the accusation of treason. I myself could not notify Schieber in detail of the suspicion concerning him that Hitler had communicated to me. Any mention would have unsettled him; and besides, Hitler himself had made light of it.

A few days earlier, I had cautiously asked Kaltenbrunner to "obtain the opinion of the SS Reichsführer as to whether it might not be better to clear up the entire business in an orderly way. . . . I believe that State Councillor Schieber is a hundred-percent safe colleague for our cause. I therefore assume that a lawful investigation of the charges against him will exonerate him. If, however, any serious reservations remain, I do not believe that, given the present stage of the war, I can accept any further responsibility for working with him in the long run—as great as this loss might be for the entire armaments industry."[22]

A few days later I received a further report, which said that Schieber's brother was deeply incriminated and that Schieber himself had commissioned a person with a poor reputation and 19 previous convictions to buy real estate for him in the Linz area.[23]

On August 7, 1944, I applied for the swords to the Knight's Cross of the War Merit Cross for Walter Rohland, Karl Saur, and Schieber, in order to emphasize the special merits of these three members of my staff. This was to be interpreted as a further demonstration of my trust and could be considered an attempt at saving Schieber's honor.

Suddenly, there was a new turn of events. Kaltenbrunner, the head of the Gestapo, had personally terminated his investigation of the charges against Schieber, and he reported that there could be no objection whatsoever to employing State Councillor Schieber in the province of my ministry since the accusations against him had not been proven in any manner. With some satisfaction, I instantly telegraphed Himmler, asking him to inform Hitler. For "I could deduce from a comment of Herr Reichsleiter Bormann's that the Führer has so far not been informed by him."[24] Such concealment, I was not unaware, was a frequently used tactic of Bormann's. When I turned to him, I still did not realize that the downfall of Schieber, Liebel, and Wäger was merely a phase toward depriving me of my power.

Although Bormann was informed of the results of the Gestapo investigation, Hitler evidently was not told; and a few days later, Bormann got Hitler to decide that Schieber "as a Gau economy leader [be dismissed] and had no right to wear the uniform."[25] The Gau economic advisers were directly under Bormann, and Schieber had been occupying this Party position in the Gau of Thuringia for years. Thus, although his innocence had been demonstrated, Schieber was relieved of his position in disgrace.

Furthermore, Hitler had meanwhile voiced qualms about awarding Schieber the swords to the Knight's Cross of the War Merit Cross. Retrospectively, I clearly see my naiveté in appealing to Bormann of all people to inform Hitler about Schieber's exculpation—something that Himmler had evidently failed to do despite the promise he had given me a long time earlier.[26]

If a member of the ministry was incriminated in this way, it was of no use for the responsible minister to inform Hitler of the results of an investigation by an SS office. The way things stood, an investigation could be terminated only by a declaration of Himmler's, for such a matter involved an internal top-secret procedure of the highest SS leaders. Hence, I again reminded Himmler of his promise to enlighten Hitler, and I asked him "to let me know whether you have informed the Führer about the outcome of the investigation in the Dr. Sch. matter."[27] But nothing happened. I realized that Hitler was being deliberately kept in the dark.

At the end of October Bormann telephoned me, saying that Hitler had ordered Schieber's discharge. On October 31 I had to summon Schieber and inform him that "the pressure of several Gauleiters upon Reichsleiter

Bormann had become so powerful" that I could no longer keep him.[28] A few hours later Schieber sent me his handwritten answer: "Without the fullest confidence of the highest leaders, a difficult office cannot be successfully occupied." He regarded "leaving after years of extremely heavy commitment and also success" as an undeserved insult. But he would retreat behind the necessities of the whole matter.[29]

That same evening Schieber, who had always been too trusting, went to Gottlob Berger, head of the SS Main Office, not only to repeat our conversation to him but also to inform him that "Liebel and [Karl] Hettlage[30] will likewise vanish from the ministry." Given Bormann's triumph, I had expressed this suspicion to Schieber. Berger, who instantly told Himmler about Schieber's report, also quoted a statement of mine: "Speer described his own position as extremely weak." Berger ended his report laconically: "I report this to the SS Reichsführer for his orientation."[31] Himmler replied the very next day: "We have to stay out of the entire complex."[32] Yet his cooperation with Bormann had made Schieber's downfall possible in the first place.

It is revealing that one month later, Lorch, the head of the Press Department of the Ministry of Economy, confidentially reported that "the retirement of one or more of three agency heads" of the Ministry of Armaments "or even all three was due to Ohlendorf. . . . This could also be interpreted," the official sanguinely went on, "as meaning that Ohlendorf as the coming strong man views the retirement of the agency heads as a tacit premise for his involvement." Lorch repeats that Ohlendorf "has made sure that the three agency heads were discharged." This confidential report by the Press Department of the Ministry of Economy might be an additional explanation for the machinations that had been occupying Hitler since the spring of 1944 through Himmler, with Bormann's participation, and that had also decisively impaired my position.[33]

Saur now took over the major part of Schieber's department. Officially, I declared that I had decided to simplify the organization of my ministry by disbanding the agency for armaments deliveries. Within the framework of this rearrangement, I said, Saur's Technical Office would now take over from Schieber's area the entire subcontracting industry, the planning of the means of production, i.e., investment planning, the organs of self-responsibility of industry for steel-making, castings, forgings, materials refinement and machine elements, welding engineering, plus the main boards of industrial organization for the electrical industry, for precision engineering and optics, for steel and iron construction, and for armaments instruments.[34]

The day after Schieber's dismissal, on November 1, 1944, I again told Hitler that Schieber had been discharged even though his innocence had just been demonstrated. Hitler waved me off with cold, unfriendly remarks. He said that countless colleagues, especially Bormann, had convinced him long ago of how unprincipled and unreliable Schieber was. He also made unfriendly, even scornful comments about Liebel and Wäger.[35]

After a year of intense intrigues, the fight was settled. It no longer made any sense to try to hold on to my position as agency head against Hitler's will. I also had to drop Wäger and Liebel. When I informed them of my visit to headquarters, they both asked to resign.

Only now, when the match was settled. did Himmler consider it advisable to report to Hitler, on November 6: "In the matter of Dr. Sch. . . . I informed the Führer that none of the charges raised against Dr. Sch. had turned out to be correct or provable. Needless to say, I had to mention that the employment of his incriminated brothers was demonstrated. The Führer told me that you spoke to him last time, and that Sch. was being used only for special assignments now. His discharge, however, was an honorable one." Contrary to his habit, Himmler adjoined a handwritten "Always Yours Truly" to his signature.[36] He was relishing his triumph.

I took Himmler's demonstrative friendliness as an excuse to ask him to make a full apology to Schieber, who, after all, served under him as SS brigade commander. To emphasize this wish, I explained that "in the past two years, Schieber has performed great services for the rise of German armaments, since, working in the armaments delivery department, he managed to take care of all subcontracting for Saur's final production to exactly the same extent that was required for the final production during these two years."[37]

And indeed, Schieber's contribution to the increase in armaments had been extraordinary. On the same day, I summed up his achievements in a letter of gratitude.

Two years ago, at my instructions, you created the armaments supply department, and in a brief time you built it up and expanded it in an outstanding and expedient way. With your excellent talent for organization you solved this difficult task superbly, and, notwithstanding all difficulties, you helped to build up and secure our present-day armaments at a decisive level. In this context, you had the difficult responsibility for one of the most important areas within the entire armaments and war production, which, furthermore, was constantly and considerably impaired by steadily repeated aerial attacks. . . . You never showed any consideration for your health or spared it in any way, and ultimately you were able to make possible things that had been considered impossible and achieve goals that had seemed unattainable.[38]

Incidentally, Himmler never answered my letter of November 10. Two weeks later I once again asked him at least to send me a letter "composed in such a way that I can use it with third parties. In this letter, your presentation to the Führer need not be mentioned. I would like to have such a letter in order to make copies accessible to the agencies that have brought charges before me against State Councillor Dr. Schieber."[39] This letter too went unanswered. Schieber was never rehabilitated by Himmler.

On the other hand, I suddenly managed to get Hitler's approval of the sword for the Knight's Cross for Schieber. I awarded him this highest civilian military decoration in a solemn session. A few days later, I also got Hitler to allow Walter Schieber[40] to compete for a prize among the best German chemists for new kinds of powder and explosives. The prize was two million marks tax-free.[41] But these were not real victories; the battle was lost.

On December 7, 1944, regarding my pleas for Schieber's rehabilitation, Himmler jotted in the margin of my letter: "Discussed with Speer verbally; settled." He had already written: "Settled. 12/7/44" on my letter of November 24, 1944.[42]

During this meeting, in which the matter had been allegedly solved, Himmler had pointed to the earnest times. We had more important things to do, he said, than to keep pursuing a matter that had been concluded long ago. Besides, he said, Schieber had been given public satisfaction by Hitler's decoration.

This sounded plausible. But his true opinion was expressed in a letter he sent to Kranefuss two weeks later, on December 22, through Brand, the head of his personal staff: "[Schieber's] citing the SS Reichsführer" in regard to his demonstrated innocence "will be in part correct and in part incorrect. Always making the proper distinction here will be difficult. Perhaps you should let things take their course rather than (which should not be the case anyway) assisting SS Brigade Commander Schieber in any fashion."[43] For the SS, Schieber remained a leper.

Chapter 6

Himmler's High-handedness in
the Ministry of Economy

Even during the years shortly before the outbreak of the war, the departmental ministers had often spoken of the SS as a state within the state. But they also spoke of power claims by the widely ramified, financially mighty Labor Front with its enormous income from membership dues paid by all workers. Then, when the SS pierced deeper and deeper into administration, this expansion of its power was eyed distrustfully even by Hitler. Gauleiter Lohse was absolutely right when in July 1944, as Reich commissar for the Eastland, he established that the Führer in no way favored the growing influence of the SS in the Reich Ministry for the Occupied Eastern Territories.[1] Hitler would have imperiled his principle of divide and rule if he had given Himmler any priority in the power structure. Keitel should rank alongside Himmler, like Bormann, Goebbels, or myself. Himmler had no choice but to know and respect this. Hence, he skillfully infiltrated his SS commanders into administrations and key positions where a direct takeover of power did not appear possible or opportune. Hitler was evidently powerless against such infiltrations. He left Himmler alone. Perhaps he also felt that all these infiltrations in the state apparatus would cause friction with the SS and ultimately lead to a unanimous opinion against Himmler, thus narrowing his power, which would be dangerous for Hitler.

The people affected by such power drives, namely the departmental ministers, could only indulge in speculations about how far the SS leaders had managed to undermine their executive power. It was well known that one or more of Himmler's confidential agents occupied important posts in every ministry; I simply assumed that Himmler was swiftly informed of major happenings in my ministry. This was, incidentally, neither an especially unpleasant nor even ominous feeling; for after all, it did not matter if Himmler's operatives investigated other people's capabilities or evaluated mine. All that counted was the measure of confidence and support that Hitler granted. And in this context, it could be assumed that Himmler was excellently informed about the evaluation of my successes by the SS adjutants posted at the Führer's headquarters. Until July 20, 1944, I had no reason to complain about lack of support from Hitler; and hence, until that date, I was relatively indifferent to the SS investigations in my area because they could not be utilized against me.

Himmler was generally considered loyal. And I assumed the same thing. But such loyalty remained on the surface. It was only while preparing this book and studying Himmler's files, the so-called "Documentary Administration of the Personal Staff of the SS Reichsführer," i.e., almost four decades after the events, that I stumbled upon certain things that dumbfounded me. As minister, I had not sensed that Himmler ruled as a matter of course over his SS leaders inside the economic administration. To mention one example: Reeder was the government deputy in the German administrative district of northern France and Belgium, and Himmler snapped at him, telling him he had to pursue policies consistent with the SS because he was an honorary commander in the SS.[2] Thus, wherever he could act to the advantage of the SS, he exerted total pressure on his SS honorary commanders, whom he viewed as vassals pledged to him, even though he kept stressing that honorary ranks in the SS involved no obligations.

A few weeks after my appointment as Reich minister, Himmler offered me the rank of Honorary Oberstgruppenführer in the SS. I could amiably refuse, for I was sure of approval from Hitler, who was distrustful of all of Himmler's attempts to confer such ranks in order to exert influence on the people directly below him. However, Hitler was typically lukewarm in making decisions regarding his closest colleagues from the period of struggle. And so he did not act directly. Especially when the issue was the spread of honorary ranks on the intermediate level of command.

In the development of the Schieber case, we saw how ruthlessly Himmler's close colleagues, inspired by him, could destroy a high-ranking SS commander both morally and professionally, even though he was under my ministerial protection. Equally instructive was the Kranefuss case, which illuminates how high-handedly Himmler dealt with Kranefuss's service in the Reich Ministry of Economy.

From the very start of my activity as Reich minister, I worked closely with President Hans Kehrl, the top staffer at the Reich Ministry of Economy. I esteemed him as an exception in the ministerial bureaucracy, but he was certainly an exception too in his relationship to Himmler. Although an SS Oberführer like Kranefuss, he displayed no signs of any dependence on Himmler's organization. Kranefuss praised "his abilities and his courage regarding responsibility." I share this judgment even today.[3]

As Kranefuss informed SS Obergruppenführer Wolff on July 24, 1942, he was to begin running a "General Division for Planning"[4] at the Ministry of Economy. This division would be subdivided into five departments:

1. For production steering, raw materials planning, and distribution. For economic expansion.
2. For industrial manufacturing requirements, coordination of labor with production, coordination of the distribution of coal and fuel production.
3. Supervision of government agencies, government associations, and war commissioners; participation in their orders.
4. Fundamental problems of regional economic management, participation in organizational and personnel measures of these intermediate authorities.
5. Fundamental problems of transportation, transportation planning, transportation management, transportation bans.

The most important and most difficult task, said Kranefuss, was the planned simplification and rearrangement of the raw materials management. Kehrl had given him "a vast as well as difficult and responsibility-laden work area." Indeed, this was a key department.

Kranefuss also wrote his intimate friend Wolff that he was willing "to take over this difficult work area only if the SS Reichsführer gave his full approval." He would accept this task only as Himmler's confidential agent and representative. He asked Wolff to get Himmler to make his decision as soon as possible. This unconditional submission was all the more surprising since the position was one of economic management within the framework of the Ministry of Economy, and the man himself was an independent industrial leader. (See Appendix 7.) For Kranefuss was chairman of the board at the important Braunkohlen-Benzin-AG (Brown Coal and Gasoline Company), known as Brabag for short. Kranefuss was even more unequivocal in professing himself to be Himmler's deputy when, in the same letter, he asked Wolff "to regard this job as well as my work at the Brabag as a command from the SS Reichsführer."[5] It was an accurate definition of the light in which an SS commander had to consider his job in a ministry.

At that time no one discussed with me this appointment of Kranefuss by Minister of Economy Walther Funk, even though it encompassed large portions of my most significant work areas for increasing production. Kranefuss would probably have had a difficult time making headway against my impulsive, unorthodox industrial leaders, who were aware of the extraordinary, if tacit, powers they had thanks to my prestige with Hitler.

In this same letter to Wolff, Kranefuss wrote that Kehrl had assigned him to work closely with me and my ministry. Kranefuss most likely sensed that difficulties lay ahead, for he asked Wolff "to speak about me with Reich Minister Speer on a suitable occasion," because he (Kranefuss) would "now have many opportunities for working with his ministry and [Speer] himself."[6] Kranefuss, as this remark implies, assumed that an intercession by Himmler's personal assistant would impress and influence a minister of the Reich. If I had agreed to accept the offer that Himmler made me through Wolff, namely, the rank of Honorary Oberstgruppenführer in the SS, then the cooperation between Kranefuss and myself, or rather, the fulfillment of Himmler's wishes as transmitted through Kranefuss, would have taken place in the aura of comradeship between SS commanders. After all, in that same letter Kranefuss stressed that he was taking the position at the Ministry of Economy out of feelings of camaraderie for SS Oberführer Kehrl.

At any rate, a note that Kranefuss had sent Wolff two weeks earlier reveals Himmler's aim of influencing my ministry. Himmler, writes Kranefuss, had already told Obergruppenführer Wolff to speak "with Reich Minister Speer in the proper manner." The times were favorable for this, Kranefuss opined in the same note, because "the activity of Reich Minister Speer and the selection of at least some of his staff members would seem to justify the hope, or rather expectation, that our position, and our willingness for cooperation resting upon it, will be appreciated in a different manner than was often the case earlier."[7] Kranefuss's wish for close contact does not seem to have come true. For on September 18, Kranefuss again urged his friend Wolff: "In the interest of my work at the Reich Ministry of Economy and for other reasons that you certainly understand, I would be deeply grateful to you if you would speak with Reich Minister Speer and also with Reichsleiter Bormann at the next opportunity, and indeed as you always do, in such an agreeable effective way. I believe that this will facilitate a great many things for me in the future."[8] (See Appendix 7.)

On August 26, 1942, Otto Ohlendorf, head of the SD, sent Himmler a report "on the intertwining of government authority and private business interests through the same people." As his accompanying letter to Himmler indicates,[9] this must have been a sharp attack on the just-established "Self-Responsibility of Industry." For in this system, the topmost principle was to have nonofficials, industrial specialists, settle crucial problems of production management. With the responsible participation of the most capable industrialists and the simultaneous exclusion of the military and civilian bureaucracy normally in charge, they succeeded—as is generally acknowledged today—in introducing the decisive change that was to lead to a multiplication of armaments performance between 1942 and the autumn of 1944.

According to Ohlendorf's testimony at his trial in Nuremberg, his report of that time consisted of comments "against the so-called self-responsibility of business, that is, against having business leaders replace the state and take over the state's authority. And this not only opened the way for corruption but was also one of the essential and fundamental reasons for the economic loss of our war."[10] As Ohlendorf further testified at Nuremberg, he had also informed Funk of this report, and Funk had approved of it. Of course, one has to admit that in 1942 the revolutionary consequences of the work method of our "self-responsibility of industry"[11] were not yet discernible. I myself was not yet quite certain whether my somewhat daring plan would really meet with the expected success.

Himmler waited five weeks before answering. Then, in his letter of October 5 to Ohlendorf, he stated that "a cessation of the damages was absolutely necessary." At the same time, he ordered Ohlendorf "to speak about these things in detail" with my office head "State Councillor and SS Brigade Commander Dr. Schieber and also with SS Oberführer Kehrl. Since I assume that both men have a fundamentally decent position, I feel obligated to clarify things bluntly and unequivocally, to expose the defectiveness, and to give them the possibility of stopping it on their own." That is how the superior speaks about the work of his subordinates.

For Himmler, it must have been natural to deal with his SS commanders Schieber and Kehrl in this manner. Thus, his letter went on to stress: "Please inform both gentlemen that I consider cessation of this damaging plan absolutely necessary."[12] This is an example of how Himmler managed his state within the state and circumvented a responsible minister. At the same time, Himmler empowered SD Chief Ohlendorf to transmit his report to Reichsleiter Bormann. Not a word that I, as the responsible minister, ought to have been informed as well.

The transmission of Ohlendorf's letter to Bormann meant interference from the Party apparatus too. This was a sign. Himmler was looking for allies in the struggle against the industrial leaders, who had been elevated by the new organizational structure. In this context, one must bear in mind that the Party—in contrast to an opportunistic Hitler—had been anti-industrial before 1933. Had I known about this intrigue, it would have scarcely touched me. After all, Hitler was totally on my side.

Ohlendorf seems to have been encouraged by Himmler's reaction. In any case, a week and a half later, on October 6, he sent another letter to the SS Reichsführer. State Secretary Friedrich Landfried, an aging, strictly Prussian-minded official who was dismissed one year later, paid in full for trying to ingratiate himself with the SS. As Ohlendorf declares, Landfried suggested transferring to him "all fundamental matters and thus all the economic matters of the Reich Ministry of Economy," whereby he would have "the rank of an under secretary." Minister of Economy Funk also approved Landfried's suggestion. Indeed, a short time later Funk received Ohlendorf for a talk. During his conversation, Ohlendorf continued his attacks against the "self-responsibility of industry." As Ohlendorf subsequently informed Himmler, he explained to Funk what effects the economic management by the Reich Ministry of Economy was having in the various areas of industry. And he "especially pointed out what difficulties were being caused by the transfer of jurisdictional tasks to individuals and organizations in industry." Funk had fully shared Ohlendorf's opinion of this issue and had approved the suggestion of making SD Chief Ohlendorf an under secretary in his ministry. (See Appendix 8.)

"The decision about me could be made only by the SS Reichsführer." That was Ohlendorf's answer to the Reich minister, according to his epistolary report. "I would agree to having this question brought to the SS Reichsführer only on condition of my maintaining my present assignment with the SS Reichsführer." This double function did not disturb Funk in the least: "Reich Minister Funk . . . intends to contact the SS RF [SS Reichsführer] immediately. My repeated condition that nothing is to be changed in my position in the Reich Security Headquarters elicited the response from Funk that he considers this connection extremely fortunate."[13]

Funk's reaction may have been a response to the impetuous activity of my newly built organization. During these months I had direct contacts with his staff members, mainly his general adviser Hans Kehrl, and I thus myself broke the rule that a minister should discuss problems only with his minister colleague, at best with the latter's state secretary. Hence, Funk could assume that Ohlendorf, the influential head of the SS Security Service, who had established his men in all branches of industry and also in the Ministry of Economy, would be powerful enough, after his installation at the Ministry of Economy, to prevent contacts between staff members of his ministry and an outside minister.

With me, Funk had always been enthusiastic about the new economic management organization known as self-responsibility of industry. Yet, as I saw to my immense astonishment in this document (preserved at the Federal Archives), he agreed with the vehement attacks of the SS against this very principle of self-responsibility.

Funk was always soft when it came to SS matters. It was rumored that the SS had a detailed dossier on Funk's dissolute love life. Certainly, his life-style offered reason enough. In the celibacy of Spandau, Funk lecherously told about his erotic excursions through Casablanca, where he would go from time to time in order to experience new variants of passion.[14]

Such a dossier must have existed in Heydrich's or Kaltenbrunner's filing cabinets. Thus, Funk presumably had banal reasons for replying that he regarded the assignment of the SD chief to a leading position in his Ministry of Economy as extraordinarily fortuitous. Shrewd and bright as he was, Funk could not have had any doubt that the energetic Ohlendorf would become the real head of the Ministry of Economy. Both Funk and Landfried, his aged and politically weak state secretary, would have unresistingly left the field of action to him.

When Bormann read the report on the alleged failure of the industrialists, he must have nevertheless pointed out to Himmler that the time for attacking our management system was very poorly chosen. After all, when I took office, it was Hitler himself who had advised me to employ industry in carrying out my task since that was where the most valuable people were to be found. At that time, February 13, 1942, he felt that we could animate the hopeless state of armaments production only by transferring responsibility to industrial leaders. I had assured him, in Bormann's presence, that I would have the industrial leaders perform most of my work anyhow. During this meeting, Hitler, in accordance with my wish, even determined that these industrial colleagues not be investigated as to their Party membership.

Furthermore, Bormann knew in October 1942 that Hitler appreciated the increasingly successful work of the industrialists. The first great triumphs were already apparent, and more important ones were soon visible. According to the "index figures of German armaments manufacturing," the September 1942 production of munitions, at 98 percent, was almost twice that of February; production of items that were harder to increase had also risen, for instance, weapons had gone up by 41 percent and tanks by 22 percent.[15] The overall performance of armaments production had risen by 58.8 percent during this period.[16]

In all probability it was due to such a warning of Bormann's that Himmler, on October 21, 1942, suddenly rejected Ohlendorf's suggestion himself. He ordered Ohlendorf not "to accept the position in the Reich Ministry of Economy."[17] That same day Himmler dictated a memorandum saying he did not approve of Ohlendorf's intention because "during the war, a fundamental alteration of our totally capitalistic economy is impossible."

Himmler also wrote that "if an office head of the Reich Security Headquarters became the ministerial director in the Reich Ministry of Economy," he "could only bump into" this impossibility of a capitalist economy. Without further explaining his rejection, Himmler continued: In that case, he said, "a witch hunt would start against [Ohlendorf and] any failure in the economy would be blamed on him or on the SS." People would say that he had disturbed the war economy. However, if Ohlendorf "does not strive for any fundamental alteration [of the capitalist system] and gives in, then he will be used up in a few months like all the others."[18] Himmler evidently felt that the time had not come for a crucial change of economic policy. However, he had always shown the ability to wait until his hour came.

Thus Himmler did an about-face in order to mask his retreat. Two weeks earlier he had demanded that Schieber and Kehrl stop the damage immediately. Now he merely asked for "a somehow personally decent man, whether it be Kehrl or [Franz] Hayler, to be given this position [which Funk had planned for Ohlendorf], someone who as a loyal follower of Funk and hence of the Reich Marshal" and, of course, Himmler, "would see his task as preventing at least the grossest messes in the economy."[19]

On October 21, 1942, the same day that Himmler rejected Ohlendorf's plans, he also changed his position on the already approved assignment for Kranefuss. All at once he was "not at all happy about the information that SS Oberführer Kranefuss" was to become "very active in the economy." He had therefore "today telephoned SS Obergruppenführer Wolff," who was ordered to inform Kranefuss of this opinion of his.[20] Himmler's note on his telephone conversation with Wolff sounds harsher. "Prohibition for Kranefuss to act politically in the Reich Ministry of Economy."[21]

This news must have been a shock to Kranefuss. Nine days after Himmler's decision, Kranefuss appealed directly to the Reichsführer: "SS Obergruppenführer Wolff has informed me that my activity in the Reich Ministry of Economy, or rather the form of this activity, has not met with your approval." Needless to say, he hurriedly added, "I will not do anything that does not have your total approval." Thus, all that Kranefuss could do was to point out to Himmler the consequences that this discrimination (for indeed, that was what the sudden removal of the SS Oberführer would be viewed as) could have for his SS comrade Kehrl: "'If my resignation after working just a few months casts a dubious or even unfavorable light on me personally, it would not particularly bother me. I consider it my absolute duty . . . to avoid anything that might have an unfavorable effect on SS Oberführer Kehrl or create any more difficulties for him in his already extremely difficult position and truly self-sacrificing activity." To emphasize how obliging he was, in the same letter Kranefuss expressed his uneasiness about conditions in his present position. "The things that I found and experience every day in the Ministry [of Economy] far surpass my worst expectations."[22]

A high-ranking leader in the economy, who was also a representative of the Reich minister of economy, thus unhesitatingly followed an order of Himmler's in a work area that was not in any way under Himmler's aegis. Yet he would have aroused Himmler's anger if he had not followed this clear-cut order without hesitation.

With such obedience, Kranefuss remained Himmler's confidant. As revealed by Himmler's calendar leaf of March 25, 1943, Himmler had taken a two-and-a-half-hour walk with Kranefuss, from 4:30 to 7:00 P.M.—an exceptional occurrence in Himmler's daily routine.[23]

I seem to have heard about this distrust toward my industrial colleagues; for at my next meeting with Hitler, on November 7 or 8, 1942, I had him expressly confirm that he had registered "with great satisfaction, the successes of the organization of the self-responsibility of industry and the far-reaching employment of engineers and technicians of factories in this self-responsibility."[24]

Six months later, all the powers that Himmler had once refused the temporary Generalreferent Kranefuss and SD chief Ohlendorf in the Ministry of Economy were now transferred to Ohlendorf at Himmler's initiative. On July 26, 1943, in a *coup de main*, I had gotten Hitler to promise that the entire wartime production would be placed under my ministry. The responsibilities for basic production like that of coal and steel were to pass from the Ministry of Economy to my ministry, as were the manufacture of consumer goods and the output of the food industry. At the same time, the agencies for raw materials, planning, and consumer goods production were to be taken over by my ministry. That was the capstone of my efforts to concentrate all German output in my hands. Furthermore, Funk's key man, Kehrl, was to leave the Ministry of Economy now and enter my Armaments Ministry as head of the Planning Division and the Raw Materials Office. During the past few months, he had more and more become my direct staff member anyhow.

After this restructuring of responsibilities, Funk, at the Ministry of Economy, was left with questions about regulation of the money economy and foreign trade, plus the distribution of consumer goods—as established by my ministry—to the population. The only important part here was the jurisdiction over *all fundamental* economic issues, which were likewise to be Funk's responsibility.

Understandably, there were still intrigues and counteractions, which delayed the implementation of Hitler's decision until September 1943.[25] This shift of responsibilities actually spelled a decisive power increase for me, and Bormann and Himmler had to eye it distrustfully. Indeed, it must have been this growth of power that moved Himmler again to take up the threads that had been spun between Landfried and Ohlendorf. On August 20, 1943, a few weeks after Hitler had promised me this doubling of my work province, Himmler met for half an hour with Funk and then another half hour with State Secretary Landfried at his Hochwald headquarters.[26] The next evening this matter must have been concluded at the supper that Himmler and Lammers had with Funk.[27]

A short time later, mid-September 1943,[28] Funk asked me to meet him in the offices of the Reich Bank president. With their gilded armchairs, heavy carpets, and marvelous Gobelins, these rooms reflected the wealth of the great promoters of the 1870s. From here, Funk directed his Reich Ministry of Economy with seeming looseness.

An order of the Reich Ministry of Food had decontrolled poultry, small game, large game, and freshwater fish. Thus, throughout the war, Horcher, a deluxe restaurant in Berlin, served pheasant at high prices, and it was as well prepared as the lobster or the caviar, which came from confiscated French stocks.

The meal, served as always at Funk's office by liveried footmen, was worthy of peacetime. First there was a soup of pressed pheasant meat, then a larded saddle of venison in cream sauce. This was washed down with an excellent Moselle, then a mild Burgundy. The sherbet was accompanied by an old champagne.

We withdrew to an adjoining salon, the walls of which were adorned with hand-stamped leather; valuable old carpets covered the floor. The furniture was hand-carved in a baroque manner; the woodwork of the heavy uphol- stered easy chairs was gilded. All these objects came from the days of Kaiser Wilhelm, when the German Reich Bank played a part in the financial poli- tics of the world.

I too must have surrendered to the enchantment of this bogus world, proud as I was that I, the son of upper-middle-class parents, could now dine at the center of financial power and play a part. The minister, always accessible and affable, told me that, with no effort on his part, he had sud- denly been summoned to the Führer's headquarters, where Bormann had surprised him by announcing that Hitler had appointed a new state secre- tary for the Reich Ministry of Economy, since Dr. Landfried was now old and tired. This new state secretary was SS Brigade Commander Dr. Franz Hayler, and his assistant was SS Brigade Commander Otto Ohlendorf.

I too had suggested to Hitler in May 1942[29] that since Dr. Julius Dorp- müller, the Reich transportation minister, was very old and tired, he should be given an assistant, the young and energetic Theodor Ganzenmüller, whom he had probably barely noticed among the many high officials in his ministry. At that time Hitler, surprisingly and without preparation, had presented the new state secretary to Dorpmüller. As I thought of that inci- dent, I considered Funk's explanation quite credible.

I also realized that Bormann must have looked with displeasure at the extension of my jurisdiction to large areas of the Ministry of Economy.[30] But I did not sense that Funk was handing me pure lies, or that there had actually been serious considerations a year earlier to which Funk had ex- pressly agreed. Even during our twelve years of joint imprisonment in Spandau, Funk never enlightened me. For me, he was always a loyal col- league, albeit one with a propensity for alcohol; and I regarded it as jeal- ousy when Milch frequently warned me against him.

When Funk returned in those early September days with his new state secretary Franz Hayler and the politically far more important Ohlendorf, this double triumph of Himmler's actually meant that my expansionist politics had failed once and for all: Ohlendorf and Hayler were part of Himmler's circle.

The redistribution of economic jurisdictions had shifted the power dy- namics in German production in my favor. As a result, Himmler may have suppressed his original qualms about exposing his own people. Just ten months earlier, Himmler had feared that Ohlendorf might be downgraded as an SS commander if the further course of armaments was positive and thus would speak against his fears. Now, quite obviously, a complete reversal of all of Himmler's intentions had taken place. Funk, known as yielding and casual, was to have his backbone stiffened. That was August 20, 1943, the same day that Himmler had gotten the manufacture of rockets transferred to his agency, thereby momentously invading my work domain; and that was the same day that he was appointed Minister of the Interior. Himmler felt that his hour had come; it was time for him to extend his power to the Ministry of Economy. The Reichsführer of the SS entered the Ministry of Economy with Ohlendorf as a leading factor. (See Appendix 8.)

It must be admitted that Himmler had made a good choice in sending Hayler and Ohlendorf into the Ministry of Economy. Both men belonged to the intelligentsia, which was better represented among the top SS leaders than in the Party. Dr. Franz Hayler, forty-three years old, a graduate of a Humanistic Gymnasium, had studied political science, in which he got his doctorate. In 1934 he was made the honorary head of the Economic Group for Retail Trade, and in 1938 he became head of the Reich Group for Commerce. Having taken part in the March to Feldherrnhalle in November 1923, he had been awarded the so-called Order of Blood. To be sure, he did not join the Party until 1931, his membership number being 754,131. The importance of his position in economy (which was significant for the SS) was underscored by his rank of SS brigade commander.[31] Upon being appointed Funk's state secretary, Hayler was promoted by Himmler to squad commander of the SS.

Ohlendorf had joined the Party in 1925 at the age of eighteen, and he had the highly regarded Party number 6531. SS Brigade Commander Otto Ohlendorf was thirty-five, hence two years younger than I, when he was called to the Ministry of Economy. Like Hayler, he had graduated from a Humanistic Gymnasium and had then studied law and political economy. Two years after passing his bar examination he became a junior lawyer, and soon thereafter a division head in the prestigious Berlin Institute for Applied Economic Sciences. In 1936 he began his lightning career at the Reich Main Security Office (Gestapo). Three years later, in 1939, having advanced to be head of the Domestic SD, he was the most important man in all of Himmler's supervision organs, which did their work in secret. Functioning under the harmless term "Security Service," (*Sicherheitsdienst*), the feared organization of the SS maintained a widespread undercover system, which had its agents in almost every office and factory. That same year, 1939, Hayler had made his closest colleague, SS Brigade Commander Otto Ohlendorf, the head business manager of the Reich Group for Commerce. From June 1941 to July 1942 he had led one of the SS operational squads in eastern Europe.[32] Under his command, as he confessed at Nuremberg, 90,000 people, mostly Jews, were murdered. He was sentenced to death at Nuremberg and executed.

Predictably, the situation grew worse. This is also obvious from a note to the chronicle of September 19, 1944. On that day State Secretary Hayler, Mayor Liebel, the head of my central office, and Dr. Gerhard Fränk, the head of the administrative division of my ministry, came to see me. The chronicle says: "The new men of the Reich Ministry of Economy and, above all, Ohlendorf, who was taken over with Hayler, have put an end to the division in the Reich Ministry of Economy. The remaining portion is being rigidly defended, and in the issue of the intermediate authority, the Reich Ministry of Economy is trying to regain lost territory. In so doing, it can rely on the Reich minister of the interior [Himmler]. Despite this discrepancy, there is still an excellent rapport between the minister and the gentlemen of the Reich Ministry of Economy."

Hayler, during this meeting, was optimistic about the overall situation. However, now that the Western Allies were on German soil and their air forces had been absolute rulers of the skies for a long time, the military facts could no longer be overlooked. I therefore seem to have made fun of Hayler's optimism. The chronicle goes on with a certain irony: "State Secretary Hayler received a green tie as recognition from the minister. This honor is a new custom, which owes its origin to a conversation of the minister about the many colors of ties and the need to reward optimism and to express it. Hence, the green tie from the box that was supplied by the Production Office is being awarded by the minister for unswerving optimism. This decoration ranks shortly before or after the Knight's Cross, according to the decorations already received by the man so honored."[33]

Soon we heard that "rumors about the rearrangements in the Reich Ministry for Armaments and War Production" were circulating. We could count on Ohlendorf's joining the Ministry of Armaments, where he would supposedly become secretary general.[34] In fact, during the first few days of November 1944, the struggle for power entered a new phase. Ohlendorf asked to meet with me and made the following suggestion: The autonomy of the individual ministries should be largely abolished and replaced by a vast, uniform Ministry for Economy, Production, Armaments, Labor, and Food, which would also include Sauckel with his powers for the labor force. Ohlendorf saw this mammoth ministry being run by me. A document I penned several weeks after my imprisonment says that Ohlendorf intended only to take the position of secretary general and Funk's personal assistant. Hayler, on the other hand, as successor to Liebel, who had just been dismissed, was to become the only state secretary and thereby my constant representative in my now all-inclusive ministry.

Funk had remained responsible for all fundamental economic problems. Moreover, since the beginning of the war, he had also had the office of plenipotentiary for the War Economy, a legally incorporated institution, which, however, had never become active because of Goering's ambition and Funk's lethargy. Thus, I could easily foresee that the intelligent, uninhibited Ohlendorf, as Funk's deputy, would appropriate all these previously dormant powers of Funk's and thereby make all decisions on the management of the entire war economy, even though Ohlendorf assured me that Funk would never be activated in his capacity as plenipotentiary. Hayler and Ohlendorf had been working together closely for years; and no doubt, with one acting as my state secretary and the other as Funk's secretary, and both of them equipped with all of Funk's powers and assisted by Himmler, they would have gained control in my ministry despite my enormous power as superminister.[35] Outwardly I pretended to go along with this hypocritical plan so as not to provoke any violent reaction, which would have been possible, given my weakened position.

Just a few months earlier, in September 1944, we had discussed, at Ohlendorf's demand, how the intermediate authorities could build up a war economy office combining the offices for food, labor, economy, and armaments. This would have been expedient if the real aim had not been to shift all power to Ohlendorf. The latter assured me that decisions in the new immediate authority would lie with me; but this new office should also utilize Funk's vested rights as "plenipotentiary for the war economy," which Ohlendorf would have directed as Funk's secretary. On September 11, 1944, my deputy Liebel sent Hayler a "brief elaboration of the possibility of combining the agencies in the intermediary authority."[36] The accompanying proposal made no mention of Ohlendorf's and Hayler's intentions. It was obviously a delaying tactic using bureaucratic means of assistance.

According to another plan of Ohlendorf's, he wanted to reach his goal circuitously, by way of Goering's comprehensive powers. Funk had already had a whole series of meetings with Goering and Lammers. Their strategy was that Goering should delegate his dictatorial functions as director of the Four-Year Plan to Funk. Officially Funk would then be in charge of this plan too; but in practice, Ohlendorf as his representative would make all decisions about the entire economy. This plan too was mooted in October–

November 1944.[37] But to make such decisions we had already had Central Planning and the planning office of my ministry for a long time, so that the whole operation was superfluous.

When questioned at the Nuremberg trial, Ohlendorf retrospectively mentioned his aims, which he now called the "Economic Administration Reform Plan" and which he had worked out in the fall of 1944. This plan, he said, called for "an orderly administration and constitutional conditions at least in the economic sector."[38]

Himmler seems to have trained a good man for every important department in his staff. In any case, one had the impression that a junior staff was being schooled, even in areas that did not concern the SS. One example, along with Hans Kammler, was Ohlendorf. Even then, he struck me as Himmler's choice for taking over the Reich Ministry of Economy.

An excellent example of the secrecy of concealed planning is offered by a memorandum that Bormann dictated on November 3, 1944, for his state secretary Gerhard Klopfer, with the remark "In an envelope": "Re: Discussion with Reich Minister Speer. According to the statements of PC [Party Comrade] Speer, I do not believe that Reich Minister Funk has been informed by Hayler and Ohlendorf of their plans to transfer the Ministry of Economy to Reich Minister Speer or, more precisely, to transfer the last responsibilities of the Ministry of Economy to Reich Minister Speer. Needless to say, Reich Minister Speer said nothing about *his* goals,"[39] added Bormann, who was always distrustful of me. However, Bormann did not seem the least bit concerned about the goals that Ohlendorf was pursuing. I had thought up what I considered a successful action against all of Ohlendorf's plans; and this action, despite my ignorance of Bormann's suspicion, would have to put his mind at ease a few days later.

Since its founding in May 1943, the Ruhr Staff of my ministry had included Dr. Theodor Hupfauer as representative of the German Labor Front in the labor squad for swift removal of air-raid damage. Hupfauer was an old Party member and probably the most intelligent of Dr. Robert Ley's staffers, which certainly did not mean very much. I had sometimes spoken openly with Hupfauer about political inadequacies and found him to be likable and undoctrinaire.

In those November days of 1944, I asked Hupfauer to meet with me again. After it began to get dark, we drove in my car to the woods outside the Berlin gates; and there I openly told him what tasks would unavoidably fall on us. I said that I saw my duty now mainly in preventing the destruction of industrial facilities in order to preserve the economic substance of the nation. Hupfauer agreed and promised to assist me unconditionally, regardless of any personal danger. He kept his promise in full.

Under the impact of this discussion, I attempted a coup d'etat. In the last few days of November I asked Bormann to agree to Hupfauer as Liebel's successor. I was primed for a longer discussion with Bormann, but he gave me his approval without reflection after I assured him that further encroachment upon the jurisdiction of the Ministry of Economy was not planned. Perhaps he sensed that the appointment of Hupfauer as head of my Central Office also meant a final rejection of the Ohlendorf-Hayler plans, for this office was regarded as the political organ in my ministry.

In the early days of December 1944 Hupfauer took over not only the Central Office but also Wäger's Armaments Office. After I received Bormann's approval, I informed the two interested parties, Ohlendorf and Hayler, about this appointment.

Chapter 7
SS Economic Ideology

Oₕₗₑₙ...

OHLENDORF AND HAYLER had claimed that they wished to simplify conditions in war production by combining and reforming the economic administration. Indeed, it would have been advantageous if the many separate economic administrations—labor, food, industrial economy, distribution of energy, coal and fuel—had been reduced to a single common denominator. But actually, Ohlendorf had very different aims. He was hoping to prepare for a transformation in basic economic policies in the postwar period. Now, at the dramatic climax of the war, he already wanted to initiate this development. His plan had a great deal to do with somewhat nebulous ideas of an economy such as had been formulated before 1933, in the early economic ideology of the National Socialists. In 1932 Hitler had explained to his economic adviser Otto Wagener that "industrialization [has] made the individual completely unfree . . . in bondage to capital and the machine." Industrialization was therefore "a work mill in which any originality or individuality is totally crushed." Only "our socialism" will lead us "back to individuality," by "radically abolishing all the specious results of industrialization and restoring this development to the service of mankind and individualism."[1]

Starting in the fall of 1943, Ohlendorf kept falling back on such notions of Hitler's, which had long since lost their validity in the practical economic policies implemented by Hjalmar Schacht, Funk, and Goering. These theories had been recently weakened even more in that I had introduced a fairly successful Americanism into the armaments organization, and this innovation was a decisive step toward the manager revolution of German industry.

On July 15, 1944, Ohlendorf, certainly one of the most brilliant thinkers of National Socialism, expounded the following ideas to the Gau Economic Advisers of the Nazi Party:[2]

"We must view and test every economic structure in terms of whether it allows the full development of the basic characteristics of the German. We must be absolutely certain whether we can fully realize in economy the elements of our weltanschauung: honor, freedom, self-responsibility, honesty, and veracity." He rejected the efficiency principle that had been introduced through my organization when he continued: "The goods we produce after the war are not so essential; what *is* essential is that we preserve and develop the substance of our biological values, thus winning the peace."

This goal, he said, was imperiled by my production principles, for they involved "notions in which the German's consciousness of freedom is identified with the consumer's possibilities of meeting his demands." A very normal axiom, by the way that we were striving for as high a production as possible in order to meet quickly the tremendous demand after the war. Ohlendorf's arguments against this were drawn from the philosophy of history: "If we can carry out our weltanschauung even in the area of economic management, then we will finally achieve that order which, deep down, allows the development of human strength to be identical with man's mission toward his God."[3]

Ohlendorf gave his speech on June 15, 1944. I had already offered my reply in Essen, six days earlier, on June 9, before a meeting of industrial colleagues and directors of large armaments plants. I had stated: "If a man attacks the self-responsibility of industry, he must be able to document his attacks. If a man puts down my colleagues with conjectures, he must realize that he can inflict the most serious damage on one of the most important instruments in the existential struggle of the German people." And, further down in my speech, I went on: "I shall absolutely not tolerate that the men who have voluntarily made themselves available to German armaments and war production be discredited by slanderous statements that cannot be documented. The work that these men have to perform is truly too serious, and the burden that they have taken upon themselves, and indeed voluntarily, is far too great. . . . The implementation of comprehensive industrial tasks can be piloted solely by men who have come from industry itself."

However, I had made concessions to Ohlendorf's qualms in that my

speech left open the form of economic management for the postwar
period: "All of us who have made ourselves available in these years, which
are so crucial to the destiny of our people, in order to bring forth the
maximum from German production, view this task as purely determined
by the war." For the duration of the war, "the self-responsibility of
industry [must be] expanded more and more and granted even vaster
powers. We cannot abandon the route that we have taken so far."[4] A short
time later, I had partial reprints of my speech and essays commenting on
our system sent to the press, which only helped to aggravate the conflict.
(See Appendix 9.)

The obvious goals of "self-responsibility of industry" included the
notion of the optimal factory, i.e., the factory achieving the highest performance with the least amount of manpower and material. "The much-
used notion of the optimal factory," Ohlendorf argued, "must be taken
with caution. One must picture the consequences of a restructuring according to the standards of optimal factory dimensions. Of handicrafts, 77
percent do not correspond to the notion of an optimal factory. . . .
Millions more people will be driven into anonymous work and shift from
artisan manufacture to assembly-line manufacture. Furthermore, such a
reshaping of industrial economy will involve a new accumulation of capital
and hence a sharpening of the gulf between poor and rich. The separation
from a small, personal business, from a personal workshop, would signify
a division between work space and living space and a general removal
from work space, which would, in turn, be bound to affect the outcome
of work."[5]

We read something similar in Ohlendorf's article "*Wirtschafspolitische
Bilanz*" ("The Balance Sheet of Economic Policies") of December 28,
1944. "I have previously spoken of how intensely the large-scale company
is viewed as an ideal type under the leading notion of efficiency and the
optimal factory, because the large-scale company seems to offer the best
possible utilization of technology and organization. Far and wide, we
therefore see small and medium-sized enterprises dying out, with a trend
toward the large enterprise, which perhaps has never been so large. We
can establish a concentration of capital that would surely have filled Karl
Marx with envy. For us, this is not a matter of indifference."[6] Elsewhere,
Ohlendorf emphasizes: "The multiplicity of economically autonomous
livelihoods is one of the most valuable strata of achievement in the entire
German national economy. We should not conceal from ourselves the
fact that during the war we have had to put up with critical invasions into
this performance stratum, for instance, the disbanding of 500,000

autonomous handicraft livelihoods for the sake of armaments." Naturally, the number of small businesses had been considerably altered by the war economy; but no statistics document an impact of this proportion.

Ohlendorf's planned "German economic order, in contrast to the capitalistic and Bolshevistic ones, aims to a powerful degree at maintaining as much self-responsibility as possible. Late capitalism, just like Bolshevism, has reached a developmental stage which allows the individual no self-responsibility and no development in his economic activity. Yet man's dignity can be granted only in an economic order that lets him live and be effective as a whole man."[7]

Skeptically, Ohlendorf asked: "Has not this war, with the constraint of mass production of weapons, launched a whole new era in mass production? Are we perhaps standing at the beginning of a whole new industrial era, which was created by the hard demands of the war and will be stamped by the period *after*[8] the war?" (These were indeed our intentions when we thought about peacetime production.) "Will industry, after masterfully learning how to mass-produce weapons and munitions, not also develop a whole new efficiency in mass-producing, say, clothing or industrially manufactured food?" This too was in part our goal, and we knew that we could achieve it with a great reduction of prewar prices. We wanted to siphon off the difference between the prewar price and the overhead in order to begin paying the war debts.

Ohlendorf saw our production methods as simply endangering his National Socialist ideals and, as we have seen, he thus agreed precisely with the notions stated by Hitler before 1942: "The period after the war will be the time of large-scale thinking, with a trend toward mammoth numbers. Obviously, mass production, serial manufacture, which were so vastly important for wartime output, will also be in effect in the postwar period. Can Europe compete with American or Asiatic mass production? If a *contest of mammothness of production* were to begin, and if this contest were to be crucial to maintaining the life and position of the German people, then Germany would have to make sure in time that it would not lose such a contest, and we could perhaps advocate deferring for a limited while the regard for the German individual, his personal life and his happiness."

The economic theoretician Ohlendorf could not foresee that this question would be answered positively by German economic triumphs after the war. At that time, he said: "No matter what the outcome of the war, if the German people devoted itself to the notion of mass production, it would have to compete with either Japanese or American mass production. But it is clear that neither would be possible without destroying the existential basis of the German people. However, if we cannot pit mass against mass, then we have no choice but to pit quality against mass." This standpoint was also consistent with our attitude. Only by means of superior quality did we in armaments production have any chance of balancing the adversary's production, which was often many times the capacity of ours. Yet even these higher-quality tanks, weapons, or jet planes (which, incidentally, always came too late) were, of course, manufactured by our methods of efficiency and series production.

"The strength and the possibilities for the German people," Ohlendorf continued, "lie in *preserving and expanding its qualitative abilities and the foundations thereof.*"[9] All this sounded very convincing, and he even seemed to be able to cite the experiences of wartime production. But Ohlendorf ought to have known that our first-class product of German quality, the BMW high-power airplane engine, was being mass-produced with automatic machines operated by Russian POWs, who had been trained in just a few weeks—although, of course, supported by technicians and trained supervisory personnel. A high-quality average can be more readily achieved in the mass process than by individual work on parts. Ultimately, Ohlendorf's theory was pure romanticism.

Furthermore, Ohlendorf doubted "*whether Germany can actually carry out a mammoth industrialization* all the way."[10] And he even cited arguments based on the superiority of the rustic over the industrial mentality. "Where are we to get, say, a guarantee of food for the people who are required for industrialization and who, on the whole, are to be drawn from the rural areas; and where, finally, are these people to come from when the inner wellspring of German peoplehood, the farm population, has dried up because of total industrialization?"[11] Now, heaven knows this was not our intention. We knew that the new production methods would require fewer workers, and thus we foresaw difficulties in reintegrating the millions of conscripted soldiers who had once worked in the production process.

"Altogether, the result would be a highly undesirable massification," Ohlendorf stated elsewhere. After strenuous work, a man cannot relax in mass, such as was practiced by the German Labor Front: "Collective baths and organized collective joys are not the basis for the development of people with whom we want to build a thousand-year Reich." This was a direct attack on the efforts of the organization that Ley had developed, "Strength through Joy," which was actually pursuing such goals. "Relaxation cannot be restricted to organized mass recovery; it can also lie, for instance, in work and in the joy in work itself, as we see in the farmer, who, in the evening after work, reflects upon today's labor and thinks about tomorrow's."[12]

I had pursued similar ideas when I was Prof. Heinrich Tessenow's assistant. Tessenow, agricultural reformer Damaschke, and others in this circle had developed theories of this kind. I now see that such ideas were backward-looking, that a modern economy cannot be steered by such old-fashioned principles. But my concern about human beings is still attracted to these statements of Ohlendorf's.

On December 1, 1944, at a meeting on sociological issues at the Ministry of Economy, Ohlendorf spun his ideas out further. "There is no doubt that in the present economic policy," i.e., self-responsibility, "the efficient use of manpower is one of the most essential program points and points of departure. As a point of departure, a goal is set for economy to achieve the greatest possible result with the least expenditure." This struck me as correct at that time, and today I still take it for granted.

"If I try to fulfill this demand without regard for the other concerns of the nation, and if I simplify these demands, perhaps superficially connect them with technology and its possibilities and then equate the rationalized, best-possible factory facilities with the utmost technological possibility, and if I see technology develop on its own with no connection to factory events, i.e., let technology itself find the ultimate form possible for technological construction or technological organization, and if I then set up this technology as a yardstick for economic development [an early formulation, incidentally, of the dangers of technological dictatorship], then the laws [probably meaning the legislators] would have no other choice than to submit to this technological construction or this technological organization."

The face of economy would "then not be determined by human-existential development," warned Ohlendorf, "but by the possibility of organization, of solidly thought, rationalist method, the best possible utilization of technology and organization!" Ohlendorf, who thereby branded the thinking of our success strategy, argued: "A nation is liveliness, is becoming and waning, as well as waning and becoming, ancestors, present, and grandchildren simultaneously. Hence, I can see economy only in broader contexts, and not economic contexts, but rather social, that is national, contexts."[13] What a lack of sophistication is expressed in those last few sentences, formulated by the man who was responsible for questions of economic policy at the Ministry of Economy within the framework of the SS. (See Appendix 10.)

On the one hand Ohlendorf was a highly qualified intellectual with great ambitions. He was sympathetic to humanitarian problems, advocated values of individuality—and yet, with his left hand, as it were, he deliberately ordered the murder of 90,000 people.[14]

Ohlendorf defended his ideas with the stubbornness of a fanatic. Despite his great intelligence and logical foundations, he refused to deny his basic romanticism. This was a quality he shared with Himmler and many other high-ranking SS leaders. As chief ideologist of economic events, Ohlendorf made it his duty to negate the technological development of our century and to project to the course of modern wars conclusions that might have been valid at the time of the French Revolution. "In closing, I might just point out that this war is not only a war of production but also a war of ideas, and that there are many examples in history where ideas have turned out to be more powerful than production figures."[15] These words were spoken in late January 1945—when the final defeat was merely a question of weeks. An example of the utopian, the downright euphoric, notions at the time of the collapse. But the surprising conclusion was inevitable after it had become clear even to Ohlendorf that German industry could now assemble weapons only from the remaining stocks of individual components, because basic production in the Ruhr had stopped in November 1944.

A few months earlier, Ohlendorf had already anticipated future wars. He must have heard about Hitler's aim—often expressed privately—to wage a new war against the United States after his victory in Europe in order to attain his goal of world domination, for which he had been designing triumphal buildings since 1925. In 1941 Hitler made this intention clear in one of his monologues at his headquarters: "Berlin will some day be the capital of the world. . . . Anyone entering the Reich Chancellery must feel that he is coming before the rulers of the world. . . . [For] if we are the masters of Europe, we will have the dominant position in the world. With the other states in Europe we will amount, with 230 million Germans, to 400 million, and with those numbers we can fight against 130 million Americans."[16]

And Ohlendorf: *"The enemies of the future, say, America,[17]* must all begin in civilization; but by then we will be able to utilize ancient cultural values and essential values and draw strength and gain possibilities from them which are not available to those who must restrict themselves to civilization."[18] *Nota bene:* These notions, voiced in the summer of 1944 and alien to reality, are theories on how to wage war beyond the continent.

In my Spandau diaries, I pursued these reflections in March 1963[19]: "Are the sentences of this concluding speech (at Nuremberg) which found so much approval in the press back then, justified? Is it correct to speak of a technological danger first caused by Hitler? Was not Hitler downright antimodern? After all, the symbol he chose for National Socialist ideology was not the modern sowing machine but the sower, not the tractor but the plow. The thatched roof was preferred over the asbestos cement roof; and modern music as the expression of our technological age was replaced by folk song. Hitler could polemicize against the 'soulless machine.' If one is pessimistic about civilization, one may understand some aspects of these strivings. But this antimodernity prevented Hitler from approaching victory: thatched roofs, old-fashioned ideas about artisan manufacture, division of the land into individual farms—all these things were contrary to the rational exploitation of German production not only in practice but far more in their ideological background. When I began my work as armaments minister in 1942, I kept coming up against such hindrances more and more, or else I fought against a rubber wall, when, for instance, I demanded the promotion of nuclear fission by all possible means, and the party organ, *Der Völkische Beobachter*, ran an article entitled 'Jewish Physics Stirs Again.' "

Typical of this intertwining with a romantic ideology was Hitler's, Goering's, and Sauckel's refusal to let German women work in the armaments industry during the war, something that came about as a matter of course in the Anglo-Saxon countries. The reason given was that factory work would damage their morals and their child-bearing capacity. Such unsophisticated feelings were not consistent with Hitler's plans to make Germany the most powerful nation on earth. Until 1942 our Reich was only seemingly ruled by standards of technology and efficiency.

When I review the matter carefully, Hitler was antimodern in his decisions on armaments as well. He opposed the tommy gun because he said it made soldiers cowardly and made close combat impossible. Or he rejected the jet fighter because he said its extreme speed was an obstacle to fighting. He had as little sympathy for jet propulsion as for rockets until 1943. He even distrusted our hesitant attempts at developing an atom bomb by means of nuclear fission, and in private conversations he called such efforts a spawn of Jewish pseudoscience.

Thus, both Hitler and Ohlendorf, and with them the majority of leading Party bigwigs, paid tribute to seemingly humanitarian ideals. The war was supposed to be won with technology, but actually technology was evil. I, too, in my summation at Nuremberg, advocated the thesis that the development of technology was the *mene tekel* of our epoch. Instead of worrying about my defense, I warned of the consequences of modern technology: "Hitler's dictatorship was the first dictatorship of an industrial state in this era of modern technology, a dictatorship that used technological means in a perfect way in order to control its own people." I continued: "The nightmare of many people, that some day nations will be ruled by technology, almost came true in Hitler's authoritarian system. Every state in the world is now in danger of being terrorized by technology. But this seems inevitable in a modern dictatorship. Hence: the more technological the world becomes, the more necessary the counterpoise of demanding individual freedom and the self-awareness of the individual." Did I realize at that time that I myself had implemented the predominance of technology in Germany? Until then mass production had been contrary to the ideological premises of National Socialism. After all, the influence of the early Hitler can be read almost word for word in Ohlendorf's adverse ideology. In many respects, Ohlendorf's notions were taken from the ideological substance of early National Socialism.

Indeed, the disagreements between Ohlendorf and me reflect conflicts that reach all the way to the student revolts. Certain qualms in our time aim at a similarly emotional world, and many things that Ohlendorf proclaimed sound like premonitions of problems with which industrial society has confronted modern states. Today, however, I advocate demands similar to Ohlendorf's. Yet I feel certain doubts when I now discover that parallels to my thinking are to be found in Ohlendorf, of all people.

Should not such connections make one skeptical? (See Appendix 10.)

PART TWO
Threats and Efforts

Chapter 8

In the Protectorate

THE INDUSTRY in the Czech territories, known as the Protectorate, had been viewed by the SS as its own domain before 1942, just as, in September 1941, after the downfall of Baron Konstantin von Neurath, the Reich protector of Bohemia and Moravia, the SS had begun seeing the administration of this country as its own province. From this point on until his death, resulting from an assassination attempt, on June 4, 1942, Reinhard Heydrich was the undisputed ruler of this territory and was largely independent of the Berlin central agencies. Even after his death, the appointment of the insignificant Karl Hermann Frank continued the tradition of assigning government offices to proven and reliable SS officers. Thus, it was not astonishing that Himmler and his staff endeavored to exploit the powerful weapons industry of former Czechoslovakia for the SS. Himmler evidently saw it as his hereditary privilege when, during the first few months of his ministerial activity, he unhesitatingly diverted the operations of the progressive Skoda Works, which included the weapons plants at Brno. To safeguard this project, Himmler succeeded in convincing Hitler in March 1942 that in the future "the Skoda Works and the Brno Weapons Works [should] proceed through their new development in cooperation with the Waffen-SS."[1] This order of Hitler's remained unknown to me for many months. This was one of Hitler's countless double-track procedures, the kind he ordered over and over again, notwithstanding the prestige of his ministers or commanders and without even so much as notifying the people in charge. This particular order was probably due to Hitler's dis-

trust of the Army Ordnance Office, which he considered all too conserva-
tive and resistant to change. Without sensing their ultimate effect, I myself
had upheld some reservations of Hitler's, which had had to be maintained
until then in certain development projects in these Czech plants with
Czech engineers, for security reasons. Now Hitler, for the first time,
ordered that the Skoda Works be supplied with captured weapons for
technical evaluation and that Heydrich be instructed of his decision.[2]

It was quite in keeping with the situation when Director General Wilhelm
Voss, head of the Skoda Works and an honorary standard commander in
the SS, assured Himmler in his first report that he was "doing his best to
meet with all the wishes and special wishes of the Waffen-SS in every respect." Precise reports covering many typewritten pages informed Himmler
about developments for mountain howitzers; for an 8 cm trench mortar with
48 rockets on the pattern of the so-called Stalin organ (multiple rocket
launcher); about an SS tommy gun; about rifle grenades; about a machine
gun with an increased rate of 1,000 shots per minute; and about an automatic rifle. These reports stated that most of the experiments were well advanced and that "the demands made by the SS Reichsführer were being
fulfilled to the utmost extent." Voss signed his letter to Himmler "your
most obediently devoted SS standard commander."[3]

Himmler was impressed. "Your report on the state of the development
projects interests me greatly. I assume that the collaboration is quite well
coordinated," he replied a few weeks later.[4]

Three days after this praise, on May 11, 1942, Voss was able to confirm
Himmler's opinion: "By concentrating all development for the Waffen-SS
in the liaison staff in Skoda and Brno weapons plants,[5] and assuring systematic, intense cooperation with the SS Ordnance Office," the development of the new weapons had progressed faster than expected.[6]

On June 4, 1942, Voss gave Himmler a new, detailed report, showing that
the development of SS weapons had indeed made strides. The 8 cm trench
mortar was almost finished, an example of the firing mechanism for the
simultaneous firing of 48 grenades was ready to be tried out; the final
model of the SS tommy gun was ready for testing; serial manufacture of
rifle grenades had begun; the new machine gun would be test-fired and
then demonstrated to the representatives of the SS Ordnance Office; and a
sample of the newly developed automatic (self-loading) rifle had been dispatched to the SS Ordnance Office.[7]

Voss's utter dependency on the SS was shown on July 10, 1942, when he
considered it necessary to report to Himmler rather than Field Marshal
Milch (in charge of air armaments) that his, Voss's, plant could develop a
bomb with very great aim accuracy: "This idea is important and urgent

enough to be examined without delay. . . . Before I approach Field Marshal Milch, may I ask you most humbly for your approval."[8] Voss saw himself as Himmler's deputy for all development projects, even those for other branches of the military.

In a long drawn-out process, my ministry succeeded in pushing back the SS armaments domination in the Protectorate. We got Hitler interested in the extent of the Protectorate's armaments capacity, which was not yet being fully utilized. Characteristically, for this reason, a relatively large amount of space in the Führer's protocols was devoted to the Skoda Works. They were mentioned 17 times, as compared with 30 statements about the far more important Krupp Works. Given Hitler's interest in matters of development and production, it was inevitable that our references to undertakings by the Skoda engineers—whom Hitler greatly esteemed also—should lead to directives strengthening our influence at the Skoda Works.

Just a few weeks after Hitler's decision to hand development of the Skoda and Brno weapons over to the SS, he accepted our guidelines for building the Czech T 38 tank, which, as the Marder T 38 tank destroyer, was eventually to be so successful in the army units.[9] Then, one week later, likewise for the army, he ordered a 24 cm cannon developed by Skoda and a 42 cm howitzer.[10] Six weeks after that, Hitler impatiently insisted on speedier delivery of these guns to the army. Within a few months the Skoda light field howitzer, together with a model from Krupp Rheinmetall, was tested by the Army Ordnance Office and not by the SS Ordnance Office.[11] Skoda suggestions for an artillery mount were submitted to Hitler, who ordered comparisons with those constructed by Krupp Rhine Metal. In early January 1943, Hitler ordered construction of more 6.5-ton aircooled Tatra trucks because of their "outstanding performance."[12] One month later, an output of at first 150 T 38 tank destroyers a month could be planned at the Böhmisch-Mährische Machine Factory.[13] Furthermore, at Hitler's orders, Skoda's experience in developing a 3 cm double antiaircraft gun for U-boats was utilized.[14] What capacities lay fallow in Czech territory!

This development allowed me to write at about the same time, April 1943, to SS Squad Commander Jüttner, telling him that the manufacture of an SS-developed weapon in the Protectorate would have to be viewed as unreal thinking. In his letter of December 14, 1942, he had expressed the "wish for manufacturing 10,000 SS 42 tommy guns" in the Protectorate, and I now informed him that this wish could not be approved because "in terms of weapons and manufacturing, no increased output over the 40 tommy gun, introduced [by the army] is to be achieved, since [this weapon] likewise shoots pistol cartridges. The production at the Brno weapons plants would mean considerable interference with the output of other instruments, including the K 98 carbine and the 3.7 cm antiaircraft gun, whose greatest possible increase was recently described as urgent by the Führer. Under these circumstances, I cannot regard as justifiable the manufacture of SS 42 tommy guns in a series of 10,000. May I please ask you to refrain from pursuing the matter any further."[15]

In mid-November 1943, I could report to Hitler "about the considerable achievements of the armaments works in the Protectorate." I also transmitted to him "the assurance of the agencies involved and the management of the plants that they have declared their readiness to take further measures to intensify their efficiency, and thereby [increase] their performance within a year to a level double that of today's."[16] There was no further mention of SS-steered production.

We had learned that since the beginning of the German occupation, the Czech territory had a capacity of several hundred Czech tanks, including all parts, even motors, etc. After Hitler's consent, the T-38, which had been developed years before, could finally get into full production. It eventually proved to be an efficient vehicle, popular with the troops. As of late November 1943, with Hitler's authorization, we were able to utilize the Czech industrial territory for the production of the so-called Czech tank. But it was only in mid-May 1944 that we were handed the SS towing-vehicle production in the Böhmisch-Mährische Machine Factory. Hitler agreed with our compromise plan of giving the SS 25 sets of T 38 frames for its own use for every 1,000 T 38 tank destroyers produced.[17] Because of such delays, it took us ten months to deliver 385 pieces (in October 1944). The difficulties caused by aerial attacks as of late summer 1944 brought the tank output within Reich territory down from 1,540 units in July 1944 to 754 units in January 1945 (not counting the T 38). In contrast, 107 T 38 tanks were produced in Czech territory in July 1944. The fact that this number could be increased to 434 units in January 1945 despite all adversities is proof of the depth of tank capacities that must have been unused in Czech territory.[18] Naturally, the established monthly output of T 38 tanks could not be attained in the spring of 1945 because of the steel shortage. But this description shows what losses were inflicted upon the army command because of the armaments policies of the SS hierarchy in Czech territory.

In retrospect, one can hardly estimate how many more tanks could have been delivered to the army in the previous years from this unused capacity. It is certainly fair to discount one year for clearing out initial administrative difficulties after the German army marched into Czechoslovakia in the spring of 1939. We would also have to assume one more year for the necessary start-up time for peak production. However, if I consider just the period from 1940 to 1943, then we may speak of three lost production years, that is, a loss of 20,000 of these light, flexible tanks—a dramatic example of the amateurishness of the SS, as well as of its inability to make use of the Czech industrial potential for its own purposes. For Hitler never had any qualms about exploiting the armaments capacity of Czechoslovakia out of basic ideological considerations. Just as, after initial hesitation, he eventually demanded that we utilize the armaments capacities of the occupied countries—France, Belgium, Holland—to strengthen the German war effort.[19]

By mid-May 1944, the final uncontrollable influences of the SS were removed from Skoda. "Reported to the Führer on the gratifying development of the output figures at the Skoda Works, with presentation of a comparison of the yields in January 1943, January 1944, and March 1944. The Führer asked that the factory be informed of his gratitude and acknowledgment, with a stress on the outstanding development performance of the plant. He registered with satisfaction that similar measures are being initiated for the Brno Weapons Works in order to bring this plant to the same performance level."[20] This report indirectly hints that the SS production at Skoda must have been low before our intervention.

In particular, Hitler was more and more impressed by the work of the technicians who were employed first by the SS and then by my organization. At the start of November 1944, Hitler expressed unusual praise for suggestions by the Skoda engineers regarding an automatic multiple rocket-launching mechanism for the 8 cm trench mortar.[21] That same day, I notified Hitler that the Skoda model had done best in a comparative test performed by the Army Ordnance Office wth various models of heavy field howitzers. On this occasion, a new kind of shell with a so-called "suction bowl" was demonstrated. Full of enthusiasm, Hitler ordered that the Czech inventor of this new shell receive a high, tax-free grant for distinguished service to the State.[22]

On March 30, 1942, Hitler had ordered the Skoda Works and the Brno Weapons Works "to pursue their new development jointly with the Waffen-SS." But now, two years later, that order was obsolete.[23] However, years were lost, as was the production of thousands of tanks, guns, and infantry weapons.

Hitler was impressed by the work of the Czech engineers and technicians. Hence, in the very last days of the war, when I was visiting his bunker on the night of April 23, 1945, he promptly acceded to a suggestion of mine concerning leading Czech industrialists and engineers; he ordered that they be saved from the revenge of the Russians and permitted to escape to American headquarters.[24] As was recently established, they did indeed arrive in Western territory, and some of them, like some of their German colleagues in construction, were taken to the United States. We may assume that they have worked there for decades.

With some irony, I would like to point out that Hitler's order was probably his penultimate official act. It was followed by his decree making Admiral Karl Doenitz his successor.

Things were now set straight in the technical area. But in the administration, we had not yet succeeded in adjusting the jurisdictions to these facts. One reason was that while I could win Hitler over for decisions on production matters, he grew evasive when it came to reducing the administrative jurisdictions of his delegated rulers in Bohemia, in the General-gouvernement [main part of occupied Poland], or in Holland.[25] I had to be content with appealing to Lammers, the head of the Reich Chancellery. Lammers would normally seek reassurance from Bormann, who would then intrigue with Himmler. Hence, the result of my efforts was bound to be negative.

General Hernekamp, the head of armaments inspection in Prague, was made my local representative. At the same time, I appointed him chairman of the armaments commission, that is, head of the highest comprehensive agency for all armaments matters in the Protectorate. Naturally, he was bitterly fought by the SS-controlled leadership of the Protectorate. In the fall of 1943 there was a violent argument between the SS-dependent Prague administrative center and my ministry. On October 8, 1943, in Berlin, after a tiring discussion between SS Obergruppenführer Karl Hermann Frank and me, a satisfactory agreement on the Protectorate could be reached. Frank's position was initially weak since he did not dare get involved in any implementation of Hitler's production orders. The ministry chronicle states: "The minister managed to get Frank to recognize Speer's right to give directives in the area of armaments. However, in order to save the face of the political autonomy of Bohemia and Moravia, Frank received the concession that all directives should pass through him."[26]

Despite this agreement, the problems did not diminish. In the trivial, daily work, SS agencies bypassed my organization more and more frequently. On March 2, 1944, in order to settle my position unequivocally, I informed Frank, as the responsible head of the German administration in Prague, that I intended to "appoint Major General Hernekamp, holder of an engineering degree and the chairman of the German Armaments Commission, my deputy for Bohemia and Moravia in order to combine my agencies in the Protectorate of Bohemia and Moravia."[27] The accompanying draft for an edict said: "In regard to the Ministry for Economy and Labor, he has the powers arising from his position as chairman of the Armaments Commission according to my edict of 10/29/43 on the distribution of assignments in the war economy. The deputy is responsible for overall direction of my agencies in the Protectorate of Bohemia and Moravia."[28]

The SS was unimpressed by such centralizing efforts, as shown by Kammler's telegram of June 13, 1944, informing Himmler that State Minister Dr. Frank had declared himself responsible "for special measures toward creating subterranean manufacturing sites or armaments factories in the Protectorate."[29] I knew nothing about such arrangements. But the resistance was blatant. I therefore sent Lammers what amounted to a policy statement on June 19, 1944, asking him to preserve the Reich authority and not to let regional governing systems undermine the direct issuing of orders from Berlin.

This request for maintaining immediate influence was important for my organs of industrial self-responsibility because, like a large concern, we could achieve optimal performance only by central control of the individual production branches. By way of complaint, my letter asked Lammers this cardinal question: "To avoid endangering the uniform issuing of orders, I cannot do without this form of organization, which is uniformly implemented throughout the armaments sector."[30] But even this intervention met no great success. On August 15, 1944, I complained once again to Lammers that "General Hernekamp, the deputy for Bohemia and Moravia of the Reich minister for armaments and war production, does not have the right to give immediate orders to the autonomous ministers . . . and must always contact the German state minister for Bohemia and Moravia" to have his orders carried out.[31]

Naturally, we can understand certain reactions of the SD deputy in Prague and his immediate superior of division III (Seibert) in the Berlin Central Office, given my successful advances and the simultaneous removal of the SS predominance in the Czech armaments industry. The Prague Security Service supported the local SS regime in its striving for power, which was interrupted by the activities of my ministry. Then, when I attempted to establish direct authority for my deputy General Hernekamp over local government agencies, I must have made the SD my all-out enemy.

The SD reported every week on the economic situation and the mood of the populace. Some of these reports were laid before Hitler. As Ohlendorf said, he tried to use these reports politically by making a tendentious selection, which he distributed to influential personalities. These reports, he told me in 1944, were to be taken as a surrogate for public opinion; uninfluenced, they were to express the popular mood in order to make it known on higher levels. When interrogated about himself at the Nuremberg Military Court, Ohlendorf again emphasized: "I was given the concrete assignment of building an economic intelligence service, of creating an organization that could draw forth, in the area of economy, all the information about faulty developments that was crucial for the National Socialist leadership to know."[32] Probably the SD under Ohlendorf's command had indeed initially seen its task as objectively informing the State and Party organs about abuses. This intention may have been sincere. But as so often in administrative processes, this apparatus had become independent, turning into an end in itself. In the curse of time, it must have developed a kind of compulsion to keep presenting new complaints, so that the now-large apparatus would not be suspected of having become unnecessary. This was bound to lead to exaggerations.

Furthermore, it was very tempting to use such an instrument for political purposes as well. Especially in the case of armaments. After Ohlendorf tried to implement his economic notions as of September 1943, the SD reports were naturally meant to serve this new direction of his as well as the preparation of his far-reaching plans to advance to the position of secretary general of the German economy. At the same time, the SD reports underpinned his views on the inadequacy of my armaments organization.

Thus, when the SD kept presenting new arguments against the reliability of industry as of the summer of 1944, Ohlendorf's subalterns knew that negative opinions on the armaments industry were not unwelcome in the Central Office of the SD. This spelled danger. In nearly all offices with rigorous chiefs, the employees turned in colored reports to avoid drawing unpleasant notice. Thus, when I visited Madrid in 1941, Eberhard von Stohrer, the German ambassador to Spain, told me that he was forced to word his reports in a tone that would not instantly be rejected by Foreign Minister Joachim von Ribbentrop. He had to conform to the official language regulations to make sure that his reports were read at all.

And then there was the inadequacy of the SD staff members. It seems as if minor employees of the firms, who had simultaneously been made subordinate organs of the "Security Service of the SS," vented their annoyance at their superiors in transparent suspicions. They had probably become megalomaniacs because of their SD positions in the factories and felt obligated to solidify these positions of trust. At the time, we were of the opinion that they regarded it as their bound duty to find unpleasant things to report at any price. This shows the nature and danger of any system of informers.

Petty reports, they would be hardly worth mentioning if they were not typical of the system that the unwholesome aspects of the labor process were composed of—a huge number of tiny intrigues by the SD or other Party agencies. Naturally, only a portion of the SD complaints, intended to show the inadequacy of the armaments administration, are still extant. But they suffice to show the tendency of manipulation from above. Luckily for me, however, they were usually unknown to me and my staffers; for refuting them would have greatly tied me down.

At any rate, I have seldom read such superficial nonsense as is summed up in the following pages.

Ohlendorf was notified by the head of the Security Service (SD) in Prague that "Reich Minister Speer is expected to come to Prague on June 30, 1944, mainly in order to inspect the Böhmisch-Mährische Machine Factory, or rather to discuss the tank program. The factory plans to have Reich Minister Speer either attend a comradeship evening of the 'Czech' employees of the plant or take a boat cruise with them." Certainly an unusual intention, which, however, would have been in keeping with my relationship to the Czech staffers. Understandably, "State Minister [Frank has] considerable reservations for security reasons, so he should not come to these functions." In fact, this plan could not be implemented. But I did visit the factory and, without requesting any special protection, standing in the midst of the Czech employees, I spoke about our armaments goal and thanked them for the achievements of Czech industry, which were astounding given the circumstances.

This SD report maliciously continues: "In professional circles, the visit of Reich Minister Speer is linked exclusively to the tank program. Particularly remarkable is the following conjecture of leading industrial circles: Department Head Saur has supposedly stated that the tank program [for the Czech T 38 tank], which he has announced for Czech territory could not be carried out in the intended form, and he will therefore have to obtain some kind of support. Even though the output so far has been at the cost of other manufacturing, this is no longer the case for the July output. However, during his Prague visit, the Reich minister will find everything in order and probably report as much to the Führer. Saur would thus be free of the ultimate responsibility, for he could point to Speer, who will be convinced of the orderly course of the tank program in Prague."[33]

The primitive nature of this speculation illustrates the intellectual level of these "supreme rat-smellers," as they were ironically known back then.

Frank probably found it necessary to write to me on August 16, 1944, because of the SD report. There had indeed been difficulties. As Saur replied on my behalf on August 28, "the hundredth vehicle [of the T 38 had come off the assembly line] on June 1, 1944. Minor problems, such as occur in any tank factory, even with well-established models, were resolved within the next few days. [Thus] the final vehicle of the hundred of the June output did not leave the factory until August 7." The final vehicles of the July output could not be delivered until the beginning of August "because of deficiencies in the original material." Likewise, in the August production, "the quota of 200 does not seem attainable, due to unforeseen difficulties. Needless to say, [in August] a peak output is being striven for with all means, and it will probably reach approximately 170."

It would have scarcely been possible, as the SD insinuated, to mislead Hitler with doctored figures. For he personally distributed the tanks that had been reported delivered. The military units would have inevitably protested that his promises had not been kept. It therefore goes without saying that Saur, in concluding his letter, declared that he would keep the Führer "up to date on the extraordinary difficulties,"[34] which would also enlighten the leaders in Prague about the resistance inflicted on us by lack of understanding on the part of the Prague administration.

The head of Division III D-East in the Reich Main Security Office, to whom this letter from Prague was addressed, was even more dissatisfied with our armaments policies. In a report on his junket to the Protectorate from October 24 to 31, 1944, he recorded his negative opinion on the ministry and its work methods. He called them catastrophic. This could certainly be read as the ulterior meaning of the following statements by this SD departmental chief for the East: "One of the most acute problems in the industrial sector is the transfer of the Old Reich industrial plants into the Bohemian-Moravian territory. . . . The transfer of the Vienna-Neustadt Aircraft Works, already discussed in several reports, showed how unsystematically the move was made, in part without heeding important production factors such as transportation! The oral discussions both in this case and regarding the transfer of a series of other production items crucial to the war effort, especially aircraft and tanks, show that these inadequacies and abuses do not occur within the framework of the factory managements, but are chiefly due to a total lack of central control for all the transfer measures." So that was the aim of this SD criticism: "In practice, every firm or its responsible committee is doing whatever it wishes. In wild competition with one another, without heeding the respective importance of each other's production, aimed only at the better connection of the factory management with the Berlin national agencies, which are completely ignorant of the local conditions, the individual firms attempt to requisition the production sites that strike them as most favorable." According to these statements, the authority in the central office must have been absolutely chaotic; yet this was contradicted by the armaments achievements even around this time, despite all the air raids and other obstacles. "It must be pointed out that not only the unfavorable transportation conditions but also the problems of manpower, food, and lodgings, as well as, above all, the security situation, are heeded not at all or too late."[35] An example of the insolence with which these lower SS ranks presumed to pass judgment on the work of prominent industrialists.

Five months prior to this SD report, on June 7, 1944, I rebuked Frank, who was protesting along the same lines: "I am not of the opinion that the Protectorate is being overburdened for the transfer of industry. The main difficulty in the Protectorate, as I see it, is not so much the shortage of manufacturing space or housing possibilities for the manpower, as the energy supply. For this reason I am already striving to admit as few factory transfers as possible to the Protectorate. . . . I shall keep on trying to make demands on the Protectorate in the area of industry transfers only if such demands can be met—albeit with difficulties."[36]

More than anything, the discussions reveal that the author of the SD report felt he had to establish the following: In contrast to the General-gouvernement [the major part of Polish territory under German rule] or the incorporated East European territories, the armaments inspection, particularly its individual armaments departments, had so far not made any efforts toward central control and planning of the transfer, much less been in a situation to carry out such a task. The personnel in these armaments agencies was generally described as poor. Thus, this attack concentrated on putting down the activities of General Hernekamp and his staff. "Such a task can be implemented," not by armaments inspection, which was under my jurisdiction, but "only by a regional [Prague] office, since all the conditions indicated, especially the political and structural ones, cannot be surveyed from Berlin."[37] We will read that a few weeks later this demand by the Security Service was approved, and that an autonomous economic organization in Czechoslovakia, subject to the Prague government, would oversee the armaments sector.

My decisions were also attacked and my opinions sharply criticized by
Ohlendorf's office, SD III D-East: "Reich Minister Speer recently raised
the problem of detaching the factories transferred to the Protectorate from
their previous company connections and incorporating them into Protectorate concerns, especially the Weapons Union [Skoda-Brno Weapons] and
the BMM [Bohemian-Moravian Machine Factories]." I saw this separation
as a way of expanding the capable, experienced administration corps of
the Protectorate concerns to these similar firms as they arrived in Bohemia
and Moravia. This could make a better working climate possible and prevent considerable friction. It was a sensible goal, even if it contradicted
the premises of the German occupation. "Such a separation," the SD
therefore opined, "is opposed by very essential political, economic, and
productive reservations, so the plan would no doubt have to be rejected."[38]
Hatred and jealousy of our successes in Czech territory are obvious in this
report, which we may assume, was received with agreement and interest in
the Berlin central office of the SD and by Ohlendorf.

In the same report by the anonymous III D-East of the Berlin central
office of the Security Service about his trip to the Protectorate, the Prague
SD was told "to keep a sharp eye" on the activities of my Prague office,
"especially since this report aims not only at halting the shortcomings but
also at using the Protectorate example in order to make positive suggestions for a better future structuring of the German economic administration in other occupied Eastern territories." Thus, the SD ambition, steered
by Berlin, aimed at drafting new forms of an economic organization, which
was based on the fact that the head of the SD, Ohlendorf, nurtured a similar ambition for the entire economy of Germany.

At the same time, Ohlendorf's Security Service, on an intermediate level,
took advantage of the ubiquitous fear of him and performed the functions
that Ohlendorf aspired to as the future secretary general of Plenipotentiary
Funk. There were larger connections, and the ideas were probably insinuated by Ohlendorf, as shown by a remark in the same report by the Berlin
SD department head for the East (November 6, 1944): "Dr. Adolf, the
head of the [Prague] Central Association of [Czech] industry, has proposed
that a central economic chamber be formed, and this well-known suggestion, which has already been treated by the II D-East in a letter to SS
Squad Commander Hayler, [should] be implemented by Bertsch in the
form that is here felt to be reasonable."[39]

According to this idea, a central organ was to be created for Czechoslovakia, corresponding to the organ for all of German economy, such as
was being planned under Hayler and Ohlendorf.

These guidelines, which the central office of the SD issued for economic policies in Czechoslovakia, are interesting enough to bear perusal despite their length. "In the Protectorate too," they stated, "the goal of a necessary unity of the German administration vis-à-vis the alien people is frequently disrupted by the Berlin agencies with their uncontrollable direct rule, which takes no account of the political conditions. Here, too, it is once again primarily the agencies of Reich Minister Speer, such as main committees and rings, which must be accused of procedures that ignore the overall political, and at the same time war-economy, necessities of the German leaders in the Protectorate. So far they have been favored in their actions by the fact that armaments inspection" under General Hernekamp (who was under attack) "is the only German economic agency in close conjunction with the rest of the German economic administration which is controlled by the state minister, and Major General Hernekamp, as head of armaments inspection, was also appointed chairman of the Armaments Commission."[40]

Since 1942 there had been an ongoing fight over the alien presence of a Wehrmacht general in the SS-controlled admnistration of the Protectorate. This struggle could be viewed as terminated in November 1944. According to the travel report, the SD section leader for the East in the Berlin Central Office had learned that "after a discussion with Speer and SS Oberführer Bertsch, Hernekamp will be transferring control of the Armaments Commission to Bertsch, and Armaments Inspection [will] sink down to subordinate significance when it is placed under a colonel as leader. . . . Such a development" would be welcome since it could be assumed "that now the committees and rings," that is, in their Prague representations, "will be held with tighter reins."[41] All in all, a reflection of my weakened position, as revealed in those weeks by the events surrounding Schieber's dismissal. Presumably the SS circles on this lower level were pinning their hopes on exploiting my political weakness in order to reestablish the original SS control of the Czech armaments industry.

Meanwhile, Soviet tank spearheads were already at the border of what had formerly been Czechoslovakia, and we, including myself, were still struggling for positions. Now that everything was settled negatively, I tried to check the course of events by resorting to a tried-and-true method of the National Socialist system: enticement to defect. Minister Bertsch, the key figure in the Prague economic administration, was not averse to taking my offer of an important position in my Berlin central office. But on November 1, 1944, Hitler went along with "Minister Frank's qualms about employing Minister Bertsch" in my ministry.[42]

These power struggles against the background of imminent destruction recall the nightmares of Franz Kafka. They were not unusual. Everywhere, the battle for jurisdictions was being fought even in the final weeks, between ministries and in the intermediate agencies, as though the Reich were invincible. Its collapse seemed absolutely inconceivable. This repression of facts was a typical reaction in the twelve years of Hitler's rule. Now, toward the end, even the ultimate conclusion would not be recognized as a reality. That is how, say, incurably ill people evade their fate. They cannot fully realize their imminent end. Such behavior was fortified by the mutual confirmation of harassed functionaries on the verge of destruction. Thus autosuggestion, such as one might find in a cancer patient, became mass suggestion within the ruling stratum.[43]

My colleagues in the armaments industry had another reason for not giving up the struggle for power in Czech territory. In France, Belgium, and Holland, a policy of preserving all industrial valuables had been pursued by the military commanders. This policy, I felt, would be endangered in Czech territory if the power in armaments were to pass fully into the hands of the SS. However, my fear turned out to be unfounded in the critical weeks of March 1945. A conversation with Minister Frank quickly led to a full agreement about not yielding to destruction orders. Eventually I also managed to win over Field Marshal Ferdinand Schörner (who was known to be headstrong) to this policy.

For months the SS had been striving to reorganize the intermediate authority in the Protectorate; and now, in the final months of the war, they succeeded. From now on General Hernekamp was no longer chairman of the Armaments Commission; he was replaced by Minister Bertsch. An autonomous organization parallel to the industrial self-responsibility, with committees and rings, was built up in the Protectorate and combined in a "commission" under Minister Bertsch. Hernekamp's position had become meaningless after this reorganization.[44] Thus, the SD report had been correct in its conjecture.

The manager of this commission was Herr Fremerey. I tried to get him to leave Frank's realm and join my ministry in order to weaken the faction against Hernekamp. On January 6, 1945, I wrote to the new chairman of the Armaments Commission in Prague, Minister Bertsch. I told him that I wanted to take over "your staff member, Government Director Fremerey, [for] the joint work of my ministry with other agencies bearing upon armaments and war production."[45]

Spurred by the notion of efficiency and performance, we had insisted that the factories receive their orders directly from the armaments ministry.[46] This corresponded to the view that only a uniformly controlled large economic space can allow great achievement, thanks to instant possibilities of balance for different production sites, even if they were separated by borders. This defeat meant that the executive boards of our Berlin agencies were now dependent on the decisions of semi-autonomous structures in the occupied countries. This solution for the Protectorate resembled Goebbels's proposal to give the Gauleiters full responsibility for all matters of armaments and war production in their Gaus. If the war had gone on, even without the catastrophes of constant bombings this solution would have automatically led to the annihilation of the German armaments industry.

After this new regulation, it is not surprising that on February 19, 1945, the SD head section in Prague, under the letterhead of III D 4, presumed to inform the Reich Main Security Office of how much coal and coke had been mined in the Moravian coal district of Ostrava and in the area of Karviná between February 7 and 16.[47] What did this activity have to do with SD duties? What purpose did all this officiousness serve apart from demonstrating the activity of younger SS junior commanders, who were urgently needed at the front? For naturally, these production figures had been reported by my subordinate agencies in order to be evaluated by the responsible division in my ministry.

It was certainly remarkable that despite their closeness to the front, both districts had mined about 38,000 tons daily, as opposed to 45,000 tons under normal conditions in the previous year; in other words, the output was 84 percent. Furthermore, despite all transportation difficulties, railroad haulage was an average of 93 percent during the ten days covered by the report. But did the SD also know that my representatives in Czech territory had promised the employees and managers that these works would not be destroyed if they kept on working until the Soviets took over?

My plenipotentiary for production in Upper Silesia and Czechoslovakia, the Austrian general manager Dr. Hans Malzacher, had agreed with me that we would not allow any destruction in the Eastern territories, since this had not occurred in the Western countries. What good would it have done? It took many months to turn the steel or intermediate products manufactured there into finished armaments. By that time the war would surely be over. Besides, due to our transportation catastrophe, so much of this material was stockpiled that the new production could not offer any additional armaments benefits for the enemy. In line with this non-destruction policy, it was only logical that the Soviets were already avoiding any action around industrial sites in Upper Silesia. Of course, Colonel

General Gotthardt Heinrici's orders made it clear that no soldiers were in these factories and that they would not be used as nests of resistance. Because of these assurances, some factories in both Upper Silesia and Czech territory operated as long as they could within reach of the Soviet artillery, which spared these targets.

In his diary entry of March 18, 1945, Joseph Goebbels criticized the prevention of this senseless destruction: "The Soviets have begun working again in Upper Silesia. The mines are operating at full capacity."[48]

One March evening, Colonel General Heinrici, the commander of the defending army in that area, Dr. Malzacher, and I drove to the Rybnik area to inspect a coal district and its steelworks. The Soviet forces were only a few kilometers away. Heinrici showed me the flashes of the Soviet artillery. But no shells were fired toward Rybnik; we were certain of that, even though the management did not even take the trouble of darkening the harsh lights of the factory. A scene of peaceful production, contrasting with the strict blackouts at similar factories on the Ruhr. Heinrici, Malzacher, and I stood there among the Czech workers, whose reactions were not unfriendly. I was told that these factories were the safest places on the long front.

Chapter 9
Armaments Industrialists Are Slandered

THE SD REPORTS on German territory were no less single-minded in attacking the work of the Armaments Inspection department, which they tried to discredit. Thus, it must have been a routine assignment when the SD reported the removal of industry from the Lodz area, on September 20, 1944. The report claimed that my ministry "did not have any comprehensive plan concerning armaments evacuation, nor had we made any provisions for it." The report went on, "As a result of jurisdictional arguments, or rather conflicts on high government levels, no central agency is keeping track of the empty manufacturing sites" and "all local offices are making an effort, which almost verges on sabotage, to make such an overall grasp difficult by not volunteering to report free manufacturing sites or by making inefficient facilities available to a bottleneck manufacturing."[1]

This criticism may have been justified. We in the central office also had the feeling that some measures were bogging down because of shortcomings. But could this inexperienced SD man come up with a better plan in a time of headlong evacuation measures? What was his accusation of sabotage aiming at?

On October 11, 1944, a second letter of the SD Head Department in Düsseldorf informed the Reich Main Security Office in Berlin that "the irresponsible bureaucratic methods of the bureaucracy were" paralyzing "the responsible initiative of the factory managers." Hence "running reports on the bureaucratization and overorganization" were necessary. Over and over again, factory managers were "complaining that the work of the many offices has so far been extremely harmful to the German armaments industry because they all want to be consulted and they all interfere, but are never willing to take responsibility and, accordingly, never really help the factories actively on their own initiative and responsibility." A reproach implying that a defective armaments organization had considerably restricted the production of weapons. After this harsh criticism, one might expect examples documenting it. But the reporter could only cite three perhaps justified but trivial cases. Their very triviality proves that the agencies of the armaments ministry were operating above reproach.

The first case: In August 1943, an SD man tried to substantiate his allegation about overbureaucratization by citing the following incident. A factory hall that had been destroyed by an aerial mine could be rebuilt four months later. "On April 1, 1944, twelve officials of the plenipotentiary for architecture in Cologne suddenly showed up" and threatened the manager with a "fine of 100,000 marks" as well as three months' imprisonment "for constructing without a permit." The matter was then supposedly quashed by another armaments authority. Although it is certain that this unreasonable act by a construction authority had no effect on production, the SD concluded that "such behavior on the part of the most important agencies [is] simply incomprehensible." As a result, "the production of highly important war material was greatly delayed or rather stopped altogether for a long time."

The second case, likewise shockingly trivial: Probably soon after the successful invasion of the Western powers in the summer of 1944, a firm in the Ruhr District wanted "seventeen new lathes, extremely important for armaments manufacture, to be transported from Belgium to their plant in Mönchen-Gladbach." The local office of my ministry had supposedly turned down the request because the documents for the release of the machines were not valid for the occupied Western territories. This red tape had presumably caused the loss of machines that were extremely valuable to the Reich.[2]

Some six weeks after this report, the SD had another complaint. "With the approach of the enemy [around September 1944], the important steel firm of Becker and van Hüllen, located on the left bank of the Rhine, has been transferred to an empty factory in Wengern on the Ruhr and is again operating with a work force of 50 men." On November 12, supposedly, some gentlemen from the motor firm of Klöckner-Humbold-Deutz appeared there, having been assigned the same space by a directive from Berlin. But the envoys from Klöckner-Humbold-Deutz had ascertained that "the factory was not suitable for their manufacture." They had, therefore, decided not to use it. However, the officious SD conjectures, "with a cancellation of the earlier transfer order, the firm of Becker and van Hüllen cannot be left uncertain as to how to carry through a second transfer of the firm.[3] Disregarding the question of whether a factory with 50 employees can be called important in the steel industry, the conflict about this small plant was already cleared up by the time the report was made.

Thus, with these three reports, the SD tried to document its discriminatory claim that mistakes had "incredibly harmed the increase in German armaments so far."[4]

Of course, in general, neither the SD nor the Gestapo would have taken any harsh or vicious action in the armaments industry. Ohlendorf had decided after much soul-searching to regard the self-responsibility of industry as a useful and effective weapon for the period of the war.

Incidentally, the SD and the Gestapo regarded one another as competitors, at least in Czech territory. There was supposedly a "danger of a gradual breaking out of valuable intelligence transmitters from the III D network" of the Security Service in the industrial sector. The State Police, "which, as everyone knows, [has] acquired an apparatus with a vast staff," is dealing "not only with pure State Police matters and defense issues, but, recently, more intensely, with reporting on departmental functions, for instance, programming," i.e., the production planning assigned to me in the factories.

The SD central office was to decide "whether immediate protest should be lodged with Office IV [the Gestapo] against this . . . activity of the State Police or whether we should first wait and watch for further development, which, however, can presumably lead to incidents sooner or later, perhaps even with Reich Minister Speer, since the State Police allegedly operate rather ruthlessly with arrests or the threat thereof, even when dealing with representatives of government agencies."[5] Such incidents were indeed overdue when the Gestapo tried to interfere arbitrarily in my domain by arresting members of my staff.

These internal conflicts between the Gestapo in Office IV and the SD in Office III are a characteristic example of the attempts of all Party organizations, even in the SS administration, to make hay at the expense of parallel agencies. Himmler's demand to simply appropriate jurisdictions was thus followed within the SS as well. For the victim, of course, it made little difference whether he was being watched by the SD or the

Gestapo. Both SS organizations were under the same roof and belonged to the same Reich Main Security Office. To be sure, an accusation of sabotage, if made by an SD member, was at first less dangerous than if the Gestapo was dealing with the same case. But in practice, it was only a tiny step from an accusation by the SD to pursuit by the Gestapo.

When interrogated at the Nuremberg Court, Ohlendorf told about the difficulties that Ley and Bormann caused for the work of the SD. And indeed, none of the top leaders cared for this institution, which unswervingly kept checking and reporting. Over and over again, Bormann rebuked Reich ministers for alleged abuses in their domains. We could only speculate that these rebukes were based on SD material. The SD suspicions thus kept causing embarrassment to the heads of the government, for Bormann ultimately used the negative material in order to solidify his own path wherever he could.

Ultimately, however, Bormann saw these reports as impairing his own dominant position in domestic politics. On April 4, 1945, the Americans and British were approaching the Elbe; the Soviet army was advancing on Berlin. The Reich was already lost except for some fragments. In this situation, Bormann still felt it necessary to send a personal letter to Kaltenbrunner, the head of the Reich Main Security Office of the SS: "The report you have handed me today is a *typical* SD report! Typical because it uninhibitedly generalizes on the basis of one or several cases or circumstances." Bormann was furious because this report claimed that the Party was railing at the Wehrmacht and the Wehrmacht was railing at the Party. After going into details about his feelings on the matter, Bormann passed his verdict. "Your reporter must have rather unsuspectingly missed what was happening; otherwise he would not make such utterly unjustified accusations. But that is exactly what I have against the SD: completely irresponsible people make allegations and accusations, while the responsible people are not even consulted."[6]

Anyone exercising unconditional power in those years was in danger of losing his perception of reality long before the collapse and even after the extinction of the Hitlerian Reich idea. Thus, when I visited Himmler at his headquarters on April 24, 1945, he saw himself, to my surprise, as an indispensable member of future Allied authorities: "Europe cannot get along without me in the future either. It will still need me as a police minister to maintain order."[7] Ohlendorf was the same. In May 1945, as ministerial director in Doenitz's 22-day administration, he was still convinced that the "government will need an intelligence service covering material problems." He suggested "making the possible function within the framework of the present Reich government the subject of an official discussion with the occupation powers." For, with the members of his SD office, he could "make it easier for the occupation powers to make an objective judgment of the conditions in Germany."[8] These words may sound grotesque, all the more so since Ohlendorf was a highly intelligent man who knew how to use his intelligence in a skillful, dazzling way. Had his many years of running the powerful SD corrupted and twisted his character? This lack of a sense of reality in a high-level SS officer will recur in many other people throughout this book. It must be viewed as resulting directly from the elite sense of mission in the SS state.

The SD rightly feared difficulties caused by arbitrary Gestapo arrests in industry. An "ordinance by the Führer for the protection of the armaments industry of March 21, 1942" provided that any legal proceeding for damage to armaments could take place *only* at my instructions.[9]

In mid-May 1944, for instance, Hans Kammler, at a meeting of the fighter staff, stated that he had had a member of my staff arrested. The man, he said, had obviously committed sabotage by causing a delay in the transfer of parts for a BMW factory to a cave in Alsace. I declared I would not put up with such arbitrary actions and, as the minutes report, "the minister will not tolerate arrests and judgments if he is not previously consulted." That very same day, I issued "guidelines for procedures regarding misdemeanors within the armaments industry." These guidelines, based on my privileges as formulated in Hitler's ordinance, provided that "a board made up of industrialists [should take] a position on misdemeanors before the courts or the SS deal with them."[10]

Just a few weeks later another arrest took place without my approval, that of Egger von Büssing, general manager of truck production. According to my letter of June 28, 1944, to Kaltenbrunner, he supposedly had utilized construction material in his factory for his own purposes, which was why the Gestapo had taken him into protective custody. My letter to Kaltenbrunner stated: "I had arranged with the SS Reichführer that all criminal proceedings occurring in my work domain should be carried out together with your representatives. The Egger case should have been dealt with in this framework," for "the treatment of the matter lies within the framework of the oral agreement both as an offense against the construction prohibitions and as an offense against the production duties assigned to him. . . . I must protest against linking such proceedings with interventions by political officers and based on political grounds."[11]

Egger was instantly released from custody. The accusations against him had proved to be invalid. Of course, such an implementation of my guidelines was purely a question of mutual power positions. But as long as Hitler was wise enough to distrust the activity of the SS in the armaments area, and as long as he did not intend to lose the confidence of technicians and industrialists by guaranteeing their personal safety, my assurance of an, albeit vague, legal solidity was still valid. I confirmed this in writing to every member of the self-responsibility organization.

To be sure, Hitler's trust vanished for good toward the end of the war. He complained to Goebbels that I had let myself "be harnessed too closely to the wagon of business" and that I should stop being the plaything of the business circles around me.[12]

Retrospectively, as I study the files, I see that dealings between the SS and my ministry began to change profoundly as early as 1944—even though there was no crucial interference in my jurisdiction. This situation contrasted greatly with the practice in 1942 and 1943 in that during those years SS actions were relatively harmless and conciliatory. Let me offer an example.

Eduard Winter, a wealthy businessman, had come to see me early in the summer of 1942 and had offered to accept any assignment, no matter how subordinate, in my organization. But despite all his capabilities as a businessman, he did not fit into my umbrella organization of leading technicians and engineers from industry. I therefore put him off. I had no idea that the Gestapo had been gathering material to use against him for some time, and that Winter was seeking support by working for me.

Before the war Eduard Winter had built up one of the largest Opel agencies in Germany. As a German branch of General Motors, the Opel Works had been confiscated as enemy property at the start of the war. Its production was restructured, and very soon Opel began manufacturing trucks for armaments purposes. On various occasions it had already become clear that Himmler was very interested in rebuilding a large-scale Opel branch factory, using a labor force of concentration camp prisoners. It is probably with this in mind that we should view the pressure that the feared Gestapo chief, SS Squad Commander Heinrich Mueller, exerted upon Opel manager Eduard Winter in the spring of 1942.

"Winter came to see me," Mueller began his report to Himmler on June 25, 1942, "and emphasized that in regard to the large tasks meant for him now [presumably in my ministry], he could take them over only with a feeling of uncertainty, since he had to conclude from various signs that the Secret State Police are collecting material against him and are planning to start proceedings against him any day. He therefore asked me to give him the opportunity for a discussion and to inform him of the charges against him." Mueller asked Himmler whether he could "show Winter the collected material within the framework of what is officially warrantable and question him about the individual charges."

The fact that Winter was of interest to the SS because of his Opel connections and knowledge is obvious from an addendum to this telegram on alloys: "As I have been informed, the acquisition of the Ne. metals[13] for the truck order has been delayed and is occasioning considerable difficulties. This imperils the delivery of the trucks destined for the Waffen-SS."[14]

After obtaining the requested permission from Himmler, Mueller reported on July 14, 1942, that "the reservations concerning Winter have been presented to him insofar as this was officially warrantable. Winter's statements were credible and also understandable, considering that he is a completely 'Americanized' businessman. . . . Winter's statements have cleared him of the charges against him. Nevertheless, as a businessman, he must still be judged with reservations from a National Socialist standpoint. I have reached an agreement with Winter that in the future, when transacting new business, and especially when making new connections, he should first inform [us] of his plans in order to avoid my learning about them from a third party, in a distorted form."[15] A characteristic formula of submission: Winter, a completely independent and also extremely wealthy man, was obliged to discuss all his business plans with the Gestapo, thereby losing his autonomy and freedom of action. Presumably, this capitulation of the car plant manager ultimately benefited Himmler's truck interests.

On December 5, 1942, the chairman of Brabag, SS Oberführer Fritz Kranefuss, had asked the head of Himmler's personal staff to promote certain industrial leaders in their SS ranks. These men included Otto Steinbrinck; Evald Hecker, chairman of the board of a large steel plant of the Ilseder Foundry; Baron Kurt von Schroeder, the banker who had helped Hitler to become Reich Chancellor; Dr. Meyer and Dr. Karl Rasche, both board members of the Dresden Bank; and finally Dr. Heinrich Bütefisch, an important member of the I. G. Farben concern.[16]

On January 11, 1943, the Reich Main Security Office sent over the requested information on the candidates for promotion. Only the data on Bütefisch are interesting, because they offer insights into the SS thoughts on the desirable or censurable qualities of an industrial leader.

"Dr. Bütefisch has a doctorate in engineering and, as a chemist, has been one of the managers of the Leuna Works since around 1928, and also has a leading responsibility since that time in planning and steering production questions of the entire IG Works," says the introduction. "On the basis of this fact, after the [National Socialist] takeover, and with the start of the first Four-Year Plan, he participated outstandingly in the planning and establishment of new nitrogen and fuel plants. Furthermore, he was and still is in charge of contractual matters of IG with domestic and foreign concerns."

What comes next shows the basic hostility of the SS toward industry, an attitude typical of Himmler as well: "He is thus generally tied to IG and to be regarded as thoroughly belonging to the company. . . . Despite all the favorable elements that can be brought out in Bütefisch's personality, one must bear in mind that such a man, because of the entire network of international business contracts which he has played a leading part in creating, basically has a mentality geared to international cooperation and international exchange of experience; such a mentality takes for granted that a business concern is a state within the state, with its own laws of life and privileges of life, which he is paid to represent." The report continues: "Illuminating his character in this respect, it is known from IG circles, for instance, that for translating his foreign contracts Dr. B. to some extent made use of an Englishman, Mr. Bridge, who was working in Leuna as a language teacher; Dr. B. explained that he was intent on the very finest nuances of his contractual English." It is a mystery why an Englishman should not undertake the translation of contracts which are meant for English or American contractees anyway. This too reveals an astoundingly hidebound attitude. Hence, it comes as no surprise when the report critically notes that Bütefisch was "also a member of local feudal associations, for instance the Leuna Golf Club. As far as his character goes, nothing negative has come to light about him." That last comment is made with reserve, almost regret; and then these words are added: "His most outstanding characteristic is extraordinary personal dexterity and strongly marked ambition. In this respect, he is said to be the most flexible of the present Leuna directors and is always striving to keep all threads of personal relations in his hand." The only truly positive feature to be pointed out is that both daughters are prominently active in the League of German Maidens.[17]

The actual reversal of mood came with the attempted assassination of Hitler on July 20, 1944. The discovery that the opposition included important industrialists led to greater distrust in the Reich Main Security

Office. Party leaders like Ley as well as Himmler himself spoke about a July 20 in industry, by which they meant that with summary proceedings of the National Court, a purge trial would have to take place for industrialists and economists too.

This was a resurgence of the old instincts for a socialist revolution, which they had had to suppress after Hitler's takeover. For a long time important industrialists were protected by dint of being irreplaceable. Kaltenbrunner told me that a whole group of people with whom I frequently conversed—illegally—had been close to the Kreisau Circle, which had also studied the problems of industrial reconstruction after a lost war. These people included my friend Albert Vögler, the head of Vereinigte Stahlwerke (United Steel Works), and the general directors of AEG and Hoesch AG, of the Bosch Works and MAN, of Demag, Hugo Stinnes, and Haniel. I had no great difficulty convincing Kaltenbrunner that these men were irreplaceable for my work and that their arrests would be very harmful to industry. Certainly, nearly all industrialists had long since become defeatists, and they did not conceal their opinion of the catastrophic war situation. Their sober mentality, with its calculating training, would not permit the fata morgana–type thinking that was spreading throughout Party and SS circles.[18]

I was likewise deeply incriminated after July 20 because the putschists had been planning to make me head of armaments production in their government. This fact must have also gotten abroad in the general public. At any rate, the SD reports that Kaltenbrunner handed in to Hitler and Bormann after the attempted assassination state that I had been arrested for collaborating on July 20. Other reports from the Reich went one step further, they reflected rumors that I had already been executed.[19]

All this would have spelled my political ruin, and my intervention with Kaltenbrunner on behalf of the industrialists would have been ignored. But Hitler did not drop me. Evidently he set great store by my abilities. In a speech to the Reichsleiters and Gauleiters, he made it clear to the Party members that his close relations with me had not suffered since July 20.[20] His words suddenly restored my political weight; I could utilize it to rehabilitate the incriminated industrialists.

One can hardly assume that people in high-level Party circles, especially Himmler, were much impressed by the validity of Hitler's statement. In any event, since early spring of 1944 the nets of the Gestapo and the SD had been drawn tighter and tighter. Because of the obvious collapse of the German defense front, and because of the assassination attempt at home, the SS was in deep water, so they desperately cast about for the people responsible for the defeat. The spying and shadowing became more and more balant now as it affected highly placed members of the government hierarchy.

When the SD or the Gestapo handed me documents on allegedly incriminated business leaders, they must have assumed that I would draw my own conclusions and dismiss these men.

In September 1944 I received news that Reuter, the general manager of Demag, had been apprehended on the initiative of the Gestapo. He had supposedly failed to evacuate the workers in time from a factory on the left side of the Rhine. Furthermore, he had left the factory in the care of a manager who, because of his language knowledge, could have negotiated with British occupation officers.

When I cited Hitler's authorization that industrial misdemeanors could be transmitted to the criminal police only through my officers, Reuter was released. As a demonstration of my unbroken affection for this outstanding business leader, I invited him for lunch the day after his release; he was my guest, along with my staff, in the Ruhr District, where I was staying at that time.

Things seemed more favorable and courteous when the Gestapo showed me documents on their investigations. This occurred seldom enough, and the assumption always was that I would personally read them in order to convince myself how dangerous the alleged machinations were.

Thus, in the fall of 1944, I was presented with a thick file on the directors of Telefunken. In this case the charges were to be taken more seriously. The document came from the central office of the Reich Main Security Office; it claimed to prove that General Manager May, together with Manager Rottgart and with the support of Privy Councillor Bücher, general manager of the AEG, was pursuing a monopoly policy in the area of valves for mainly political reasons. All these men were supposedly old Center Party people (a moderate Catholic party). Furthermore, Friedrich Lüschen, head of my main committee for electrotechnology, together with his deputy Heinz Freiberger, had been aiding in these endeavors, since they too were of "Catholic" leanings. This was a ridiculous claim, of course, and all the more absurd since Lüschen was a manager at Siemens and would never have supported any monopoly by the competing AEG company, Telefunken.

However, the files included copies of letters and notes presuming detailed knowledge. The material had to come from employees of the firm. After my successful refutation of the nonsensical accusation, the Gestapo withdrew its charges. The gathered reports, they said, were to be evaluated not as "veracious" but only as "information material."

A few months later, on December 20, 1944, the SS mounted new attacks against Lüschen. The head of communication services for the SS Reichsführer—a bizarre title, quite in keeping with SS nomenclature—complained that I had appointed Lüschen "representative for concentrating development and production." Actually, I had assigned Lüschen to reduce programs, a step necessitated by the air raids.[21]

As I wrote to the head of SS Intelligence, "it is a completely unjustified imputation if you feel that you must reject this commission because of company interests. I therefore regret that I cannot support your opinion. Whatever differences of opinion exist between the plenipotentiary for Wehrmacht Communication Services and Deputy Dr. Lüschen will be settled my me." I thus shifted the level of conflict from the SS plenipotentiary to the plenipotentiary-general of the Wehrmacht; at the same time, I reserved the right to settle any conflicts. I also asked my staff member Dieter Stahl "to get the Lüschen matter over with as quickly as possible, otherwise there will be endless discussions about the concentration deputy." In January 1945, after my return from a trip to see Field Marshal Walther Model, I was to be notified of appointments and dismissals.[22]

By now it was early February 1945, but Lüschen still required my protection. He came to me and read me a quotation from *Mein Kampf*: "It is the role of diplomacy to make sure that rebellion is not only the right but the duty of every member of a nation when the facilities of government power are carrying that nation to its destruction."[23]

I had already told Lüschen to restore order to railroad communications (which had been destroyed by bombing attacks) and to give top priority to all the industrial assignments necessary for this reconstruction. The end of the war could only be a few weeks, at most a few months, away. Thus, we were already setting ourselves a prepeacetime task.

Kaltenbrunner was loyal enough to send me Gestapo reports on SS attacks on the shipyard industry. I generally had the impression that Kaltenbrunner wanted to cooperate with me. However, I did not realize that he was nevertheless concealing a great deal from me. The files I perused in the Federal Archives after my release from Spandau gave me my first insight into the two faces of Kaltenbrunner's loyalty.

On November 29, 1944, Kaltenbrunner sent me an SD file on the shipyard industry. Once I saw the nature of the charges I composed a reply, in which I pointed out several basic facts. The accusation was that we had not attained production goals of the newly designed U-boats. I fully admitted that this program, which I had promised Doenitz, had not been achieved. "Nevertheless, Grand Admiral Doenitz is very satisfied with our performance and acknowledges that in the field of naval technology it is a unique performance," i.e., that of Otto Merker, the industrialist responsible for all shipbuilding—namely, to take less than nine months not only to develop two new U-boats but also to produce them in the first serial prototype and to deliver a considerable number of submarines every month in that series. All the difficulties were well known. They were certainly known to Grand Admiral Doenitz. He consciously put up with them, since he had no choice. "All that counts for him is to obtain new U-boats in order to remount his U-boat weapon, since his old U-boats are no longer capable of fighting the enemy. . . . We fully realize that such interference in an industry will raise problems. Similar conversion difficulties have emerged with the Panther and Tiger II tanks, and others will come about with the radical conversion of air armaments. My colleagues will try to keep these deficiencies to a minimum. Now, Merker is a man who has unreservedly committed himself and his good reputation to a cause that could quite easily have failed; one must therefore see to it that he be given a certain protection and that any attacks upon him be rebuffed as sharply as possible."[24]

More and more wasted time and energy while the war slowly drew to an end. But I could not just take Kaltenbrunner's reports on my staffers and toss them into the wastebasket; the charges were much too serious. In November 1944, Purucker, an SS standard commander, came under fire. He had supposedly been doing private business with foreign countries. As SS Obergruppenführer Berger, chief of SS headquarters, accurately wrote to Himmler on October 27, 1944, Purucker was "one of the most important men under Reich Minister Speer in the manufacture of light and heavy artillery weapons." In its efforts to produce infantry weapons in Buchenwald and Neuengamme, the SS was largely dependent on his goodwill. Purucker was actually under Berger's protection, since in addition to his regular duties, he also belonged to the staff of the SS main office. Berger put in a good word with Himmler for the victim of the attack: "Dr. Purucker is suspected," wrote Berger, "of collaborating with two other gentlemen to sell a German patent for a machine gun to France." The accusation, like nearly all SS charges, seems to have been unfounded, for a trial against the industrialists ended with their being declared innocent. Berger reported to Himmler that he had thoroughly investigated everything beyond that. It was very obvious, he said, that the general judge of the SS, Dr. Fischer, "had had personal reasons for pursuing the proceedings against Purucker and bringing charges at the very moment that the two main defendants were declared innocent."

Here too, the best defense was a good offense; so I let Berger know that I was proposing Dr. Purucker for the Fritz Todt Pin, a decoration for outstanding performance as an engineer, and for the Pioneer of Work. Berger thereupon wrote Himmler: "Reich Minister Speer personally asked me a total of four times to finally rehabilitate Purucker and promote him to SS Oberführer at the next term. I am now being pestered daily by the Speer Ministry."[25]

We could not do without Purucker's ability and energy. So eventually everything petered out and he remained in his position until the end of the war.

From a subjective viewpoint, how strange it was that the leading minds in the system should be not only chiefs but also victims. They lived under the pressure of the sinister, incomprehensible atmosphere of being constantly observed. They never knew the extent to which their statements were being carefully gathered in order to be used against them some day by Himmler and Bormann. They could then expect Hitler's disfavor. For we were all observed, and we knew we were. Around May 1942, soon after becoming minister, I met for lunch with Colonel General Friedrich Fromm in a private room at the famous Berlin restaurant Horcher. Our conversation began with a discussion of the possibility that a microphone might be installed in the room, even though the normally harmless use of the space spoke against this. In early November 1944, I quite openly told Otto Merker, the head of my Main Committee for Shipbuilding, that my telephone was being tapped at Himmler's orders.[26] I cannot say that this awareness of constant spying shocked me. We were far too accustomed to this system and the risks involved in it.

In his memoirs, the successful fighter pilot Johannes Steinhoff, later a NATO general, tells of a dangerous step he and Adolf Galland and another comrade took. On January 4, 1945, they visited SD chief Ohlendorf and tried to convince him of the necessity of replacing Goering, whom they called incompetent. This dangerous attempt soon proved unsuccessful. It was not Goering but the fighter pilots who were criticized for lack of fighting spirit. Ohlendorf demanded a certainty of victory from the three highly decorated officers. When the discussion became heated, Ohlendorf played his trump. He ordered someone to start a gramophone. They heard the following:

"This is Galland."

"This is Speer," replied another voice. "Galland, I would like to talk to you about the aerial defense of the Ruhr District. I'm extremely worried."[27] The needle was lifted from the record. The secret of the incriminating sentences to follow was not revealed. But the very knowledge that such a recording existed was bound to have an effect.

Adolf Galland did not tell me about this discovery, which must have been frightening for him. For this highly successful fighter pilot never held back what he wanted to say on the situation. The further course of the recorded conversation must have contained utterances that could have been deadly for him.

But nothing happened. Himmler despised Goering because of his shortcomings and indolence.

Chapter 10
Denunciations

UNCERTAINTY OVERCAME ME whenever I thought of the bugging techniques practiced by Himmler's and Goering's offices. And this uncertainty was increased by the insecure feeling that my own ministry must be employing agents of Himmler's who reported on me or on the members of my staff.

In December 1943, groups in the Todt organization fought my efforts to grant self-responsibility to the building industry. (These were groups left over from Fritz Todt's [Speer's predecessor in the Ministry of Armament] administration.) If my plans had been carried through, the Todt organization would have lost a good deal of its power. There must have been personal reasons as well, which presumably were connected to the treatment of one of Dr. Todt's leading staffers, Xaver Dorsch. When Fritz Todt had crashed to his death in February 1942 and I had taken over all his duties, Dorsch was quite right to feel ignored.

In the spring of 1944 the office of the personnel department in my ministry contained a sealed cabinet, which was opened at my orders. Its files revealed that a member of my ministry had written to the Reich Main Security Office requesting information on the political reliability of those close members of my staff who were to carry out my orders for a self-responsible building industry.[1]

"It was observed here," a man named Seeberg (a very low-level employee unknown to me) reported[2] to the SS, "that the following employees are devoted to the movement externally; but, internally, they do not stand wholeheartedly behind the State and the movement. I therefore request an investigation and replies to the following questions:

a. What were the political inclinations of these people before the *Machtübernahme* [Hitler's accession to power]?
b. What circles do they frequent?
c. What is their political conduct off the job, participation in local groups, willingness to donate money, etc.?

The following people were to be politically incriminated:

Ministerial Director Eduard Schönleben, one of Dr. Todt's oldest and most loyal colleagues. When I replaced Todt, Schönleben had sided with me, and he enjoyed great prestige among the employees of my ministry.

Carl Stobbe-Dethleffsen, whom I had put in charge of the entire construction industry in the spring of 1943 against the wishes of the leaders of the Todt organization. He could be regarded as my representative for the introduction of a certain self-responsibility in the construction industry and a more efficient solution for the distribution of assignments.

Ministerial Director Hugo Koester, one of the most distinguished members of the Planning Office, which was headed by Hans Kehrl.

And Dr. Paul Briese, ministerial councillor in the construction department of the ministry.

The Gestapo's response is not extant. But in any case the matter was decided against me. During the months of my critical illness, Dorsch attained his goals. In May 1944 I had to give up my efforts toward making the constuction industry independent and dismiss Stobbe-Dethleffsen. Dorsch, with Hitler's support, had become the decisive head of all construction matters in the Reich.[3]

After taking over my ministry, I had established that any conflicts between the heads of large companies should be settled among themselves, without interference from the bureaucracy. However, if they could not settle their differences, then they were to come to my office. Thus, on August 16, 1944, a meeting took place between Paul Pleiger, our plenipotentiary for coal and also chairman of the board of the Hermann Goering Works, and Walter Rohland, the assistant chairman of the Reich Association for Iron and also chairman of the board of the Vereinigte Stahlwerke (United Steel Works). The conflict between these two important industrialists had become embittered and had reached a personal level. According to the ministry chronicle, the discussion was "dramatic, but fruitless. . . . Pleiger refuses to compromise; he is irritated and aggressive. The minister is angry at this incompatability despite his urgent wish for mutual agreement, and he rebukes Plieger for this with sharp words. He emphatically demands cooperation between the Hermann Goering Works and the rest of the iron industry, and he orders Pleiger to join the executive committee of the Reich Association for Iron. Pleiger grows more excited than usual, and the good personal relationship between the minister and Pleiger seems jeopardized in the heat of the conversation."[4]

A week earlier I had informed Pleiger of my intention "not to deviate from the principle of self-responsibility in industry; i.e., all decisions in factories will be made in my name through the organs of industrial self-responsibility to the extent that they consider it necessary. . . . It would be an extraordinarily offensive thing if this principle could be implemented only by force in the iron industry of all places, which is one of the most important for me in these difficult times."[5]

Such differences of opinion are not unusual. Conflicts that can lead to quarrels occur in any government. In the Third Reich, however, such incidents promptly assumed a political dimension. The chronicle notes: "The iron industry and the fight over its leadership are not an internal matter of the industry or of the Armaments Ministry alone. One should not overlook the fact . . . that the SS Reichsführer is dealing with the matter. In his individual reports, discord in the leadership is construed as sabotage of armaments."[6]

The fear of Himmler and his apparatus was ubiquitous even in this period when I had vast power.

In the last nine months of the war, more and more charges and accusations were addressed by outsiders to the Reich Main Security Office. This was a result of the strengthening of the SS, which many people in that pessimistic landscape of destruction saw as the final optimistic and dynamic force. Indeed, the SS bureaucracy kept working through the last months of the war as though there were no end in sight.

One day I received news from a man I barely knew. His name was Dr. Ungewitter, and he was a leading official in the Reich Chemistry Agency. He informed me that industrialists were quite openly talking about the end of the war. A report issued by SS Sturmbannführer Backhaus, the Personal Assistant of the food minister, said that Dr. Ungewitter had made statements about the practice of large industrial concerns "which come very close to high treason. Dr. Ungewitter has claimed that large industrial firms are already neglecting armaments work and have switched to peacetime production, that leading men in industry are openly speaking against the

Führer. Dr. Ungewitter has declared his willingness to repeat this information to higher persons." When Dr. Ungewitter was asked to state "this information to SS Brigade Commander Ohlendorf," he reported that he had already brought these charges.

The same letter also accused the head of the Wintershall Company, General Manager Rosterg, and his manager Werthmann of defeatism: "A Frau Halfmann, whom I know to very reliable, an old National Socialist, asked to meet with me, in order, as she said, to regain her faith in National Socialism. Director Werthmann had stated to her that National Socialism was bankrupt, that the Führer had no overview of the situation, that industry and business already saw the war as lost, and that the present state would doubtless collapse. For these reasons, he said, [German] industry was already striving for relations with foreign industry. It was clear that in the future only industry could guarantee that Germany would play a part in the circle of nations."

The letter writer was uneasy because Director Werthmann had stated in this conversation that he knew that the Reichsführer had similar notions, "for his boss, General Manager Rosterg, was a friend of the SS Reichsführer and constantly frequented his home."[7] It is conceivable that Himmler was merely interested in learning the opinions of internationally prominent industrialists by pretending to agree with them. But I also consider it possible that he actually had a similar attitude.

Himmler's personal chief of staff, Brandt, visibly nervous, merely informed Backhaus that his statements were very interesting, but that it would be more expedient to discuss them orally.[8] Himmler's staff was not at all satisfied with this dilatory treatment. The very next day, SS Hauptsturmführer Meine of Himmler's personal staff sent Brandt a warning note: "I assume from your remark 'resubmission in Hochwald' [camouflage term for Himmler's headquarters] that you wish to speak with SS Sturmbannführer Backhaus. Shouldn't something be undertaken by us first? The reported statements are, to my mind, of such a grave nature that a careful investigation is advised immediately. They tend to leave one with the impression that a second Twentieth of July is being prepared within industry. The fact that General Manager Rosterg is involved is certainly regrettable for both him and us. But his name should not keep us from clearing the matter up as quickly as possible."[9]

I never learned about Dr. Ungewitter's denunciation. Kaltenbrunner's loyalty did not go very far, it seems. Even when the deadly charge of high treason was brought against one of my most important staffers, he did not inform me. I also first learned about the following charge only just now, from the files. In November 1944 SS Squad Commander Meinberg, the assistant chairman of the Hermann Goering Steel Works, brought charges against his rival in the steel industry. He gave Himmler a letter from Hans Günther Sohl, the assistant chairman of the board at Vereinigte Stahlwerke, who was also in charge of the entire ore supply for the iron and steel works in the Ruhr District. The informer added a comment: "It is a crime to see how frivolously the Ruhr is being supplied with German ores. All the documents mentioned in the correspondence have been made available by me to the Main Office of the Security Police."[10]

The alleged political crime referred to the supplying of Salzgitter ores to the Hermann Goering Reich Works; Meinberg must have been interested in their sale. The ores were of a poorer quality than the Minette ores from Lorraine or the Swedish ores, which Sohl naturally preferred. In the meantime, however, the Minette mines had been overrun by the Western armies, and the Swedes were delaying their deliveries more and more because of the deteriorating war situation. Furthermore, the nonstop attacks on the transportation system of the Ruhr had cut off all supplies from this industrial area. The sudden worsening of the situation had not been foreseen by Meinberg or Sohl, whom Meinberg now accused of gross criminality. On October 19, 1944, Meinberg wrote to Sohl that the Ruhr Works had constantly refused, not only in the past few years but even in 1944, "to stock up on Salzgitter ores. After going through my documents, I must abide by the accusation that the Ruhr Works have failed in a downright frivolous manner to fulfill the demands of the war for supplying the steel works. The Ruhr steel works would never have come to this pass if you, Herr Sohl, had enabled them to stock up in the past, when it was possible."[11]

Sohl replied to Meinberg on October 25, 1944, with superior coolness: ". . . the measures for laying in ore supplies for the Ruhr were not geared to the possibility that Swedish ores and Minette would stop at the same time, that the Reich railroad would be in a crisis at the same time, and that the water routes would be disrupted." The Ruhr supplies of iron ores, he pointed out, had risen from 4,435,000 tons on January 1, 1940, to 7,571,000 tons on January 1, 1944. "Hence, there can be no question that the Ruhr works have neglected laying in ore. On the contrary, a systematic stockpiling has been underway." Then Sohl switched to a counterattack. He accused Meinberg of presenting the matter "as if the Reich Works had merely, for reasons of war economy, carried through an increased delivery of Salzgitter ores. In my opinion, however, these long-past negotiations are concerned only with a stubborn representation of factory interests, which I recognize as such."[12]

Himmler hesitated to take up the charge with the Reich Main Security Office, especially since the issue was purely one of war economy and not politics. With offensive coldness, he ignored Meinberg's claim that this was a kind of political crime. He replied with one single sentence: "Thank you for your letter of November 2, 1944, and the accompanying news about the situation of coal deliveries and coal supply."[13]

Another denunciation came from people working in industry; I learned about it from Himmler. He had gone to the personal trouble of sending me a memorandum[14] with a friendly accompanying letter;[15] the memorandum had been obtained by Kaltenbrunner from the Air Ministry. Cautiously and judiciously, Himmler wrote me that "many things in this memorandum may be wrong" or "may be seen wrong and not correctly recognized. Nevertheless, I believe that a number are of utmost interest." Himmler recommended that I weigh a few points with care; he himself "as a layman [could] judge them no more than certain other things. I know your view that a layman can sometimes see things better than experts." The last sentence was certainly accurate in regard to my opinion. The memorandum was allegedly written by "top experts in the development of air defense and the Luftwaffe"[16] in August 1944. In it, the collapse of fuel production was the occasion for charges. Fuel output had gone down from 5,850 tons daily to 120 tons on July 21, 1944, i.e., to 2 percent. The enemy air offensive had almost reached its goal. In September we managed to raise production to 5½ percent, but even that spelled the collapse of the Luftwaffe for lack of fuel.

The title of this 15-page memorandum was "Leadership Deficiencies in the Air Force and the Air Industry." The top leaders of the Air Ministry were charged with negligence in planning, developing, and manufacturing new types of airplanes.

Indeed, a number of things in this ministry were in a bad way. Goering was blatantly not held responsible since "before the entry of the United States into the war, he earnestly pointed out that we must work with all possible means to at least maintain qualitative superiority at all times." It was not clear whether this was caution or tactics. The true reason "for the loss of our quantitative superiority in the air" was "to be sought in the wrong measures taken by the RLM [Air Ministry]. . . . New ideas and developments" were "much too hesitatingly checked, brought to construction, tested, constantly changed, and then, usually under the pressure of the events due to many alterations, were still not ready for mass serial production. . . . [The Air Ministry] did not take prompt and emphatic measures against unfruitful representations of interests by competing firms, so that constant delays occur with urgently needed new types and instruments."

The example, cited in this context, of the delay in planning the Ta 254 fighter plane is truly stunning. Great hopes had been pinned on this aircraft for fighting bombers. Its removal was necessary, however, because the program was to concentrate entirely on the new jet fighters, especially the Me 262. Moreover, it was obviously a mistake to replace the 2,500-HP Junker motor with a Daimler-Benz motor; the latter was not yet ready for production. Incidentally, Goering had been personally responsible here. However, most of the charges in the memorandum are unjustified, even in retrospective, for instance the allegedly poor decision to cancel the Me 163 with rocket propulsion. After all, this aircraft had no flying range worth mentioning. Likewise, it was a correct decision to halt a parallel development of the jet engine (this development was known as the "Lorin aeroengine").

It was absurd to attack the decision to halt production of the Fritz X, a remote-control rocket dropped from airplanes. The He 177 planes meant for this bomb could no longer be used; they were too defect-prone and too slow. The authors of the charge were unable to indicate how the bomb could be used if no transport aircraft was available.

The development of an antiaircraft rocket to be shot from planes had been given up in favor of an antiaircraft rocket launched from the ground. This was done even though Professor Gladenbeck had allegedly guaranteed that it could be developed and made ready for production within six weeks; the ground-air rocket would allegedly require more than a year before it could be serially manufactured.

On the same day that Himmler sent me this memorandum, I happened to issue a directive saying that "a speedy solution to the problem of target-seeking board-to-board rockets" had to be found. I empowered Dr. Gladenbeck "to use all means to create a safely functioning complete model." Gladenbeck was to be supported as far as possible in carrying out his assignment and "his directions [were] to be obeyed in all cases."[17]

Kaltenbrunner's report, transmitted by Himmler, rebuked the cessation of developments, most of which had been stopped in order to concentrate on other, more important projects. In other words, the very objective that was expressly demanded six weeks later in a further indictment from the Air Ministry. It was not easy to find one's bearings in the multiple interests of the denouncers and SS agents. This was the case back then; and today, in the activities of skillful lobbyists, it is still difficult to decide on the development and introduction of new weapons.

The indictment closes with the statement "that not only has development of a research result always taken years after research has ended; but also that after development has ended, a purely military test by the military before the abatement of research has again taken and still takes several years. The road from invention and research to development, military testing, and ultimate employment normally requires many years within the Air Ministry and Luftwaffe."[18]

Long development periods are the cardinal problem in all air forces in the world. Only seldom do chancy decisions work out, for instance England's hasty introduction of the Spitfire. On the other hand, serial manufacture of the revolutionary new XXI U-boat brought production problems that gave the Gestapo grounds for investigation. At my orders and on my responsibility, we dared to skip the test of a prototype in order to save one and a half years. A decision that would have paid off; for ultimately, we were ready for production by November 1943, within half the normal time.

The memorandum "Leadersip Deficiencies in the Air Force and the Air Industry" of September 5, 1944, did not comfort the people involved; it unsettled them. The existence of the document was sure to get around in the Air Ministry and make the responsible officials fear that the notions and suggestions of the SS agents could have consequences. If the heads of development projects wanted to concentrate on just a few plans (even at the risk of holding back other promising ideas), they needed the full protection of the state. But this was difficult because the SS and the Gestapo formed a second power, which was unpredictable.

There are two replies from my ministry to Himmler's letter to me of September 5, 1944. First, I informed Himmler on September 16, 1944, "that I can get involved in the development of aircraft after the Reich Marshal has agreed to give up his rights. As in other areas, for instance in the development of weapons, tanks, etc., I have created a 'Development Main Commission for Aircraft.' " This was to be chaired by Dr. Lucht of the Messerschmitt Works. He was "no technical designer. But after long reflection, I am convinced that the designers have bogged down in feuds and are too willful [to assume] leadership in developing airplanes."[19]

Saur's reply of October 8, signed by me,[20] tried to clear up misunderstandings by pointing out that preliminary tests were still being made with the Lorin aeroengine, even though it was showing great disadvantages next to the jet engine, which was now in serial construction. "Opinions still diverge widely today in research and professional circles," Saur declared. He could also clarify another item mentioned by Himmler: Gladenbeck could never keep to the short development period promised for his airplane rockets "since fundamental development problems still [had] to be solved."[21]

SS Standartenführer Klumm, personal assistant to the chief of SS headquarters, reacted to Saur's reply to Himmler by sending another letter on November 15, 1944. But even before that, on October 18, he had tried to influence Himmler. Evidently Himmler's friendly and delaying letter to me was not the sharp reaction that the people around him had expected. In fact, one can generally establish that the middle stratum of leaders in the SS conducted themselves far more radically than Himmler himself. On a letterhead of the chief of the SS headquarters, Klumm sent Dr. Brandt, Himmler's personal chief of staff, an organizational proposal. This would give Himmler a decisive role in air armaments—and also bring his ambitious subordinate new activities. Along with this letter of October 18, 1944, he transmitted "a request from men in the Air Ministry" [who], "even without any effort on my part, [would have] made this statement." This statement, he said, came from the circle of the engineering corps, which had actually gotten into difficulties with Saur's shirt-sleeve methods. Basically, this memorandum must have agreed with the one in August of that same year. Accoring to Kaltenbrunner, it too had been composed by "top experts in the development of air defense and the Luftwaffe." After all, only the engineering corps of the Air Ministry could be considered top experts.

The new memorandum expressed the suspicion that "forces are at work to stop war-decisive measures." This was a barely disguised hint that the Gestapo might deal with the matter at some point. "Events keep proving more and more," Klumm declared, "that a change must occur in the commanding positions if all the projects are not to go awry at the last moment." Thus, they wanted to evade Saur's dictates. "I can only keep reemphasizing that we have the better inventors and instruments, yet they are not having any effect. They are not even being developed by the RLM [Air Ministry], even though they have been ready for many, many years and could be used for the new construction of aircraft and offensive instruments."[22]

The memorandum accompanying Klumm's letter went even further than Klumm had gone. "Ruthless tactics [should] be used chiefly if there is a clearly demonstrable failure by influential men in the armaments industry and the Wehrmacht," which might have referred to Saur, Milch, and me. "During the course of the war, many a soldier and numerous technicians have constantly been forced to wonder why the higher German leadership quite obviously makes the wrong decision . . . in individual cases. This observation is so incontestable that none of the explanations normally cited in such cases will suffice." This tacit charge of high treason could refer to Field Marshal Milch, state secretary in the Air Ministry, who was incriminated anyhow in the eyes of the SS. The "roots of the evil [lie] in having incapable men occupy important offices, in rivalries between offices, selfish efforts by industry, a lack of a sense of responsibility, organizational deficiencies, and in other human weaknesses."

However, the example of the development of an antiaircraft (ground-air) rocket makes it clear that the authors of the two memorandums could not be the same. The first memorandum assails the fact that the project of a plane-to-plane rocket was given up for the sake of the antiaircraft rocket. The second memorandum, in contrast, voices the opposite reproach, that "the employment of an antiaircraft rocket [would be] possible today with fair certainty [on the basis of an early reduction of] "five ongoing projects to not less than two projects." In reality, however, as Saur pointed out in his reply, the test steering mechanisms for this rocket were not yet at the stage where they could go into production. And an antiaircraft rocket could obviously not go into production before they were.

The authors of the memorandum, however, are unmoved; they conclude that everyone must be made to realize "that a wrong decision will have personal consequences and might even cost them their lives. Such a stance will undoubtedly scare off the huge number of orators and semi-ignoramuses and clear the path for the most capable men again. . . . Various agencies are fighting over their positions"—a correct observation, no doubt—"and indeed to the misfortune of the German people. . . . These are high-placed men who obviously believe that the normal standard set for every German does not apply to them."

The memorandum ends with the demand to create a new agency in Himmler's headquarters under the inoffensive designation "Technical Watch Force." This office would have to "render harmless these incapable men who have revealed their incapabilities in a cruel lesson for the German people." Thus, it would be a kind of execution place. "This . . . agency could almost bring about a turn in the war with its decisions."[23] I would assume that it would have made the war end earlier. The members of the Luftwaffe engineering corps who lent their names to this memorandum were evidently quite inexperienced in politics. If their suggestions had been implemented, they would have brought about their own doom. For the desperate situation could no longer be stopped. No wishful thinking could help. Even if all developmental mistakes had been stopped, it would have had no effect on the imminent end of the war.

Himmler's reaction to the letter of October 18 was ambivalent and, at least for Klumm, disappointing. It also contrasted with the apparent loyalty he had shown me several weeks earlier by benevolently sending me Kaltenbrunner's material. For on October 30, 1944, Dr. Brandt answered Klumm on Himmler's behalf that he was forced "unfortunately to send him a negative reply. The thought of establishing such an agency under the SS Reichsführer is good," Himmler said in praise; "it would certainly have positive results." But then comes a remarkable concession: "However, its implementation is obstructed at the moment by difficulties that cannot be cleared away."[24]

At that very same time, late October 1944, the intrigue against three of my department heads had succeeded, thus documenting that my power was broken. In regard to all steps leading to an expansion of his position, Himmler always considered very thoroughly what negative reactions they might elicit from Hitler. Hence, he had to be careful not to offend Hitler by suggesting a new agency of this sort. In regard to industry at that time, he must have felt like a spider in a net, a spider that can observe but never strangle. For Hitler still saw the achievements of the armaments industry as amazing, and he knew that the industrialists were responsible for them. Himmler could not become active, for he could not skirt the guarantee of protection that Hitler, in his own interest, had given the industry. However, it was Saur who had long since become the guarantor of an anti-industry policy. His prestige kept rising with Hitler, whereas Hitler reproached me for defeatism.

In the winter of 1944, Hitler had turned to the marshals and generals during a discussion of the situation and said: "We are lucky enough to have a genius in the armaments industry, and that genius is Saur!" A few months later, on March 28, 1945, i.e., several weeks before the end, Hitler must have been even more unrestrained in formulating his appreciation of Saur. Goebbels wrote in his diary on that day: "The Führer considers Saur as having a stronger personality than Speer. Saur sticks to things; if necessary, he will use force to carry out a task assigned to him. Quite a contrast from Speer." On March 31 Hitler added: "Saur exceeds Speer in energy as well as in a skill for improvising."[25] Indeed, in his will Hitler made Saur my successor in all my functions.

It was certainly not moral qualms that kept Himmler from agreeing. For he himself was always quick to demand executions for alleged failures. Thus, on September 9, 1944, he demanded that von Axthelm, general of the antiaircraft branch, determine "the men responsible" for an unsuccessful defense against a bomber attack on the Brüx hydrogenation plant, "put them on trial, and have them sentenced."[26] Even in the still relatively calm times of 1942, he threatened the navy through Gottlob Berger, the head of the SS main office. Himmler, said Berger, "would at some point have to deal with the various faulty designs of the navy. He need merely remind them of the infamous magnetic torpedo ignitions, whereat one might ask whether the gentleman responsible for them has already been stood up against the wall."[27]

In regard to this drastic comment, one must point out that such threats had long since become ineffectual because they were usually not followed by any execution.

In a further letter, on November 15, 1944, Klumm again got worked up. He had meanwhile learned of the reply that Saur had drafted to Himmler. Klumm was especially angered by Saur's statement that "opinions on the possibilities [of development projects] still strongly diverge today in research and professional circles." This, said Klumm, outlined "all the madness of our development works in the Luftwaffe and also in the army." This madness had brought us to the point of having a thousand things in development. Why not "thoroughly ram a few experts through for projects that are considered good, push them on to the test, and then simply let the test prove whether it is possible or not? Theoretically, I can argue about something or other for a thousand years, but the yes or no of it is established only by practical demonstration." The SS leadership he said, had set itself the goal "of pushing ahead with all its might" anything in air armaments "that comes from the lips of outstanding experts and that can be seen as especially favorable." In plain words, this meant that the SS leaders were presuming to grab hold of the development of air armaments, but were now being held back by Himmler's measured letter.

Klumm continues: "That is what I wished to achieve by employing plenipotentiaries in the individual categories of remote-controlled bodies, torpedo weapons, etc. In one category we succeeded in launching such a plenipotentiary under Speer; in the briefest time, he cleared up all the confusion in the area of remote-control bodies. Development, manufacture, and testing are in the same hands, and we are advancing at the best possible speed."[28]

The members of my ministry had also been trying for months to concentrate manufacture and development, quite in keeping with an edict that I had gotten Hitler to issue in June 1944. (See Appendix 11.) In the discussion of the armaments staff on October 3–4, 1944, i.e., six weeks prior to the SS attacks, Saur, for instance, had established for air armaments: "In order to finally clean up the plethora of test models, construction series, variants, and changes in old and new models [in air armaments], HDL (Chief Service Leader) Saur has directed that all orders from the Development Main Commission for Aircraft that are not reconfirmed within fourteen days be cancelled. Until then, all models are to be thoroughly discussed by the Commission, and special importance is to be placed on the veto power of Herr Frytag, Herr Dr. Heyne, Herr Dr. Haspel, and Herr Klinker. The fact of cancellation is to be expressly communicated to the firms."[29]

Even before these attacks by the SS, a change in the climate had become apparent. The industrialists who had previously been trusted and, basically, liked by Hitler were now more and more exposed to threats. Gauleiter Sauckel, authorized by Hitler to command all the German and foreign labor forces, declared in semipublic speeches that the factory managers could be spurred to greater achievements only by rigorous measures. Once a few of the directors lost their heads, the others would know what they were dealing with, and production would go up.[30] This contradicted my fundamental attitude that threats of concentration camps would never get engineers and scientists to increase their performance. And after all, the memorandum that Himmler had sent me on September 5 was nothing but an order to drive the development engineers ahead by threatening them with draconian punishments.

That was why I had personally appealed to Hitler on September 20, 1944, four weeks prior to Klumm's massive assault. The assassination attempt on July 20, 1944, had, I said, "supplied new nourishment to the distrust of the reliability of my large group of colleagues in industry." The Party, I went on, was convinced that the people closest to me were "reactionary, economically one-sided, and alien to the Party." Furthermore, they claimed that my ministry and the industrial self-responsibility that I had built up were to be designated "as a reservoir of reactionary business leaders or even as hostile to the Party."

In response to these charges, I insisted that "performance could be increased only through the organization of the self-responsibility of industry and through the *voluntary* readiness of the factory managers." I was challenging the strivings of the SS and the Party directly when I continued: "I do not believe that the alternate system, of coercion, factory plenipotentiaries, or extensive investigations and punishments, can be successful even if quotas are not filled. At any rate, I regard it as extraordinarily dangerous at the present moment to spark any discussion on the expediency of one system or another and to thereby bring uncertainty into industry. The Party circles have declared 'that one must finally force the armaments industry to work with more modest standards' or 'that now different times have begun, demanding different methods.' " I asked Hitler to renew his promises: "With the exception of criminal incidents, any arrests, dismissals and appointments of managers, and any appointments of commissioners and special representatives in the factories can be made only by the Reich Minister for Armaments and War Production. This obtains also in regard to misdemeanors that the manager has committed and that can be prosecuted under the penal code, for instance hoarding of material and manpower, false information on factory needs, on the employment of machine tools, etc." I made the following addendum to these demands: "[Hitler] must make a clear decision on whether, in the future, the self-responsibility of industry, based on confidence in the factory managers, or a different system should rule industry. In my opinion, the responsibility of the factory managers for the factory must be maintained and brought out as strongly as possible, because, naturally, such responsibility can attain the highest achievements. It is my personal viewpoint that in this decisive time, one should not fundamentally change this system after it has fully proved its worth so far. I consider it necessary that a clear decision be made on your part, which will also plainly show the outside world the direction that the leadership of industry shall follow in the future."[31] But this decision never came, because Hitler had delegated it to Bormann and Goebbels. In fact, this letter aroused indignation and resistance from both men. Nevertheless, a few days later I succeeded in getting Hitler to sign an appeal drafted by me to the German factory directors. The appeal basically confirmed what I had asked of Hitler.[32]

Such directives of Hitler's were still binding. In December 1944, Erwin Barthels, the commodore of my transport fleet, was arrested by a commissioner of the Secret State Police even though a judicial inquiry of the Hamburg district attorney's office had arrived at a negative finding. I informed Kaltenbrunner that "Barthels has a leading position in my operation, and on the basis of his achievements he is irreplaceable for me." Also, "the material coming to light so far [does] not justify such a drastic procedure against this highly meritorious man." Kaltenbrunner instantly gave in to my request for Barthels's release.[33]

At that time, the Gestapo must have received many accusations based on personal motives or rivalries. Himmler and his staffers must have long since grown tired of these charges, for many of them were simply not followed up on.

In mid-November 1944, during the successful attacks on my office heads, Schaaf, the resolute opponent of Saur, also lost his field of duties.[34] Until then he had been Schieber's constant representative in my ministry and had also been in charge of vehicle production. I insisted that he be appointed general manager of BMW.[35] Thereupon, Hille, the chairman of the board of the BMW Works, had turned to a middleman in the SS to intrigue with the Gestapo against Schaaf with "an exposé of the conditions in the board of directors and management of BMW." "A fierce power struggle [is] taking place in the Bavarian Motor Works," according to the report of this middleman, SS Company Commander Wolf.[36] Supposedly, the board of directors had decided in November 1944 "to make Schaaf chairman of the board. Hille refused to go along with this decision. He apparently managed to get Gauleiter [Paul] Giesler to interfere. Of far greater interest to us than this struggle for personal power position are the accusations that Hille has made against Schaaf in political terms. As Hille alleges, Schaaf has taken measures to let the factories transferred to Markirch and Bitschweilen (in Alsace) fall undamaged into the hands of the Americans." In this respect, Schaaf had followed the unofficial line of the ministry. Furthemore, "Hille reports that Schaaf has discussed in a large circle in what way one can cooperate with the Americans when they appear at the gates of the Munich plant." Indeed, Schaaf had been careless enough, when he was in a relatively large group, to discuss how one could protect German industry against fanatics, including Gauleiter Giesler. To make matters worse, Wolf was also told that "Schaaf had quite unabashedly made defeatist remarks."[37]

Three days after this memorandum, on December 29, 1944, I dictated a rebuke to Hille for appealing his dismissal "to the Chancellery of the Führer and also to Gauleiter Giesler" without informing me of his objections. I told my staffer Clashes to proceed against Hille "with the goal of 'loss of the position of managing director' when the investigations [were] concluded."[38]

I evidently did not know that the matter was also being handled by the Gestapo. Wolf's incriminating report had been transmitted to Dr. Brandt, Himmler's personal assistant, who, on January 9, 1945, asked Kaltenbrunner, the head of the Security Police and of the SD "to investigate Hille's political charges against Schaaf. If the Gestapo is already dealing with the procedure, then may I ask you to inform me of the present state."[39]

In the next few months nothing happened. Interest in the matter had obviously waned. Brandt's March 15 deadline for a resubmission had been tacitly changed to April 15. Perhaps the Gestapo itself was now reckoning with the end of the war. But it is more likely that the SS was simply overworked in these last few weeks of the war.

Finally, on February 5, 1945, Bormann personally spoke to Himmler. He said it was about "things picked up in the BMW Works II, Bruckmühl, Upper Bavaria. Presumption of sabotage in the manufacture of a tested rocket for fighting enemy fliers." Bormann asked Himmler "to urgently order an investigation of the allegedly sabotaged firing stage. My official, Party Member Elberding, will be available in this case too for a meeting with the head of Technical Office VIII, SS Squad Commander Professor Dr. Schaab."[40] It was consistent with the overall line in those days to construe setback as treason.

However, Himmler, who was already flirting with other goals in mid-February, passed the matter along with a weary gesture. "This memorandum on the presumption of sabotage in the manufacture of a tested rocket for fighting enemy fliers" was handed over to Hans Kammler, whom Hitler had long since put in charge of the planning, production, and employment of all rocket weapons. Himmler asked Kammler to take charge of the matter.[41]

Chapter 11

Baking Fumes, Geraniums,
Fir Tree Roots, and Atomic Bombs

IT WAS THE WISH OF HIS STAFF that Himmler was to personally get rid of the mistakes in air armaments. One ought to assume that with such trust by the SS leaders in Himmler's genius, the SS must have made remarkable progress in their own developments. Indeed, Himmler devoted his special energy to them, but in the usual bizarre and eccentric way that corresponded to his abstruse behavior. The grotesque results of this amateurish and excessive zeal show what consequences an overall interference by the SS would have had in developmental projects of air armaments.

Milch feared friction with the SS. He anxiously made a point of cultivating his relations with them. I therefore assume that this was the reason why he sacrificed two hours of his working day to discuss Himmler's chimeras on February 2, 1942. For on that day an insignificant SS Untersturmführer[1] recommended by Himmler discussed development problems with the field marshal. "The greeting and the form of the discussion were cordial and personal," the Untersturmführer boasted. "Further meetings were planned for the very near future." As a result of the two-hour conference, SS Untersturmführer Helmut Zborowski could state that the following matters were to be examined under his responsibility.

1. Possibilities of increasing the performance of the Me 109;
2. Border ranges or penetration depths of P.[rocket] bombers;
3. Technical expenditures and development time for R[rocket] long-range missiles with a 200- and with a 500-kilometer range.

Anyone familiar with the problems besetting Wernher von Braun's team when they were trying to successfully complete the A-4 rocket at that time can only be astonished at the lack of expertise and the insolence of the Untersturmführer.

The very next day after obtaining Field Marshal Milch's basic agreement, Zborowski went to Pleiger's representative in the management of the Hermann Goering Works. This man, SS Squad Commander Meinberg, "stated that he is basically prepared to plan the large-scale manufacture of long-range missiles simply on a hunch that their military employment can be guaranteed when the development is terminated. SS Squad Commander Meinberg promised that he would speedily transmit the designs of the 500-kilogram bomb."[2] (This was probably meant as equipment for the rocket bombers mentioned under point 2.)[3]

Eisenlohr, the engineer general of air armaments, had to interrupt his certainly more important work in order to travel to Graz with Zborowski on February 5, 1942. Dr. Siegfried Uiberreither, the Gauleiter of Styria, himself a high SS commander, instantly promised to build a rocket-development plant in his Gau. He repeated "his past promises that he would do everything he could to support this project." He would let them know as soon as he found a suitable location or suitable factory facilities.[4] It is characteristic of the high-handed conduct of the SS that Gauleiter and SS Commander Uiberreither had made these promises to the SS leaders much earlier, that is, before conferring with Milch. The deadline set for these preparations was February 25, 1942; for the SS prided itself on working significantly faster than other agencies.

Thus energy, material, and construction systems were wasted on a layman's ideas only because it was generally known that Himmler was interested in fantastic future projects and was also quick to view their rejection as sabotage against Germany's victory.

Zborowski's report went to Pohl, the head of the chimerical SS industrial empire, which would indicate that if these goals had been realized, the SS Economic Office would have been interested in the implementation of this production.

Naturally, the inadequacy of the technical background would have been revealed at some point. The project is never mentioned again. Himmler focused his interest on the promising development of the A-4 rocket, as will be discussed later on.

In general, this Zborowski seems to have been one of the visionaries whom the development offices did not care to turn down outright because they were aware of his connection to Himmler. Evidently, one year earlier,

Zborowski got Himmler excited over "oxygen turbines." "For tactically sufficient underwater periods, they" would allow submarines essentially higher underwater speeds . . . than the surface speeds of commercial and military ships."

On February 26, 1943, Zborowski, who had meanwhile been promoted to SS Obersturmführer, wrote to Himmler. The letter indicates that the SS Reichsführer had set up a "meeting on February 24, 1943, on the flagship *Erwin Wassner* to discuss possibilities of increasing the underwater speed of long-distance U-boats." Of course, Himmler could not possibly set up such a conference. But that is almost beside the point, since Zborowski could then report to Himmler: "Chief Engineer Captain (Eng.) Thedsen, after examining the technical proposals, for which he consulted members of his staff, was extremely surprised and enthusiastic at their effect. These proposals offer the technical solution for the U-boat problem that is most urgent for the future, since the effectiveness of U-boats is being strongly restricted because of the sea routes that the enemy keeps expanding and controlling with his air force. The enemy air force compels the boats to dive, in which state they cannot manage to fire since their speed is at this time so much slower than the enemy's. A pursuit under water and advance into a favorable firing position is intrinsically impossible. . . . Because of the crucial effect on future naval tactics and thereby on the course of the war, Captain Thedsen will have the necessary work started through Grand Admiral Doenitz. Clearly realizing that the most crucial things often fail because of petty disagreements, a procedure was agreed upon in order to prevent these interferences as far as possible from the very start. To avoid arousing the resistance of the appropriate experts, some of whom have been assigned the described predictable problems for years without solving them, it was agreed that there would be no originnaming of the process or the mention of any name, and the proposed suggestions would be transmitted as wishes and solution proposals of the 'Front,' especially the 'Technical Staff of the Commander-in-Chief of U-boats.' "[5]

The navy must have been deliberately misleading Zborowski. For a few weeks later, after Doenitz's promotion to Supreme Commander of the Navy on January 30, 1943, the construction of the new U-boats was theoretically ready. By doubling the electrical propulsion and multiplying the energy stored in the accumulators, they would have a larger underwater radius and an underwater speed surpassing even that of destroyers.[6] Moreover, some time earlier, they had successfully tested a factory-ready U-boat with the hydrogen superoxide engine developed by Walther, so the next generation of U-boat weapons was already technically established.

Nevertheless Rear Admiral Hans von Friedeburg, the commanding admiral of the U-boats, assigned Zborowski "to offer you, Reichsführer, his heartiest gratitude and his best greetings through me." This was a subaltern formula of greeting, totally out of character for a man like Friedeburg, who had the courage to commit suicide after signing the armistice with the British forces under the Doenitz government.

On March 5, 1943, Dr. Brandt replied that Himmler "was delighted by your letter of February 26, 1943. Keep him up to date at specific intervals on the practical effect of this positive discussion."[7]

One month later Himmler was pleased to learn that Rear Admiral (Eng.) Thedsen[8] had had "his engineering staff examine the proposed suggestions and the documents left with him. . . . The examination proved that they were correct and valuable. On the basis of this finding and in keeping with the cited report of February 26, 1943, the Commanding Admiral of the U-boats has personally ordered and assigned the K [Kriegsschiffbau, i.e., Naval Construction] Office of the OKM [Oberkommando der Marine, i.e., Supreme Naval Command] to develop and build 'oxygen turbines,' and to equip boats with these turbines."[9] Even if this had been the case, these turbines would have taken several years to develop and test. But the naval command evidently only wanted to avoid angering Himmler, so it pretended to go along with even absurd suggestions.

The highest-level officers and industrialists were harnessed for such nonsense; and bizarre inventions were worked on by the very experts whose time was already occupied to the utmost by urgent development projects. All these abuses had to be put up with. The most peculiar proposals were made. On January 4, 1943, Himmler personally asked me to abolish the direction indicators and large headlights on automotive vehicles. The indicators, he said, were hardly necessary considering the small amount of traffic; and the headlights were not used anyway because of the blackout regulations.[10] On the occasion of a report[11] in the Führer's headquarters on April 17, 1943, he recommended to Hitler that side arms be burnished so that the flashing of the shiny weapons would not betray attackers during night attacks. It made no difference whatsoever that such attacks were hardly common at that time.

Himmler's curiosity about the latest developments was feared by us because of the constant danger that he might interfere with development work, disrupting it with his amateur initiative. On May 14, 1943, for instance, Himmler met with Porsche in Hitler's headquarters only to appraise the 188-ton Maus [mouse] tank, which was demonstrated to Hitler in a wooden model.[12] Early that same year, Himmler had heard that Hitler, after watching a demonstration of the Flettner helicopter, had remarked that this project was highly worthy of support. Just one year earlier, on January 27, 1942, Himmler had sent for the designer[13] to pick his brain about the project in an earlier stage of development. Neither the heavy Maus tank nor the Flettner helicopter had anything whatsoever to do with Himmler's work areas.

In August 1943, according to my protocol, a third party, probably Himmler or his representative, told Hitler about a new infantry defense weapon. Hitler was very enthusiastic and instantly ordered that this "Gerloff combat pistol" must "be supported in every way because of its extraordinary importance . . . especially in order to decide as soon as possible which ongoing development projects and manufacturing can be stopped."[14]

But Hitler's enthusiasm was unfounded. The protocol of a meeting with the head of army armaments, Colonel General Fromm, on January 21, 1944, soberly reports on this combat pistol: "Weapon proclaimed as wonder weapon; at 70 meters, it has 3 meters horizontal and 4 meters vertical dispersion. Next demonstration, late January. End of development not yet in view. Test piece in repair. Shells wobble at a combat distance of up to 100 meters."[15]

Such failures and defeats could not discourage Himmler and his agents from constantly supporting apparently revolutionary developments. If such ideas came from the experiences of SS troops, they could sometimes be sensible. Thus, the three-ton Maultier track-laying vehicle, supported by the SS Reich Division, was an excellent development. In the first few days of January 1943, Hitler made up his mind that an output of one thousand pieces a month was to be prepared. A further increase, he said, was to be speedily striven for within the framework of the possibilities of the three-ton type.[16] The SS commander who developed this SS crawler-type vehicle was handed an award of 50,000 marks by Hitler.

Often, however, it was Hitler who stimulated Himmler's boundless imagination. In mid-June 1943 he reported on Hitler's proposal: A new material, known as durofol, now had to be "used on a large scale for the manufacture of a new invention. . . . Thus, if we want to use durofol, we must make sure of greater output since it is being produced by only one factory. I ask the head of the SS Economic Administration Main Office to investigate instantly this question" of a second factory "and to make suggestions when he reports to me."[17] At the same time, Himmler ordered the SS Command Office "to build a noninflammable durofol car as quickly as possible. If the experiment succeeds, then we will have solved the iron problem in automobile construction."[18] As everyone knew, Goering once wanted to force the construction of cement locomotives for the same reason.[19] Himmler also told his representative Kammler that he was placing "the greatest importance on this new material." He assigned him "to undertake the testing immediately and to make durofol T-girders, which, according to scientific calculations, are supposedly much more solid than steel girders. Please keep me informed on the development of the experiments. If they succeed, we would be extricated to a great degree from the iron shortage for construction. Furthermore, durofol supposedly does not burn."[20]

On June 25, a disillusioning Jüttner reported that this durofol was artificially compressed wood with an "elasticity module of only 280,000 kg/cm^2 as opposed to 2,200,000 kg/cm^2 for iron. This lack of elasticity limits the applicability of the material so that it cannot be used for manufacturing the bodies of automotive vehicles. It would be suitable for smaller parts of the automotive construction, for instance gears, door handles, window frames, and the like."[21] An accompanying report of Office X of this SS Main Command Office explained: "Basically, a substitute for nonferrous metals and for aluminum. At the moment, only for smaller objects up to around 500 millimeters in the largest dimension, e.g., door and window trimmings, interior parts of vehicle bodies. The largest parts so far are factory-made fenders. Self-supporting body parts have not yet been manufactured since models are not produced; they are planned for the future, corresponding to the more advanced development in the U.S.A. (Ford). A disadvantage will be that injuries (dents) are not repairable; instead, they require complete replacement of the part involved."[22]

Kammler's statements were likewise negative: "The manufacture of T-girders is not considered expedient since, on the one hand, the material for this purpose is much too expensive, and on the other hand, the stampers would be very ,large and expensive. Furthermore, as already mentioned, the process would be worthwhile only for very large series. . . . Since durofol is nowhere as solid as ingot iron (durofol bending strength 2.910 kg/cm^2 as opposed to 3,500 to 4,500 kg/cm^2 for iron), the profiles would have to be considerably larger under an equal strain."[23] Once again, a project of Himmler's had failed.

The impotence of the German Luftwaffe against enemy bomber squads naturally aroused universal criticism. Himmler did all he could to cultivate this criticism of the already discredited leaders of the Air Ministry.

In October 1943, Himmler received Dr. Plendl (a doctor of engineering), whom Milch, Doenitz, and I had made our mutual representative of high-frequency research. On January 7, 1944, Plendl sent Himmler a ten-page report on research projects in the area of high frequency, even though this was outside the jurisdiction of the Reichsführer, who, moreover, had no background in this discipline. At the same time, Plendl announced that "in August 1943, with the agreement of the Reichsführer SS Economic Administrative Headquarters, a high-frequency research institute has been set up at the concentration camp of Dachau." The head of the Institute, he said, was SS Obersturmführer Schröder. "The institute has exclusively prisoners for its employees, to wit, as scientific director the prisoner Hans Maier, former director of the central laboratory of the firm of Siemens & Halske, and another twenty or twenty-five prisoners who are graduate engineers, physicists, and technicians in specialized areas. The necessary measuring instruments, measuring tools, and machine tools will be prepared by the Reich Agency for High-Frequency Research, Inc., and research assignments will be made by the B.H.F. [Bevollmächtigter Hoch-frequenz-Forschung or plenipotentiary for High-Frequency Research]." It is certain that such specialists would have done more successful work in freedom than under the command of a technically ignorant SS Obersturm-führer.

"To make even untrained prisoners of concentration camps useful in a much greater degree for the purposes of high-frequency research," Plendl's letter to Himmler continues, "a research workshop is now being completed in the Gross-Rosen concentration camp on the basis of special support by the SS Reichsführer. This research workshop comprises four barracks roughly 1,700 square meters in area. The construction of the barracks will presumably be finished by early March. The use of the barracks is planned as follows: one and one-half barracks will house the institute now located in Dachau, and the remaining two and one-half barracks will house the actual research workshop. As soon as the barracks are finished, 150 to 200 prisoners, commanded by one engineer and five foremen, provided by the Reich Agency for High-Frequency Research, shall be assigned to high-frequency work, first in the exploitation of booty instruments, tubes, etc., and then, to an increasing degree, in work like the construction of measuring devices, instruments, and individual parts for the needs of high-frequency research. The high-frequency work capacity thus created can, if needed, also be used for the purposes of the SS Reichsführer, for instance the tasks that are assigned by you to Sturmbannführer Siepen, without any intermediate agency."[24]

The final line of this letter clarifies something that we did not know. Himmler had established his own research office "without an intermediate agency," i.e., uncontrolled by Colonel Geist, who had been set up in my office to centralize air-defense research. Scientifically trained prisoners were then siphoned off for special SS developments instead of doing their regular work in their usual jobs at their companies.

Himmler was equally heedless when interfering in development projects of other Wehrmacht branches. Thus, with all the means of his authority, he promoted the development of a navy speedboat, even though the naval command would not have been interested. On April 30, 1944, Himmler informed SS Standartenführer Kloth in his raw materials office that a certain SS Standartenführer Frosch would be visiting him. This man, said Himmler, had been assigned "to develop and implement an important invention. Support him with all possible and impossible means."[25]

The project, as Himmler wrote to Frosch on the same day, was "the testing and implementation of the 'Zisch' flying boat. You are responsible to me for making sure that this war instrument, which is extremely important for the German war effort in the land and sea war, will be ready for serial manufacture and employable in the shortest possible time. I want the first series to be in use by September 1, 1944. In case of any difficulties caused by any agencies, you are to telegraph me immediately."[26] Pohl too was asked "to receive SS Standartenführer Frosch of SS Headquarters in the next few days. He has been assigned by me with implementing a brand-new invention. I would like the manufacture of this invention to take place exclusively in our workshops as far as possible."[27]

This flying boat was the development of a single-hull speedboat of the Wankel Test Workshops in Lindau. In an aerodynamic form, this boat was to cut through the waves like a fish; equipped with a torpedo and armed with a 3.7 cm twin antiaircraft gun, it would attack enemy ships at a high speed. The project was among the group of small combat weapons that were being manufactured or developed at that time for the navy under Admiral Heye.

This development was not unusual. Similar projects were being worked on everywhere. The only extraordinary aspect was Himmler's arbitrary interference with a development meant for the navy. On May 6, 1944, Himmler then personally inspected the Wankel factory near Lindau.[28] The Dornier Aircraft Works, assigned special projects for the aircraft program, were using the factory space of the Wankel Test Workshops. On June 19, 1944, Himmler had Herr Frosch "go to the Wankel Workshops as soon as possible to get a picture on the spot of how the Dornier Works are being run. The SS Reichsführer requests a report."[29]

One month later, on July 19, Wilhelm Keppler, Hitler's former economic specialist and Himmler's agent, assured Himmler how important he felt the development of this flying boat to be. He wrote him: "I have heard that you spoke with the Reich Marshal about having Dornier clear the Wankel plant in Lindau, but that Herr Dornier has not stopped bothering you and intends to bring the matter personally to the Führer."[30]

On August 2 Frosch met with Kühl, the director of the Dornier Works. Dr. Kühl said that the Fighter Staff had need of this factory space. He had been "informed by General Staff Engineer Lucht of the Fighter Staff in charge of immediate measures, that the evacuation of the Wankel Test Workshops has been put off until September, and only then will the actual decision be made." At that time the Fighter Staff had the far more important task of multiplying the output of fighter planes within as short a time as possible. "Director Kühl states that he is merely yielding to an order from the Fighter Staff, since the chairman of the Fighter Staff, Herr Saur, accused him of not asserting himself emphatically enough in favor of Dornier in the Wankel matter."[31]

But the SS was more powerful than the Fighter Staff. On August 5 Frosch declared: "Herr Major Schubert, Technical Officer with the Reich Marshal, called me up on 7/31/44 to ask me if Wing I of the Wankel Test Workshops can continue to be used by Dornier. I replied that I would be going to Lindau on the same day to examine the matter on the spot. On 8/5/44 I informed Major Schubert by telephone that I *must* insist that Wing I be cleared. Major Schubert declared that he would inform the planning office of the Fighter Staff accordingly, that Wing I is required by the Waffen-SS [*nota bene*: for naval purposes] and is therefore to be evacuated by Dornier."[32]

My people also capitulated. Colonel Geist, the head of my office group for development in the Technical Office, informed the Raw Materials Office in Himmler's personal staff that, at the behest of the Main Committee for Shipbuilding, he had sent the leading designer of the flying boat, Graduate Engineer Büller, to a discussion with Wankel in Lindau, and he was taking two designers and two draftswomen along. Likewise, a Dr. Eglin had supposedly been released on July 26 by the Sachsenberg firm for the Wankel firm, and he would "then clarify the employment of the Büller design group."[33] Thus, Himmler's drastic conduct was successful.

However, this assistance from my staff was not enough for Himmler. As he noted in a personal memorandum, Dr. Krimm, professor of aircraft construction at the Technical Universty, was ordered to go to Lindau immediately with Graduate Engineer Neumann. "Dr. Krimm, who performed the fundamental calculation for the flying boat," Himmler further ordered, "is to remain in Lindau until August 15, 1944, in order to carry out the follow-up calculations of the design changes. Admiral Heye has sent Wankel a naval engineer, Lieutenant Engineer Wendel." This man was to familiarize himself with the flying boat. "In terms of personnel, the work staff is now complete, so we may begin laying down the 'flying boat' very soon, assuming that Dornier evacuates Wing I at Wankel. After conferring with Reich Minister Speer and Herr Saur, and considering the important manufacturing to be done by the Dornier Works," Himmler's memorandum went on, as though he were in charge of armaments, "I myself have consented to let the Wankel Works be housed for now in factory wings until the Dornier Works can move into their subterranean transfer workshops in three or four months. The improper conduct of the Dornier Works is entirely clear to Speer, Saur, and me. It is equally clear that the Wankel Works will regain their factory."[34]

According to Himmler's notions, the boat was to go into production within one month, in September 1944. He had no sense whatsoever of how much time it takes to develop a new prototype and prepare it for serial manufacture.

The flying boat haunted the SS files until the final weeks of the war. As late as March 12, 1945, an SS Sturmbannführer named Luditz, of the Pioneer Inspection division of the SS Command Main Office, wanted "to speak to SS Standartenführer Dr. Brandt about the flying boat matter." Meanwhile, the general disorganization had spread all around. Luditz had "so far not succeeded in his efforts . . . because of the evasive movements of the various departments of the SS Command Headquarters."[35]

It was only when checking through the "Documentation of the SS Reichsführer," that I realized that Himmler also had a Technical Office next to his own Raw Materials Office. Today I feel that Himmler may conceivably have been building up a kind of shadow administration which would some day replace the heads of the major departments in my ministry.

It struck me as unnecessary and wasteful for the SS to develop its own weapons. Offering the possibilities of rapid advancement and the military prestige of its divisions, the SS drew important people into its realm, thus depriving the army.

Dr. Schwab, the head of the SS Technical Office, could have had a leading role in my ministry. On November 24, 1942, appearing before the Ministry's Munitions Commission, he had made demands for restricting superfluous developments. These demands supported our own ideas; but they contradicted the ideas of the imaginative Himmler and especially Hitler, who, faced with the war situation, was thinking more and more earnestly about miracle-working weapons. Schwab declared: "Hundreds of developments are taking place in all possible areas. Each development is important and each one can some day advance us in some combat area. But considering the overall technical situation of the war, the vast majority of all these developments will not be of decisive significance for the war during the next three or four months. It is possible that in two years we [could] possess a tank weapon or an artillery weapon that would put us in a position to defy any possible tank breakthrough. But this hope is utterly illusory if the enemy does not leave us this [necessary] time."[36] That was the exact policy of my ministry.

In the spring of 1942, Colonel General Heinz Guderian and his experts, who were provided by the General Staff of the army, were convinced that the great offensive toward the Volga and the Caucasus was a waste of armaments material. They felt that instead, it would make sense to employ the increased armaments output solely for building up a solid defense front. Exceedingly late, on August 3, 1944, Schwab joined this line of thinking, which was based on a realistic appreciation of the German armaments capacity. In his paper to the Tank Commission, Schwab explained that in the development of motorized antitank gunners, "the emphasis should lie on defense technology." Schwab recommended the construction of light antitank gunners, for "industrially speaking, we [can] not compete with the construction of the heaviest tank models, whose achievement lies in the solidity of the tank and the penetration power of the heavy guns. For the antitank gunners, we have to put speed and efficiency foremost, with a relatively weak armor plating, in order to perform quick tactical movements. The armor has to be strong enough to resist light automatic weapons up to 2 cm. A speed of at least 60 kilometers per hour on open terrain must be aimed at."[37] The later success of the light T-38 Czech tank in the fall and winter of 1944 proved that the General Staff and Schwab were both right.

The more difficult the military situation became, the more Himmler expanded his realm of power. His breakthrough to becoming Hitler's most versatile and, formally, most powerful satellite was something he owed to the events of the Twentieth of July, 1944. Previously, the SS Reichsführer had been Hitler's minister of the interior, head of the Gestapo, and head of the police. As commander in chief of the army reserves, he now penetrated positions tenaciously defended by the Wehrmacht; he also assumed command of the home army, was responsble for the reactivation of army divisions, and could decide on distribution of army weapons. Furthermore, soon after the Twentieth of July, he became Hitler's plenipotentiary for the reorganization of the front deployment of millions of soldiers and officers in all three Wehrmacht branches, including the Todt organization. A short time later, in December 1944, he became commander of several divisions on the Upper Rhine, and in late January 1945, of an army group on the Vistula. But all these things were not enough for Himmler. While he was supposed to stabilize the front, he also tried to contribute to changing the course of the war with bizarre ideas for armaments.

The responsibility for developing and producing weapons, however, remained with my ministry. But when Himmler was made commander in chief of the army reserve, he finally had an official pretext for interfering in development and production matters. Himmler made SS Obergruppenführer Jüttner his representative in all army reserve matters. (See Appendix 12.)

To inhibit Himmler's and Jüttner's hunger for power, I wrote to Jüttner on August 10, 1944: "I am worried that with the present plans to demonstrate new weapons to SS Reichsführer Himmler and yourself and also with other individual measures, there may be attempts to act against this edict" of Hitler's for the concentration of armaments and development "and his implementation orders. I would therefore like to ask you to first call the Reichsführer's attention to this edict and its content so that he does not make any decisions in ignorance of this edict. The directive you have signed to halt a portion of the developments at your instructions and to admit a further portion to be halted, contravenes this edict on the concentration of armaments and wartime production. We wish to go a great deal further in the restriction of development than is expressed in your directive."[38]

On June 19, 1944, at my suggestion, Hitler had signed an edict "for the concentration of armaments and war economy." In accordance with this edict, I issued the following order on July 21, the day after the assassination attempt: "All research and development work is to cease immediately unless my written approval for exception and continuation is applied for by August 31, 1944. The resumption of research and development work requires my consent. The beginning of work before the issuance of my consent is prohibited. . . . To the extent that presumable bottlenecked raw materials or bottlenecked products are to be used in the objects to be developed, the quantity and the quality of the materials to be employed or the quantity and nature of the products are to be indicated, so that the feasibility of later production can be cleared up in advance."[39]

This edict was aimed also and particularly against Himmler's innumerable activities, which made demands on valuable development capacities for mostly useless objects with no prospect of success.

The opposite was effectuated. On his own, as though it were a matter for the SS leadership, Himmler had received Dr. von Holt on September 9, 1944. Dr. von Holt was one of the leaders of Wasag,[40] which was subordinate to me; and Himmler picked his brain about the focal points in the development of defense rockets against bombers, a problem of air armaments, which were likewise my responsibility during that time. One week later, on September 15, 1944, Dr. Brandt, the head of the SS Reichsführer's personal staff, sent Dr. von Holt a suggestion made by SS Unterscharführer Glätzer to revolutionize guidance technology.

Going by his experiences, said Dr. von Holt, he could vouch for the implementation of a ground-air rocket guided to bombers by light impulses, so far as his experiences "concern the rocket propulsion and the energy questions. . . . Since, on the other hand, the perfect functioning of the automatic control system is a precondition for the 'peacock's eye' and 'lark' devices and for that of Unterscharführer Glätzer, I am asking you to obtain an accurate report from Professor Dr. Föttinger on the present stage of the development of the automatic control," von Holt asked Himmler's chief of staff. The request that Himmler take personal charge of this matter is reinforced: "Professor Föttinger's report would be all the more desirable since the rapid termination of the development of the automatic control system is dependent on externals, which, as Professor Föttinger informed me on Friday, are no longer contingent on his side."[41] Thus, Dr. von Holt was asking Himmler to intercede personally in order to remove abuses. To be sure, the automatic control of rockets was the unsolved problem of all ground-air defense rockets. But even the Wasag director himself must have foreseen that his dangerous request would be bound to cause not only disquiet but also difficulties.

Himmler, however, with the apparent reasonableness of an outsider, made the following lapidary remark about the rocket problem: "Just shoot one off. We've got the possibility of practical testing every day, unfortunately!" Von Holt hastened to assure him that this wish "expresses the heartfelt thoughts of both Professor Föttinger and myself, and we will constantly do our best to carry out this task."[42] This tortuous statement hints at a fear of not satisfying Himmler. However, these side channels to such an important man as Himmler also undermined the authority of my employees and made their orders seem secondary. Professor Föttinger, incidentally, was the head of the prestigious Institute of Technical Flow Research at the Technical University in Berlin-Charlottenburg.

In these last few months of the war, there were more and more of these eccentric ideas of dilettantes. But they had to be seriously followed up because of Himmler's authority. An unknown firm named Elemag in Hildesheim had sent a suggestion to SS Obergruppenführer Lauterbacher, Gauleiter of South Hanover–Brunswick; the firm proposed the idea of "using remote control to switch off electrical devices." In an amateurish way, it claimed that the insulating material of the atmosphere "is generally unheeded because of the naturalness of its existence; but ultimately, it constitutes the insulating foundation of all electrotechnology; and it is established that by removing the insulating effect of the atmosphere, one makes it impossible for any electrical device of a familiar construction and implementation to function. The present state of technology offers the possibility of influencing the insulating material of the atmosphere for the task at hand. It is well known that ultrashortwave electrical vibrations of certain frequencies also develop the ability to yonize [!] the atmosphere they permeate, thus causing a reverse electrical reaction: in other words, they transform the insulating material of the atmosphere into a voltage conductor."[43]

Instead of sending this utopian proposal on to my ministry, where it would have simply been filed away, Gauleiter Lauterbach dispatched it to Himmler on November 13, 1944.[44] Himmler asked his Technical Office for its opinion on this proposal. With a seriousness out of all proportion to this trivial matter, the response was that the procedure was absolutely impossible; all the means to be made available would have to be designated as lost in advance.[45]

In early January 1945, the Soviets were at the Vistula; and Himmler, as commander in chief of eight divisions, was still futilely trying to save the situation on the Upper Rhine and establish himself as general. At the same time, however, he was busy with the notion of miraculous weapons that would solve all strategic problems. In this case, too, Himmler was not satisfied with the clear-cut rejection by his own office. That very same day, January 8, 1945, he handed the suggestion for transmuting the atmosphere into a voltage conductor to the highest scientific authority, Dr. Werner Osenberg, the head of the planning office of the Reich Research Council. One month later Osenberg's opinion was sent to Himmler. In keeping with the importance of every wish uttered by Himmler, the letter was sent from Northeim to Berlin by special messenger, as a notice on the letter indicates.

Osenberg's letter was bound to dash all of Himmler's hopes. The result of the investigation was "that this [proposal by Elemag] is unrealizable given the present stage of technology. Elemag's statements themselves lack any deep understanding of the technological and physical processes involved, so it cannot be recommended that this agency be assigned the implementation of the necessary research."

Obviously Osenberg had instantly realized that this proposal was scientific humbug. For fear of any possible reproach, he nevertheless consulted further top-notch scientists. "Since similar suggestions are constantly being made, I have asked several noted scientists for a basic opinion on these issues." By way of preliminary reply, he could present a verdict by "Professor Meissner, who has special experience in the field of electromagnetic waves, as well as an opinion by Dr. Radstein, the head of my testing division. Once I have received the still outstanding reports, I will give you a comprehensive survey of the present state of development in this area."[46]

The two experts that Osenberg mentioned in his letter are extant. Dr. Radstein, head of the testing division of the Reich Research Council, stated after three pages of detailed explanation of basic physical concepts that "no success of the sort desired can be achieved with the means known today or even with means to be attained in a short time."[47]

After a thorough discussion, Professor Meissner of the AEG Research Institute came to the following conclusion: "The suggestions lack any physical and technological sense of the fundamental processes. Hence, and also according to the technological state of things now, it is completely useless, and it would only be a waste of time, to go into the physical details."[48] Even today, the files reveal the panicky urge for action unleashed by any query from Himmler. Who would want the burden of being responsible for the loss of the war?[49]

In the area of chemistry, too, Himmler felt sure of his judgment. In January 1945 he energetically pursued the insane idea of producing fuel from fir tree roots. This idea was not just born out of the imminent catastrophe. As early as May 1943 Himmler had pursued a similar idea. He had quite seriously informed Pohl about an invention that could "catch the exhaust fumes from bakery chimneys" for "the manufacture of alcohol. Bakeries like our bakery in Dachau could supply 100 to 120 liters of alcohol of this sort daily. Please look into this matter and see whether we can do the same thing with [all] our bakeries."[50]

An SS Hauptsturmführer named Niemann must have then made a report that angered Himmler. Of the 4 million hectoliters of alcohol produced in the last year of peace, he said, not more than 0.6 percent could have been obtained from all the smoke of all the bread factories put together.

On October 17, 1943, an angry Himmler wrote to Pohl: "Employ a different SS commander for these experiments. SS Hauptsturmführer Niemann strikes me as being absolutely negative toward the entire question. I don't like the tone of his report either. I am of the opinion that in wartime, the yield of even small quantities of alcohol is important. I do not believe that we are now producing 4 million hectoliters of alcohol in the war. Accordingly, the percentage of alcohol obtained from smoke would be essentially greater if an accurate and objective investigation were undertaken. Perhaps, at the next opportunity, we will discuss this orally."[51]

Six months later, another crazy idea came up. On March 31, 1943, SS Sturmbannführer Dr. Joachim Caesar, head of the Agricultural Division in the concentration camp at Auschwitz, wrote to Himmler's staff about the possibility of obtaining oil from geraniums. The very next day, Himmler wanted to know "what contains oil" in a geranium. He felt that a larger quantity of geranium oil should be procured and that SS Obergruppenführer Pohl should have one hectare of geraniums planted. In any case, he said, he wanted this problem to be dealt with systematically.[52]

In January 1945 Himmler was off on a new trail. His interest was aroused by a report of the Information Service (December 28, 1944) about the Japanese manufacture of high-octane gas for airplane engines from fir tree roots. "As reported officially, this airplane fuel can be produced in a relatively easy process and is already being industrially manufactured in Japan. In November, the [Japanese] Ministry of Agriculture and Commerce introduced a five-month campaign for increasing production throughout the country. . . . Experiments have shown that this product is equal, if not superior, in quality to the high-grade octane gasoline obtained from petroleum. . . . Experts explain that the older the roots are, the greater their oil content is. For instance, 375 kilograms of buried roots that had aged approximately 10 years yielded 54 to 72 liters; roots buried for 2–3 years yielded 45 liters."[53]

To Himmler's eccentric mind this news was a godsend, considering that our production of plane-engine fuel was almost at a standstill. On January 9, 1945, he had Dr. Brandt write to Privy Councillor Wagner in his capacity as Standartenführer: "Would it not be possible to ask Ambassador Oshima whether the Japanese would be willing to give us more detailed information about obtaining the oil and the processing thereof? The SS Reichsführer would be very interested in this."[54]

A few days earlier, on January 5, 1945, before this inquiry was made, SS Obersturmführer Lipinsky was dispatched to Himmler from his SS armored division.[55] On January 18 Himmler spoke to Lipinsky "about his special assignment, the extraction of gasoline from roots." Pohl was instantly informed that Lipinsky would report to him after leaving his division. "The SS Reichsführer asks you then to discuss the necessary particulars with SS Obersturmführer Lipinsky and to support him in every possible way."[56] At the same time, Dr. Brandt informed the SS Command Headquarters that Himmler had "given Lipinsky a special assignment in his area of chemical expertise," and for this reason he had had him transferred for the time being to the SS Economic Administrative Headquarters.[57]

Pohl was more circumspect than his superior. On January 23, 1945, he wrote to Brandt in order to let Himmler know: "According to our information, Japanese fir trees contain a great deal more oil than our German ones; and to all appearances, this oil quantity is increased by decomposition when the roots are aged by being buried in the ground. This burial in the ground is a well-known manufacturing technique in Japan. Thus swords that are meant to be particularly sharp are wrapped in straw and then buried in the ground or under horse manure; and the same method is used to transform soy mush that has been buried in the ground into the soy sauce that is part of the Japanese daily diet. For the indicated reasons, I believe that it is not possible for us to produce large amounts of fir oil for gasoline, especially since the fir roots, which are prepared in some probably secret way, have to age in the ground *for several years*."[58]

In a reply from Himmler's "Personal Staff," Pohl was to be told that in the Reichsführer's opinion, "SS Hauptsturmführer Lipinsky would, under the circumstances, be more effective in the armed forces at this moment than in carrying out this research assignment, the results of which cannot be achieved quickly. I have therefore seen to it that the transfer of SS Hauptsturmführer Dr. Lipinsky to the SS Economic Administration Headquarters has been rescinded."[59] This letter was evidently not dispatched; the text was crossed out, the date is missing, and no copy of the letter exists.

Plainly, Himmler kept pursuing his false hopes. On February 1, 1945, Lipinsky informed the head of the Personal Staff: "I have taken on two scientific researchers for the research assignment. They are Dr. Hans Brückner [an engineer], now at the Chemical Physical Experimentation Institute of the Navy, and Dr. Horst Luther [an engineer] of the Reich

University of Posen, Institute for Inorganic Chemistry and Chemical Technology. Both gentlemen have obtained their positions with the help of Professor Osenberg. The release of Dr. Luther should not pose any problems, since his boss, Professor Kröger, has consented willy-nilly. In regard to Dr. Brückner, the Reichsführer will probably have to intercede, as has been discussed. I can not speak to Obergruppenführer Pohl until February 3 because he is now on a business trip. At the orders of Obergruppenführer Gutberlet, I can no longer go to my division. I have to be processed out officially."[60]

Himmler's undashed hopes can be gleaned from a telegram to Lipinsky of January 28, 1945: "The SS Reichsführer has promoted you to SS Hauptsturmführer in the reserve of the Waffen-SS, effective as of 1/30/45. Congratulations."[61]

A few months earlier, Himmler had been hot on the trail of new explosives. On June 22, 1944, he had announced "that with the progress of technology, explosives are suddenly emerging whose speed and effect overshadow the newest explosives of our retaliatory weapons."[62] In my ministry, we had long since come to realize that an atomic bomb (that was the only thing he could have meant) could not be produced before the winter of 1945, when, as we calculated, our entire armaments production would reach a standstill because all our chromium reserves would be used up.[63]

Himmler was reticent in the area of atomic research. Nevertheless, he rebuked me for neglecting it, precisely because of the consequences of nuclear fission. Himmler's letter is not extant. But my reply shows that I was forced to defend myself. On September 23, 1944, "in order to prevent misunderstandings," I informed Himmler of the following: "There can be no doubt that research must go on even in wartime, and indeed very intensively. It would certainly be most agreeable if we could give research complete freedom and be satisfied with granting it the stimuli that promise to be of the greatest use for the war effort. However, we cannot proceed in this way, as shown by the fact that our foundation in research, exactly as in development, is far smaller than that of our enemy. We can achieve results that would be of essential importance to our war effort and that would promise a lead over the enemy if we carefully weigh the deployment of energy and means in both development and research, and if we form points of main effort for concentrating our strength. But then it would be necessary to have a clear picture of what kind of research is being done and what could be attained with the work that is being pursued or planned. On the basis of this picture, we would then have to limit or even halt the allocation of assistance to those projects for which the necessary capacity is lacking, albeit without imperiling of the central tasks. . . . It goes without saying that in the approval of research projects, we must follow different principles than in development, because goals and prospects of research projects cannot be evaluated as accurately as the goals and prospects of development projects. Ultimately, however, the main issue in research is that projects advantageous to the war effort should be given preference, while we hold back those projects that challenge or hinder the concentrated advancement of the important projects."[64]

After receiving Himmler's letter, I had instantly communicated my opinions to Goering in his capacity as chairman of the Reich Research Council, for, as I said, these were "fundamental reflections on the theme of the control of research."[65]

At the start of the final year of the war, however, the question of missed opportunities resurfaced. Ohlendorf interfered to a huge extent with atomic research in a letter of January 25, 1945. He accused me of neglecting a discipline that had been labeled "Jewish science" for many years, and he rebuked me for not paying the necessary attention to atomic research. He insisted that a building slated for atomic research be erected despite the desperate state of the war. Relatively cool, I replied that "the present stage of the war absolutely [will not permit] the commencement of construction project SH 220 despite all encouragement of nuclear physics. You know that I was personally interested in nuclear research and that I have granted it all possible support. For this reason, may I ask you to have Professor Gerlach of the nuclear physics section of the Reich Research Council apply to me again in about three months. I will then try to help again."[66]

The downright grotesque part of this correspondence was that Professor Gerlach was also my deputy for nuclear physics, so that I was asking Ohlendorf to have Gerlach apply to me, his superior. I did this only to avoid provoking Ohlendorf, who was head of the Security Police and the Security Service. As a precaution, I had already written to Professor Gerlach on December 19, 1944: "Because of urgent tasks, I am unable to come into personal contact with you and your work. However, I place extraordinary value on research in the field of nuclear physics and I am following your work with great expectations. . . . You can always count on my support to overcome difficulties inhibiting your projects. Despite the extraordinary demands made on all strength for the armaments industry, the relatively small resources for your work can always be obtained.

Please address yourself to me or Dr. Goerner as before, if you need my help."[67]

All these orders and arrogance on the part of the SS and especially Himmler reduced our capacity for research and development and created uncertainty about the command channels and areas of responsibility. (See Appendix 13.)

Chapter 12
Infiltration by Special Deputies

Oₙₑ OF THE TIME-TESTED METHODS in every bureaucracy is infiltration by means of special assignments. Thus, on November 28, 1942, Pohl contacted an important leader in the construction industry. Because of the new course of "the self-responsibility of industry," the Reich Ministry of Economy had set up "Reich Associations" to guide production and approve new factories or expansions of existing ones within their production area.

He had heard, Pohl wrote to Himmler on November 28, 1942, that they were planning to create a "Reich Association" very soon for economic control of the "stone and earth" domain, i.e., the production of building materials. "The state is thus relieving itself of immediate administrative work," Pohl went on in his letter to Himmler. "At the head of the Reich Association, there is a responsible entrepreneur, who enjoys the trust of the Party and the state and is endowed with very far-reaching powers. In the 'stone and earth' domain, there is no such Reich Association as yet. But we have to reckon with private entrepreneurs taking over the leadership of a Reich Association for Stone and Earth in the near future. This would also cover our factories" in the stone quarries and brick manufacturing "and practically place them under someone else's control." Pohl said that he had therefore contacted SS Brigade Commander Dr. Schieber (at the time a confidential agent of the SS) and discussed "whether it would not be expedient for us to seize the initiative and, with the endorsement of Reich Minister Speer himself, begin to establish a Reich Associa-

[153]

tion and take over its leadership. SS Brigade Commander Dr. Schieber is quite in favor of this possibility, even though, of course, we will have to overcome considerable resistance both in Speer's ministry and in private industry. Nevertheless, I consider it necessary to initiate the required measures. . . . As in other special areas, the leadership of the Reich Agency for Stone and Earth, now run by State Secretary Schulze-Fielitz, would have to be linked in a personal union with the leadership of the Reich Association for Stone and Earth, since the functions of the Reich Agency would have to be transferred to the Reich Association. May I ask you to consent to my pursuing the matter in the above terms and getting the Reich Ministry of Economy to transfer the control of the Reich Association and the Reich Agency for Stone and Earth to me."[1]

Himmler quickly sent Pohl a positive reply. For in contrast to his hesitation in response to Ohlendorf's plans for infiltrating the Ministry of Economy, this would be the substructure for his diverse plans in postwar construction. Naturally, the opposite of what Pohl had stressed in his letter was also true: If the Reich Association were taken over by the SS as planned, then the factories in the stone quarries and the brick industry would be practically under the control of the SS. "The SS Reichsführer is very much in agreement," he informed Pohl, "with your initiating the establishment of a Reich Association and taking over its leadership. The SS Reichsführer felt that you should make sure, above all, of support from the Reich Ministry of Economy."[2]

However, there was no need to call for an agreement with Funk. To add emphasis to his request, Pohl had addressed an unusually sharp letter to the Minister of Economy at the same time that he sent his letter to Himmler. "The economic group for stone and earth[3] recently formed committees for the East to discuss and debate the question of starting and transferring the individual factories for stone and earth in the new Eastern territories. In their formation, these committees have ignored both me and the firms that I have founded and supervise: Deutsche Erd- und Steinwerke, G.M.B.H., and Ostdeutsche Baustoffwerke G.M.B.H. [German Earth and Stone Works, Ltd., and East German Building Material Works, Ltd.]. I find this even more peculiar since these factories I manage are not only the largest enterprises and hence pay the largest contributions in their branch of industry, but also because I believe that my work as acting administrator of over three hundred fifty brick plants, tile factories, fireclay factories, and other manufacturing plants for construction materials in the newly won territory in the East has demonstrated that I with my staffers am capable of running factories in the particularly difficult conditions of Eastern Europe and thereby being of use to industry. I would be very grateful to you, dear Herr Reich Minister, if you could see to it that the Eastern Committees of the Economic Group for Stone and Earth were to have the managers of my enterprises participate in accordance with the great importance of their companies."[4]

The letter makes clear that the SS had long since taken over the acting administration of over three hundred fifty brick plants and other factories for construction materials in occupied Russia and had prepared to take them over after the war. They had done so even despite the fact that after the first three months of tempestuous advances in Russia, Rosenberg of the Ministry for Eastern Europe had agreed to the SS running only sixty factories in the occupied territory. One may assume that a similar number of factories in the construction materials industry were already being run by the SS in occupied Poland as well.

There seems to have been some resistance. For three months later, on February 17, 1943, Himmler had to telephone SS Brigade Commander Klopfer (Bormann's state secretary) about the matter. However, Himmler and Pohl did not succeed in accomplishing their goals. The head of the Reich Agency remained the responsible representative of the stone industry.

While Ohlendorf was still held back by Himmler, Pohl, despite Ohlendorf's failure, tried to obtain the leading position in the Reich Food Ministry. Pohl's ambition seems to have been unbounded in these months of the second Russian war winter. Just four days after his letter to Himmler of December 2, 1942, in which he had requested control of the production of construction materials, he sent a new letter to Himmler, pointing out: "As is the case in the armaments industry, the organization and leadership of the food industry, as the war continues, are becoming more and more obscure—to the detriment of supplying high-quality foodstuffs to the people. Whereas in the armaments industry, Reich Minister Speer has clearly worked out the leadership line and the organization of industry has been considerably simplified by the reintroduction of self-responsibility, with its powers delimited, this is not the case in the food industry. Indeed, only very few clear-sighted men have so far realized the necessity of clearing up the completely entangled conditions. At this time, the following offices are operating in the area of the food industry: next to the Reich Ministry of Food and Agriculture and the Ministry of Economy, in the occupied territories, the agencies of Operation East, the Food and Agriculture departments of the various civilian administrations, the various Reich agencies and main associations (e.g., cattle, eggs, grain, gardening). . . . Then there is the Food Administration in the Four-Year-Plan Agency. The Supreme Command of the Wehrmacht, for the sake of supplying army sections everywhere, is creating or stimulating its own facilities. In the civilian sector, for instance, the Reich Health Agency and the German Labor Front are endeavoring to put up factories in order to open up new sources of scarce foodstuffs for the people under their aegis."

After four pages of explanations, which actually offer a good picture of the complicated management tasks of the diverse competing agencies, Pohl concluded: "The above inevitably points out that, similar to the armaments industry or labor deployment, centralizaiton must be created in the food industry too. This centralization can be accomplished only by a plenipotentiary, equipped with all necessary powers and bearing the title of *General Manager for the Alimentation of the German People*." Enclosed with the letter was a work plan for this "general manager": ten pages exhaustively outlining Pohl's future powers.[5]

In his letter to Himmler, Pohl emphasized: "In case you ever decide to discuss this issue with the Führer, I would like to point out that the assignment of an SS commander appears highly expedient because then the entire organization of the SS and the police will offer the best guarantee for the most effective realization. . . . I am also honest enough to admit that this task would be eminently attractive to me. I would also be prepared to devote myself to it with all my strength while retaining all my present duties."[6]

Himmler, however, did not feel like releasing Pohl for this task: "The idea of a general manager is very tempting, but I would nevertheless prefer to reject it." We "would be involving ourselves in an area that does not actually concern us in its gigantic responsibility. We must guard against this, for the potential of what we can accomplish as the overall SS and police force is already amply realized. Furthermore, I believe that the war will make other demands on us in other areas, and we will have to strive to meet these demands. I also believe that it would be dangerous for the overall development of the SS if now, in its present dynamics, it were to move too far from its fundamental line and go along paths that are ultimately peripheral. The truth is that by operating effectively in our own sector, we can set a good and active example everywhere. That is what I see as our mission: to be a vanguard everywhere here. But, in my estimate, we should not be anything more."[7]

Himmler did not act with such restraint when dealing with the goals of his construction and industrial empire, as shone by his positive response to Pohl when the latter wanted to place the Reich Agency and Reich Association for Stone and Earth under the SS.

"The potential of what we can accomplish . . . is already amply realized," Himmler correctly said when rejecting Pohl's idea. He thus contrasted with his ambitious top leaders in the SS, who had boasted that they could solve the most difficult development problems of air armaments by employing specially authorized delegates from their own ranks. It was only a seeming contrast, however, for Himmler had tried repeatedly to interfere in areas outside his jurisdiction.

In February 1943 Hitler had established a three-man committee made up of Bormann, Lammers, and Keitel to check ways of releasing industrial manpower that could replace the armaments workers entering the Wehrmacht.[8] The system always responded very slowly to emergencies. And typically, this edict was supplemented nine months later, on November 27, 1943, with a further order of Hitler's to simplify the Wehrmacht administration. Again, another three months went by until, on March 24, 1944, Hitler's representative, Artillery General Ziegler, began to build up his organization. Certainly the army was not interested in hurrying with measures that were bound to cause difficulties, friction, and unforeseeable annoyances within the Wehrmacht administration. I had been well acquainted with General Ziegler for a long time. He often told me about his army days in the Weimar Republic when, acting on behalf of the Reichswehr, he had negotiated the military budget with the parliamentary parties and had had to deal with complaints and attacks. Since Ziegler had conducted this delicate business for many years, he must have known how to handle a difficult task with political tact.

Hitler's order foresaw the formation of six commissions. SS Squad Commander Lörner was to chair the first one, which was supposed to simplify provisions. Lörner was also in charge of food and clothing for concentration camps, which was certainly no recommendation for his assignment, since the chaos, misplannings, disorder, and corruption in his own operations areas were indescribable. The Buildings Commission was to be chaired by Paul Pleiger, head of the Hermann Goering Works. His deputy was Hans Kammler—indicating how important the position of this head of all SS construction affairs had become. The sixth and most important commission, for simplifying administration, was to be run by General Manager Röhnert and SS Squad Commander Frank.

In a letter to Himmler (which Himmler honored with the handwritten note "Very interesting"), Pohl regretted "the formation of six commissions. Nor do I set great hopes on the appointment of famous industrial leaders to chair these commissions. I had occasion to speak with Röhnert and Pleiger. Both realize the difficulties of the task and are pursuing it very earnestly. But I doubt whether they are tackling it correctly. If it is believed that one could reform the administrative organization primarily by reducing personnel, then this is a fundamental error. One has to change the system, i.e., make things in the administration simpler; people will then drop off on their own because they will have no more work. However, things in administration can be done only by the old, trained administration man who is *inspired with revolutionary drive*. Frank, for instance, is that type of man."

It is obvious that Pohl is referring to Frank without expressly naming his candidate when he goes on: "If they had therefore appointed a completely experienced, but absolutely resolute administration man as simplification *dictator*, then they might achieve a greater success than with these six commissions, which employ over one hundred people [underlined twice in the original]. This, Reichsführer, is my personal opinion."

Here, Himmler scrawled his note across the letter in inch-high Gothic script: "I think so too." Pohl concluded his letter: "I believe that this action will not turn out any differently from the previous ones under General von Unruh, namely like the Hornberg shooting. And this is highly regrettable."[9]

The sixth commission, which was supposed to simplify administration, was the first to convene. In his introductory words, Ziegler, the old fox, suggested "the creation of a 'Ministry of War,' which will be small but endowed with the highest powers. It should uniformly align the administration of all parts of the Wehrmacht, i.e., the army, the air force, the navy, the Waffen-SS, the police, the Todt organization, and the Reich Labor Force, together with their staffs. The realization of this organization is necessary all the way down to the defense groups and garrison administrations. This is the only way that, in my opinion, I can report a true success in simplification to the Führer."[10] Ziegler had thus reached into the drawer to pull out the still-latent call of the army for a uniform Wehrmacht organization, which was also in the simplification program of the Goerdeler administration. Naturally, this idea, although thoroughly reasonable, was thwarted by a distrustful Hitler's efforts toward division. On April 24, 1944, Pohl very proudly informed Himmler that it was "not saying too much when I claim that we have carried off a great success, and primarily by means of Frank's fearless and courageous stance."[11] Frank's enclosed report said that he had tried to make clear in "a one-hour off-the-cuff speech . . . that the greatest difficulties and nearly all setbacks are due to the concatenation with the army administration." Hence, in Pohl's opinion, the SS administration, which was viewed as exemplary, was not to be reformed so much as the army administration, which was made a scapegoat. Its inadequacies were listed "very freely and openly" by Frank, although surely not to the delight of the army generals who were present: "The flood of red tape, the complete confusion of the most important of all war laws, the Operation Wehrmacht Entitlement Act, which had originally been so clear and simple, but had long since been tattered to obscurity by two thousand edicts. The abominable state of affairs caused by all the forms to be filled out, the displacement of clerks, the technical and material impossibility of equipping a newly formed unit with all the valid regulations, the exaggerated principle of checking and policing, the long-strangled willingness of garrison and unit paymasters to carry out their responsibilities, the mania for having every bit of trivia decided on from above, as well as the years of delay in centralizing pay." Ziegler, "to my satisfaction emphatically understood my statements. General Ziegler particularly said: 'It is fully clear to me that, as Herr Frank has correctly said, we must take completely new paths. I believe that I am one with the chairman when I say that the only person who can head this staff is Squad Commander Frank. After his statements, I realize that the work of the commission will have unforeseeable effects and repercussions on the general administration of the state in terms of a complete reorganization of public administration even after the war.' General Ziegler then criticized the departmental complexes of the ministerial authorities." He was quite aware that it was tactically intelligent to have an SS commander for this almost insoluble task; the man would then be responsible in Hitler's eyes for the failure of his assignment. "Thus, I have become the man responsible for the attempt to reorganize the administration of the German Wehrmacht," Frank continues. "The findings of my staff will be presented to the Führer by General Ziegler as soon as possible. If they are approved, then a man is to be assigned the task of carrying out, adding to, and supervising these proposals. In other words, he will practically be vested with the highest powers as head of the Wehrmacht administration."[12]

Pohl shared Frank's satisfaction at his presumed success. "This is how the matter stands," he informed Himmler when sending him Frank's report. "We, the SS, are at the helm in this commission. Frank spoke so impressively," Pohl went on, "that Ziegler more or less gave him the command over the entire association. . . . This may be a complete reversal of the method planned initially by Special Agent Artillery General Ziegler. But it is in keeping with what I described in my above letter [April 13, 1944] as a prerequisite if this most important reform of the army in the past hundred years is not to turn out like the Horberg shooting. The responsibility we thereby assume is enormous. But it is borne gladly and cheerfully. We know what we owe you and the SS."[13]

However, it seemed as if Himmler caught Ziegler's intentions faster than Frank or Pohl. On May 15 he wrote back that he was delighted at Frank's report: "The task lying ahead for you and Frank is very great." Apostrophizing Pohl as responsible for the mission, he simultaneously establishes that in his opinion it is not, as General Ziegler plans, an assignment bound to Frank personally. This is a task for the SS, so Pohl as the superior shares responsibility for success, needless to say. Not only was he skeptical about success ("I hope you manage to achieve at least some of the goals"); he also had his qualms about measures going too far: "Regarding the unified Wehrmacht administration, please let me know whether everything should be done jointly for the Wehrmacht and the SS. I do not consider a uniform administration corps proper. The possibilities for blaming failures on us would be too great in many cases. I have no objections whatsoever to making the regulations uniform and reducing them to a common denominator for the Waffen SS, the Wehrmacht, navy, air force, etc. But the implementation must be separate,[14] whereby, of course, an agreement can be reached in places where something can be done jointly." With unusual warmth, Himmler honored Pohl as "my dear Pohl" and signed the letter "Yours truly, H. Himmler."[15] But the documents do not reveal the further course of this enterprise, which began with so many advance laurels and was promptly sabotaged by Himmler himself. All that is certain is that the Wehrmacht administration was never even remotely unified. This egotism, understandable from the viewpoint of the SS, shows once again that these were naked power struggles when, for instance, the SS insisted on having Himmler as supreme commissioner of air armaments, with SS assistant commissioners. A few months later, when Himmler was personally appointed Hitler's deputy for the Wehrmacht reform, he displayed his inability to wipe out abuses in his own absolute power realm, even though he and his staffers could so clearly formulate their sharp and facile criticisms of failures in other agencies.

As is noted in my ministry's chronicle on August 23, 1944, General Ziegler had "little luck with the Führer's assignment to unify and simplify the administrative offices of the Wehrmacht and the military units. As simple as it may be to set up a new agency next to existing ones, it is hopeless to move three officials or administrators from three chairs to two or even one. General Ziegler complained to the minister on August 23. He also tried to reproach the minister that no military or ministerial agency can tell him what to do. The minister had to hint that it was his own fault if he does not have enough authority for the task the Führer assigned him. Since a return to the front troops is no longer open to Ziegler, it looks as if the great host of unemployed generals will soon expand by one more."[16]

My own ministry was scoured by the SS for possible thinning out of personnel. In June 1943, when the "Protective Corps of the Todt Organization" consisted of one hundred Germans from the Reich and eight hundred from the outside, these nine hundred were conscripted for service in the Waffen SS. I protested to Himmler: "Sufficient protection of our construction sites for the Todt Organization is the unconditional and necessary prerequisite for carrying out the missions that the Führer has assigned me." In the Balkans, urgently needed raw materials like copper, chromium, bauxite, molybdenum, and asbestos were being mined, and I reminded Himmler of the partisan threat to those areas.[17] Curt and unwilling to discuss the matter, Himmler declared that the men in question could not be exempted: "If these men do not wish to be regarded as deserters as of August 1, they must be taken over into the Waffen SS. The head of SS Headquarters, SS Squad Commander Berger, will take the younger men from the Protective Corps in exchange for older men to replenish it. You will certainly concur with this solution."[18]

It was surely no coincidence that Himmler's staff took up the general issue of the protective commandos one week later. These commandos were a stumbling block if for no other reason than because of the police nature of their missions. In mid-June 1943, an SS standard commander named Rhode turned to SS Standard Commander With, who, as representative of the SS, was "on the staff of the Führer's special deputy Infantry General von Unruh." The latter, in turn, assigned the task of finding human reserves in the Wehrmacht and the administration, thus had the same mission as General Ziegler. A fine example of parallelism in Führer assignments.

However, With shielded the Protective Corps of the Todt Organization, which he described as necessary for guarding the large Todt Organization camps of foreign laborers and the supplies of raw materials. It had been Wehrmacht generals, he pointed out, who had set up this protective corps, filling it with Frenchmen who had fought in the French Volunteer Legion in Russia. Thus, he said, it was not a police organization, which, naturally, could not please Himmler. "I believe," With continued, "that the SS Reichsführer has not been quite correctly informed in this matter. If we did not approve of these self-help measures of the Todt Organization, then we would be forced to make the Reich German police available to a considerable degree. Given the well-known surrogate situation of the headquarters of the regular police, such an action would, in my opinion, encounter difficulties."[19]

The entire case was an example of the efforts made to provide Hitler with impressive news of successes. If the Protective Corps of the Todt Organization had been absorbed into the Waffen SS, then it would naturally have continued to perform the same duties. Needless to say, Himmler would not have waited to impress Hitler by presenting these several thousand men as an economy measure in the Todt Organization.

One day later, With penned a detailed report to Himmler about the state of construction of the Atlantic Line; his report, incidentally, was objective and even positive. But it was characteristic of the situation that Himmler, without my knowledge, took in such reports about matters beyond his responsibility or control.

A few weeks later, a further thrust was directed against leading employees of the Todt Organization who had honorary SS ranks and were thus registered with the Command Office of the General SS instead of with SS Headquarters. They added up to 77 men in the central office of the Todt Organization, plus construction experts in charge of aboveground building.[20] Naturally, Himmler was interested only in those employees under forty; and he requested reports on their degree of fitness and training.[21] The upshot of the investigation was that of the 77 alleged draft dodgers in the Todt Organization, only 18 were classified as fit for active duty.[22] From a distance of nearly forty years, the true issue has long since become meaningless. But the most striking thing in these files is the meticulous way that the highest officials dealt with such totally insignificant matters.

At the dramatic climax of the war, which has long since assumed a somber course, Himmler (the chief of police, the minister of the interior, and the SS Reichsführer) is still perusing the personal documents of 18 members of the Todt Organization. Finally, after twelve weeks, in February 1944, "the SS Reichsführer has gone through the personal documents," as the SS Headquarters reported. Himmler responded mildly, for meanwhile I had dropped out because of illness, and he saw sure ways of directly involving Xaver Dorsch, the head of the central office of the Todt Organization. This investigation of soldiers who had eluded the SS had stretched over the considerable time of six and a half months. And the conclusion was: "The SS Reichsführer said that we must contact the Todt Organization and make it realize that it cannot be in the interest of these men to keep them classified as exempt, especially since 18 of them are fit for active duty."[23] It is obvious that if these 18 top employees had been drafted as simple soldiers, they would scarcely have had the same importance for the war effort as at their jobs in the Todt Organization.

General Ziegler had failed. The problem of simplifying the administration in order to get more soldiers was never resolved. A snort time later, someone thought of conscripting younger men from the ranks of experts and specialists in the armaments industry, which would have meant extraordinary difficulties for development and production. I decided to tackle the problem at its root. On July 20, 1944, the day of the anti-Hitler putsch, I sent Hitler a long memorandum, on which I had worked for some time with General Ziegler's support. My maneuver was to get Himmler to take over the task that General von Unruh and General Ziegler had been unable to complete in over a year. My memorandum construed the task more widely than it had previously been defined. I wanted not only to simplify the administration but also to clear up the discrepancy between the active troops and the services behind the lines. General Ziegler had contributed valuable material on statistical data and other facts for my memorandum. There were 2.3 million soldiers fighting in 210 divisions as opposed to 10.5 million who had been drafted into the Wehrmacht. Aside from this disproportion, I suggested solving the special problem of saving manpower by reducing excessive demands on the supplies personnel for these 210 divisions. I included Ziegler's original demand to unite the new independent administrative branches and subdivisions of the three Wehrmacht forces as well as the Waffen SS, the Todt Organization, and the Reich Labor Service. I had also arranged with Ziegler to try and persuade Hitler to assign this task to a man "who would pay no heed to the prestige of the organizations involved. . . . The supreme command of the Wehrmacht does not have the clout to carry out such measures harshly enough. It is therefore necessary, for determining who are combat-fit men in the Wehrmacht and industry, to find a person who is vested with all powers and who—although in concord with the Wehrmacht branches—will ultimately have the possibility to bring about the necessary decisions against these Wehrmacht branches too from you, my Führer."[24] In the given state of things, this person could only be Himmler.

Before July 20, 1944, Himmler enjoyed remarkable prestige with leading military men because he was one of the few critical observers of the situation. It was quite obvious that at times he was rather open about stating his concern that Hitler was not properly evaluating the military situation. In the summer of 1943, I had conspired with Kurt Zeitzler and Heinz Guderian to convince Hitler that he should yield the supreme command of the army to one of these two colonel generals.[25] To my astonishment, Guderian had also mentioned Himmler. I had previously assumed that the army leaders regarded Himmler as their most powerful rival. Thus, in my venture, I was combining tactics and real hopes in Himmler's energy.[26] At that time, I did not yet know about the intrigues against me that were piling up in Himmler's files.

On August 2, 1944, Hitler decreed that Himmler should take over this task. Likewise, a memorandum of mine to Hitler had preceded Goebbels's appointment as "Reich Representative for Total War." I dispatched both memorandums, fully ignorant of the change soon to come on the scene. For just a few days later, to my surprise, my name appeared on the cabinet list of a Goerdeler government and permanently weakened my position, even though I knew nothing about the nomination. I was soon to learn that I had strengthened my rivals.[27]

Goebbels, the new Reich Representative for Total War, appointed his second in command, State Secretary and SS Squad Commander Werner Naumann, his deputy for the new position. Roughly four weeks to the day after my memorandum, Berger, head of SS headquarters, submitted a large-scale plan to Naumann for organizing the work of this Reich Representative for Total War.

A truly new order would be as follows:

1. The Reich Minister for Armaments and War Production will set up the production program.
2. The working groups and committees will establish the machine capacity of the factory.

3. The general representative for labor will construct the production structure of the factories.
4. The central registration office for all people in Germany who are able-
   bodied and subject to military service will release the volunteers for the
   front; it will receive its orders from the planning division of the Reich
   Representative for Total War.[28]

Examined more closely, point 3 meant that I would be deprived of
responsibility for factory processes, the most important problem in an
armaments industry.

Berger's plan provided for an "Agency for Central Management of
People," to be headed by the SS Reichsführer or a representative appointed
by him. This agency "will work closely with the Führer's representative,
Reich Minister Dr. Goebbels. The Central Agency will comprise:

three representatives of the previous substitute defense office of the
  Supreme Command of the Wehrmacht (army, navy, air force);
one representative of the Waffen SS;
one representative of the headquarters of the regular police;
one representative of the Reich Labor Service;
one representative of the Todt Organization and Army Ordinance office;
one representative of transportation;
one representative of the Ministry of Labor;
one representative of the Reich Youth Leadership;
one representative of the NSKK.

This list did not include a representative from the Armaments Ministry,
even in a subordinate position. Himmler had his chief of staff inform
Berger that he had "read the suggestion and written on it by hand: 'Very
good.' "[29]

Berger, in the same letter to Goebbels's state secretary, used the most
naive arguments to explain why my principle of self-responsibility had
collapsed.[30] A factory manager simply reflected that a doubling of output
requires a doubling of manpower; and the German entrepreneur saw the
unique chance "of acquiring a huge factory at the expense of the Reich.
He was most carefully taken care of [in this endeavor] by a series of
agencies of the [Ministry of Armaments]. Every wish of his was fulfilled;
he felt as if he were in a fairy tale."[31]

In reality, however, the very opposite was the case. According to the
statistical abstract of the Ministry of Armaments, the number of workers
directly employed in armaments had risen from 5,385,000 domestic and

foreign workers and POWs to 6,097,000 from July 1943 to July 1944. This rise of 712,000 represented 11.6 percent.[32] In contrast, the armaments index during the same period had zoomed from 229 to 322,[33] i.e., 40.6 percent. Production almost quadrupled for every additional worker, which was naturally due to the efforts of entrepreneurs in regard to greater efficiency, conveyor-belt manufacturing, and modern machines.[34]

In his memorandum, Berger had pilloried not only the management of the armaments industry in general, but especially the commissions of my deputies, who had been sent by the Armaments Ministry directly into the defense plants. "They tried to clear up the facts of factory demands by inspecting the factories. However, the number of members kept growing steadily, so that visits by commissions of ten to twenty members were no rarity. . . . These constant inspections and visits make a very bad impression on the employees and contribute nothing to raising or increasing their morale."[35]

In a certain sense Berger's criticism was valid, but it came five months too late. In March I had already sent out an edict to all agency heads in the Armaments Ministry; I objected that "recently, a bad habit has developed of forming special huge and mostly overstaffed committees, commissions, etc., for investigating the most diverse matters and establishing facts *in situ*. . . . I therefore prohibit any further participation by members of my agencies in such superfluous commissions, and I demand that you resolutely reject such nonsense and put an end to it in your departments."[36]

When Himmler was asked to reorganize the Wehrmacht organization, one of his duties was "to investigate and simplify the entire organizational and administrative foundations of the army, the Waffen-SS, the police, and the Todt Organization for the purpose of economizing on manpower."[37] But Himmler simply passed on his assignment; three days later, he stated that SS Obergruppenführer and General of the Waffen-SS Oswald Pohl had been charged with carrying out this assignment.[38] Shortly before the end of the war, he was finally ready. On January 29, 1945, Pohl handed in his proposal for cutting manpower in the Todt Organization. A long, well-thought-out paper illuminated the system of this organization, which had been in charge of all construction projects since May 1944. Pohl had drafted a moderate letter from Himmler to me: "On the basis of the Führer's order of August 2, 1944, which you are familiar with, I am now investigating the organizational and administrative foundations of the Todt Organization with your consent; my goal is to suggest measures for releasing greater numbers of men for the front. The first completed work is now before you and deserves serious consideration, especially because a reduction of some 20,000 men is considered possible. Before I approach the implementation of this proposal on the basis of the Führer's order of 8/2/44, may I ask you for your opinion."[39]

This threat of an executive action is a good example of how commissioners, deputies, and other representatives were repeatedly used for outside interference in existing organizations. Pohl's draft remained idle. Himmler never wrote me a letter. And everything was soon obsolete anyhow.

Today, I can read in my senseless reactions of that time my awareness of a growing impotence during the last few months of the war. On January 8, 1945, I wrote Himmler an indignant and insulting letter, which, retrospectively, merely shows me the extent of my helplessness.

Himmler had once again gotten Hitler to sign one of the feared edicts that were not first discussed with the people affected. Lammers had often urged Hitler to sign such edicts only after he, the "Reich Notary," as I called him, had obtained the consent or noted the reservations of all the people involved in order to let Hitler have the final decision in any conflicts. But Hitler had always been averse to such administrative methods, and also too impulsive and too convinced of his own infallibility to submit to such limitations.

Thus, on December 28, 1944, at Himmler's suggestion Hitler had assigned a new task to the same SS Obergruppenführer Frank who was supposed to reorganize the Wehrmacht administration. Frank was now told to bring about an increase in the use of "machine reporting," and to submit the appropriate orders to Hitler. My ministry had recognized the importance of the Hollerith system many years earlier and had obtained and stored significant data in order to obtain information quickly in countless intricate armaments problems. We also had a comprehensive personnel file with immunerable evaluations. The importance of such data collections as a control instrument need not be emphasized in the decade of computer processing. It was certainly evident to Himmler too.

I therefore wrote to Himmler on January 8, 1945, that when I had taken over the Ministry of Defense from the Supreme Command of the Wehrmacht, I had also fully taken over the machine-reporting system under Lieutenant Colonel von Passow. "It is incontestably established that the entire machine-reporting system is anchored in my ministry, *in terms of both the personnel and the material.* I am the main assigner since the machine-reporting system is constantly employed by me for swift reporting of the entire armaments industry and war production. Doubtlessly, the head of my agency for machine reporting, Lieutenant Colonel von Passow, did not represent my interests quite irreproachably at the negotiations with SS Obergruppenführer Frank, as I can gather from a note written by von Passow." Presumably, von Passow had been intimidated by the SS power as personified in a squad commander. "I have therefore ordered von Passow," my letter to Himmler went on, "to avoid any further negotiations with SS Obergruppenführer Frank. In case negotiations are necessary, SS Obergruppenführer Frank is to address the head of the central office, Dr. Theodor Hupfauer, the superior of Lieutenant Colonel von Passow. I would be grateful to you if you would wait with the edict, which was erroneously submitted to the Führer, and put it into force only when an agreement on all issues has been reached between SS Obergruppenführer Frank and Dr. Hupfauer."[40]

Himmler's response was one of irritation: "I would like to say the following in all bluntness: I believe that it suffices that [the machine-reporting system] was taken away from me as commander in chief of the reserve army and head of army armaments[41] not entirely without the action of your ministry. I cannot possibly be prohibited in any way from introducing into the reserve army the machine-reporting system (which I introduced into the SS long ago) and from centralizing the machines existing there. I consider it out of the question that I may be forced by your objection to hand over this purely internal measure in the reserve army to the Ministry of Armaments and Munitions and thereby resort to antediluvian earlier methods for my leadership tasks."[42]

I submitted to the given situation: "Of course, there is no reason for removing from my ministry the machine-reporting system, which I have previously employed almost exclusively with assignments and which I also urgently need in the future for armaments tasks." My deputy Hupfauer, I said, had come to an agreement with Frank by formally recognizing Frank's authority as provided in Hitler's edict.[43] The final skirmish. Driven into a corner, I was virtually fighting with my back against the wall.

But just a few days later, a conversation between Saur and Hitler brought a 180-degree turn. Saur, an office head in my ministry, deployed his overwhelming influence with Hitler. To my astonishment, he succeeded in convincing Hitler that he would have more and more difficulties with Himmler in his capacity as commander in chief of the reserve army. Hitler, who had long since become unpredictable, then saw to it that the Army Ordnance Office would instantly pass from Himmler's control to that of

General Walter Buhle, who was head of the Army Staff in the Supreme Command of the Wehrmacht.[44] On February 1, 1945, Hitler signed the appropriate edict. To support the prestige of Himmler, who was thus losing a great portion of his responsibility as commander in chief of the reserve army, Hitler promoted him to supreme commander in chief the very same day.[45] But in practical terms this meant nothing. It was a mere change of nomenclature.

PART THREE
The Failure of the Economic Empire

Chapter 13

The Disorderly Concern

In EARLY JUNE 1944, I informed Hitler "that, needless to say, I will always support the SS Reichsführer in the expansion of his manufacturing plants; however, I would first like to establish a clear area of responsibility, for his plants must submit to the same supervision as the others involved in armaments and war production. I could not accept having a Wehrmacht branch [which obviously meant the Waffen SS] taking a self-sufficient route while I have devoted two years of great efforts to unifying the armaments of the other three branches of the Wehrmacht." My protocol goes on: "The Führer agreed with this opinion and is ready, if need be, to inform the SS Reichsführer of this. I have stated that I will try for the time being to clarify the matter personally with the SS Reichsführer."[1]

Roughly one week later, this meeting took place in Himmler's private villa, his headquarters near Berchtesgaden. One year later, shortly before the end of the war, Himmler suddenly told me that this villa housed his mistress and that she had given birth to a son there. Proudly, like a petty clerk, he reached into his wallet and drew out a photograph of the young, attractive woman and the child.

In June 1944 he was not as open about his private life. But he confided that his plans to build a huge industrial concern had failed only because of the inadequacy of his men. He said he intended to develop SS-owned steel production all the way to the finished product; and in a longer conversation, he expounded on his motives. He had frequently talked to the Führer, he said, about the possibility that hostility toward the SS might someday dominate German politics after Hitler's death. At this point, the SS was dependent on the financial allowance from the Reich Minister of Finances, which, of course, spelled complete dependence of the SS on the head of state. This did not matter, said Himmler, so long as the Führer was alive. However, the Führer agreed with him that it would be expedient to make the SS independent of the national budget on a long-term basis by having it construct its own factories as a financial foundation.

At the end of his disclosure, Himmler told me that he lacked a brilliant man to help him build up his SS concern. Could I recommend someone? I was somewhat embarrassed. On the one hand, I didn't care to name an industrial leader, who would be putty in Himmler's hands and turn against me. On the other hand, it was better for me to have a person of my choice in this position. I thought of Meindl, the Austrian head of the Steyr Works, whom Goering planned to make my successor anyway. However, a man that powerful would soon be a factor not to be ignored in the force-field of intrigues. So I wondered whether to suggest Hans Kehrl to Himmler. However, Kehrl would have overblown his assignment and worked toward a mammoth enterprise.

In the end, I suggested Paul Pleiger, who had built up the steel concern of the Hermann Goering Works and managed it with great energy. Pleiger was known for the courage of his convictions; he occasionally even disagreed with Hitler. He would make sure not to build up an SS concern that would compete with his own life's work. In no event would he be a spineless instrument of Himmler's. I did not foresee that Pleiger would be totally submissive a short time later, when Himmler turned on the thumbscrews in regard to petroleum drilling.

Himmler assured me that he had no intention of building up any production that would not be under my supervision. To be sure, I had occasionally had different experiences with his agencies; but I accepted his assurances as true for the time being.

The man actually responsible for these years of efforts to build up an SS industrial empire was Oswald Pohl, the head of the Economic Administrative Headquarters of the SS. In contrast to Ohlendorf, Pohl advocated self-responsibility of industry, since he considered it an effective plan. On December 2, 1942, he had written to Himmler: "In the armaments industry, Reich Minister Speer lucidly worked out the guidelines, which considerably simplified the organization of industry by reintroducing the principle of self-responsibility."[2] In this respect Ohlendorf, as a critic of self-responsibility in the Ministry of Economy, was his rival. At the Nuremberg Trial, Ohlendorf testified that he had wanted to force Pohl and the Economic Administrative Headquarters "to show the hand of the SS concern. We [Franz Hayler and Ohlendorf] told him unequivocally that we would not tolerate any further expansion of this SS concern, whether at home or abroad. In the course of this conflict, Himmler summoned me together with Hayler, the state secretary of the Ministry of Economy, to Berchtesgaden in the summer of 1944 and told us why we must not pursue these policies against his industrial activity. We refused to go along with him, but in Hungary he had created a *fait accompli* by securing the Weiss Concern through a business transaction."[3]

This event had occurred while I was convalescing in Merano after an illness of more than two months. My ministry chronicle said: "SS Obergruppenführer Kaltenbrunner has descended upon the minister for a visit, as announced, to check all security measures. The real issue, however, is the economic adviser for Hungary. The minister is discussing the matter with Dr. Schieber, Kehrl, and Rafelsberger. Liebel, General Wäger, Dr. Schieber, and Hayler are being flown to Merano on April 4 by a JU 52 to discuss the economic adviser for Hungary. The nomination is being made to the Führer through Liebel: Hasslacher as deputy for economy under the Reich deputy in Hungary."[4]

Enclosed with the letter was a draft for an authorization appointing Hasslacher, to be signed by Hitler. Himmler, Funk, and Minister of Food Ernst Backe had already agreed to this proposal, according to the letter. (See Appendix 14.)

While we were conferring, Himmler had already pulled his strings. Without informing us, he had appropriated the only important entity in the small Hungarian industry. In a memorandum, Himmler wrote:

1. The largest armaments and industrial concern in Hungary is the Manfred Weiss Concern. It belongs to the relatives of the Manfred Weiss/Korin families and is composed of Jewish and non-Jewish members.

2. If Hungary is to be economically exhausted for Germany and totally exploited in its armaments potential, it is necessary that Germany get hold of this armaments industry with all its potential as well as this concern with all its foreign-currency possibilities.

3. By means of negotiation with only this goal, which will help us win the war, the following possibility now exists:

A. The Weiss/Korin families have asked the SS Reichsführer to take over the trusteeship of the Manfred Weiss Concern, of which 55 percent of the shares are in the hands of Aryan members of the family and which can be disposed of freely.

B. The 48 members of the Weiss/Korin families are assured by the SS Reichsführer of being allowed to emigrate to Portugal or Switzerland. Of these 48, 36 are Jews, 12 are Aryans.
C. Nine members will remain here as hostages for the duration of the war.
D. The Jewish families will receive 3 million Reich marks in free foreign currency to establish an existence abroad and also as compensation for the net profits that the family will lose because of the trusteeship.
E. The trusteeship, for now, will last 25 years.[5]

Naturally, it was absurd of Himmler to claim that the transfer of the concern to the SS had for a goal only "to help us win the war." It was precisely for the sake of an orderly war economy that I had to oppose this private SS deal of Himmler's. Hitler agreed with my objection, even though the transaction was as good as concluded. But Hungarian Prime Minister Sztoja went back on his word, and before Saur could appeal to Hitler, the contract had become valid by means of Sztoja's approval.

The Weiss Concern, an important defense enterprise, was the only well-ordered production at Himmler's disposal. It was to be the foundation on which the SS planned to build its own weapons manufacture. Himmler viewed it as the kernel of a huge concern for the SS, which was already or would be producing infantry weapons in Buchenwald and Neuengamme, trucks in Brandenburg, high-frequency machinery in Ravensbrück, and was even bottling mineral water for the needs of the SS on its own account. Himmler was on the watch everywhere, seeking any possibility of becoming active in industry.

Himmler had been working toward this goal for more than two years. Thus, on January 11, 1942, by means of an order of Hitler's, he took over the "manufacture, expansion, and management . . . of the foundries in the Volkswagen Works, especially the light-metal foundries." With Hitler's promise that it would also be responsible for the factory, the SS could feel that it was in charge of production. The Führer's order said: "The SS Reichsführer will employ the necessary manpower from concentration camps. He will assume responsibility for the implementation of this assignment within the shortest possible time. The factory must be in operation by 1942 at the latest."[6]

This edict had been submitted to Hitler by Porsche and Werlin, the "Führer's deputy for motor vehicles." Porsche had resolved to forge ahead with the project of the Volkswagen Works even in wartime conditions; and he thus managed to realize a major portion of his plans. It was only four weeks later that I became responsible for all these matters upon being appointed Minister of Armaments. Six weeks later I gave Hitler reports by the appropriate group leaders of my newly created self-responsibility of industry; these reports explained that the additional capacity of the light-metal foundry of the Volkswagen Works would be necessary only if all Volkswagens were equipped with light-metal cast parts. However, Hitler had already decided that only the vehicles and amphibious trucks meant for Africa should be fitted with such light-metal components.[7] Thus, Himmler's order had been nullified by the events.

Porsche promised Pohl to exert his influence with Hitler in order to get him to change his negative decision. Two weeks later Pohl was optimistic that "on the basis of his [Porsche's] personal negotiations, the investigation will have a positive outcome, leading to the release of the construction." But because of my interference, the release "for establishment of the light-metal foundry could not be completed as yet. Under these circumstances, the deadline indicated in the Führer's order for the operational start of the light-metal foundry in autumn of 1942 cannot be met."[8] In the same letter, Pohl informed Himmler that the SS had taken charge of construction and that the lodgings for guards and prisoners were ready. The employment of prisoners could now begin.

The shell had already been greatly advanced in earlier years. According to my decision of April 28, 1942, it was now to be completed by the SS. But not for the light-metal foundry, because the building was to be used for another top-priority armaments purpose.[9] This decision wrecked Porsche's and Himmler's desire to set up an efficient SS-run light-metal foundry in the Volkswagen Works. A few months later, in September 1942, I finally decreed that the "further construction of the shell for the light-metal foundry" was to be halted "for reasons of wartime economy."[10]

This action contrasted with Dr. Todt's yielding ways. My predecessor, as I could see from the letters and accounts he left behind, had always been quick to give in to wishes of people close to Hitler. A Party veteran, he was far too close to the circles of the Party and the SS. Of course, I could count more readily on Hitler's support and endure a power struggle.

On July 7, 1942, SS Squad Commander Jüttner suggested to his superior that they "acquire about one-sixth to one-tenth of the overall capital [of the Steyr Works], thereby ensuring an influence on the board of directors. The Waffen-SS," he had been told, "was very interested in the production of the Steyr Works, for instance cars, tanks, and weapons." He had "secretly learned" about the planned sale of the parcel of shares "from Meindl, the general director of the Steyr Works, who is an honorary SS Oberführer."

(Once again, it is clear how honorary ranks put seemingly independent industrial leaders in the service of the SS.)

Pohl argued against this idea, since the ownership of shares would not imply any influence on the distribution of output. As everyone knew, the Supreme Command of the Army was in charge of distribution. Furthermore, Himmler had decided "not to expose [himself] by means of extensive participation in industry." The use of the word *expose* indicates that vaster plans were in the making. In industrial expansion, he said, they had to follow the axiom of "limiting our industrial undertakings, and in such a way that every undertaking has some kind of meaningful relation to us."[11] Himmler tersely replied to Pohl that he fully agreed with him "that the SS ought to stay out of this matter."[12]

The fact that Himmler had no interest in a block of shares and was actually and persistently pursuing other goals in weapons production is revealed in his letter of February 8, 1944, likewise to Jüttner: "Increased equipping of our units with medium-sized and heavy trench mortars [is] absolutely necessary. . . . We must see to it that we [get] such a manufacture in a concentration camp factory in as large a quantity as possible [illegible word] with the goal of receiving a large number of mortars for our troops aside from the quantity to be delivered to [the Supreme Command of the Army]."[13] Thus, Himmler planned to quietly siphon off a part of armaments production in his own concentration camp factory, which was outside the army's and my control.

Naturally, Himmler and his men also constantly tried to expand their peacetime capacities during the war. In September 1942, when Himmler returned from a trip through cities damaged by bombs, he instantly told Pohl: "We can help in your sector with our strength in the following area: the large-scale manufacture of door and window frames. I hereby order the start of this large-scale manufacturing. I ask you to undertake it in as many camps as possible, since the need is enormous. I imagine this manufacture in Dachau, Buchenwald, Sachsenhausen, Lublin, and Stutthof. Have the Todt Organization give you a standard type, especially for the window frames. The manufacturing is to begin within ten days at the latest. . . . Similarly, I ask you to consider whether we should not convert one of our brickworks to the production of roofing tiles. I am thinking especially of Neuengamme, because Hamburg, Bremen, Lübeck, and a great number of cities in western Germany could thus be supplied."[14]

Even when Himmler did not say so explicitly, every offer of help had the goal of implementing the intended production under his control, i.e., of eventually incorporating the factory under his imperium. When Porsche failed to build up the light-metal foundry of the Volkswagen plant with Himmler's assistance, he appealed to Himmler again. "Professor Porsche," Himmler wrote to Pohl on March 4, 1944, "visited me today. He would like us to take over as a concentration camp factory a plant for a secret weapon, located in a mine underground and requiring 3,500 workers."[15]

On June 19, Kammler, the top SS leader for the production of the V-2 in the Central Works, reported: "According to the assignment of the SS Reichsführer, I will support with all my power Professor Porsche's plans for transfer to the Central Works. My deputy in the Central Works will immediately contact Professor Porsche about the details."[16]

The Führer protocols make no mention whatsoever of this new weapon. It was certainly not the "flying saucers," which extreme right-wing circles now claim were secretly produced by the SS toward the end of the war and concealed from me. Our technology was quite remote from such flying objects. Nor could it be the 188-ton Maus tank, which Porsche advocated; or Porsche's as yet unmanufacturable project of a heavy diesel engine for the Panther and Tiger tanks.[17]

Often it was difficult to determine the best item advocated by all the tenacious lobbyists who tried to boost their own products and put down their competitors'. Countless types of wood- or coal-combustion generators had been developed for producing gases to run automotive vehicles. Himmler too had his pet generator, developed by Kristen; this project had gotten further than the one to extract gasoline from fir tree roots. When Himmler replaced Colonel General Friedrich Fromm as commander in chief of the home army, one of his first measures, just ten days after taking office, was an order to Jüttner, his representative in the new office. In regard to the "Kristen generator tested within the framework of the SS," Himmler told Jüttner to introduce it first throughout the entire home army, then later among the front-line troops, and to press for the fastest delivery possible. Heedless of the fact that my ministry was responsible for such a decision, the order went on: "You are to negotiate immediately with the Speer ministry so that the generators can be manufactured in large quantities and without any obstructions." However, Himmler instantly rescinded the demand for cooperation. The next sentence established that the responsibility was to be given to "an officer both qualified and undaunted by any obstacle . . . no matter what his rank. The smaller his staff and the greater his success, the more readily I will promote him. This man's advancement depends on the quick and successful completion of his action. On the fifth of every month, I would like a report on how many Kristen generators have been produced, how many have been placed with the home army, and also how many automotive vehicles the home army has. This number must be known anyway."[18] When it came to promotions, Himmler did not have to stick to the list of ranks; and he made ample use of this freedom.

We were relieved when the generators, fueled by charcoal, briquettes, or coal, did not overly disappoint our expectations, and the vehicles at least operated halfway.[19] But twelve days later, despite all difficulties that prevented the flawless operation of these generators, Himmler's imagination went one step further. Someone must have told him that generators can also be fueled by peat. Himmler instantly told Pohl to enlarge his imaginary industrial empire. "By establishing large peateries, that are to be set up as concentration camp factories, the peat requirement for all German generators [is] to be assured. All the exact agreements are to be made with SS Obergruppenführer Jüttner."[20]

It took Pohl two months to formulate his answer. Meanwhile, he went on "an information tour of the various peat regions." After that he informed Himmler that there were two kinds of peat, of which black peat alone was suitable for fueling generators. Black peat can be extracted only by machines in "peateries that are 5 to 8 kilometers long, with excavators and pressing machines racing over the surface. The bouquet of all the enterprises and authorities in the peat sector is extraordinarily variegated. However, any accomplishments have so far been mainly outside—as usual— in the factories. The ministries, in contrast, have founded associations. The latter have then usually secured large peateries for other purposes, for instance to fuel electric plants, "and have placed themselves upon [the peateries] like slimy jellyfish. So here, we're going to bring some life into the joint." These were the same old claims, undaunted by any setbacks, that only the SS could achieve increased performance, not the organs of the Ministry of Economy or Armaments.

During the winter, "several peateries were tackled, and the necessary preparations were [made] with prisoners for spring production." The SS would also be taking over a peat coking plant, in East Friesland, "sort of a blast-furnace plant in miniature. I want to establish a concentration camp here." Six thousand tons of peat coke a month could be obtained in this way. In November and December, he continued, he would set up an additional 40 to 80 charcoal piles, each with an output of 6 tons of peat coke a month. "As the man in charge of peat," Pohl had "appointed a layman, namely SS Sturmbannführer Dr. Mischke, head of the Nordland Publishing House." In our armaments organization, we always tried to get the finest experts. Now, Pohl respected my achievement, i.e., increasing armaments production as an architect, but he did not accept my system of delegating this task to real, top experts. With the self-confidence of a layman, he said, in regard to appointing the head of a publishing house, that it was "always better to get an impartial and unencumbered man with a sound understanding of such tasks than a weisenheimer who is too filled with expert knowledge to ever get around to cutting peat. Mischke has proved that he can do the job. For the implementation of the work, a new company must be founded, Torfverwertungs GmbH [Peat Exploitation, Inc.]."[21] A new link in the chain of SS factories.

Himmler was satisfied. To be sure, it took him almost another four weeks to write to Pohl, by way of Dr. Brandt, and tell him that the SS must "get involved to the greatest possible extent so that we may have sufficient latitude for the great tasks after the war, when gasoline will no doubt still be scarce. The SS Reichsführer feels that in this area, we can easily be among the largest entrepreneurs."[22] It is almost poignant to see Himmler still clinging to his idea of establishing large-scale SS-owned concerns for peacetime—at the very end of the war, despite all the setbacks.

On November 11, 1944, I sent a memorandum to Hitler pointing out "that a loss of the Rhenish-Westphalian industrial region will, in the long run, be intolerable for a successful continuation of the war."[23] I had turned to Bormann five days earlier to make it clear to him that "the successful continuation of the [aerial] attacks on the transportation system [in the Ruhr] could cause a production catastrophe, which would have decisive significance for the further course of the war." The enemy had developed a new tactic of bombing railroad and navigation facilities in order to cut German war industry off from the Ruhr coal and thus paralyze it. By early November, there was no doubt that this plan had worked. "Ten railroad stations [in the Ruhr] are now fully inoperative; another 46 stations can operate only to a limited degree," I told Bormann in the further course of my warning. I then went on: "The factory situation is accordingly tense; the daily output of cars in the fourth week of October has dropped to 7,786 cars as compared with 18,700 cars last year."[24]

It was obvious that Himmler would instantly go to the Ruhr to take a personal look and put everything in order again. On November 3, 1944, he sent me a telegram: "I'm here in the West. Among many problems, one—the lack of freight space—may be the easiest to deal with, by speeding up the construction of generators for trucks. The more oppressive the transportation situation here becomes, the more important the transportation by automotive vehicles and the more important the generators for them. What can be done here to bring back quick and thorough help?"[25]

Thirteen hours later, Himmler himself offered detailed information on what had to be done to get the better of the crisis and prevent catastrophe. "The more I speak with the individual Gauleiters," he told me, "the more convinced I become that the transportation calamity [a euphoric term for a total catastrophe] which we are all familiar with and which is due to the aerial situation, can be controlled to some extent by a large-scale shift of transportation to automotive vehicles."[26]

The lack of 11,000 railroad cars a day, each one of which had been transporting 12 tons of coal for distances up to 500 kilometers, could have been made up for only by an estimated 44,000 trucks with a loading capacity of 3 tons. These trucks were not available. Nor would the road network, which was greatly damaged by air raids, be adequate for this mass— not to mention that low-flying aircraft would have shot up these truck convoys, making them inoperative and thus also blocking the roads. Himmler's advice was obviously sheer madness.

Berger must have gotten wind of Himmler's generator crotchet. Three days later he offered Himmler "100 automotive omnibuses and 30 trucks. [He] has no fuel, however. The small reserve that I have secured from Slovakia is something that I would rather save for very special cases. Today, I asked Reich Minister Speer to help me and make generator facilities available for reconstruction."[27]

Himmler triumphed. The "SS Reichsführer is delighted that 100 automotive omnibuses and 30 trucks are available. He asks you to see to it that the reconstruction for generators is speedily carried out."[28] Himmler sent this message to Berger in an urgent telegram. It was inconceivable that any of my department heads would have dared to bother me with such trivia.

Himmler could not fail to exploit this Ruhr crisis, which could presumably decide the outcome of the war. He used it to get back to his idea of building generators. In a telegram of November 3, Himmler complained to me: "However, each one of the Gauleiters [at a joint meeting] lamented that no generators are to be had and that the inventors and designers of generators in this area are subject to such difficulties and harassment that the Ruhr cannot get any coal generators even though it has masses of hard coal. I believe that very great pressure must be applied. Perhaps it would be possible for you to appoint a man with dictatorial powers to deal brutally with the issue of hard-coal generators with no consideration for industrial sensibilities."[29]

I courteously replied: "Now that Dr. Schieber is leaving the Armaments Supply Office, I am going to disband the Central Office for Generators, which in part operates quite bureaucratically, no doubt, and I will assign the integration and speedy resolution of the generator problem to Nagel, the head of my transport units, an extraordinarily efficient man, endowed with common sense. Incidentally, the difficulties in supplying generators for industrial needs are partly due to the fact that the Wehrmacht now has top priority on the production of generators." One may conclude from the last sentence that the officer Himmler had demanded in his letter to Jüttner of August 1, 1944, the officer "who would not shrink from any obstacle," had been unable to bring about any additional output. For all my courtesies, I made my dissatisfaction clear to Himmler: "I always find it a pity that matters in my jurisdiction are brought to your attention during your visits, although the Gauleiters previously had countless opportunities to discuss solutions to these emergencies directly with me, whereas during my next visit to the Ruhr I may receive complaints about matters in your jurisdiction—the police, the fire department, or air-raid protection."[30]

Of course, in a sense, the five Gauleiters of the Ruhr were right to use Himmler's political pressure. Because as a result of this pressure, I made 8,300 anthracite-fueled generators available to them. That was nearly twice the production of all types of generators in the month of November; the output had dropped to 4,700. (See Appendix 16.) But I could not help telling the Gauleiters: "The greatest difficulty in employing these generators will be the acquisition of the required amounts of anthracite. That is the reason why these generators were at first held back. I ask you to take note in advance of the difficulties which may crop up."[31] The buck had been passed to the Gauleiters. Let them see how they could cope with the problems of assembling the generators and obtaining fuel.

I told Himmler: "I hope it will be possible to resolve the foreseeable difficulties in obtaining the necessary quantities of fuel. But if this is not possible in the Ruhr, where can it be possible?"[32]

On November 21, 1944, Himmler thanked me for my two letters, but responded only to my reproach that he was dealing with issues that did not concern him: "Regarding your remark that it was a pity that complaints about your jurisdictional area were presented to me during my visits, while you were informed of complaints about the police, the fire department, or air-raid protection, I would like to say that the meeting in Klein-Borkel was a discussion concerning all matters and jurisdictional areas. I only regretted that [your] State Secretary Schulze-Fielitz declared that he was not responsible for pretty nearly anything. Thus, for instance, nothing much came out in the very important area of generators. That was why I had to inconvenience you with my telegrams."[33]

This propitiation did not mean much. For in that session with the five Gauleiters, Himmler had high-handedly promised Gauleiter Dr. Meyer that he would get him allocations that were not even at his disposal. The next day Gauleiter Meyer had wired Himmler to confirm: "As per yesterday's discussion, I inform you of installation possibilities of 600 generators in four weeks."[34] On November 25, 1944, with the normal delay of 20 days, Himmler passed the wire on to SS Standartenführer Kloth, the head of the Raw Materials Office in the Personal Staff of the SS Reichsführer. Kloth was to take immediate charge of the matter.[35]

On December 27, 1944, after another four weeks, Kloth reported that he had transmitted Meyer's request to my ministry. The speedy allocation of 415 generators had been promised to him, he said.[36] Had Meyer addressed himself to me directly, he would not have had to wait eight weeks for this decision. But, precisely in these last few months of the war, many old Party members trusted in Himmler's initiative. He deceived and scintillated by making swift promises. I was more cautious and more sober in this respect.

Chapter 14

Semiprecious Gems, Poison Gas, and Dandelions

Himmler tried to expand the economic influence of the SS in all areas. He even set his sights on the products of basic industry, the production of raw materials. But there was no such thing as systematic action in the expansion of SS industrial interests. Occasionally Pohl claimed that he looked upon the vertical organization of self-responsibility in industry as a model, but such assertions existed only on paper.

The extant documents certainly reveal only a fraction of the projects that were planned or were being carried out; for instance, the fact that in the spring of 1942 Himmler got Gauleiter Erich Koch, Hitler's deputy for the Ukraine, to surreptitiously give him the right to exploit a quartz deposit near Zhitomir. Field Marshal Milch was alerted by his technical office on April 2; for "with the present stage of high-frequency technology," a lack of quartz was "a powerful obstacle, especially for the ultrawave areas, which are so important for the war effort." In October 1941, Milch was told, the Technical Office had gotten wind of a large quartz deposit near Zhitomir in the Ukraine, a deposit kept secret by the Russians. The size was sufficient to abolish the highly critical quartz shortage in Europe for decades. The report continues: "In late January 1942, at the behest of the Reich Ministry of Economy and the Reich Minister for the East, the Reich Commissioner for the Ukraine [Gauleiter Koch] appointed the De Boer firm by way of operational order to take over the trusteeship for administering and exploiting the mines near Zhitomir. In early February

1942, the De Boer firm was then discharged by a telephone communication from the Reich Commissioner for the Ukraine; in late February 1942, this discharge was orally confirmed on the occasion of a meeting in Kovno with Gauleiter Koch, who stated that the De Boer firm must be replaced by the SS, since there were political interests to be represented. . . . The Technical Office LC-E 4 sees a great danger that the quartz deposits, which are so important for the war effort, permitting us in large part to keep pace with our enemies in high-frequency technology, are not being exploited in accordance with the war situation. We therefore urgently request the intercession of Herr State Secretary [Field Marshal Milch] in order that the demand of the Technical Office may be recognized, namely that the exploitation and utilization of the quartz deposits near Zhitomir should be transferred unequivocally to a responsible agency, if possible the Luftwaffe."[1]

Even though I did not take charge of air armaments until two years later, I felt that my interests were imperiled in regard to a flawless allocation of quartz to all three armaments branches. Fully imbued with my almost unrestricted power, which Hitler had given me in these first few months of my activity, I soon wrote Himmler a clear letter, partly in support of Field Marshal Milch in his predicament. I was on close, familiar terms with Milch, and his position in regard to Himmler was weak. "Field Marshal Milch," my letter said, "has sent me the enclosed report from the Technical Office of the Luftwaffe. According to this report, the quartz deposits near Zhitomir, which are so crucial to the war industry, have so far been mined by the De Boer firm in Hamburg. Even though the De Boer firm has an assignment from the Reich Ministry of Economy and from the Reich Minister for the Occupied East European Territories, the Reich Commissioner, at the beginning of February, ordered the firm to be replaced because, allegedly, political interests are to be represented. The De Boer firm is to be superseded by the SS. I cannot agree to this action, which constitutes interference with an extremely important measure crucial to the war effort. I must demand" (Himmler was probably unaccustomed to someone's using this word with him) "that the De Boer firm, Hamburg, undertake the mining, and I would be grateful to you if you instructed the head of Economic Headquarters not to place any obstacles in the path of the De Boer firm in its continued work and to refrain from transferring the exploitation of the quartz deposits to the SS."[2]

Meanwhile, I had contacted Alfred Rosenberg, the minister for the occupied East European territories, to protest the transfer of this quartz deposit to the SS. Perhaps Pohl had some vague glimmering of this protest.

On June 9 he wrote to Himmler: "Since Reich Minister Speer has declared in a secret letter to the Ministry for the East that you, Reichsführer, have agreed to the employment of the De Boer firm, I am planning to ask the Reich Commissioner to recall me as fiduciary. Please inform me of your decision."[3]

Pohl could predict Himmler's reaction to this untrue assertion. The answer came just as he could have wished. Dr. Brandt, the head of Himmler's Personal Staff,. wrote to SS Squad Commander Sachs on July 1, 1942: "Yesterday the SS Reichsführer stated that in his letter to Reich Minister Speer he intends to propose the following arrangement: The SS Reichsführer wants to leave the proprietorship in its present state, i.e., have the exploitation done by us. But he commits hmself to supplying quartz in that amount that has been needed so far by industry crucial to the war effort."[4] Pohl received a copy.

I too felt that Himmler would not let go of his booty without a struggle. Two days earlier, on June 29, 1942, my complaint had triggered a counter-order from Goering, who was already politically weakened, but surprisingly delighted to make a decision. Goering ordered that "this transfer be canceled and this quartz deposit be made available to the Reich Minister for Armaments and Munitions for proper utilization."[5]

Two weeks later, Pohl felt that people had been going over his head. He reacted in annoyance: "After my appointment as fiduciary [for Zhitomir] by the Reich Commissioner for the Ukraine, an all-out witch-hunt began. The Supreme Command of the Army, the Luftwaffe, the Navy, and all civilian agencies that require communications devices for army supplies are laying claim to the Zhitomir mine because in the Old Reich all quartz deposits for producing communications devices are exhausted. The East Ministry [Rosenberg], because of the personal intercession by Reich Minister Speer, has instructed the Reich Commissioner for the Ukraine to recall me as fiduciary and put the special firm of De Boer in my place. The Reich Commissioner for the Ukraine [Koch] has therefore urged me to give up my trusteeship in favor of the De Boer firm. At my petition, however, he has ordered the De Boer firm to sell to me at cost the semi-precious topaz stones obtained at Zhitomir." It seems, as we will read, that these semiprecious stones interested the SS as much as the quartz deposit. Pohl's letter to Himmler continues: "On the basis of this state of affairs, I have therefore declared my willingness to give up the trusteeship, especially since I wanted to prevent the SS Reishsführer from being abused on one side or the other in the struggle between the Reich Commissioner and the Ministry for the East."[6]

Alarmed by Pohl's unexpected renunciation of the trusteeship, Himmler turned to me one day later. He probably did not intend to go into my gruff letter. Instead, as was frequently his way, he wanted to confront me with *faits accomplis* on the basis of his at times excellent relations with Koch, the Reich Commissioner for the Ukraine. "I am unfortunately replying only today, after almost three months, to your letter of April 20. May I ask you to leave the present state of proprietorship as it is. However, I am ready, needless to say, to make the usual yield available to war-crucial industry. You may rest assured that the utilization of the quartz deposit, as determined by us, will proceed as necessary. The Reich Marshal, whom I have also addressed about this quartz deposit, has been instructed by me in the same terms, and he is in agreement."[7] Himmler began in a casual form, asking my approval, only to state his decision instantly. Goering, too, he said, was merely informed of his decision; and naturally, the Reich Marshal did not care to wage a power struggle with Himmler over a quartz deposit.

On July 25 he wrote Pohl through Dr. Brandt that the yielding of the trusteeship had been a rash action. He also rebuked Pohl: "The Reichsführer stands by his decision, which he formulated in the letter of July 15 to Reich Minister Speer. The SS Reichsführer asks you not to give up the trusteeship. Basis of negotiation: The SS Reichsführer will give the De Boer firm any quartz deposits uncovered during the war. Otherwise, we will remain the proprietors." Squad Commander Berger, the feared partner in the Ministry for the East, "should represent this viewpoint of the SS Reichsführer accordingly in the Ministry for the East."[8]

However, Himmler had lost the struggle. One month later he wrote a reproachful letter to Pohl: "Unfortunately, your premature renunciation of the trusteeship of the quartz deposit in Zhitomir has now led to our not obtaining it for the moment; for shortly after your letter arrived, Gauleiter Koch concluded a contract with the firm in question for the duration of the war. I have now reached an agreement with Gauleiter Koch, allowing us to take over this contract after the end of the war. I therefore intend to conclude a contract with him today for peacetime. I only ask you in the future, when we have such matters in our hands, not to release them without asking me. I somehow very much regret the loss of this wonderful quartz deposit."[9]

Himmler's letter to Erich Koch, mentioned in his letter to Pohl, was dispatched on August 26, i.e., one day later. The crux was Himmler's interest in semiprecious stones: "Dear Erich. Referring to our conversation about the quartz deposit in the Zhitomir area, I would like to ask you for the following:

1. To conclude a contract so that after the end of the war, when the contract with the Hamburg firm runs out, we can lease this quartz deposit.
2. Would it be possible for me to lease a topaz deposit somewhere now?
3. Please send me the regulations on the almandines and other semiprecious stones and also the rules pertaining to the collecting of such semiprecious stones. I would under no circumstances wish to do anything illegal. [an astonishing resolution for Himmler.] On the other hand, I would regret it if here, in the surroundings of the headquarters, where such stones are to be found, they could not be collected or purchased."[10]

Pohl now had to show his hand. "The Ministries for the East, Economy, and Armaments drastically opposed our installation as fiduciaries and sided with the De Boer firm because of its many years of experience in the area of quartz mining. I myself was persuaded that at this time, a systematic and economical exploitation of this quartz deposit could be guaranteed only by the De Boer firm, whereas we do not have the necessary specialists at our disposal. Since quartz can be mined only in summer, and the exploitation of the deposit was urgent for war purposes, I considered it my duty, in respect to Reich Minister Speer's communication, to give up the trusteeship, especially since all the other army agencies" (and this was certainly not unwarranted) "felt that we were laying claim to the quartz deposit only because of its topaz stones." He believed, Pohl concluded in resignation, that other agencies had also taken a fancy to the mined topaz stones. That was a bizarre contradiction in one and the same letter. He had only just established the inability of the SS to properly mine the indispensable quartz deposits; and then a few sentences later, Pohl accused the Commissioner General of the Ukraine and the other agencies involved of preventing his appointment chiefly because of the desired stones.[11]

This quarrel soon proved academic. On March 18, 1943, the Supreme Command of the Wehrmacht had to ask Himmler, who was assigned the fight against partisans: "In early March gangs assaulted the quartz-mining area 40 kilometers northwest of Zhitomir and destroyed part of the factory. Since this is the only deposit of quartz for high-frequency technology in all of Europe, any disturbance of its systematic mining will be highly disadvantageous to the German war industry. It is therefore necessary to fight and clear the space northwest of Zhitomir of gangs—and to assure permanent and sufficient security of the quartz region. We ask you to inform us of the intended measures."[12]

After the victory over France, there were serious discussions about the idea of a huge colonial empire in Africa, with the partial annexation of the Belgian and French colonies, for instance in the Congo or Chad. This idea was by no means a pipe dream of SS Squad Commander Hennicke, who, after the successful French campaign, sent a sober business report to his friend Karl Wolff, Himmler's chief aide. Hennicke suggested building gigantic concentration camp factories in the colonies after the war. "The copper and tin mines, the building of roads and dams, the diamond, gold, and silver mines for the jewelry industry will offer a fabulous labor opportunity for the concentration camp inmates, who are to be found so profusely in Europe. This will keep the settlement space in Greater Germany clean. Government plantations will provide work for the colored peoples."[13]

Hitler's peace offers to England, one goal of which was this notion of a gigantic connected African colonial empire, were curtly rejected by Churchill's government. So Himmler had to bury the dream of German rubber plantations in Africa. Somewhat as a surrogate for the rubber plant *Taraxacum kok-saghyz*, Hitler made Himmler aware of a dandelion plant that only grows to a few centimeters in height (*Taraxacum bicorne*) and whose roots are 1½ percent natural rubber.

Two and a half months before the start of the Russian campaign, Himmler wrote to an SS Sturmbannführer named Vogel that Hitler had stated that "originally, we had sugar cane only as a colonial product. The domestic beet, which had always existed, was not taken into account. But then someone hit on this idea, and the beet was cultivated more and more for a higher sugar content until the present-day sugar beet evolved." Now, there was a plant "that supplies a large amount of rubber. The seeds of this plant supposedly come from Russia. [Pohl should] procure seeds of this rubber plant, which we wish to propagate as fast as possible. Furthermore, I ask you to report to me on this plant, its cultivation, and the manner in which rubber is obtained from it. In this connection, I would like to indicate another plant, next to the dandelion, which also grows in our forests, namely wolf's-milk, the sap of which, in my opinion, is even stickier than the milk of the dandelion."[14] Measuring the gumminess in this way, the dictator and his police chief discussed the rubber content of dandelions.

It was only one year later, on June 23, 1942, that Hitler "expressed the intention of possibly assigning Himmler the task of planting." For he was far from satisfied, we are told, with the statistics on rubber farming. He asked who was responsible for the planting—a cogent question, given the chaos of jurisdictions.[15]

Hitler could certainly find no more obliging or more enthusiastic subaltern than Himmler for carrying out such a fantastic project with energy and relentlessness. But, as he did so frequently, Hitler hesitated. Himmler likewise waited six months to answer Hitler's question about who was responsible. The system always reacted very bureaucratically, even when Hitler's wishes were in the background.

It was not until February 1943 that Pohl reported on the status of the matter. "The following agencies are in charge of cultivating and farming the [*Taraxacum*] *kok-saghyz* plant:

a. in the Four-Year Plan, the deputy for Automotive Vehicles;
b. in the Four-Year Plan, the deputy for chemistry;
c. the Reich Ministry of Food;
d. Reich Agriculture [the Farmers' Association];
e. in the SS Reichsführer's office, the Economic Administrative Headquarters;
f. the Kaiser Wilhelm Institute for Breeding Research;
g. the Research Office of the DAF-Volkswagen Works;
h. the processing industry."

This was a jumble of overlapping jurisdictions; and presumably nothing happened because each agency counted on letting the other agencies take care of the project. The SS, Pohl went on, had already been called in, for "tiny samples of all attainable seeds are being sent to the SS Reichsführer's office at the concentration camp of Auschwitz. . . . Furthermore, the German Labor Front is now setting up a laboratory in Auschwitz so that individual stems and plants can be examined for rubber content right away." At the January meeting of the "Plant Rubber Co., Inc.," it was stated, according to Pohl's report, that "in the year 1943, a surface area of circa 40,000 hectares can be planted with [*T.*] *kok-saghyz*, using the available seeds. . . . With this year's tillage, enough seeds should be harvested to enable the tillage of 100,000 hectares in the year 1944. In the year 1944, a yield of 8,000 tons of rubber can be expected from this farming surface." This meant some 800 kilograms of rubber for every hectare.[16]

Since late 1942, delivery of natural rubber by blockade-breaking ships had been clearly impossible. The quantity of natural rubber sank from

23,500 tons in 1942 to 5,100 tons in 1943 and 2,300 tons in 1944.[17] This diminished balance of our natural rubber supplies must have increased activity; and it also explains Hitler's wavering until this moment. Of course, we have to recall that our chemical industry had meanwhile succeeded in so greatly improving the quality of synthetic rubber that the addition of natural rubber was no longer necessary for tires or components subject to great stress.

Hitler, in contrast, still counted on rubber from the *T. kok-saghyz* plant. In June 1942 he wanted to put Himmler in charge of this mission. By February 1943 Pohl had delivered his report. It was only on July 23, 1943, that Hitler carried out his previous year's intention and gave Himmler "the responsibility for the greatest possible production of plant rubber." Himmler told his SS commanders who were responsible for the intended farm areas: "In every possible way that you can, support the production and extraction of plant rubber and its processing in your areas. . . ." This would be done "by the systematic transfer of elderly women and children, whom we will take from the cleared partisan areas" and use as manpower for farming *T. kok-saghyz*.[18]

Himmler's journal says that on April 15, 1943, he studied this plant for three hours. On June 24 he conferred once again with Stahl, a farmer, for one hour, and on November 30, 1943, for three hours. Nine months later, on April 20, 1944, Himmler spent a great deal less time studying the dandelion: only one and a half hours.[19] For meanwhile, he had received a sobering letter from Kehrl, my courageous department head. This letter of March 30, 1944, contained a report from the Society for Plant Rubber and Gutta-percha, February 23, 1944. The report, which had been sent to Kehrl as head of the Planning Office in my ministry, explained: In 1942–1943, 137 tons of rubber could indeed have been extracted from this plant. However, because of the retreats from Russia, the arable areas were now lost. In the spring of 1944, according to this society (which, since July 1943, had been under a Deputy for Plant Rubber of the SS Reichsführer), 20,000 hectares of Polish territory would have been replanted with *kok-saghyz*. A surface ten times the size of Grunewald (a Berlin recreation area) would have yielded a root harvest of 10,000 tons. But since the roots contained only 1½ percent natural rubber, one could expect a yield of only 300 tons of natural rubber. In order to meet our most urgent needs, we had to process some 24,000 tons of synthetic rubber. What did 300 tons of rubber signify against 20,000 tons?

Fifteen kilograms per hectare was one-fiftieth of the 800 kilograms per hectare that Pohl had promised on February 12, 1943! These 300 tons of natural rubber, as noted in the memorandum of the "Society for Plant Rubber and Gutta-percha," could be extracted with an expenditure of 60,000 to 80,000 workers. The society calculated production costs of 32 to 35 marks per kilogram of natural rubber as opposed to the official rubber price of 2.70 marks.[20] The 300,000 kilograms of rubber extracted from the *T. kok-saghyz* plant would thus cost some 10 million marks, corresponding to a yearly recompense of 125 marks per capita for 80,000 workers,[21] aside from the other overhead (likewise listed in the report). Now, a report of April 14 from the Raw Materials Office explained that these workers would be employed only part-time for this purpose.[22] But even if we take this fact into account, then the payment would scarcely suffice for proper food, clothing, and lodging. Hence, an unrealistic calculation, unless one applied the cost standard of concentration camps to these 80,000 people.

Hitler's imagination may have spawned the idea of spending years growing dandelions; but the cultivation of *kok-saghyz* by the SS was characteristic of Himmler's insistence on fantastic production goals. All these plans, however, were soon canceled automatically by the rapid advance of the Red Army in Polish territory. The dandelion was not farmed.

Himmler could always be easily won over to untested processes. When he promised Hitler he would build up a gigantic output of brick for his grand constructions projects, he made the mistake of believing the inventor of a new manufacturing system. Himmler committed the entire brick quota on that system without first having it examined by experts. The idea turned out to be an utter disappointment. All the facilities had to be converted to normal production methods, and the resulting losses were great.

Now, he once again waxed enthusiastic when he was approached by Wilhelm Keppler, an SS squad commander and once Hitler's influential adviser in economic matters. In June 1944 Keppler asserted that he had achieved great success in his development work. A new chemical process would, he said, raise the yield of lead/zinc works from 60–75 to 98 percent. A plant for producing 20,000 tons of lead and 8,000 tons of zinc a year was to go into immediate construction—naturally, without anyone's bothering to obtain permission from my Raw Materials Office. "You once offered me the prospect of setting up a shortening factory by using the necessary manpower from concentration camps. May I ask you if it might be possible to do the same thing for working ores and setting up the required factory. We would need about 1,500 men, including, of course, the proper skilled workers." As usual in such cases, Himmler showed great interest. "In regard to your wish to have 1,500 men made available to you for mining ore and setting up the factory, it would be best if we discussed this personally. I could decide to allocate the manpower only if the responsibility of the works were transferred to me in full. The factory would have to be built in such a way that aerial attacks could do little or, better, nothing to it." More clearly than usual, Himmler made the offer of manpower dependent on his being completely in charge and on having his offices take over the management.

These plans proved to be illusory.

The rich manganese ore deposits near Nikopol, Bulgaria, were threatened by the Russian advance in early November 1943.[23] It was obvious that German armaments could not count on them much longer. Meanwhile, industry had found ways to stretch our considerable manganese stocks from 12 to 18 months, i.e., until autumn 1945. Nevertheless, in December 1943 Hitler evidently calculated a much longer duration for the war. He indicated that geologists ought to be called in "to establish whether other manganese supplies could be found, say in the Carpathians, Hungary, or Slovakia."[24]

As usual, the SS once again tried to put a foot in the door. At a meeting on May 8, 1944, Hans Frank, the governor general of Poland, sent out an expedition to Zabie, Galicia, where a manganese deposit had been reported. He appointed SS Hauptsturmführer Jordan as head of this expedition, and he, in turn, was to report directly to Frank. Right after this meeting, Frank wrote to Himmler: "Regarding the Galician manganese ore, I have just had a detailed discussion in the presence of State Secretary Koppe [also SS and police chief of the Generalgouvernement] and SS Hauptsturmführer Jordan. Jordan, with the best possible support, will go on a three-week expedition to the area in question next week; and there he will definitively establish both the manner and size of the deposit and the possbility of commencing the work and the transportation as soon as possible. I therefore suggest that the visit of SS Obergruppenführer Pohl to Krakow, which you have promised, would be more expedient if it takes place after Jordan has returned here from his expedition; for then we will know the clear points of departure for the company to be founded. You may rest assured that I will give you every conceivable assistance in this matter."[25]

Ten days later, in a letter to Himmler about a meeting with the governor general, Wilhelm Keppler reported: "The centralization of metal research in a Berlin staff" (an open criticism of the agencies subordinate to the Raw Materials Office of the Armaments Ministry) was "totally disadvantageous in practice. As in other areas, centralism has now become an evil that absolutely must be abolished, at least in places where centralism threatens to paralyze the energies of portions of the sphere of power in the Greater German Reich." This was a parallel to the SS struggle in Czech territory against the centralization of the armaments industry in my ministry. "The completely dilatory manner of treating metal research is not the fault of the Generalgouvernement, but rather exclusively that of the complete failure of the centralistic positions in the Reich. The SS Reichsführer fully agrees with the governor general in this respect."[26] Indeed, after earlier experiences with Himmler's agencies, my groups and committees must have had little taste for leaving any newly discovered manganese deposits to the SS.

Himmler used the occasion of his visit to Krakow to advance the expansion of his armaments empire. "The SS Reichsführer," said Keppler, "would like to have an investigation of whether it would be possible to promote directly the output of weapons and munitions [in the Generalgouvernement] without heeding the somewhat clumsy apparatus of Speer's Reich ministry. . . . The governor general promised this and also raised the question of whether it would be possible to set up a special infantry gun factory somewhere in a mountain glen; he would then order the matter to be pursued as quickly as possible."[27] Thus, in the internal conversation of these three high-ranking SS commanders, the masks were dropped.

Frank's state secretary, SS Squad Commander Koppe, had always been helpful in talks between the Armaments Commission and General Schindler. I was therefore all the more astonished in retrospect at what Koppe said in a meeting on June 3, 1944, which was chaired by Governor General Frank and was meant to advance the policies decided by the three high-ranking SS leaders. The double-dealing Koppe stated: "There are many things that might be treated differently. I am thinking especially of the blast furnaces and the mixed-ore mining. Here, we ought to call in the SS Reichsführer. I consider it quite possible to boost the extraction of iron. But the concerns and the trusts don't like the Generalgouvernement mining too much iron ore. Unfortunately, the leading men in semiofficial positions [meaning probably those in the self-responsibility of industry] can become effectively active and simply refuse to let this happen. That is why I would consider it proper to establish a few steel mills here which have nothing to do with this coterie. We will set up blast furnaces where we consider them necessary. Messrs. [Hermann] Röchling et al. evidently fear that there is too much of a shift toward the East."

Frank replied to Koppe: "Thus, they are deliberately pursuing the policy of holding us back with our iron production."[28] They were quite bluntly discussing an SS-owned industry, which was to be built up in open opposition to the ruling organizations in armaments. An instructive example of the disorganization and dissolution of all state authority in the late period of the Third Reich, which is frequently viewed even today as a perfectly functioning political machine.

After the Nuremberg Trial, high-ranking representatives of the U.S. Department of War Production spoke with me in order to get to know our organizational forms. Previously they had picked the brains of many of my staffers. In the concluding session, the leading mind on the American commission noted: "When we had problems with institutions of democratic society, we often regretted that our 'ministers' were not vested with all powers like Speer. Just a stroke of Speer's pen, and all conflicts are resolved. That was how we pictured your position. Well, now that we've studied the work methods of your authoritarian system in armaments, we are forced to see that you and your staff members had a much harder time than we did, with this chaos of jurisdictions, intrigues, and usurpation of power."

My qualms about assigning major armaments tasks in Poland were based on the chaotic conditions of that country, which made costly investments seem useless. On March 29, 1943, I forcefully made Hitler aware of the inadequate armaments possibilities in the Generalgouvernement: "The manpower pool is poorly fed, so the workers have to buy food on the black market, causing a loss of half their working time. Also, coal is poorly distributed, etc. As a result, it is absolutely impossible to exploit the armaments industry already existing in the Generalgouvernement. For these reasons, a shift from the West is out of the question, even though the armaments industry in Poland would be up to it."[29]

That same day, I went to see Himmler in his nearby headquarters, located inside a comfortable Pullman car in a forest. I wanted to inform him of my worries about Poland and ask for his support.[30] Two months later I repeated the argument to Hitler: "The uncertainty in the Generalgouvernement will not permit any shift of armaments manufacturing to that territory, even though it would be quite suitable for large-scale production."[31]

But to either Frank or Himmler such obstacles did not seem worth mentioning. Then too, there was the total incapability of their subordinate organizations, which began projects in every possible field without having the requisite mental and technical leadership capacities.

Evidently the efforts of Himmler and his organization to establish SS-owned industrial plants had multiplied as of the spring of 1944. This may have been due in part to the weakening of my position during and after my illness. However, the cause might also be sought in the conception, approved by Hitler, of an independent, industrial empire for the SS. What had previously been a hunger for power now became a system.

In October 1944 Gauleiter Greiser reported from Posen that the founding of the brown coal works in Konin, as well as the construction of a major power plant to be fueled by these works, was making good progress. (Two years earlier, before he even became minister of the interior, Himmler had high-handedly "approved of having the Gau self-administration[32] lay claim to the concessions for mining brown coal as revealed by drilling.)[33] Himmler answered Greiser two weeks later: "I share your delight about the positive test results concerning the brown coal mined in Konin. In normal circumstances, the mining of coal in the Warta Gau would have been highly advantageous. But it is especially valuable in the next few weeks and months. How can we advance the extraction of coal with utmost energy? If is it to be done by strip mining, then I could assist you with prisoners."[34] A copy of the letter was promptly dispatched to Pohl.

Manganese-ore mining, iron smelting, armaments manufacturing in Poland, lead and zinc smelting in the Reich territory, Porsche's secret manufacturing at the Central Works in the Harz Mountains—all the SS-owned armaments factories were striving to expand in the last year of the war. But these efforts were to no avail.

The extraction of mineral oil was to round off the planned combine. When Germany was already heading toward doom, Himmler appealed to Paul Pleiger, the general manager of the Hermann Goering Works, whom I recommended to Himmler for running his concern. Himmler asked him to take part in exploiting hitherto unknown oil sources. "I have often been told that there are promising oil deposits in central Germany which have not yet been drilled for, much less tapped. I ask you to let me know whether you have also heard of this deposit and to give me your opinion on this matter."[35] In officialese back then, the word *ask* was a lesser form of the word *command*.

Pleiger understood this diction and replied without delay, even though he was responsible solely to Goering and in no way to Himmler: "I have heard of assertions about oil deposits in central Germany which have so far not been explored. I consider it absolutely indispensable to do exploratory drilling there immediately. I would be grateful to you if this work could be carried out jointly by us."[36]

But even this offer of cooperation between the SS and the Hermann

Goering Works was not enough for Himmler. This case makes clear what was going on behind the scenes. On August 15, 1944, an SS Hauptsturm-führer wrote the following file memorandum: "After the SS Reichsführer dictated the enclosed telegram to State Councillor Pleiger, he ordered me to call up SS Squad Commander Meinberg and inform him that the SS Reichsführer would like to have the answer in a certain form. The SS Reichsführer also said that it was a matter of playing ball. Since the tele-gram of 8/6/44 was not satisfactory, I called up SS Squad Commander Meinberg once again and told him in detail the wording desired by the SS Reichsführer. The telegram of August 10, 1944, then arrived."[37] Meinberg was one of Pleiger's closest colleagues. A few months later, he accused my deputy Hans Günther Sohl of high treason.

This telegram of August 10, 1944, which compiled with Himmler's wishes, is distinguished in two points from Pleiger's first wire. First of all, he is now suddenly convinced that the work must commence immediately. And secondly, Pleiger, who was normally impervious, kowtowed to Himmler, as desired, and actually asked him to permit the Goering Works to operate in tandem with the SS.

Hans Marsalek, in *Die Tat*, reports on how similar deals came about. In July 1942 there were difficulties because of the SS's profit share in a cinder-processing factory on the grounds of the Hermann Goering Works in Linz. Himmler finally turned to Pleiger, writing laconically: "Please be so kind as to inform your people that for all Pleiger/SS enterprises, fifty-fifty is the sacred law."[38]

Two days after Pleiger's submission, Himmler dropped his mask of courtesy and gruffly told him: "I find it incredible that these oil deposits have not yet been exploited. I regard it as your national duty to deploy all your energy and overcome any difficulties in order to proceed without delay in drilling and—if you are successful—in developing these deposits. I must ask you for a telegraphic report on your progress in seven days."[39] Himmler did not use such unfriendly terms even with Pohl when giving him orders.

Three days later Pleiger respectfully informed Himmler that a large drilling rig had been sent off to the established drilling point west of Bernburg. The drilling, he said, would begin in three weeks.[40] It is aston-ishing that Pleiger did not demand any further preliminary evaluation by the Mining Office, whose expertise was recognized even by the Allies after the war. However, such a consultation would have taken months and per-haps roused a threatening Himmler to violent measures. Like an obedient pupil, Pleiger reported on August 16 that the drilling rig had arrived; on

September 12 that concrete foundations, water pipes, and lighting equipment had been erected; on September 26 that the drilling tower had been set up, the powerhouse erected, and the engines installed; on October 12 that the assembly work was done; on October 26 that they had been drilling since October 18, but had made very little progress; on November 8 (even more pessimistically) that a depth of 50 meters had been reached, but that the daily progress amounted to only 4 or 5 meters because the cutting tools were worn out after 4 meters; on November 15 that they had reached a depth of 119.5 meters, but that hard, mottled sandstone permitted daily progress of only 6 meters.[41]

Pleiger then lapsed into silence. But despite the situation of the war, Himmler admonishingly inquired on January 6, 1945: "How are our oil deposits doing? I haven't heard anything for a long time and I'm extremendously anxious."[42] On January 13, 1945, Pleiger replied tersely (for Himmler's influence was blunted by his failures as commander in chief on the Rhine): "Depth, 634 meters. Mountain very hard."[43] Hence, since November 14, the average daily progress had risen from 6 meters to 8.6 meters.

Meanwhile, Himmler had lost interest. Easier triumphs were beckoning in the form of extraction of gasoline from fir tree roots.

Himmler's ways may have been unsystematic. But within his plans, was a reasonable goal to try and assure the extraction or exploitation of certain basic products, like manganese, lead, zinc, coal, and mineral oil, for his operation. In the spring of 1944, the army had refused to produce N-material; it was allegedly an inextinguishable burning chemical mass, similar to the legendary Greek fire. Himmler ultimately wanted to bring the production of not only N-material but also the nerve gas sarin into the hands of the SS.[44] Sarin was our most modern weapon, many times more effective than any previously manufactured war gas. Moreover, there was no defense against it because the gas masks and filters known at that time offered no protection.[45] Sarin could thus someday be an inestimable factor, at least for extortion, in an internal German struggle between the Wehrmacht and the SS. And after July 20, such considerations could no longer be viewed as absurd.

In early 1944 Hitler had stated that he had made up his mind to assign both the testing and the manufacturing of N-material to the SS. I pointed out to Hitler "that the operation of a chemical factory [should] if possible remain within the overall chemical industry." Hitler changed his mind. But he wanted "to charge the SS Reichsführer with testing and evaluating N-material and only then deciding with me whether the production of N-material will remain in our hands."[46]

On July 7 Hitler again ordered General Buhle, the head of the army staff, to have "the SS Reichsführer speedily perform further experiments with N-material."[47] Three weeks later I spoke to Hitler about the SS's intention of simply going ahead and manufacturing N-material without first testing it: "I convinced the Führer that for the time being the Waffen-SS should not take over production; it would be enough of the Waffen-SS tested N-material. Today, I still consider it a mistake for the Waffen-SS to take over production of N-material. For only I.G. Farben has the specialists necessary for the constant innovations in the chemical process. . . . Another reason why I cannot agree to the Waffen-SS taking over the Falkenhagen production is that a facility for manufacturing a crucial chemical warfare agent is located next to and in connection with the N-material. A Tandem factory management does not seem reasonable. Sarin, the combat agent manufactured in Falkenhagen, is the most valuable and most modern of any chemical combat agents and is six times as effective as any previous one."[48]

Jüttner's report on the experiments was negative. N-material, an expensive failure on the part of the Army Ordnance Office, could not be used. "The Führer reads SS Obergruppenführer Jüttner's report on N-material. The Führer asks them to ascertain once again whether a fire can be started in a tank when it is shot through by incendiary projectiles containing N-material. In the experiments, the gasoline fumes that arise from a running engine during combat should be present."[49] Such detailed instructions are a good example of how Hitler tried to interfere even in small matters.

Hitler no longer spoke about having the SS take over the manufacture of N-material. But despite the negative findings of the highest experts in the SS, the SS had unhesitatingly appropriated the factory, which was valuable because of sarin production. In early November 1944, Schieber, who was about to be dismissed because of Himmler's intrigues, performed a not undangerous duty by making me aware of SS machinations: "Problems have arisen in Falkenhagen because the Waffen-SS is already manufacturing N-material there, the workshops and general manufacturing facilities are overburdened to excess, and these machines are now to be moved into bunkers to boot. All this adversely affects the expansion of sarin production. . . . We most sharply protest against the SS measure." For as soon as the SS had established itself in the factory, it would appropriate the sarin manufacture for operational reasons.[50]

The conflict soon became illusory. By October 11 I had to inform Field Marshal Keitel that because of the collapse of the chemical industry, the basic materials zyanogen and methanol were exhausted. Hence, on November 1 the production of tabun and sarin was suspended.[51]

Chapter 15
Himmler Takes Charge of the Rocket Program

The TECHNICAL DEVELOPMENTS on which our weapons construction concentrated in the spring of 1942 were at the threshold of revolutionary breakthroughs. We were about to produce a large automatic rocket as well as a jet engine, which had already been tested. And we were on the verge of breaking the sound barrier with an MeZ 63 rocket. Without these advances made during the second half of the war, today's technology would be inconceivable. During exchanges of opinions after the war, Western experts confirmed that we had a three-year lead in these areas of technology. It was only in atomic research that the Americans had outstripped us with tremendous efforts, leaving the Germans behind after our initial head start.

A thirteen-ton rocket, developed in strict secrecy under the code name A-4, was truly a technological miracle for that time because of its various qualities. It rose vertically from the ground and was kept vertical by a new type of localizer beam, until, at a distance of 500 kilometers, it steered itself toward the target area with relative accuracy.

This was an achievement exceeding all expectations. And I forgot any qualms I would have felt if I had soberly compared this costly solution with our technological predicament. For we did not even have the explosive devices that would have made such an expenditure worthwhile.

However, the A-4 rocket was fully in keeping with Himmler's notions that seemingly fantastic innovations would decide the war in our favor. Hence, this development exercised a draw on Himmler like a magnet. And he was not bothered by the fact that as SS Reichsführer he had no jurisdiction in this area. Actually, this even strengthened his urge to interfere and to support the project. In case of failure, he would have to claim no responsibility; and in case of success, he could point out his contributions.

On December 16, 1942, Berger, Himmler's chief of headquarters, reported that the military experiment institution at Peenemünde "is still deeply impressed by the visit of the SS Reichsführer." At the same time, Berger transmitted a request from Lieutenant Colonel Stegmaier, who was, after all, in charge of Peenemünde. Stegmair wanted Colonel Walter Dornberger, head of the A-4 project, "to come to an official meeting with the Führer together with the developer Dr. [Wernher] von Braun, in order to discuss the possible uses of the instrument, along with the pros and cons, and to listen to the intentions and wishes of the Führer in this connection. The intentions established by the Führer would then provide a clear direction for the now partly ongoing preparations for the operation. Please give me further orders."[1] Thus, direct lines were set up from a competent army officer to involve Himmler's authority directly and to circumvent Colonel General Fromm (in charge of the project and still hesitant about it) and me (who was responsible for production).

Penning the word *Führer* in his own hand, Himmler added this welcome letter to the file that was meant for the meeting with Hitler. On January 23, 1943, Himmler pursued this matter further after adding "Colonel Dornberger and Braun once to the Führer" in accordance with point 8 of his meeting with Hitler.[2] This was in keeping with Berger's suggestion.

Ten days later Stegmaier asked "for a decision of the Führer by way of the Reichsführer: Instrument A-4 contains a series of electrical equipment. Assigning these matters to the electrical industry is very difficult, since the free volume here is very limited. It is extremely urgent to have a decree of the Führer give the A-4 program priority over the radar program. This can also be justified by pointing out the quality of the A-4 as an attack weapon in contrast to the radar program as a part of defense. . . . The decision is vital since the already urgent deadlines cannot possibly be kept if no change occurs."[3] Aside from deliberately undermining the authority of my ministry, such a change of priorities could have easily increased our military inferiority because of our limited capacity in this area. This letter was promptly brought along to Berger by Stegmaier. In his letter to Himmler, Berger explained that the brief report indicated "that things have come out of the first experiment and that so far the [A-4] can be employed up to a distance of 180 kilometers, albeit with no precise aiming at a target and with a dispersion of 5×10 kilometers. The gentlemen request the involvement of the SS Reichsführer."[4] In this way, it was easy for the SS to infiltrate.

Nine days after Himmler had received this blunt request to interfere in military and armaments matters, he repeated his wish that "Colonel Dornberger [be ordered to see] the Führer."[5] Evidently Hitler was still not favorable to the project, for Himmler noted that he had to keep repeating his requests. Clearly resigned, he asked Berger to discuss the Peenemünde demand with me after all.

On April 17, 1943, Himmler had his third Peenemünde meeting with Hitler in several months.[6] Colonel Zanssen, the military commander of Peenemünde, had been accused by the SS of being hostile to the regime because he was a devout Catholic. After his meeting with Hitler, Himmler ordered Berger to tell the Gestapo "to investigate these espionage matters in the ranks of the Catholics."[7] But in mid-June Colonel General Fromm sent an angry letter to Himmler, pointing out that Zanssen was by no means a committed Catholic. On the contrary, as Fromm informed Himmler with his typical irony, Zanssen was married to a Protestant and had had his children baptized in the Protestant Church, which would indicate that such accusations were unjust. Kaltenbrunner confirmed Fromm's statements in a letter to Himmler.[8] But this was not the last attempt of the SS to gain control of rocket production in this manner.

On May 26, 1943, a rocket had made its first successful flight, a distance of 265 kilometers. It struck only 5 kilometers off target. It seemed as if they could start manufacturing the A-4 despite all risks. I could therefore take the chance of presenting Dornberger and Wernher von Braun to Hitler on July 8, 1943. Hitler appeared impressed. That same day he ordered us to get "the missing manpower, if it could not be obtained elsewhere, from the production of the general Wehrmacht equipment." He also decreed "that *only Germans* should be employed in the manufacture of the A-4."[9]

Just two days after Hitler's decision to give top priority to the production of the A-4, Himmler went to see Hitler again. Himmler protested that the three most important men involved in the A-4 project, Major General Dornberger,[10] von Braun, and Steinhoff, had flown to Hitler together and in an unsafe Heinkel 111 to boot. He maintained that such joint flights should be prohibited because they were too risky. "The Führer told me to have Lieutenant General Rudolf Schmundt order the three gentlemen in question, on behalf of the Führer, not to fly together anymore."[11] It was Himmler's habit to interfere even in trivial matters, thereby reminding the people involved that he was interested in what they were doing.

On July 25, 1943, Hitler signed an edict prepared by myself: "The greatest output of A-4 missiles is to be attained as swiftly as possible. . . . The German plants that manufacture the A-4 missile, as well as those supplying the component parts, must instantly be supplied with skilled German workers. . . . The Reich Minister for Armaments and Munitions is to direct the A-4 program."[12] My authority was unrestricted. Only German workers—as Hitler had first determined two months earlier—were to implement the project; and we were to avoid Sauckel's program of forced laborers, which would simply promote the infiltration of spies. However, I was to remain in charge for only four weeks.

According to his calendar entry, Himmler was in Hitler's East Prussian headquarters, the Wolf's Lair, on August 19 and had supper with Bormann. He normally had a talk with Hitler after such suppers.[13]

That same evening, accompanied by Saur and his staff of experts, I arrived at Hitler's headquarters. Then or on the next day, we talked to Hitler about aerial damage in Peenemünde, Schweinfurt, Nuremberg, and Regensburg. An edict of Hitler's was to regulate the position of the Todt Organization within the Wehrmacht; a further edict was to make 500 more skilled workers available for the bottleneck in the manufacture of crankshafts. Next, we discussed the problems generated by the Russian advance in the Donets area for the industry which had just been rebuilt; and finally, we talked about the production of antiaircraft guns and antitank guns.

At some point Hitler brought up the manufacture of the A-4 and the necessity of keeping it top secret. In this respect, he said, he had received a cogent suggestion from Himmler: Our concern about any betrayal of this highly crucial armaments project could be reduced to a fraction if the work were done by prisoners of concentration camps. Himmler, he said, had told him that he could guarantee all the necessary manpower for the project. Skilled workers and even scientific specialists would be removed from the concentration camps and used in the construction of the rockets. Furthermore, he had asked a young, energetic construction expert, who had already proved his outstanding ability, to take charge of the enterprise, in case Hitler agreed with the proposal.

Neither Saur nor I cared for this new development. We remembered our negative experiences with unsuccessful earlier programs, when all the blame had been placed on us. We remembered Himmler's threats to my staffers when he had failed in his plans to build up his own armaments production in the Buchenwald and Neuengamme concentration camps. But Hitler was quite taken with Himmler's idea; and he ordered Saur and me to go to Himmler as soon as possible to discuss the details with him.

The very next afternoon, we went to Himmler's nearby headquarters in Hochwald, where we met with him from three to four P.M.[14]

Himmler instantly surprised us with the news that Hitler had just appointed him minister of the interior. Until then, Himmler, as head of the German Police, had, strangely enough, been subordinate to Wilhelm Frick, the minister of the interior. To be sure, Himmler was as untroubled by this bureaucratic defect in his legal position as I was by the lack of any legal authority in production control.

However, there was one other area in which Himmler departed from the reserve he had previously practiced in the government realm. That same day, he conversed with Funk about the appointment of Ohlendorf and Hayler to the Reich Ministry of Economy. Naturally, in our meeting, Himmler was aware of his strong position—both as minister of the interior, because of Ohlendorf's delegation (as the leading figure in the Ministry of Economy), and now as Hitler's representative for the manufacture of the A-4. Himmler played out his triumph to the hilt: "This time, I require a first-class staff of your engineers, who will have to be responsible to both of us for the strict execution of the Führer's orders. On my side, I have assigned Kammler, one of my most capable SS commanders. I ask you to reflect on whom you wish to place at his side. I would agree to Degenkolb,[15] if he proves capable. This will be the largest and most important armaments task that the Führer could assign. You heard him say so himself. We will carry it out. For the SS and myself, it is an obligation to translate the Führer's will into action. I gave him my promise and I keep my promises! I expect that you will contribute your share to the solution." Hitler, he said, had placed his hand on Himmler's shoulder when saying good-bye and had emphasized: "I am relying particularly on you and your energy. You are my guarantee for a punctual, precise implementation of my orders."

At the close of our meeting, Himmler again stressed that in contrast to other SS armaments projects, coordination between SS agencies and the technical organizations of the "self-responsibility of industry" must absolutely be guaranteed for this highly technological achievement. This, he said, was the express wish of the Führer, who had already agreed to everything—which was Himmler's hint that he would permit no discussion of his decision. Finally, he told me that the Führer had requested that we continue this discussion with him that very same evening.

In February 1942, when appointing me minister of armaments, Hitler had told me to ask him for a meeting in case of any conflicts so that he could deploy his full authority in my favor.[16] This time, he had authorized Himmler to enfeeble any protests of mine by ordering me to come to him.

Thus, we went back to Hitler's headquarters. Hitler talked enthusiastically about the consequences of A-4 attacks on London. In March 1942 Hitler had demanded an unrealizable program of 3,000 A-4's per month.[17] But he did not repeat this demand, since his interest in the rocket had waned. However, in the spring of 1943 a demanding but feasible program was set up. It reduced Hitler's original demand to one-third and provided for a production increase of up to 950 A-4 units each month by December 1949. However, on this day in August 1943 Hitler gave free rein to his imagination. He demanded an absolute minimum of 5,000 A-4 rockets within the shortest possible time. The thing I had always feared was here: tangible success was imperiled by immoderate demands.

The debate with Hitler and Himmler went on until early evening. My reservations about technical difficulties with such a complicated missile went unheeded. My argument that the assignment could be compared only with the mass production of a recently developed racing car made no impact.[18] My anxieties were caused not only by the thought of all kinds of technical difficulties, but also by the predictable conflicts that, as experience taught me, would come from working with the SS.

But Hitler could not be stopped. "This will be retribution against England. With this, we will force England to her knees. The use of this new weapon will make any enemy invasion impossible. For the south and southeast of England can now be dominated by us."

The outcome of the discussion was noted in the minutes as follows: "The Führer, on the basis of a—*and not my*—suggestion had ordered that all measures must be renewed in order to push forward the construction of the required manufacturing facilities and the production of the A-4 together with the SS Reichsführer, with a powerful employment of his manpower from the concentration camps. The Führer has decided that the existing facilities should continue to be emphatically set up and used for manufacture as transitional facilities until a definitive manufacture can be guaranteed in safe places and in a safe form with the greatest possible use of caves and other proper bunker positions. The final development plant should, in accordance with the suggestion of the SS Reichsführer, be set up in the Generalgouvernement in connection with the troop drilling grounds that belong to the Reichsführer."[19]

The next day Himmler conferred for one and a half hours with Pohl, Kammler, and Glücks (Pohl's representative in the administration of concentration camps).[20] They seem to have jointly drafted an unusually sharp and icy letter, which was handed to me the very same day: "With this letter, I inform you that I, as SS Reichsführer, in accordance with our agreement of yesterday, do hereby *take charge* of the manufacture of the A-4 instrument." The previous evening Hitler had established that all measures were to be taken in tandem by the SS Reichsführer and the minister of armaments. Now, Himmler categorically established that he would take sole responsibility for carrying out the Führer's assignment. Himmler continued: "Today, I have discussed the entire assignment with my men and I am convinced that we can absolutely carry out the promise to deliver 5,000 A-4's in the shortest possible time." (Himmler's "shortest possible time" was to stretch out to 18 months. The 5,000 A-4's were not completed until January 1945.)

Himmler's letter went on: "I have transferred the assignment to SS Obergruppenführer Pohl, placing SS Brigade Commander Dr. [Hans] Kammler as the responsible director under him. I ask you to receive SS Brigade Commander Dr. Kammler personally in the next few days, so that he may be instructed by you yourself in all demands; and, vice versa, so that he can also tell you all the necessary prerequisites for the implementation of the assignment, so that it can be approved and secured in the first few days. You can rest assured that the SS will not disappoint the Führer or you in this task, which is vital to the war effort."[21]

Himmler was to address the SS squad commanders in Posen on October 4, 1943, and as a catch phrase for his speech he jotted down: "Competence conflicts. The man who succeeds is competent."[22] In his speech, he then stated: "Whatever must be achieved for Germany, for the SS . . . is to be implemented by the man who can implement it, and he must be willing to take total responsibility."[23]

Himmler had also acted according to this philosophical principle, as it were. After our experiences with Himmler following the failure of his projects in Buchenwald and Neuengamme, this letter was not an attractive prelude.

Yet this decision should have been completely welcome for me. We had no reserves of manpower; and now Kammler had to take responsibility for this industrial capacity, which had to be built up. Furthermore, I felt that this assignment would satisfy Kammler's ambition. Later on, to keep him away from my actual work area, I tried to give him the military responsibility for launching this and other V-weapons.

As had been made clear by the Ohlendorf case, the SS had a "crown prince" for the Ministry of Economy. However, Himmler made long-range plans for other important ministries as well. In the SS, it was already said that Kammler was to be developed as my successor.[24] Such men, selected by Himmler, were infiltrated whenever a gap appeared or a mistake was to be abolished. They would then gain influence bit by bit in their work area.

And indeed, Himmler succeeded with his decisive stroke against my previously unchallenged authority by the circuitous route of developing and manufacturing the new rocket. Kammler, who made an extremely fresh, energetic, and ruthless impression—comparable to Heydrich's—had begun by taking over relatively small tasks of the A-4 production within the overall armaments area. Then he had assumed responsibility for rocket launchings, which was actually a military task. Finally, he obtained the production of all special weapons on the basis of rockets; and at the close of the war, he also received responsibility for manufacturing all jet airplanes. At the last minute, Hitler put Kammler in charge of all air armaments. Thus—just a few weeks before the end of the war—he had become commissioner general for all important weapons.[25] Himmler's goal was achieved. But there was no more armaments industry.

Very soon we had the same situation as with Buchenwald and Neuengamme. The explanations of the first phase were followed by one delay after another. To be sure, six weeks after the decision, Himmler appeared in the Central Works and, playing himself up as lord of the enterprise, announced that the Supreme Command of the Army had previously failed to assign the manufacture of A-4 rockets to the Central Works, Inc. Hence, further assignments were not made. But this was yet another unfounded reproach. And one day later Kammler could correct it: "According to an oral communication from Major General Dornberger on October 16, 1943, assignment of Supreme Command of Army to Central Works was signed on October 14 [i.e., one day before Himmler's visit]. . . . Alleged reasons for delays: Budget and anti-infiltration considering the high amount."[26] It took another three days for Assignment no. 0011/5565/43 to be issued in writing. It called for the "manufacture of 900 A-4 instruments per month up to an overall number of 12,000 units." Their final assembly would be at a "standard price of 40,000 marks apiece. The overall price: 480 million marks."[27] Nine hundred A-4's a month was the production goal that Degenkolb had set for himself; it was way below Hitler's demand for 3,000 instruments a month.

On October 20, 1943, Kammler wired Himmler that "a discussion with Colonel General Fromm" had taken place "in accordance with an *order* from the SS Reichsführer." That same day Major General Dornberg, it said, had received an accurate compilation on the still missing personnel, material, and equipment, as well as drawings. He had been given a five-day deadline by Kammler to take care of the matter. "I will then inform you of results." Nevertheless, two full months had passed since Hitler had given the assignment to the SS; and they were still dealing with preparations.

An agreement was reached on the same day about establishing an underground testing site for the development of an "America rocket" with tenfold propulsion power. Large caves were to be hollowed out in the mountains near Traunstein. Kammler reported to Himmler: "After a bombproof testing location was found by telegram and approved by Major General Dornberger, the Waffen-SS today received the assignment from the Supreme Command of the Army to carry out the construction project. According to the meeting with Colonel General Fromm on October 20, the preliminary project will be set up by us by November 10. Colonel General Fromm and Reich Minister Speer will then unequivocally clarify and create the necessary conditions for the construction. The preliminary work has begun today. I ask that the SS Reichsführer be notified accordingly."[28] (See Appendix 16.)

In the Central Works, the cave district in the Harz Mountains, where the production of the A-4 was being prepared, conditions were scandalous and actually interfered with production. In early December 1944, Dr. A. Poschmann, chief physician of the Todt Organization, told me that he had seen Dante's Inferno.[29] A few days later, with more and more complaints from the management of the Central Works, I went to inspect the production personally. The ministry chronicle noted about my inspection: "On the morning of December 10, 1943, the minister went to inspect a new plant in the Harz Mountains. The implementation of this tremendous mission required the maximum strength of the men in charge. Some had even reached the stage of having to be forcibly sent on vacation in order to restore their nerves. The plant was visited to the depth of the shafts and viewed from an airplane overhead. The visitors were guided alternately by Director Degenkolb and Brigade Commander Kammler."[30]

After roughly one hour's inspection, we returned to the construction barracks. What did I see? Expressionless faces, dull eyes, in which not even hatred was discernible, exhausted bodies in dirty blue-gray trousers. At the approach of our group, they stood at attention upon hearing a cutting command and held their pale-blue caps in their hands. They seemed incapable of any reaction. Two and a half years later, I was to wear the same clothing but not remove my pale-blue cap when a subordinate inspection official approached me in Spandau prison.

The prisoners were undernourished and overtired; the air in the cave was cool, damp, and stale and stank of excrement. The lack of oxygen made me dizzy; I felt numb. Oddly enough, I thought of the Greek prisoners of war who dug out the caves of Syracuse two thousand years ago. Just a few years earlier, I had visited the caves with Magda Goebbels and the sculptors Arno Breker and Joseph Thorak. I had shuddered at the heritage of cruel centuries. Now I saw bleaker scenes than my imagination had pictured in Syracuse.

The SS Commanders probably knew how visitors reacted to this horrible sight. For they promptly offered us a glass of spirits, which I quickly gulped down—contrary to my habit. When I asked for statistics on the high mortality rate in the camp, I was told about the inadequate medical attention and the sleeping barracks of the people in the unventilated caves.

I then ordered the construction of a barrack city for the 10,000 inmates.

Five weeks later, on January 13, 1944, the chronicle says: "The minister has received Dr. Poschmann, who, as physician for all the agencies in the ministry, has painted the state of health at the Central Works in the blackest colors. The rapid construction of this factory and the naturally unhealthy conditions would have an unfavorable effect on performance without sufficient medical attention. The minister has agreed that the necessary medical measures must be made up for so that the amount of illness can be reduced in the factory."[31] One day later, on January 14, 1944, I saw to it that the Central Works were inspected again—this time by Stobbe-Dethleffsen, head of the Construction Office in my ministry, and two of his closest colleagues, Schönleben and Berlitz. The entry in the chronicle goes: "In order to obtain a personal impression of the underground labor and the employment of the concentration camp prisoners of the SS, Stobbe-Dethleffsen is inspecting the Central Works construction project on January 14 together with Waffen-SS Lieutenant General Kammler, Schönleben, and Berlitz."[32]

Several days later, on January 18, 1944, I was taken to Professor Gebhardt's clinic with a leg ailment. I did not resume my work until four months later, in early May.

However, the barracks were erected within three months after my order. A former inmate, the Frenchman Jean Michel, reports: "In late March or early April 1944, the barracks were put up; the deportees, many of whom had not seen the sun for months, could finally all sleep outside the tunnel. The tunnel now served only as a laboratory, a storehouse. On the other hand," Michel continues, "Albert Speer maintains in his memoirs [*Inside the Third Reich*] that after his visit of December 10 he undertook various steps to improve the sanitary conditions of the deportees at Dora and its 31 branches. That may explain the medical peculiarities: teeth care, camions des deistage. I repeat: It is possible that the German scientists and engineers at least had the intention of a more humane attitude toward the deportees. If that is so, then the power of the SS must have been greater. No great improvement came of the intentions."[33]

In a footnote on the attempts of my staffers to improve the working and living conditions, Michel remarks: "To be objective, I [Michel] quote these passages from the memorial of the camp at Dora: 'In March 1944, Savatsky [Speer's representative in Dora] demanded and received from the SS permission for the prisoners to eat their soup outside; then in May–June, for sleeping barracks to be set up in the main camp; and finally in July, for the workers to be lodged in blocks reserved for them alone.' "

Likewise, Dr. Poschmann, head physician of the Todt Organization, tried to help: "The first deliveries of additional food, medications, vitamin preparations, etc., from our stores in the Ministry of Armaments and the Todt Organization aroused a great protest from Kammler and [Robert] Ley," Dr. Poschmann wrote to me on February 13, 1978. "Nevertheless, with your and Professor Brandt's backing we kept supplying the laborers and prisoners.[34] They were even given medication and vitamin preparations so that they might supply one another in the camp, to which the medical personnel of the Todt Organization had no access. However, the medication was taken from the prisoners upon their entry into the camp. We then supplied the sick and weakened prisoners ourselves on the labor sites."[35] On August 5, 1944, I thanked Dr. Karl Brandt, the "Commissioner General of the Führer for Medicine and Health," and I asked him to continue this action. "For I am convinced that the additional medical and sanitary attention is one of the essential measures for increasing performance in the factories."[36]

Indeed, the conditions of prisoners in the Central Works did improve, as shown by the statistics: In December 1943, when I visited the Central Works, 630 of the 11,000 prisoners died, i.e., 5.7 percent.[37] But in August 1944, the mortality had gone down to 100 deaths out of 12,000 prisoners, i.e., 0.8 percent.[38]

Himmler must have been all the more annoyed by this interference in "his" rocket manufacturing because none of his boasts had come true. In January 1944, only 50 of the slated 650 rockets came off the assembly line.[39]

In mid-March 1944, Himmler had made a second drastic attempt to intimidate the staffers in the development of the A-4 project and make them submissive after his attack on Colonel Zanssen nine months earlier had failed. Without my knowledge, he had Wernher von Braun and two of his "most important colleagues" arrested for armaments sabotage. It required the most strenuous efforts and my personal intervention with Hitler to cancel the arrests. On May 13, 1944, Hitler promised me "in the B matter [that] so long as he is indispensable to me, he will be exempt from any prosecution, difficult as the general consequences might be."[40]

On May 12, 1944, a bare two weeks after my return from several months of illness, I tried to reduce the SS influence on my offices by re-arranging the distribution of assignments in the A-4 program. The SS Economic Administration Headquarters was then basically left with the expansion of the Central Works. It provided as manpower the prisoners needed for expansion and production, and they were solely under the disciplinary control of the SS. The development and testing of the A-4 was now returned to the Supreme Command of the Army, namely the Army Ordnance Office, and was placed under General Dornberger's aegis. The special A-4 committee of my ministry, chaired by Degenkolb, set up the production program; it secured the technical production requirements and provided for the punctual allocation of machines, components, and materials. In contrast to Himmler's unauthorized control demand, the manufacture was under the management office of the Ceneral Works, which was in turn under the direction of the management provided by the organizations of self-responsibility, which management was in turn responsible to Demag director Georg Rickhey.[41] My position was strengthened after my reconciliation with Hitler, so I could act tough with Himmler.

However, my attempt at reducing the power of the SS leaders over the entire manufacturing process failed very soon. After July 20, 1944, Himmler had succeeded Fromm as "Commander in Chief of the Reserve Army and Head of Army Armaments." On August 6, 1944, he put Kammler "in charge of all preparations for achieving the employability of the A-4. . . . You are responsible only to me as well as to SS Obergruppen-führer Jüttner [chief of staff of the Commander in Chief of the Reserve Army and chief of staff of army armaments]." In his new wealth of power, Himmler did not even consider it necessary to bother maintaining form by sending me a copy of this order.[42] Meanwhile, I was incriminated because my name had been discovered on the ministerial list of the conspirators.

A short time later, Kammler wrote to Saur, making Himmler's vague authorization more specific. Five days later I protested to Jüttner: "As I see from a letter of Dr. Kammler's to Herr Saur, the SS Reichsführer, in his capacity as supreme commander in chief of the reserve army, has given the latter the responsibility for the *manufacture* and utilization of the A-4 instrument. The only agency responsible for the manufacture of the A-4 instrument *under me* is exclusively the A-4 Special Committee chaired by Herr Director Degenkolb, who is under the overall responsibility of Herr Saur. I ask you to change the order of the SS Reichsführer to Herr Kammler accordingly after a discussion with me."[43] But I got almost nowhere. Even in minor details, Himmler was now much more careful about retaining control of all A-4 matters. The appropriate ministers had the right to give Hitler suggestions for awarding the Knight's Cross of the civilian War Merit Cross. Himmler now took the initiative here too. On September 28, 1944, he got Hitler to approve the Knight's Cross for Dornberger and two of his colleagues in the A-4 project, Riedel and Kunze. Slipshod and disrespectful, he added in a wire to me: "I think it would be best if the formal suggestions were handed in my you."[44] I let Himmler wait six weeks for my answer: So far, the following have been suggested for the V-2: "Herr Rickhey [director of the Central Works] and Herr Kunze, plus, from the area of the head of army armaments, General Dornberger and Dr. Thiel, one of the designers (died in action)." The actual initiator of the rocket development, Wernher von Braun, had been ignored by Himmler. I found this grotesque. I wrote to Himmler, saying it struck me as "necessary to honor [Wernher von Braun] with the Knight's Cross of the War Merit Cross since he has been active as the closest colleague of General Dornberger since the start of the A-4 development ten years ago."[45]

That winter, on December 31, 1944, Himmler did not even consider it appropriate to reach an agreement with my agencies on his "delimitation of the work areas and responsibility in the area of the A-4 program." The distribution list for this order does not even include my ministry. The order was only to be sent to my ministry "by way of a postscript." An obvious insult, for, translated from officialese, it meant that I was not to deal with the matter. This seemingly insignificant detail is more important for understanding the decree than its long-winded content. Next came further decrees from Himmler and Kammler, which, however, altered in no way the fact of the total takeover of the A-4 development and production.

In April 1943 Degenkolb had slated a daily production of 30 units as a future goal. Hitler had thought of three times that number. But the

Army Ordnance Office had endorsed Degenkolb's forecast and given the industry an assignment of 900 units a month.

However, according to the calculations that the Central Works sent to the Supreme Command of the Army, only the following units could be delivered:

January 1944	50
February	86
March	170
April	253
May	437
June	132
July	86
August	374
September	629
October	628
November	662
December	613

In twelve months of that year, the total amount was thus 4,120 units.

January 1945	690
February	612
Until March 18	362

For two and a half months of 1945, the total was 1,664 units.[46]

In early April the prisoners had been moved into the barrack city, and production had zoomed upwards. In June and July it went down again because of countless technical changes. It is astounding that a daily production of 21 A-4 rockets continued month after month, from September 1944 until the end of the war, despite the armaments reduction caused by the transportation catastrophe on the Ruhr. The high production figures in spite of all difficulties in the last months of the war reveal that Degenkolb's goal was attainable.

However, there was a visible difference between the effectiveness of the Central Works and that of other SS manufacturing endeavors. This difference was due to the close cooperation between the SS leaders and the members of the Ministry of Armaments. The goal that Himmler had always striven for was realized: that the technicians and engineers of armaments should run the SS works under the control of the SS. Kammler, according to Jüttner's edict of December 31, 1944, should utilize the organs of "industrial self-responsibility."[47] Industry remained "fully responsible for

industrial manufacturing." And why should Himmler assume this responsibility after his representative Kammler could make the fundamental
decisions and after my organization under Degenkolb had produced 613
A-4 rockets despite the collapse of the armaments industry in December
1944?

It was precisely because of this partial responsibility of industrial experts
that the production result contrasted so sharply with the constant failures
of the SS in the concentration camps, which they also managed.

But all these efforts were useless as long as our gigantic rockets transported quite conventional explosives to their targets. We did not have the
atomic bomb. Hence, the entire production was actually a failure, no
matter how successful.

Chapter 16

The Cave Fantasy and Its Consequences

IN THE SPRING OF 1943 Hitler had asked that "a long-term effort be made to manufacture the most sensitive products, like crankshafts, bevel gears, electric devices, etc., in factories that are totally under concrete protection." Hitler considered this protection urgent, and "the transfer to the East of the Reich only conditionally valuable."[1] This was certainly a far-sighted directive; but it could not be carried out. Merely to protect the most important manufacturing against bomb damage, millions of square meters of manufacturing areas would have had to be moved underground—and right in the middle of the extremely tense late phase of the war. Not to mention the additional strains put on the construction industry because of bombing damage.

On October 10, 1943, Goering made a similar demand. Because of "constant enemy interference with the aircraft production program [we must] set up bombproof manufacturing sites as rapidly as possible, at least for engine production and special bottlenecked parts. To the extent that the utilization of large caves, cellars, nonoperating mines, and unused fortress facilities in the home-war area and in the occupied territories is not possible, factories must be placed under concrete protection. For now, I consider it necessary to set up at least six or eight such factories on a large scale."[2]

One year later, in the spring of 1944, Hitler was to complain bitterly that I did not carry out his orders and Goering's demands. The resulting conflict nearly ended with my dismissal. I had quite decisively argued that it was impossible to fight bombers with concrete; and the armaments industry could not be brought under the earth or under concrete even with many years of work. Moreover, to our good fortune, I added, the enemy was attacking armaments production in the widespread delta of a river with many arms. By protecting this delta, we would merely force him to attack the area where the industrial river was concentrated in a deep and narrow riverbed. I was thinking of chemistry, coal, power plants, and other things that gave me nightmares, for instance the transportation network.[3]

Himmler was more active than I was. In August 1943 he turned to one of the many organizations in which able-bodied men were dodging their front-line service, the "Cave Demonstration Division in the Military Science Institute for Karst and Cave Research of the SS Karst Defense Unit." Himmler ordered this bureau to draw up a register of German caves. The 11-page report was divided according to states. It listed 93 caves of which some 10 would have been of interest if transportational access to them would not have spelled a disproportionately high expenditure. The largest cave, the "Ice Giant World" of the Tennen Mountains, lay in the middle of high, inaccessible mountains.

Himmler's Cave Demonstration Division then felled his project automatically on August 25. The memorandum said that aside from the difficulties of opening them up, the caves normally did not offer the conditions that must be expected of "arrival and departure possibilities, ventilation, humidity, temperature, and solidity of rock." Experience "showed unequivocally that the use of machines—and similar facilities—in caves would very quickly result in far-reaching damage to all manufacturing equipment because of the relentless water. Furthermore, work-related daily presence in caves often [causes] severe problems of health."[4]

But Himmler refused to be disheartened by this negative information from his own agencies. A few weeks later the SS Ancestral Heritage Office was told to "confer with all the existing experts on the homeland as well as other private scholars, of whom there must be a considerable number," and they were to work out a scientific compilation of the existing caves.[5]

My own ministry attempted to gather data on useful caves a few months later. A few of them were slated for expansion, so the SS arrived at closed doors. The Ancestral Heritage Office informed Himmler that "in light of the war-vital necessity," it was not possible simply to go over the head of the Ministry of Armament. Himmler replied that these caves had to be left to armaments, but that it was important "not to give away the caves, but to maintain the claims to a later return."[6] Gain property, hold on to property—that was Himmler's constant watchword, even in the final phase of the war.

Kammler, who was an engineer with a university degree, displayed abilities where the SS bureaucracy of the concentration camps had failed. His success was sensational in regard to A-4 manufacturing. "In an almost impossibly short period of two months, he [transformed] the underground facilities [in the Harz Mountains] from a raw state into a factory." I wrote him that this feat "does not have an even remotely similar example anywhere in Europe and is unsurpassable even by American standards." Whereby I admitted my admiration for American production methods.[7]

Kammler's astonishing performance induced me to entrust him—as I informed Himmler on December 22, 1943—"with special construction assignments." Anxiously, though, I restricted my authorization: "However, I am greatly concerned that the practical implementation of these construction projects take place in closest contact with the Main Committee for Construction, which is responsible to me for the scheduled and efficient construction of all building objects within the Reich territory. For the same reason, the use of leaders in the construction industry is to be regulated only in closest contact with the Main Committee for Construction. The right of disposal over these firms and experts in the German construction industry must remain with the Main Committee for Construction. I ask you to issue appropriate directives to your agencies."[8] I had already had experience with Kammler's vehement urge to take over my leading experts. In early March 1944, Goering too, still in charge of air armaments, appointed Kammler his representative for the "Kammler special constructions."[9]

In early December 1943, Himmler heard that there were supposedly tunnels near Reichstadt, Crossnow, and Spalle. "The Führer has suggested that they are to be used for setting up underground factories," Himmler wrote to SS Obergruppenführer Koppe, who was responsible for the Generalgouvernement. "Find out whether this has already occurred. If not, then transfer armaments factories there in your capacity as [Frank's] general deputy [for armaments in the Generalgouvernement] or in cooperation with SS Obergruppenführer Pohl. Then report to me when this has been done."[10] The project also fitted in with Himmler's goal of an SS-owned armaments industry in Poland.

After a delay of six weeks, Brandt replied to a (now lost) report of Koppe's, whose negative findings had angered Himmler. He said "that, needless to say, a factory could not be placed in the tunnel. The tunnels should, however, be used as roads; and appropriate shafts and spaces could be excavated in the mountain from the tunnel." Furthermore, "we must set about creating a large number of subterranean things." The wording was amateurish, and the matter was none of Himmler's business.[11] At the same time, Himmler ordered Pohl to "begin the expansion. Workers should, expediently, be taken from Auschwitz. The SS Reichsführer asks to be informed as soon as the first plans are ready."[12]

After a pause of three weeks, Pohl reported that the tunnels were very suitable as storerooms. The discussion with Agency Ia of the military district command responsible for Krakow had revealed "that all the tunnels have been made available by the Führer Headquarters to the Wehrmacht commander in chief of Krakow for strong important military supplies. Hence, nothing further can be undertaken by us in this matter."[13] Such reports, according to which Hitler, Himmler, or other leading agencies interfered with matters that should have been dealt with by government counselors, move like a red thread through my experience of those years. The feeling of impotence, aggravated by the military situation, caused something like an escape into details. To return to this example: The simplest way would have been to have someone on Himmler's staff question the subordinate officials in other agencies in order to establish whether the caves were already in use. But since Hitler and Himmler were personally involved, then of course a Pohl or a Kammler had to deal with the matter himself, even though it did not correspond to his rank. As the files reveal, special planes were even used for inspecting the location.

As the war advanced, Himmler interfered more and more insolently with the affairs of my ministry. Usually he turned to Kammler with regard to large-scale construction projects churned out by his brain, which was indefatigably preoccupied with new ideas. Thus, on May 8, 1944, he said: "I believe we ought to consider whether we should build subterranean factories as underwater factories. Purely as an amateur, I picture it as follows: sheet walls should be built on some lakes, the water pumped out, the factory constructed in concrete in the ground, and then the water let back in over it."[14] One can imagine the response of specialists in the construction and armaments industries when reading such recommendations by one of the most powerful men in the Reich.

Two and a half months later, Brandt sent out reminder notes about the underwater manufacturing idea. And when there was still no reaction, he urgently repeated his demands two months later.[15] But Himmler's letters could not be found. Plainly, they had gotten lost in the business shuffle. Schleif, a subordinate SS commander, apologized to Brandt with a Turkish proverb: "The devil interferes in hurried matters."[16] Which induced Brandt to make the macabre comment that "one should not be disrupted by the devil's game; one should at most laugh at him as a philisopher [sic in the original]."[17]

Concerning the matter itself, however, Kammler had to reply in the negative: "The construction of underwater factories—as the Reichsführer suggests—is certainly possible; however, because it demands vast preparation, construction site facilities, and, above all, specialists, the expenditure would be so great that these ideas could not be carried out in a hurry. . . . After the war, however, the matter will by all means be scientifically investigated so that we may have the practical consequence of building facilities for underwater factories on a large scale."[18]

Himmler wanted to have the last word. The matter was settled. But, he felt, "it would certainly be good to utilize the many bodies of water by installing rails to put trains carrying fuel there. On the one hand, they would thus be more out of sight than out in the open; on the other hand, they cannot be shot at and ignited in the water. Please investigate this proposal and let me know what possibilities exist here."[19]

Once again an investigation had to be made merely because one of the powerful figures around Hitler took pipe dreams seriously without knowledge or jurisdiction in this area. After a suitable delay of four weeks, Schleif replied in Kammler's name: He had "taken up and investigated the SS Reichsführer's suggestion. However, the installation of rails in water would involve extraordinary construction difficulties, aside from the fact that the tracks leading up to these underwater rails would have to be built aboveground and would thus offer a clue for aerial reconnaissance. The fuel trains cannot be destroyed by incendiary bombs, but they are still extremely vulnerable to attacks by explosive bombs, especially those with penetration depth. Sighting underwater targets as deep as 30 meters offers no problems nowadays." Cautiously, to keep from annoying or angering the top superior—which would have been detrimental to any promotions—the SS Obersturmbannführer added that he "will in any case continue pursuing this suggestion and keep you up to date on any results of the investigation."[20]

On December 17, 1943, Himmler proposed a new ingenious action to Pohl. He sent Pohl plans that had been worked out at his behest by a standard commander. "See to it with all possible speed that such subterranean workrooms and factory rooms are set up in all our stone quarries. . . . I would like the tunnels, however, to have at least 50-meter-high, if possible 100-meter-high, roofs wherever this can be done. I envision that by summer of the year 1944 we can be installed as new cavemen in as many places as posssible in these factories, which are the only ones that are really protected."[21]

The answer again took five weeks, which would have overtaxed my ministerial patience. Pohl, with evident delight in instructing his boss, re-

plied that his experts had investigated the possibility of installing armaments factories in the granite quarries and that he had discussed the matter
with them. The stone formation in granite deposits is fractured; the tops
of the caves would not bear up. None of the quarries had an 80-meter
depth. But Pohl's most important argument was that the construction of
caves "would make the use of our stone quarries for obtaining ashlar highly
dubious, even though this task was planned for peacetime. When building
a cave, one cannot obtain blocks suitable for ashlar. One only gets rock
material that can be used for roadstone and asphalt."[22]

That same December of 1943, Himmler hit upon another idea. He ordered SS Oberführer Fritz Kranefuss to ask Dr. Carl Krauch, the head of
all German chemical companies, whether hydrogenation plants could be
installed underground to shield them against air raids. The reply from the
"Plenipotentiary for Special Questions of Chemical Production in the Four-
Year Plan" was negative:

"Blasting out large caves from the natural rock in order to install such
factories [would have] to be discounted from the very start because it would
require three or four times as long a construction period. . . . Furthermore,
[there would be] serious reservations about installing hydrogenation plants
underground. . . . Above all, we must consider the high danger of explosion
of hydrogen/air mixtures and also of any escaping hydrocarbons, which
tend to explode almost inevitably at very low percentages (2 or 3) and at
high percentages (70 or more). . . . The extreme operational danger and
the high vulnerability to sabotage in such a factory are obvious. Moreover,
any explosion would practically always destroy the entire factory with its
employees, while any factory or air damages in normal hydrogenation
plants have so far always affected at worst only portions of the factory."[23]

Himmler yielded to the technical realities and had Dr. Brandt of his
Personal Staff reply that the SS Reichsführer was fully sympathetic with the
operational reservations.[24] But this one time, he was in the wrong. Eleven
months later Himmler could enjoy a belated triumph. On November 3,
1944, SS Oberführer Kranefuss, general director of Brabag, informed him:
"After the various heavy air attacks on the fuel plants since May, I
heard in the course of the summer that now [subterranean] transfer plans
are to be processed and implemented. . . . Regrettably, what remains is
that six months were surely lost if not a whole year, and that once again
the bitterest experiences were necessary to bring about appropriate decisions and their implementation. Unfortunately we cannot count that this
plant" (the subterranean installation in the so-called Kirchleite, a large
wall directly on the Elbe) "can begin operations before August of next
year."[25]

Dr. Brandt thanked him on behalf of Himmler: "This case is yet another proof that the SS Reichsführer is always right," which seems a bit exaggerated after the mostly absurd suggestions of the past. He had, however, assumed, Dr. Brandt mordantly said, "that a verdict presented to the Reichsführer by Professor Krauch would be so well founded as to be considered practically irrefutable."[26]

The triumph, however, was moderated. The plants in question were small factories with an ultimate capacity of 50,000 tons in production, partly by coal liquefaction, partly by processing oil shale, partly by distilling crude oil. However, the damage caused by aerial attacks from May to December 1944 ran to a monthly average of over 160,000 tons. By early 1945 no underground plant was operating well enough to supply usable fuel.[27]

Once, in a group of slightly intoxicated SS commanders, Karl Gebhardt, Himmler's old friend and confidant, made an unabashed comment. He said that in Himmler's opinion, "Speer is a peril; he has to disappear." What was the background of these words? Could they have been caused by my independent position in Hitler's court or my sometimes insulting bluntness when anyone interfered with my area? Or did Himmler wish to remove the obstacle blocking his armaments ideas?

The motive may have been more serious. Karl Hanke, my old friend from the early years of the Third Reich, the former lover of Magda Goebbels and now Gauleiter of Silesia, had asked Hitler's Munich architect, Hermann Giessler, in March 1944 to take charge of urban planning and building in Breslau. Hanke said that there were various reasons for not giving this assignment to Speer. In his memoirs, which appeared thirty years after the war, Hermann Giessler reports: "He wanted to confide" one reason to me for the reserved attitude toward Speer: "He had very clear notions about Speer's goals. . . . He was exceedingly worried; it couldn't work out; the Führer ought to be told. . . . He asked me whether I knew that Speer was planning to succeed the Führer? Yes, I had heard about it, but I regarded it as gossip, an arrogant misreading of Speer's personality by the people around him. Here, the wish was the father of the thought. No, Hanke protested, there was more to it. He didn't want to burden me with all the junk, but the Führer had to be told, and he couldn't get to see him."[28] Could it be such rumors that turned Himmler against me?

After all, Hanke was not only Gauleiter of Lower Silesia, he was also a high-ranking SS commander; he must have informed Himmler, and Himmler must have felt that such ideas, which were not all that unreal, were interfering with his plans. The ruling strata of the army (represented by generals who were friendly with me—Kurt Zeitzler, chief of the general staff, and Heinz Guderian, the well-known tank general, as well as Friedrich Fromm, head of the reserve army, plus my friend Field Marshal Erhard Milch, state secretary in the Air Ministry)—looked upon me as one of several possibilities if Hitler were suddenly to step down in one way or another. Himmler must have realized this. All these generals feared an SS regime that would threaten their very existence. At the time, I did not even know that Claus Stauffenberg, Karl Goerdeler, and the men around Beck and Treskau had long since worked out far-reaching plans that ultimately led to an attempt to take over the government on July 20, 1944, with the help of the army.

At any rate, Himmler must have felt so threatened in his position by me that he did not shrink from attempting to murder his own minister of armaments, and he almost succeeded. I use the term "murder" reluctantly; but the people closest to me and I were already convinced that I had just barely escaped a serious attempt on my life.

After my collapse on January 18, 1944, I went to the Sanatorium of the Red Cross in Hohenlychen to be treated by Dr. Karl Gebhardt, the most famous knee specialist in Europe.[29] I did not know that this place was an SS institution and that Gebhardt was an intimate friend of Himmler's. By then I was reluctant to receive any medical attention from the SS. And indeed, a series of bizarre events took place during the next two months of a serious illness. First, I was confined to bed for twenty days as therapy for a bloody effusion in my knee joint. Against all medical practice, a cast was put on my left leg, which was kept motionless. Nothing was undertaken by way of gymnastcs to prevent the danger of thrombosis. The first time I got out of bed, alarming symptoms appeared: sputum containing blood, violent pains in my chest and back, difficulty in breathing. The head of a special clinic for knee and leg operations must have known that the danger of thrombosis is always present after a long period of bed rest, especially back then, when there were no anticoagulants.

Three days after I first sat up on the edge of the bed, the picture was as follows, according to Gebhardt's report:

"February 8, 1944. After getting up this afternoon, sudden intense pain in the left back musculature." Gebhardt concealed the fact that on that afternoon, I had handed him my handkerchief with brownish sputum containing blood. His report went on: "The examination revealed pains in the muscles of the back, left side, extreme when pressed; the auscultative examination revealed wheezing. The findings on the lung do not exclude the possibility of a muscular rheumatism." That same evening, Gebhardt gave me a good rubdown with bee venom, mixed with glass splinters, to fight this alleged attack of rheumatism, and he administered eleudron, a sulfa drug.

I am somewhat reluctant about repeating this report here. Considering the sufferings in the Central Works, where there was no medical assistance, much less clean beds, the report seems out of place. However, the issue is not my own person. Quite simply, the mentality of a "political physician" can be followed in this example.

"February 9, 1944. The pain in the muscles of the back persist with the same vehemence; breathing, coughing, and, at times, speech are troublesome. . . . The auscultative findings are the same as before; the slightly creaking sound over the left lung is somewhat stronger." Gebhardt evaded the truth: "These findings are to be explained by the poor breathing because of the pains on the left side."

On the same day, Gebhardt's internist offered an opinion that was closer to reality: "Lungs: No certain sound contraction, very rough breathing, countless almost crude rubbing sounds over the left lung. . . . Diagnosis: dryly circumscribed pleurisy."[30] But Gebhardt would not be swayed by this internist. The next day, February 10, 1944, Gebhardt insisted on his misdiagnosis of a violent rheumatism. He wrote: "The muscles are extremely hard, almost cramped, and very painful when pressed. The pains are so strong that the use of narcotics was necessary. The auscultatory findings are the same, indicating an acute muscular rheumatism. . . . The muscular rheumatism is to be treated with methyl-melobrin and painkillers."[31]

After my release from Spandau, I asked several physicians to reconstruct Gebhardt's therapeutic methods on the basis of the medical report. These physicians were the internist Professor Bock of Tübingen University, former chairman of the German Society for Internal Medicine; X-ray specialist Professor Frommhold, also of Tübingen; and Dr. R. Bauer, retired radiologist of the Berlin Charité Hospital. Their findings were unequivocal: such basic mistakes could not be tolerated even if made by an orthopedist.

Professor Friedrich Koch, the internist at the Charité Hospital and a close colleague of Dr. Ferdinand Sauerbruch, was altered by my secretary Annemarie Kempf. He was put in charge of my case, with the support of Karl Brandt, the "Plenipotentiary for Hygiene and Health" and, even more important, a member of Hitler's private circle (like myself).

On the night of February 10, Koch, equipped with special authorization, took over the treatment. In his first medical report, Professor Koch wrote: "In accordance with the course of the illness, the symptoms could only be interpreted as an embolism. The examination revealed a massive sound contraction with no sound of breathing over the entire left lung all the way to the shoulder blade ridge, in back and in front to the clavicle. This condition [became] extremely ominous during the night of February 11 and in the daytime on February 12," i.e., three days after Koch had stopped all medication and prescribed complete rest. "Extreme difficulty in breathing, blue coloration of the skin, considerable rapidity of the pulse, up to 120, high temperatures; tormenting dry cough with sharp pains over the left side and coughing up of blood. The patient had total bed rest and was not allowed any excitement or further medication; on February 14 there was a turn for the better, which continued quite amazingly until February 15."[32]

Given the state of medicine in those days, a lung embolism was a dangerous, potentially terminal illness. I survived because Koch took over my case. But if anyone had tried to increase my weakness, who could and would verify the result of such efforts? Gebhardt seemed to be making a persistent effort, and he kept trying.

A few days after this crisis, Professor Koch told my then friend Robert Frank that during those three perilous days Gebhardt had asked him to perform a small operation, which would have endangered my life. At first Professor Koch pretended not to understand; and when he then refused to perform the desired operation, Gebhardt grew evasive. He claimed he had only wanted to test Koch.[33] Robert Frank begged me to hold my tongue, for Profesor Koch was afraid of vanishing forever into a concentration camp if I did anything in the matter. Viewing the period carefully, I see that such intentions did not stir me so deeply as they might now seem to have done when I write them down. In such a system, I had to reckon with the same type of danger as the leading Romans in the days of the Claudians.

Shortly before the end of the war I asked Koch what had taken place at that time. But he would only confirm that he had had vehement arguments with Gebhardt about my case. When Koch was interrogated by an American officer on May 12, 1947, he made no statements about these events. Perhaps he hesitated only because Gebhardt was being tried at Nuremberg for surgical experiments on prisoners. His trial ended with a death sentence.[34]

During my forced sojourn at Hohenlychen, Xaver Dorsch, my representative in the Todt Organization, was already furthering his career. On March 5, 1944, he supported Hitler's plan to construct six or eight large concrete bunkers such as Goering had envisioned in October 1943. Each was to be 100,000 square meters in size and take in portions of the endangered production of aircraft.

Hitler had agreed with Himmler over a year before that about the necessity of the concrete protection. Now he only repeated his old demand when he told Dorsch: "The measures initiated" for the safety of the armaments industry by means of caves and bunker construction "are not to be carried out as temporary measures under any circumstances. . . . They are the prelude to a far-reaching and definitive transfer of all German industrial factories under the earth, since this is the only way to create long-term conditions for preserving the manufacturing plants in case of war."[35]

The following day, March 6, 1944, Himmler summoned Dorsch for a meeting from 3:00 to 4:30 P.M. We must constantly bear in mind that Himmler had nothing, absolutely nothing, to do with these matters and that according to the government rules of procedure in the Third Reich, he had no right to confer with anyone on my staff. But Himmler had known Dorsch from the time they were young. The two men were still intimate, and Dorsch was also one of the "Old Fighters" who had taken part in the March to the Feldherrnhalle in November 1923. Thus, Himmler had no difficulty interfering in my ministry. One hour after meeting with Dorsch, Himmler conferred with Kammler.[36] Three days later he visited Goering in his Castle Veldenstein, and the two men had an unusually long conference: from 11:30 A.M. to 7:00 P.M., including luncheon in the castle. This was all the more conspicuous since they were anything but friends and rarely met.[37] They certainly must have discussed the prospect offered by Hitler's assignment for Dorsch. But everything seems to indicate that Himmler tried to persuade Goering to extend the SS influence to at least managing those factories in which prisoners worked. That very day, he dictated a letter to Goering emphasizing that greater speed and therefore greater results could be expected in the factories if the responsibility of the SS were to be increased in them. In an accompanying letter, Pohl suggested installing the SS as responsible managers wherever prisoners worked. For according to his experience and knowledge, the mere employment of prisoners did not suffice. Thus, during my illness, the SS was unabashedly striving for control of countless private industrial plants—even though it was totally unable to supply leaders with the necessary qualifications.[38]

My secretary, Frau Kempf, soon realized that the direct telephone line she had had installed from the hospital to my ministry was being tapped by the SS, and that they were also keeping a record of who was visiting me and for what purpose. In this situation, Himmler must have been intent on keeping me supervised in an SS hospital as long as possible. Despite my malaise, which gradually turned into distrust, I naturally did not know what Koch later reported with many details in his sworn statement: "I was of the opinion that the humid climate of Hohenlychen had an unfavorable effect on Speer's recovery, and after examining the patient and finding him capable of being transferred, I suggested sending him to Merano. Gebhardt violently opposed this suggestion. He took refuge behind Himmler; and he telephoned the Reichsführer several times about this matter. I had the impression that Gebhardt was exploiting his medical position to play some sort of political game. But I did not know what game, nor did I concern myself with it, because I only wanted to be a physician. I made several attempts to change Gebhardt's mind; but finally I had enough, and I asked to speak with the Reichsführer personally. In a telephone conversation that lasted roughly seven or eight minutes, I succeeded in getting Himmler to agree to Speer's transfer to Merano. It struck me as very odd that Himmler had any say in a medical matter, but I did not beat my head about it because I deliberately refused to concern myself with matters outside my sphere as a physician. I would also like to remark that I had the impression that Speer was overjoyed when under my protection."[39]

Indeed, I gradually felt that Koch's protection was indispensable now that I had discovered that Kurt Daluege, the SS and police general, and an old rival of Himmler's since the early months of the Nazi regime, was stationed only a few rooms away in Hohenlychen. Daluege had bluntly complained to me that he was being held in the clinic against his will on the pretext that the condition of his heart made a release impossible. Yet he said he felt perfectly healthy. Which was in keeping with the impression made by this strong, tanned man. Daluege declared that Gebhardt was keeping him in Hohenlychen allegedly only for his own sake, and that he could not judge how serious his illness was. In this matter, Koch stated: "Gebhardt took a similar attitude when I was summoned to treat Police General Kurt Daluege. I felt that he [Gebhardt] and the powers behind him did not want Daluege able to perform."[40]

Things had reached that pass when a mysterious attack took place. The Eighth American Air Force raided a hospital in Templin only 18 kilometers to the southeast. Like Hohenlychen, this hospital was located on a land bridge between two lakes. One could only suspect that the Americans had made a mistake and that they knew of my presence here. After the bombing of the Templin Clinic, countless seriously wounded patients were brought to the Hohenlychen Hospital. It was felt that Gebhardt feared a repetition of the attack and that he wanted to be rid of a patient who was dangerous in many respects. At any rate, a few days later I traveled to South Tirol in a special car of the national railroad.

En route, I stopped at Klessheim Palace, near Obersalzberg. In a telephone conversation with headquarters, Goering told me that Gebhardt had notified him of my critical heart ailment and that he felt bad that there was no prospect of improvement. He said I was a "wreck incapable of working," which had also been reported to Hitler. However, Dr. Brandt took it upon himself to enlighten Hitler about the excellent state of my heart. What could Hitler have thought when given such conflicting information?[41]

It is only in the sinister terms of medical politics that we can understand Himmler's ulterior motives when, during my stay in Klessheim, he told Gebhardt on March 20, 1944: "Aside from the medical responsibility that you have assumed for Reich Minister Speer, I am assigning you, at the Führer's orders, responsibility for the safety of Reich Minister Speer during his four-week holiday. Within the framework of this responsibility, *only your orders* are binding and decisive."[42] Hitler had agreed to this, certainly without guessing that this assignment tacitly put Gebhardt over my physician, Professor Koch. I thereupon invited Koch to Merano as my private guest. But if there were conflicts, Koch's judgment meant nothing, that of Himmler's confidant everything. Thus, despite my departure from Hohenlychen, these orders to supervise me prevented any change in the situation.

Despite urgent tasks in his Hohenlychen Hospital, Gebhardt spent the next six weeks in Merano—a sign of how seriously he took his task of supervision. For by assuming responsibility for my "safety," Gebhardt could also keep an eye on my private sphere. Until then I had avoided protection by the SS; and thus I was not one of those functionaries who were accompanied night and day by a unit of some four to six SS men. These functionaries included men like Doenitz, Keitel, Goering, Goebbels, Rosenberg, Funk, and other ministers. It was only now, in Merano, that Gebhardt summoned an SS escort to protect me. The SS men had to live in my home, while Gebhardt himself resided in Merano. However, the leader of the SS escort was a decent and modest person. We had already gotten to like one another when he had served in Hitler's escort unit. Hence, my fears were soon allayed.

A bit later, on April 18, I was challenged in an unusual way by Goering, who had just recently conspired with Himmler about the armaments factories. A discussion chaired by Goering took place over the six large-scale

construction projects that Dorsch was to take charge of. I had expressly
sent Dr. Gerhard Fränk, my trusted colleague of many years, as my personal representative to the meeting. But Goering, unmoved, refused to
allow him into the conference room.

After this insulting rejection of my representative, I felt it was unavoidable to use my influence with Hitler. Professor Koch reports in his sworn
statement: "I had a second collision with Gebhardt, the "Reich physician"
of the SS and police (as his title was), "when Speer was in Merano. Speer
asked me whether I felt he was healthy enough to fly to Obersalzberg, probably to Hitler." This visit took place on April 19, for on April 20 Koch had
to leave Merano at Gebhardt's demand. "I said yes, on condition that the
plane did not fly above 1,800 to 2,000 meters. When Gebhardt learned of
my decision, he made a scene. He rebuked me, saying I was no 'political
doctor.' Here, as in our first run-in at Hohenlychen, I had the impression
that Gebhardt wanted to keep Speer a prisoner. Gebhardt was a confidant
of Himmler's and was very active politically. In his profession as a physician, he also pursued political goals. The flight to Obersalzberg did not take
place [at first]. I believe that today I can explain why Speer was being held
prisoner. A short time later, Speer was removed from his leadership of the
Todt Organization, which was given over to Ministerial Director Dorsch.
I assume they wanted to prevent Speer from talking to Hitler."

Indeed, Himmler had to fear my personal influence with Hitler. For if
I had managed to get to Hitler, then Himmler might not have succeeded in
taking away my leadership of the Todt Organization in the occupied territories and of all construction in Germany and introducing an SS control
in all private armaments factories.

However, Dorsch was enough of a professional to realize that Himmler's
assignment would confront him with insoluble problems and his failure
would spell a loss of prestige with Hitler. In any event, Koch reports:
"Shortly after this scene, the following happened: Ministerial Councillor
Dorsch, who was in Merano on that day, asked me to examine him since
he was feeling under the weather. After examining him, I established that
his heart was not sound and that he urgently needed rest. I advised him
to take care of himself and to consult me later on in Berlin, where I wanted
to examine him more thoroughly. Gebhardt learned of this decision, and
we had a violent collision. He again used the phrase 'political doctor.' He
said that nothing could be done with me. Everyone knows that Dorsch is
supposed to take over an important position now, and if someone is to
take charge of an important position at higher orders, then the doctor must
declare him healthy no matter how ill he may be.' "[43] Hence, Gebhardt

must have been informed precisely and immediately about the development at Obersalzberg by Himmler or his staff.

These unauthorized actions of Koch's were too much for Gebhardt. The very next day, citing his authorization, he ordered my guest to leave Merano without delay.

On April 19, because of the crisis generated by these humiliating efforts, I knew that the only thing I could do was to write to Hitler. My letter said that it was illusory to begin these huge construction projects, for "it would require great efforts to meet even the most primitive demands for lodging the German employees, the foreign workers, and also rebuilding our armaments factories. I am no longer faced with the choice of tackling long-range construction. . . . I constantly have to halt the ongoing construction of armaments plants in order to guarantee the necessary prerequisites of the German armaments output for the next few months." However, I said, Dorsch could remain in charge of construction in the occupied terrtitories.[44] Incidentally, I telephoned Goering to ask Hitler to dismiss me.

Himmler must have been called about this affront. As evidenced by his calendar on April 19,[45] he promptly met for an hour with my office head SS Brigade Commander Kehrl, who, as a member of the Reichsführer's circle of friends, remained in intimate contact with him. (This circle of "friends" consisted of industrialists and acquaintances who paid for their membership with large contributions to the SS.) Himmler went to the Berghof right after this conference. A meal with Hitler was followed by a discussion with Bormann. But then Kehrl flew to Merano the next day, remaining there for two days:[46] At the time I had no reason to doubt his loyalty. I also believed that he would put his relationship with me over his relationship as an SS commander to Himmler. However, I do not recall that he instructed me about the climate of the conversations about my ministry.

On April 22 Himmler, fully aware of his superior position, wrote me a letter whose unfriendliness is reflected even three weeks later in my answer. I said I would have "considered it more correct if you had first discussed the reproaches" (in his letter of April 22) "instead of communicating them to me as facts." These were serious attacks by Himmler against the technical leadership of the A-4 production, Degenkolb and Rickhey.[47]

On April 23 I again asked if I could fly to Obersalzberg. But again Gebhardt refused, citing his authorization as Hitler's medical representative. He bluntly declared that he had to prohibit my flight for reasons of health, even though six days earlier Professor Koch had raised no objections to my flying to Hitler. I acquiesced and asked my friend Milch to inform Hitler at the next opportunity of my intention to resign; Dorsch's power seemed to be definitively solidified. All I wanted to do now was to speak with Hitler in this situation and perhaps even obtain his permission to leave office.

I threatened Gebhardt, saying I would consult Hitler's physician, Dr. Brandt, and I also hinted that I could telephone Hitler at any time. To which Gebhardt hesitantly stated that Himmler would have to decide personally. He thereby openly admitted that it was Himmler who forbade my flying to Hitler; the medical pretext was no longer at issue. After this threat, Gebhardt informed me that Himmler was willing to let me fly, but only on condition that I go to see him before meeting with Hitler. Himmler had thus finally shown his hand.

When I paid my forced visit to Himmler on the morning of April 24, 1944,[48] he insolently spoke of "facts that can no longer be revised": construction had been separated from the Armaments Ministry, and Dorsch, a time-tested Party member, had been put in charge. This, said Himmler, had been definitively decided days ago in a discussion with Hitler, in which Goering had also taken part. He knew, of course, that I had struggled against it; but he was giving me good advice, he said. I would only increase Hitler's anger if I resorted to unreasonable actions, such as resigning my post. I had been delaying Hitler's program to transfer German industry promptly under concrete or into caves. Now, Dorsch was Hitler's independent plenipotentiary for construction, but I would still be left with armaments as a decisive area of jurisdiction. On such occasions Himmler did not flaunt his triumph. On the contrary: he visibly attempted to treat me with great friendliness and not make me feel my defeat.

Strangely enough, I put up with Himmler's presumption. Although I was one of the most successful ministers in the Reich, I did not even protest anymore. As if paralyzed, I agreed to everything. But I wanted to clear the decks anyway, and I did not mind that the area meant for Dorsch would be removed from my jurisdiction. After all, the implementation of these six or eight superdimensional constructions would have to fail in this phase of the war.

A short time later, according to the SD report of July 2, 1944, there were rumors in Berlin and Halle that "Minister Speer had been dismissed after remonstrances by Dr. Ley, Gauleiter Sauckel, and Professor Krauch, the plenipotentiary for the Reich Chemistry Group, because he [Speer] had neglected aircraft production."[49]

Leaving Himmler, I then went to see Hitler in the Berghof that same day, April 24.[50] However, Hitler avoided discussing my surrender to Himmler. Suddenly, it was he who would not accept the dismemberment of the unified organization that I had so arduously developed. He resolutely contradicted my suggestion, inspired by Himmler, to put Dorsch in charge of construction. To my amazement Hitler emphasized, while standing with me face to face, that everything would stay as it was. I would remain the head of all German construction.[51]

Two days later, on April 26, I took Dorsch along to Hitler so that he might hear the new decision from Hitler's own lips—a decision tantamount to an about-face.[52] Again, one day later, on April 27, Himmler sent for Dorsch and met with him for half an hour around noon.[53] Although newly confirmed as head of construction, I was no more informed of the gist of this conversation than of the preceding ones.

In reality, everything remained as before. Dorsch stayed in office and ran the construction industry, for I was not even capable of taking over this task myself. I was merely given suggestions, for instance the wish "that the construction of caves necessary for ball bearing production [have] to be assured before the 'fighter-plane factories.' "

Upon hearing of this decision on May 13, 1944, Hitler stressed that as far as he was concerned, "it goes without saying that 160,000 square meters of bombproof factory space which can thus be gained must be evaluated exactly as plants constructed in concrete above ground. His goal is to have the most important defense factories in safety."[54] The result was that after months of conflict, Hitler's illusory order to build six bunker factories, which Dorsch had promised him would be completed by November, no longer had the urgency that Hitler had once dictated. That same day I got Hitler to sign an order for Dorsch, stipulating that he was to prepare monthly reports to present to the Führer. These reports were to be structured as follows:

1. The number of square meters of cave space already, or in the process of being, prepared every month for construction in the existing caves or tunnels.
2. The number of square meters of caves that are gained every month through new facilities.
3. The number of square meters of concrete construction that can be completed each month.[55]

During my illness changes had also occurred in the power structure of the actual area of armaments. With the setting up of a comprehensive arm of my ministry, the Fighter Plane Staff, and, later, with the Armaments Staff replacing it, I necessarily, if tacitly, gave up portions of my own jurisdiction. For ultimately the new organization—and I agreed to this—was put under the aegis of the hyperactive Saur. Letters and directives awaiting my signature kept accumulating on my desk. But they now bore the dictated sign TA (*Technisches Amt*-Technical Office). I had little say in bringing about these orders. A short time later Kammler's authorization as special deputy for cave construction was expanded. I had been validated but deprived of power. Things went past me, as I had seen during my visit in the Central Works, even though I had not admitted this development to myself.

Chapter 17
Kammler's Realm

THE FIGHTER PLANE STAFF, founded in late February 1944, was a product of crisis. The stubborn and concentrated air attacks by the Allies on our air armaments made it obvious that our plans to increase the output of fighter planes were wrecked. Big Week—a series of Anglo-American air attacks on German aircraft factories during the spring of 1944—was a success.

The representatives of various ministries and agencies got together at a large conference table in my ministry; the meetings were chaired by Saur.[1] Their aim was to do away with this bombing damage. The catastrophe had given birth to a new formula, not only for organization structure but also for power: All members of the Fighter Plane Staff had to submit to the directives of the chairman, even in their own areas, which were not subject to my ministry. For instance, even during the session, the representative of the national railroad promised to carry out certain orders. There were no jurisdictional conflicts. The representatives of the national departments realized the necessity of such measures. After all, they could also lodge protests after the fact. But no protest was ever lodged. Strictly speaking, this was a preliminary stage to the "concerted actions" of the postwar period.

Dr. Kammler, an engineer, had been a regular member of this Fighter Plane Staff since its founding. He carried out measures that Saur ordered, within the construction sector, for moving industrial objects—to the extent that such tasks were not reserved for the Todt Organization. These measures were top priority. For instance, the necessary contingents for barracks construction were allocated to such projects. Because such allocations contrasted with the meager rations of 1943, the SS construction administration managed to raise its camp capacity.

"According to an order of Himmler's, the employment of prisoners for the so-called transfer construction measures," the head of Agency B in the SS Economic Administrative Headquarters stated, "was the responsibility of General Kammler and not of Agency D. However, not in his capacity as head of Agency C [construction], but personally. He had his own office for this and the title of 'Special Deputy of the SS Reichsführer.' "[2] On March 4, 1944, Goering too put Kammler in charge of transfer underground. The general could thus enjoy all the advantages of a twofold office, citing one or the other as he saw fit.

Professor Bartel quotes Georg Rickhey, the former general director of the Central Works: "Kammler had unusual power through the SD department, which he was personally in charge of; he could order the arrest of any person who, in his opinion, interfered unwarrantedly with the measures he ordered. Since Kammler constantly made ruthless use of this power even against SS officers, there was absolutely no way that other people or agencies could interfere with the employment [of prisoners], which was the most important aspect of Kammler's technical duties."[3]

Kammler's "Special Staff" was headed by "Dr. Kammler's Construction Bureau," with its main office in Berlin. This office commanded several "SS Special Inspections," which were distributed throughout the Reich and, in turn, headed the regional "SS Command Staffs."[4] The files reveal that the SS remained in charge of employing and controlling the prisoners used under Kammler.[5]

Under Kammler, a relentless but capable robot, there was a new development in the spring of 1944; ultimately it threw hundreds of thousands of prisoners into the production process under the harshest conditions. Yet it gave these hundreds of thousands a chance to survive. The effects of Kammler's hectic diligence is described by Rudolf Höss, who was running the concentration camp at Auschwitz: "It now turns out that the armaments industry has an enormous need for manpower, but that they are not making any progress with the construction of lodgings. The Todt Organization has been called in to build these armaments labor camps. For lack of other manpower, the Todt Organization likewise requires prisoners. Where can they be housed? Maurer [of SS Economic Administrative Headquarters] is off on inspection tours day and night and is forced to reject most of the emergency housing, since it lacks even the most primitive features. This causes a further delay in the labor operation. Himmler is furious; he sets up an investigation commission with special powers to discover the culprits. Auschwitz is crammed with prisoners waiting to be transported to the armaments camp. New transports by [Adolf] Eichmann are rolling in, stuffing Auschwitz even more. The transfer underground of the most important parts of the armaments industry is, naturally, advancing very slowly; they've lost at least two years. Himmler has installed Dr. Kammler as his commissioner for this project. Kammler can't work magic either; and weeks, even months are going by with no essential progress. The air war causes delays, obstacles, often a paralysis of months. Himmler keeps driving; his promises torment him."[6] This depiction of Kammler's labor operation obviously refers to a long period, presumably from the summer of 1944 to the spring of 1945.

On June 21, 1944, in his speech to generals at Sonthofen, Himmler reported that "large underground factories are being built [by prisoners]. In the past few weeks, we have used this manpower at a speed that would not have been considered possible, to create, within eight weeks, ten underground factory spaces with an overall floor surface area of tens of thousands of square meters."[7] A feat remarkable in both organization and technology had indeed been performed. Six months later Kammler reported to the SS Reichsführer about the "factory surfaces of bombproof underground plants completed [by the SS] in 1944 on the orders of the Herr Reich Minister for Armaments and War Production."[8]

The accompanying graphic description revealed that by January 1, 1945, a total of 425,000 square meters underground or in bunkers had been completed by the SS. These 425,000 square meters correspond to a covered surface about 200 meters wide and 2 kilometers long. Kammler had thus used draconian measures to carry out a program that nearly fulfilled Hitler's demands for 600,000 square meters in six large bunkers. A forecast attached to the report said that this surface area would be increased to 1,025,000 square meters by June 1, 1945. But this would no more have altered the situation than our overall planning, which provided for 3 million square meters. Basically, it was all futile; Hitler's goal of shielding the entire armaments output from air raids was unattainable because the overall dimensions were too great. Furthermore, this program was nonsensical in regard to air strategy. In those very same weeks, the enemy was paralyzing the transportation network, so only the tiniest portion of production could have been moved.[9]

On May 26, 1944, I took part "for the first time in a session of the Fighter Plane Staff, which, chaired by Saur, [had] been extremely active since February 28 and presented unexpected output figures." The chronicle then records in the next paragraph: "SS Squad Commander Kammler, who is forming a new construction column with his army of concentration camp inmates, a column that the minister must put back into the proper front from time to time, reported on the construction work."[10] (See Appendix 16.)

Kammler's consruction brigades greatly increased the number of laboring prisoners. According to information from Himmler in early March 1945, the concentration camps had 480,000 healthy and 120,000 sick prisoners.[11] This figure chimes with a statistic claiming that on January 15 the German concentration camps had 487,290 male and 156,000 female inmates.[12] Of these inmates, 137,500 labored in the Todt Organization.[13] Eugen Kogon similarly states that 530,000 prisoners survived the tortures of the camps.[14]

Incidentally, it must be noted that according to the figures of January 15, 1945, 36,454 soldiers were employed to guard the 487,000 male prisoners. A newly formed infantry division had an average strength of 11,000 men; thus, over three divisions were tied down because of the prisoners.[15]

These labor policies of the SS commenced roughly in late 1941 and were expanded as the demands of the German armaments industry increased. There is no doubt that these policies contributed to the relatively large number of survivors. However, a new danger loomed in the final weeks of the war, since Hitler kept emphasizing that with the approach of the Allies, the concentration camps were to be blown up with all their inmates. Himmler confirmed this threat on March 12, 1945, in a conversation with Kersten: "If the National Socialist Germany is to perish, then its enemies and the whole gang of criminals that are now in the concentration camps are not to experience the triumph of emerging as victors. Let them share the annihilation. This is the clear order of the Führer, and I must see to it that this order is carried out precisely and thoroughly." However, in the further course of their talk, Himmler promised Kersten that he would ignore this order.[16]

Still, I knew of this threat by Hitler, and therefore, in my last speech, dealing with postwar Germany, I stated: "In the concentration camps, the political prisoners, and hence also the Jews, are to be separated from the asocial elements. The former are to be handed over unscathed to the occupying troops. Any punishment of political prisoners, including Jews, is to stop until further orders."[17] From today's perspective, the clause about asocial elements shows me how incomprehensibly I was trapped in the mentality of the regime.

At this time, even Himmler would probably have agreed with these lines. Such efforts fitted in with his policies during the final weeks; in the end, he was negotiating with Count Folke Bernadotte about the rescue of concentration camp prisoners.

In general, Himmler had always insisted on his precedence in the hierarchy, and had therefore always summoned me to meetings in *his* headquarters. He visited me in my office only once, around the middle of March 1945. My department head Theodor Hupfauer and I had just returned from a long journey. We had managed to get the commanding generals and civilian authorities to halt the scorched earth policy for the sake of the oil wells in Hungary and the coal district and industrial area in Czech territory.

At the same time, Kaltenbrunner announced to Hupfauer that he was also stopping by. This duplication was cause for worry. We were concerned that reports on our trip had reached Kaltenbrunner and Himmler via the Gestapo offices, and we feared an imminent SS action against us. But the visit was innocuous. Kaltenbrunner had indeed received reports on our extensive travel activities. But he merely urged his old fraternity brother Hupfauer to proceed more cautiously and not to attempt obstructing Hitler's express orders. He avoided any excessive sharpness when he pointed out that such refusals to carry out orders were punishable by death. His tone remained oddly comradely.

At the same time my conversation with Himmler one floor below likewise had no real substance. Himmler sought contact with me in amiable words; even today, I still do not know what he was after. In any case, he did not repeat the general advice that Kaltenbrunner had just communicated to my staffer. I, for my part, tried to make it clear to him that his intimate friend Martin Bormann had to be "put on the shelf" in this situation, "taken out of circulation," because in his radicalism he opposed any attempt at moderation. I suggested that Himmler replace him. This suggestion must have been based on rumors that Himmler had maintained a sober judgment of the situation and was ready to draw the proper conclusions. However, my suggestion did not meet with Himmler's approval. Cool and reserved, he declared in an official tone that he would accept such a charge only from the Führer himself. But he did not flare up, did not even threaten to inform Hitler of this conversation. Thus, despite everything, we had become accomplices in some way. Actually, Himmler may have been the only officer in the Nazi hierarchy who had any power at this time. Did that justify an attempt at working together? Except through Himmler, there was no way of opposing Hitler and Bormann. Crazy, futile actions in the darkness of the hour after midnight.

On March 27, 1945, Hitler issued his "last great assignment in the area of armaments." He ordered Kammler, who had meanwhile been promoted to SS Obergruppenführer, to take command of air armaments. "He is receiving the greatest powers from the Führer," Goebbels wrote in his diary on March 28, 1945."[18] In October 1944, when urged by his SD staff to take harsh executive measures in air armaments, Himmler had replied that at the moment, immovable difficulties obstructed the path. Now, a ruthless SS officer had been ordered to take the harshest possible steps in air armaments in order to bring about a turn of events during the last few weeks of the war; and Himmler found himself left out.

Twelve days before this decision, on March 18, 1945, I had informed Hitler that we could safely expect "the final collapse of German industry" in four to eight weeks, after which there could be "no military continuation of the war."[19] Thus, Kammler's assignment was one of the utopian solutions that people chased in this desperate situation, even though a sober review made it obvious that the bell had tolled. Nevertheless, Hitler believed he could save the situation merely by reassigning a position to someone else.

Under my aegis, armaments of the three branches of the Wehrmacht and also the Waffen-SS (with a few illegal restrictions) had been with difficulty unified. Now, the dismemberment of this union would have ruled out any possibility of improvised activation, even if our industry had still been intact. Only the balancing possibilities of the overall industrial capacity as united in my ministry would have permitted the implementation of a single urgent special assignment. The area that Hitler ripped from the totality of industry on March 27, 1945, had no chance of pulling itself out of the slough. But in desperate situations, Hitler often tended to break up things that belonged together.

Three days after telling Goebbels about the imminent change in the air armaments structure, Hitler stated: "The Führer wants to implement a very small air armaments program, but push it through as powerfully as possible. It must be carried out under any circumstances. Goering feels he has been put in the corner because of the authority granted to Kammler; but nothing can be altered in this. The Führer rejects the reproach that Kammler was not installed earlier. He says he only got to know about Kammler during the organization of the employment of our V weapons. He is nevertheless the right man to activate the Luftwaffe in its reduced state. We must now act according to the principle by which the Soviets acted in their great military crisis; that is, we must become as primitive as possible and try to make the best of our situation. . . . In any event, he [Hitler] is determined to put the Luftwaffe in order. I too believe that he will succeed, for the Luftwaffen generals are cowards, just like the army generals, and as soon as they feel their master over them, they will obey."[20]

On April 3, 1945, Hitler again had "very long negotiations with Obergruppenführer Kammer, who now has part of the responsibility for reforming the Luftwaffe. Kammler is doing an excellent job, and great hopes are being pinned on him."[21] Not faith but brutality can move mountains, it seems. Which was something Hitler, Goebbels, Bormann, and Ley agreed about in these last weeks of the war. This made the situation different from the last few weeks before Napoleon's surrender.

I assume that Kammler too was quite aware of the hopeless military situation. Nevertheless, he had to carry out his mission. First, grotesquesly enough, he delegated the implementation of his task to his construction organization. The "Construction Inspection of the Waffen-SS and Police Force for the South of the Reich" thus became the bearer of Hitler's final hope in the southern area of Germany, which was almost totally divided by now. Extant telegrams demonstrate the dilettantism displayed by Kammler and his construction staff. For instance, on April 3 the head of this "Construction Inspection" transmitted an order of Kammler's. According to this order, SS Obersturmführer Mataré, who was also liaison officer to groups VI, VIII, and IX of the Todt Organization, was put in charge of the special assignment for jet planes and the silver program. An Obersturmführer—this corresponded to the rank of a lieutenant colonel—was carrying out a special mission for Hitler, an assignment on which the very existence of the Reich depended. The effect of the new activities was meager; it could not be otherwise with such poor staffing. Thus, in the same telegram, the head of the Construction Inspection writes that he intends to "employ SS Obersturmführer Dauser, message center Munich, for urgently recommended settlement and pile program." Such a settlement program would have taken roughly nine months; and it is a mystery what advantages it might have had for the special mission. The telegram goes on: "Please inform SS Sturmbannführer Dr. von Gliszinsky accordingly. At the same time, please wire back information on where Sturmbannführer Dr. von Gliszinsky is now serving. He cannot be reached in Minden."[22]

Four days later, the same powerlessness is shown by a wireless message that a man named Herr Karl was supposed to transmit to Kammler. According to this message, the underground facilities in Kirchbichl, Tirol, have been reserved by Steyr for the 603 Daimler-Benz aircraft engine.

Professor Messerschmitt suggested that Junkers transfer this aircraft manu-facturing there with all component parts; the rooms, according to this wireless, were suitable. Kammler was to decide, "if necessary, to give Junkers the order to carry out the transfer and to notify the Steyr firm that it must leave."[23] My general guidelines stipulated that such detailed measures were to be decided by subordinate offices in the self-responsibil-ity of industry.

The impressiveness of the titles were in reverse proportion to the pros-pects of success. Thus, in a wireless of April 8, 1945, Mataré was desig-nated "Representative of the Plenipotentiary of the Führer for Jet Engine Aircraft." The reports that were proudly transmitted by this Representa-tive of the Plenipotentiary of the Führer for Jet Engine Aircraft had the most trivial significance. An unknown Colonel Pretzell had "decided that Emmerich, Inc., in Weingut II [probably the project of an underground factory] will receive 4,000 square meters of manufacturing area within 7 days, an additional 1,500 square meters within another 5 days, and a total of 7,500 square meters by May 1. Any further interior installation has been stopped. But the outside construction is continuing according to plans. Tomorrow the first special transport of cement is to arrive from Blaubeuren."[24] One week later, an SS Obersturmbannführer named Staed-ing, who called himself "Plenipotentiary of the Führer for Jet Engine Aircraft," had notified Professor Messerschmitt and Director Degenkolb, likewise by wireless, that he had "transferred" himself and his "agency from Halle to Dresden. What can I do for you or for the [Me] 262 from here? The Protectorate can also be considered. Where else do you need help?" the communication ended, as if he were capable of providing assistance, even though he was already clearing out.[25]

Documents to be found in the archives today are both terrifying and laughable. SS Headquarters, once all-powerful, was about to confiscate a truck from the Junkers aircraft firm for military purposes. Kammler wired SS Headquarters that "according to the Führer's order, jet planes have priority over military planes. Am therefore not in position to release desired truck."[26] Meanwhile Kammler, as revealed in the wire, had re-moved himself from Hitler's vicinity and moved to Munich. Given the expected failures, it could be dangerous for him to remain near Hitler.

On April 16, almost three weeks after Kammler had received his mis-sion from Hitler to change the course of the war, he came to his senses. "In concordance with Reich Minister Speer and Hauptdienstleiter Saur," he made "Director Degenkolb Plenipotentiary, at the Reich Ministry for Armaments and War Production, for Manufacturing the [Me] 262."[27] But for some time now, Degenkolb had been the ministry's industrial pleni-

potentiary for the manufacture of jet planes. And so Hitler's assignment
bounced back to my ministry. Thus, as the same communication reveals,
there were now two plenipotentiaries, one designated by Hitler, the other
by Kammler. A subtlety glimmers through the words of the radio message
even one generation later: Kammler did not really make Degenkolb a
plenipotentiary; he appointed him "to" the Armaments Ministry, which
was meant to indicate that he was attached to me, but not as my subordinate. This is also revealed by the fact that Kammler thereafter referred to him as "his" plenipotentiary.

To reemphasize the change in power, Kammler, the "Plenipotentiary of
the Führer for Jet Engine Aircraft," wired Frank, the head of the Messerschmitt branch in Regensburg, that very same day: "According to order of
Führer of March 27, 1945, all powers previously vested within the framework of the Reich Minister for Armaments and War Production for Me
262 have been transferred to me." Kammler thanked Frank "for the work
he had done so far," and then continued: "I have asked Herr Director
Degenkolb, my Plenipotentiary for the Manufacture of Me 262 in the
Reich Ministry for Armaments and War Production, to contact you about
further cooperation."[28] To be sure, this seems to have been more of a
protocol matter, such as when ministers resign because of a change of
sovereign only to be reappointed the very next day. A jotting on this wire
underscores the burlesque quality of such efforts: "No connection exists
with Regensburg." Most likely, a man as reasonable as Degenkolb played
along in this production game merely to avoid any conflicts with the SS,
who might have executed him as a saboteur.

Perhaps Kammler felt the same way. As though to provide a grotesque
end to these charades, he came to me in early April in order to say good-
bye. For the first time in our four-year association, Kammler did not dis-
play his usual dash. On the contrary, he seemed insecure and slippery with
his vague, obscure hints about why I should transfer to Munich with him.
He said efforts were being made in the SS to get rid of the Führer. He
himself, however, was planning to contact the Americans. In exchange
for their guaranty of his freedom, he would offer them the entire technology of our jet planes, as well as the A-4 rocket and other important
developments, including the transcontinental rocket. For this purpose,
he was assembling all development experts in Upper Bavaria in order to
hand them over to the Americans. He offered me the chance to participate
in this operation, which would be sure to work out in my favor.

Later, Jean Michel says, in his book *Dora,* which deals with conditions
in the Central Works camp: "Thirty years have passed, and the same conclusion still urges itself upon me: SS Obergruppenführer Hans Kammler

was the only man who had sufficient authority to induce the Gestapo to propose his strange bargain. Kammler was the only man who could have them tell the Allies in November 1944: 'I can negotiate with you about the future of the secret weapons. . . .' His urgent wish for contact, his desire to manipulate the French Resistance, is comparable to the sadistic double game of a cat with a deported mouse. This simile accurately depicts the given facts of the somber negotiations launched by Hans Kammler."[29]

The SS then allowed the transport of engineers and officers of the A-4 development project to the skiing village of Oberjochin Allgäu, under the leadership of General Dornberger. Wernher von Braun was a member of this group in the Bavarian mountains, which then surrendered to American troops. But Kammler did not join them. Rumor has it that he was shot in Prague by his own SS aide in the last days of the war. Perhaps the aide was acting as a representative of the loyalty inherent in the SS ideology.

PART FOUR
The Fate of the Jews

Chapter 18

Hatred and Rationality

THROUGHOUT 1942 the agencies of the Armaments Inspection in Berlin tried to prevent the deportation of Jews employed in the armaments industry. Looking back, it is hard to determine the extent of humane sensibility behind the argument that this manpower had to be kept for the production process. It probably varied from case to case. However, the files reveal attempts to employ more and more Jews in the Berlin armaments factories, which, for the time being, automatically kept them from being transported to the East. Yet when reading those old documents today, I perceive a lack of statements in the decisive language that I used when opposing Himmler or Kaltenbrunner in trivial matters. My ministry was very cautious in its attempts to improve the situation of the Jews; and certainly, the reason very often was simply to retain their labor.

Himmler and the Gestapo acted with moderation even in cases in which they leveled accusations against the industrialists. Sharp threats are as rare in these files as draconian measures. But the latter cannot be ruled out, since the extant material seems full of lacunae. On the other hand, the anti-Semitism that had been the crux of all speeches and actions during the years of Hitler's struggle for political power had simply aroused a sharp fight by the Jews against the National Socialists. Ultimately, the very existence of the Jews was at stake. And it is astonishing that these Jews, who were allegedly so powerful in Germany before 1933, were not even able to struggle effectively against this petit bourgeois movement of the National Socialists. The justified struggle of the Jews against their arch-

[247]

enemies increased the anti-Jewish hatred of the Party to such an extent that it refused to make any exceptions or go back in any way.

In all issues dealing directly or indirectly with the fate of the Jews, there was no mercy. It was scarcely possible to make exceptions. Any independent action spelled personal danger. A leading Party member could be accused of unreliability, personal failure, even corruption. Hitler and Bormann put up with this if they had to. But they never permitted anyone to stand up openly for the Jews. Any such stirring meant instant loss of rank and prestige and a plunge into the void. I personally witnessed only a single open protest. It was at Obersalzberg. Henriette von Schirach expressed her agitation to Hitler about the mass transports of Jews which she had witnessed up close in Holland. Henriette was one of his most intimate friends from the early days. That was why she could always say an insubordinate word or two, which might from another person have aroused Hitler's sharp reaction, for she was fairly spontaneous in her boldness. Yet he never did react sharply. Now, however, she had said something in favor of the Jews. That very same night, the Schirachs had to leave the Berghof. And Hitler never again received them.

In the meeting of September 20–22, 1942, Hitler ordered Sauckel to transport all Jews working in the Reich's armaments factories to the Eastern concentration camps. This mainly referred to the Berlin Jews. Since the fall of 1941, the Armaments Inspection III and the Party had been struggling over the continued presence of these Jews in the city and hence in the factories. As early as August 15, 1941, demands made by the office of the Berlin Gauleiter had led to restrictive measures against the Berlin Jews. The Food Agency for the City of Berlin informed the Berlin Armaments Inspection that "Jewish workers may no longer receive supplementary rationing cards meant for workers doing long shifts, heavy labor, and the heaviest labor, even though they are in these categories. Furthermore, non-Aryans may no longer receive the same food as the Aryan manpower in an armaments factory. The Food Agency for the City of Berlin is supplying the canteens of the armaments factories with the following additional food for Aryan workers: rice, noodles, bacon, margarine, etc., in order to make the meals tastier and more nutritious. From now on, the warm meals of Jewish laborers" must "be prepared in a special kitchen [and] only on the basis of their food-rationing cards. Nor are Jews to be permitted to eat in the same canteens or lounges as Aryans."[1]

In September 1941, a few weeks after this directive, Goebbels categorically demanded the total removal of the Jews from his Gau of Berlin. In a ministers' conference, at which Gauleiter Jordan (Dessau) was also present, Goebbels demanded: "The Berlin Jews must be evacuated or grouped in a ghetto."[2] Just a few weeks later, the deportation began.

The files of my predecessor, Todt—I was still an architect at this time—contain the following report: "In October 1941, without the Armaments inspection first being given an opportunity to express its opinion, a resettlement of the [Berlin] Jews in the East suddenly began. The Jews involved in urgent manufacturing were not to be evacuated for the time being. But since, for varous reasons, the deportation was to be in terms of families, greater and greater amounts of important manpower were nevertheless included and thus lost to the armaments factories."[3]

Four weeks later, on November 15, 1941, the Berlin Armaments Inspection reported in greater detail: "The removal of some 75,000 Jews from Berlin, of whom some 20,000 are in important jobs (over 10,000 alone are employed in the metal sector), is also interfering with the question of labor replacement. There is no possibility of replacing this manpower with German workers through the Labor Office. Another 15,000 Jews are to be evacuated by December 4, 1941, and then the rest as of February 1942. The Jews working in the armaments industry should, if possible, be removed from the factories after the termination of the evacuation measures. For this purpose, the Berlin Labor Office has reached certain agreements with the Gestapo."[4]

And indeed, the first transports of Jewish men and women began on October 1941 and lasted until January 25, 1942. During these three months, some 8,000 Jews were sent to their destiny in ten trains.[5]

"For lack of replacements for experienced workers and for lack of transportation space, the scheduled further resettlement of the Jews was halted in early 1942," goes a report of the Armaments Inspection III, October 1–December 31.[6] But at the same time, the remaining "Jews, who had frequently been working individually in factories, were now assembled in closed groups, factory sections, or Jewish shfts. Here, they worked separately from the Aryan employees. They were overseen solely by Aryan foremen or masters."[7]

One month later, on February 8, 1942, when I took office as minister of armaments, I was confronted with an acute lack of weapons and munitions of all kinds. The generals calmly informed me that the speedy filling of this gap would determine the further course of the war. For because of the winter defeats in Russia, which was covered with ice and snow, the troops had lost most of their equipment; and now, in spring, they were practically weaponless to face the enemy, who was about to switch to an offensive.

This emergency alone led to a slowdown in transporting Jewish workers to the East. And I could cite it as such in my first conversations with Bormann, a few weeks after taking office. On March 13, 1942, Bormann, "at the suggestion of Reich Minister Speer," released a circular to the agencies. Among other things, he said: "If directors of armaments factories in individual Gaus continue employing Jews in the future, they are not to be reproached for this, especially since they are acting in accordance with a directive from the Reich Minister for Armaments and Munitions. I ask the Gauleiters to defend the directors of armaments factories employing Jews in accordance with this directive, to protect them against attacks and the suspicion of pro-Jewishness, and to provide for the necessary enlightenment of the population as far as necessary." Without asking for Bormann's permission, I published this announcement on March 31, 1942, in the first issue of my ministry's bulletin *Nachrichten* ["News"], which I myself had launched and which was sent to all directors of German factories.[8]

However, Goebbels in his fanaticism, which, in many respects, was the driving force behind all anti-Jewish measures and at times even surpassed Himmler's, would not put up with this. On May 12, 1942, he wrote in his diary: "Still 40,000 Jews in Berlin. Transport to East difficult since most are employed in armaments factories and are to be deported only in families."[9] Five days later Goebbels returned to this theme: "We are trying to evacuate to the East larger numbers of the Jews still remaining in Berlin. One-third of all Jews still living in Germany are in the capital of the Reich.[10] Naturally, this condition is unendurable in the long run. It is due chiefly to the fact that in Berlin fair numbers of Jews are employed in the armaments industry and, according to one regulation, the heads of their families cannot be evacuated either. I am striving for a cancellation of this regulation and I am going to try to get all the Jews that are not employed in factories crucial to the war effort out of Berlin."[11]

The rule about not breaking up Jewish families was due to considerations of expediency. It was believed that this was the only way to ensure satisfactory performance. Hence, one family member working in an armaments plant meant protection for all the rest. This can also be seen from the fact that as late as November 1941, "of some 75,000 Jews in Berlin [only] 20,000 are employed in important jobs."[12]

There is no doubt that Goebbels intensified even Hitler's radicalism. But it took four more months until September 22, 1942, when Hitler gave the order to Sauckel, who was in charge of manpower, to exclude the Jews once and for all from all armaments factories in the Reich. I pointed out to Hitler that the loss of Jewish workers would gravely interfere with the armaments industry. But Sauckel assured us that he could offer a complete replacement by using foreign laborers; and thus, my argument had no weight. Whatever I felt beyond these considerations of expediency, I cannot determine today with any accuracy.

On September 30, 1942, Goebbels triumphantly noted in his journal: "The Führer is once again expressing his determination to get the Jews out of Berlin under any circumstances. Nor is he impressed by the economists and industrialists who tell him that they could not do without the so-called Jewish precision work. All at once Jews are being lauded everywhere for their high-quality work. People keep advancing this argument to us in order to request protection for them. However, the Jews are not as indispensable as they are presented to be by our intellectuals. Given the fact that we have 240,000 foreign workers in Berlin alone, it will not be too difficult to have foreign workers replace the remaining 40,000 Jews, of whom only 17,000 are employed in the production process anyway. The Jewish precision worker is becoming more and more of a standing argument for the intellectual philo-Semitic propaganda. This shows once again how easily we Germans tend to be overfair and to treat political necessities with resentment, rather than with cool reason."[13]

Starting on October 19, 1942, the food for working Jews was so greatly curtailed as to threaten their ability to work. From that time on, they received no cards for meat or eggs.[14] It must be a sign of resignation that the files of the Armaments Inspection do not record any protest effort against this measure.

Four weeks later, on November 23, 1942, Himmler announced to SS junkers: "The Jew has been resettled outside Germany."[15] This was rash, for there were still all the Berlin Jewish workers who were tolerated in the production process, as shown by Sauckel's circular three days later: "In accordance with the head of the Security Police and the SD, the Jews employed in labor are to be evacuated from the territory of the Reich and replaced by Poles resettled from the Generalgouvernement. The so-called 'qualified' Jewish workers will be left in the factories until the Polish replacements have been sufficiently familiarized with the work processes within a training period that is to be determined in each individual case. This will ensure the utmost restriction of lost production in the individual factories."[16] The comprehensive powers with which Sauckel and his agencies were vested allowed him to establish when the replacement could be viewed as adequate. This state of affairs was repeatedly criticized by me and my agencies, because by means of it nonexperts interfered with the production process.

An entry in the war journal of the Berlin Armaments Command for

November 9 shows that these imminent transports were known about two weeks before Himmler's announcements. "The non-Aryans, including the Jewish workers employed in armaments factories, are soon to be evacuated from Greater Berlin. This will affect several plants, especially in the precision engineering branch, where a large number of Jewish women are working. The evacuated Jews are to be replaced by Poles."[17]

But, oddly enough, another three months went by and nothing happened. Then, in the last few days of February 1943, Goebbels called me up and was extremely resolute in declaring that no Jews could remain in Berlin any longer. He said that Sauckel had just given him his definitive promise to replace these Jewish workers with Poles. He was absolutely fed up with statements from factory managers to the effect that performance would go down in that event. One could, said Goebbels, rely on the word of Sauckel, an old Party veteran; he would keep any promise he made.

In other areas, however, I got along well with Goebbels. In these months, he made sure that radio, newsreels, and newspapers emphasized the importance of armaments production. This action had a good effect on my personal prestige. The public recognized me as one of Hitler's most important colleagues in the war effort. I was weak enough to tell Goebbels that under these circumstances I could not approve any more objections.

A few days later, on February 27, the evacuation took place. It was explained by Sauckel one month later, on March 26, 1943, in a circular. When cross-examining me at the Nuremberg Trial, Justice Robert Jackson asked me about this text: "In agreement with the Herr Reich Minister for Armaments and Munitions and me, the SS Reichsführer, for reasons of state security, has removed from their jobs those Jews who have so far been employed in factories and not in camps, and he has assembled them in a closed operation or for removal."[18]

During the past two years, Privy Councillor Bücher, chairman of the board at AEG [the electric corporation], had been especially active in making sure that as many of the Jews working in his plants as possible would be exempted from the transports. I had been on good terms with him since my days as chief architect of Berlin, and we could always speak confidentially with one another. Hence, right after my discussion with Goebbels, I made an appointment with Bücher. He was shocked at my news. He kept softly repeating: "We will never be forgiven for this. Someday we will have to pay dearly for this sin." It was no use my trying to tell him that there had been no possibility of pretext for me. Deeply disappointed at my yielding, he took leave of me. After the Twentieth of July, it was established that Privy Councillor Bücher had conversed with other industrialists about Germany's future in a post-Hitler era. However, I intervened with Kaltenbrunner, and any further prosecution was halted.

For over three years, these Jews had had jobs in Berlin factories, especially in the electrical industry; their work had provided some security for them and their families and had even kept them their apartments. But now their hour had come.

On the day of the evacuation, the Armaments Commander of Berlin made the following entry: "On February 27, all the Jews in the work process, ca. 11,000 in the armaments sector, were removed suddenly with the speed of lightning. Since many of the Jews were employed in closed divisions, and some in important programs, every effort had to be made to replace them without delay. This was possible only by taking on all the Western workers who arrived in the first half of March exclusively for this purpose and by allocating all other available manpower, especially from the actions for obligatory registration and measures for closing factories. This prevented the halt of certain manufacturing, and only a few interruptions occurred due to the training period of the new workers."[19] Thus, Sauckel did not keep his promise. The adequate replacements were never supplied. The gaps had to be filled with manpower originally allocated for other kinds of production. Despite our emergency situation, Sauckel did not leave room for a training period for surrogate manpower, which had been a condition for the evacuation of the Jews.

In January 1942, Himmler had planned to employ 150,000 Jewish workers in Reich territory. And that September, he had still spoken of 50,000. Now, one year later, we had lost the final 20,000 specialized workers.[20]

Nevertheless, Goebbels was still unsatisfied. He angrily wrote in his diary a few days later: The Berlin Jews "were assembled with lightning speed on this past Saturday and are being deported to the East within the shortest possible time. Unfortunately, it has turned out that the better circles, especially the intellectuals, do not understand our Jewish policies and are partly on the side of the Jews. As a result, our action was betrayed prematurely and a whole bunch of Jews slipped through our fingers. But we will get hold of them anyway. In any case, I shall not rest until at least the capital of the Reich is totally free of Jews." A short time later, he repeated his lament: "The Jews were supposed to be arrested on one day, but because of the shortsighted behavior of industrialists who warned the Jews in time, this plan was a fiasco. All in all, we could not lay hold of 4,000 Jews."[21]

The war diary of the Armaments Command of Berlin does indeed reveal that of the 11,000 Jews still working in the armaments sector, some 4,000, i.e., one-third, managed to escape the roundup because they had been warned in time. Many of them may have gone underground and been hidden by friends until the end of war. A goodly number survived, for instance Dr. Ernst Ludwig Ehrlich, today director of B'nai B'rith. He has told me that at that time, my ministry provided numerous endangered Jews with cards that actually were to be given only to my important staffers. The cards instructed the army, the police, and the SS to let the bearer pass freely. Dr. Ehrlich used such a card to reach the Swiss border unmolested, and there he succeeded in getting across.[22] I have never been able to find out who the courageous man in my ministry was who launched this action on his own initiative.

The Party was shocked by the response of the population. In late 1941 Goebbels had complained to Hitler in my presence about the Berliners especially: "Introducing the Jewish star has led to the very opposite of what was to be achieved, my Führer! We wanted to exclude the Jews from the folk community. But the simple people do not avoid them. On the contrary! They show sympathy to them everywhere. This nation is simply not yet mature and is full of maudlin sentimentality!"[23]

The entries in Goebbels's diary make it clear that the harshness of the war had actually increased the population's distaste for the anti-Jewish measures. It was not just the better groups, especially the Intellectuals, who did not understand our Jewish policies and sided in part with the Jews, as Goebbels stated. Himmler was just as explicit as Goebbels in his speech to SS commanders in Posen on October 4. With sarcastic humor (which often expressed his anger), he said: "And then they all come, these fine eighty million Germans, and each one has his decent Jew! It is clear that the others are bastards, but this one is a first-class Jew."[24] Two days later, Himmler once again attacked the pro-Jewish mood of the German people: "Just think for yourselves how many Germans, even Party members, have addressed their famous petition to me or some agency, saying that naturally, all Jews are bastards, but that so-and-so alone is a decent Jew, and we mustn't do anything to him. I venture to claim that, judging by the number of petitions and the number of opinions, there were more decent Jews in Germany than the number that existed nominally. You see, we have so many millions of people in Germany who have their famous decent Jew, that the number is already larger than the [overall] number of Jews."[25]

But this changed nothing. On March 9, 1943, Goebbels wrote in his diary: "In the Jewish question, [Hitler] approves of my actions and is expressly assigning me the task of making Berlin totally free of Jews." One week later: "One simply cannot trust Jews in any way. I have once again emphasized to the Führer that I consider it necessary to get the Jews out of the entire territory of the Reich as fast as possible. He approves of this action too, and has ordered me not to rest until not a single Jew remains in the territory of the German Reich."[26]

When I recall the fate of the Jews of Berlin, I am overcome by an unavoidable feeling of failure and inadequacy. Often, during my daily drive to my architectural office and, after February 1942, en route to my ministry from the city highway, I saw the crowds of people on the platform of the nearby Nikolascee Railroad station. I knew that these must be Berlin Jews who were being evacuated. I am sure that an oppressive feeling struck me as I drove past; I presumably had a sense of somber events. But I was rooted in the principles of the regime to an extent that I find hard to understand today. Slogans like "Führer, command, we obey!" or "The Führer is always right!" had a hypnotic effect; especially on those of us who were in Hitler's immediate proximity.

Moreover, one preferred to focus on the concerns that were almost overwhelming. Perhaps it was also an unconscious numbing of the conscience when we buried ourselves totally in work. This immersion in our work had something almost neurotic about it.

In the days of Stalingrad, and then more and more often afterwards, Hitler repeated suggestively and in a gloomy undertone that we should not have any more illusions. "There is only forward. The bridges are burned behind us. Gentlemen, there is no going back." We all sensed that monstrous things were happening, and that the road to the past would be blocked for each one of us. We never spoke about this, not even among friends.

Chapter 19

Unreasonable Actions
and Resistance in Poland

REINHARD HEYDRICH WAS ALWAYS COOL and self-controlled: he formulated things with a sharpness that seemed intellectual. On October 4, 1941,
just three months after the invasion of Russia, he was very clear-cut in a
discussion with Gauleiter Meyer, who was Alfred Rosenberg's representative in the Ministry of the East. Heydrich's statements boiled down to
the fact that the German industrialists were pro-Jewish. This recalled
Goebbels's and Himmler's suspicions that German industry was sabotaging
the unambiguous Jewish policies of the Reich.

There was a danger in the occupied territories, Heydrich declared, "that
in many cases, Jews would be claimed as indispensable workers by industry, and that no one would make any effort to obtain other manpower
to replace the Jews. This would destroy the plan of totally moving the
Jews out from the territories we have occupied."[1] Thus, months before the
Wannsee Conference, Heydrich was treating the plan of "totally moving
the Jews out" as an inalterable fact. The word *annihilation* was avoided,
in keeping with linguistic policies. But the meaning was obvious. Where
were the Jews to be moved to if even the East European territories were
to be *judenfrei*?

Heydrich was thus only confirming the general line that Goering had
sketched in a letter a few months earlier: "Jewish manpower must be
used for heavy manual labor. . . . We must see to it that Jews are used only

[256]

in production that would not suffer any remarkable interruption if this manpower were quickly removed. . . . At any rate, we must avoid letting Jewish workers become irreplaceable in important manufacturing."[2]

Nevertheless, plans for employing Jewish workers in armaments factories went on. The directives contradicted each other almost daily. Thus, in these very months, as of May 1942, Lieutenant General Schindler, the Armaments Inspector of the Generalgouvernement, kept working at replacing Polish and Ukrainian skilled workers in Wehrmacht factories in the Generalgouvernement with 100,000 Jewish skilled workers.[3] This project, after all, chimed with the plans followed not only by Himmler but also, at the same time, by Obergruppenführer Pohl with me and my staff. On June 20, 1942, Schindler then announced his intention of negotiating directly with Pohl in order to move shoe and clothing factories from the Reich to the Generalgouvernement and operate them there with Jewish workers.[4]

For a long time there had been no clear-cut line. On June 21, 1942, one day after Schindler took this step with Pohl, a tar paper factory in Tarnov reported a halt in production because all Jewish workers had been deported.[5] At first this was a single case. But on July 19 Himmler gave the decisive order. He told SS Obergruppenführer Krüger, his deputy in the Generalgouvernement, that the resettlement of the entire Jewish population of the Generalgouvernement must be carried through and finished by December 31, 1942. After December 31, 1942, no persons of Jewish background were to reside any longer in the Generalgouvernement —unless they were in the assembly camp in Warsaw, Krakow, Czestochowa, Radom, or Lublin. "All other places of work employing Jewish manpower will be terminated by then, or, in case their termination is not possible, will be transferred to one of the assembly camps. . . . Any foreseeable deadline extensions are to be registered with me in time, so that I can make sure of assistance early enough. All applications by other agencies for changes or permission for exceptions are to be submitted to me personally."[6]

That same month, the Armaments Command of Warsaw kept trying "to deal with the SS and police leaders and other agencies in order to remove the rising difficulties and assure the Jewish manpower necessary for manufacturing. [Also,] residence permission for the close family members of the Jewish workers [should] be obtained. . . . In the ghetto itself, [there is] great unrest and the agitated crowd is massing in the streets. . . . The necessary order [was] preserved with the use of violence." Partial success seemed imminent, for "the [Armaments] Command established with the police and other civilian agencies exactly which factories are to continue operating in the ghetto with Jewish manpower."[7]

In the next few months, Himmler's gruff order of July 19 led to a conspicuously powerful reaction by the Wehrmacht, which was involved in a great deal of important manufacturing. However, these conflicts ended with the total victory of the SS over the army. Two and a half months later, General Gienanth, the military commander in chief of the General-gouvernement, was replaced at Himmler's demand.

Before returning to the general events, I would like to offer an individual case in Przemysl in order to show what problems were caused on a lower level by Himmler's order. A memorandum issued by SS Hauptsturm-führer Fellenz on July 27, 1942, reveals that a "new order from the Higher SS and Police Commander for the East, SS Obergruppenführer and General of the Police Krüger, [set] the age limits for the remaining Jews employed in labor as 16 to 35 years of age. . . . The interests of the East Railroad and the Wehrmacht [are] to be heeded as much as possible." He, Fellenz, as SS deputy for the district of Krakow, had therefore "permitted that in real cases of exception, Jews who are special workers, e.g., foremen in a special skill, can remain for the moment even if they exceed the age limit. [Also,] in keeping with the prevailing regulations, residence permits for the wife and children may be issued along with the residence permit for the man."[8] Here, too, as in Berlin, a surprising consideration for the family.

Himmler's order seems to have been treated loosely in accordance with local conditions. Major Lietke, the local commander of Przemysl, must have had bad experiences with such promises of the SS. For on that same July 27, SS Untersturmführer Benthin, the head of the Security Police in Przemysl, reported that Lietke had learned "that about 95 percent of his Jewish workers were slated for deportation. [He] pointed to Wehrmacht work that he had urgently to carry out. In particular, the local commander emphasized that the main supply camps for the southern armies are located here [in Przemysl], and that he urgently needs workers for this. If no adjustment could be found, then he would complain to the military commander of the Generalgouvernement [General Gienanth]." At the same time, the local command of the army in Przemysl reminded SS Untersturm-führer Benthin of an order that openly contradicted the SS directives, which not only was addressed to all local command officers, but which also had been delivered by special couriers of the military commander in chief: "Re: labor employment of Jews. As already communicated orally through the aide-de-camp, [it is now] ordered that longtime Jewish employees are to be instantly barracked and placed in safe military custody in order to prevent any interference with supplies for the front lines and with urgent work. It is also requested that further Jewish manpower be made available to as great an extent as possible, since, at the orders of the Intendant of the Military Commander in Chief of the Generalgouvernement, a new construction program is to be launched in Przemysl and the Army Construction Office, as well as other agencies, have submitted requests for an increase in the amount of manpower."[9]

After that the district captains, i.e., the local civilian agencies, "were not to [have] any more control over the Wehrmacht Jews. Instead of receiving the salary paid previously, they are to be taken care of by the Wehrmacht. The Wehrmacht is to appoint its own Jewish councils. This special treatment is to prevent the repetition of interference from civilian agencies," i.e., the SS too, "in regard to the Wehrmacht Jews." SS Untersturmführer Benthin, the head of the SS Agency for External Affairs in Przemysl, instantly reported these directives to his superiors, which were obviously directed against the SS. He transmitted details that had been communicated to him orally by Local Commander Lietke; these details were really explosive enough. "The Wehrmacht Jews [are being] housed together inside the present ghettos. They have been placed under *military protection*. The local commander said verbatim that within the framework of his jurisdiction he is going to build up a model Jewish community. Furthermore, he intends to install a company of soldiers to guard them for the time being, which, however, will presumably not be carried out."[10]

But, with an arrogance illustrating the power of the SS even on the lowest level, Benthin stated that he would not go along with the Wehrmacht directives. The local commander "can complain. But exceptions [will be made] on the basis of the prevailing regulations for exceptional cases only for, say, irreplaceable top workers." Naturally, Benthin went on, "Party circles are strongly criticizing the planned social improvement of the Wehrmacht Jews. The treatment of the Jewish question is a spectacle of German disunity. The Wehrmacht Jews will once again think back longingly to the days when they were still under the protection of the German Wehrmacht." A Ukrainian, said Benthin, had remarked that "the exemption of Jews for the Wehrmacht [had] demonstrated that even the Germans cannot get along without Jews. Many attempts have been made in their history to exterminate the Jews, but this has never completely succeeded. The remaining remnants then always became the gravediggers of their persecutors."[11] Such open language in an official report unmistakably indicates the ongoing annihilation of the Jews.

But even Paul, the district captain in Przemysl, felt it necessary to interfere. On August 24, 1942, he commented on the issue of the "position of Aryan manpower to replace the Jews in Przemysl." He said that "all the Jews employed in the Wehrmacht can eventually be replaced by Aryans. He only required "the appropriate powers, to get hold of the still unproductively existing manpower." He said he would "utilize the Ukrainian bishop of Przemysl." He could also "see to it that the workers are decently fed and clad. He intended to let the Poles and Ukrainians employed by the Wehrmacht benefit from the social care meant for the Jews."[12] This was an example of the many proposals submitted by insignificant subordinates merely to attract attention by demonstrating zeal and thoroughness. Of course, these were empty words. Poland was a chaotic country with a traditionally disorderly administration, which the Germans had often described even before the war as a "Polish mess." And now Poland lacked the necessary executive structure for these administrative measures. To expect the bishop to take over such functions was a grotesque misjudgment of the situation.

Ignoring all directives of the military commander in chief, the SS simply got down to business. On August 3, 1942, one week after the army's rebellion against the SS's deportation plan, the Supreme Field Command of Warsaw, and then two days later the Supreme Field Command of Radom,[13] reported that the police were already shipping out Jews. Important work, for supplying the army could no longer be carried out. For instance, the front-line supplies of food were now imperiled.[14] In this dire situation, General Gienanth felt it was expedient to call in Armaments Inspection, which was in my jurisdiction. He thereby circumvented his superior, Field Marshal Keitel, from whom he could not expect support anyway.

Next, on August 15, a futile discussion took place in Krakow between representatives of Armaments Inspection of the Generalgouvernement and representatives of the SS. According to the minutes of Armaments Inspection, "the SS representatives declared: In the opinion of the Reich Marshal, we must get away from the notion that the Jew is indispensable. Neither Armaments Inspection nor the other agencies in the Generalgouvernement are willing to keep the Jews until the end of the war. The orders that have been issued are clear and hard. They are valid not only for the Generalgouvernement, but for all occupied territories. The reasons for them must be extraordinary." These somber words again point to the Holocaust. "Under these circumstances, it does not pay to train Jews for skilled work.

"Captain Gartzke emphasized in contrast to this that Armaments Inspection needs Jews, since work orders are mounting. For instance, a Heinkel plant is being transferred to Budzin because the one in Rostock has been damaged. He stressed that it would be impossible to replace overnight the Jews employed as trained workers in the factories of the Armaments Inspection."

Eventually, they reached a compromise, which was initially applied to the Warsaw Ghetto, the most important labor site. "The Jews employed in the factories of Armaments Inspection are to be assembled [as a part of the overall ghetto] in a special armament ghetto; they will thus have no more contact with the other Jews. A sifting of these Jews in terms of age groups is being tabled for the moment in order to prevent impairing the factory output important for the winter campaign." As a result of this session: "During the clearance of the ghetto in Warsaw, 21,000 Jewish workers were assured until the end of the year for the production crucial to the armaments industry and the war effort."[15]

This agreement, however, did not comply with Himmler's intentions, for it left the army factories a certain independence. Hence, it lasted only two days. On August 17, 1942, Lieutenant General Schindler was informed by Obergruppenführer Krüger, in the presence of several administrative officials of the General governor, that the Warsaw Ghetto would be dissolved altogether, and all previous agreements were to be viewed as invalid. All Jewish manpower would be taken over by the SS in the future and only then be made available to the armaments industry—which was fully in keeping with Pohl's efforts to promote his industrial ambitions by way of the Jews.[16] Armaments Inspection, although deprived of power, was to supply the barracks; this would have meant an economic waste, for the Jews had previously lived in houses, which would now be empty. Furthermore, given the shortage of barracks, this demand was unfeasible.

In any event, all this boiled down to months of interrupted output, for the factories had to move and their operations had to start up again under pressure after new buildings were erected and the machine tools were set up. This spelled no small amount of trouble for the SS, as had been made clear by the examples of Buchenwald and Neuengamme.

On September 5, Field Marshal Keitel—as though it were his own private affair—outdid Himmler, who had at least granted the further employment of Jews already working in the armaments industry. Keitel had not been in charge of armaments since March 1942,[17] when Armaments Inspection was transferred to me. Nevertheless, he ordered Military Commander in Chief General Gienanth: "The Jews employed in the Generalgouvernement by the Wehrmacht for military auxiliary services and in the armaments industry are instantly to be replaced by Poles, that is, non-Jews. The implementation is to be reported."[18] Naturally, Keitel knew that his edict would cause the greatest difficulties because it was simply impossible to replace Jewish manpower with Poles. Hence, this was nothing more than one of those infamous "cover letters" which Keitel used to shield himself against possible reproaches from Hitler. In case Hitler mobilized against the army agencies rebelling in Jewish issues, Keitel, as usual in such case, could pull out his useless letter and be sure of Hitler's praise.

With this backing, Himmler telephoned SS Obergruppenführer Wolff four days later, on September 9, 1942. Wolff, who was staying at headquarters, was simply told "Milit[ary] C[ommander] in Gen[eral] Gou[vernement] must be dismissed."[19] Presumably, countless reports similar to that of the local SS commander Benthin had been landing on Himmler's desk. After the previous events, he could be certain that Keitel would give in to his demand for replacing the rebellious general.

Nine days later, on September 18, 1942, the general quite openly opposed the implementation of the directive from his superior. Despite Keitel's order,[20] he refused to release the Jews to the SS. In a long, cool, matter-of-fact letter, he informed Keitel's command staff, that is, the Wehrmacht Command Staff, of the inevitable production losses if the Jews were to be removed from Wehrmacht manufacturing. Naturally, Keitel was notified of the substance of this letter.

Even if Himmler had not demanded his dismissal, this letter was bound to lead to Gienanth's immediate removal, especially since he had not even shown restraint in his language.

Gienanth, now fighting both Himmler and Keitel, was unmoved in pointing out that "so far, the Generalgouvernement has been directed to release Polish and Ukrainian workers for the Reich and replace them with Jewish workers. For the utilization of Jewish manpower for the war effort, purely Jewish factories or partial factories have been formed [and] Jewish camps set up for employment in the factories. According to government documents—Main Division for Labor—the sum total of commercial workers [in the Generalgouvernement] is somewhat more than one million, including 300,000 Jews. Of these, some 100,000 are skilled workers. In the individual factories working for the Wehrmacht, the number of Jews among the skilled workers keeps shifting between 25 and 100 percent; it is 100 percent in the textile plants making winter clothing. In other plants, for instance in the Fuhrmann and Pleskau vehicle factories, the key workers, the cartwrights, are chiefly Jews. The saddlers, with a few exceptions, are Jews. For uniform repairs, private firms employ a total of 22,700 workers now, of whom 22,000, i.e., 97 percent, are Jews, including some 16,000 skilled workers in textiles and leather plants. A purely Jewish factory with 168 employees manufactures harness fittings. The entire production of harnesses in the Generalgouvernement, the Ukraine, and partly in the Reich is dependent on this firm."

The deportation of Jews, usually beginning without any notification of Wehrmacht offices, had brought "great difficulties for supplies and delays in immediate production for the war effort. Work on the top-priority 'winter' level cannot be completed in time. The immediate removal of the Jews would bring about a considerable reduction in the war potential of the Reich and hold up supplies for the front lines as well as for troops in the General gouvernement. In the armaments industry, there would be serious production gaps, between 25 and 100 percent. In the automotive repair workshops, there would be an average performance drop of about 25 percent, i.e., an average of 2,500 fewer vehicles would be repaired every month. As has now been established, top-priority war-crucial orders, especially for winter needs, have been placed in the Generalgouvernement by the most diverse agencies of the Wehrmacht without the knowledge of Armaments Inspection or the Army Industry officer in the Generalgouvernement. The punctual completion of this work will be impossible because of deportation of the Jews."[21]

The fact that Keitel's order could not be carried out was confirmed by the director of the Main Labor Office, Warsaw, which was under the aegis of Gauleiter Sauckel. At a meeting on September 15, the director stated that he was unable to provide even one Pole to replace the Jews.[22] Likewise, the head of the Przemysl branch of the Labor Office declared: "A removal of able-bodied Jewish manpower would be tantamount to a failure of the measure" to recruit more Poles for German industry.[23]

The plenipotentiary for labor, i.e., Sauckel, would have "to do without 140,000 Poles, who were to be sent to the Reich by the end of this year," General Gienanth wrote to the Wehrmacht Command Staff, if they hoped to even partly prevent the catastrophe of a collapse of the armaments industry in the Generalgouvernement because of the removal of the Jews. The Jewish skilled workers, he said, could be replaced by unskilled Polish farm workers at best only after a year's training.[24] My staffers and I were informed about these events and thus about the imminent production losses by the Armaments Office of my ministry, which combined all Armaments Inspections. Sauckel, for his part, was probably informed by the Main Labor Division in the Generalgouvernement (which he was in charge of, after all) about the consequences of Himmler's and Keitel's deportation plans.

Because of this open conflict, an armaments discussion with Hitler took place on September 22, 1942, and Sauckel was included at my request. He openly sided with me, using, as I did, the arguments of our agencies. When faced with the choice of doing without either valuable supply production or 140,000 Poles, who were urgently needed in German farming, Hitler stated tersely: "The Führer agrees with Gauleiter Sauckel's proposal to have the Jewish skilled workers remain in the Generalgouvernement."[25] Hitler had yielded to economic pressure. Keitel's cover letter had been penned too early; Hitler had decided against his rash order.

That same day, Himmler noted a telephone conversation at 10:30 P.M. with SS Obergruppenführer Wolff, who told him about "Speer's (Saur's) wish, concerning Jews in industrial plants."[26]

Himmler probably felt that this decision of Hitler's had gone over his head. It was in keeping with his character that he transformed Hitler's decision in favor of Sauckel into a wish expressed by me and thus having only conditional validity. Ten days after Hitler's decision, on October 9, 1942, Himmler modified his directive of July 19 that the resettlement of the entire Jewish population of the Generalgouvernement had to be completed by December 31, 1942. But otherwise, he stuck unyieldingly to his industrial goals. He again ordered that "all the so-called armaments workers who are merely working in tailor, fur, and shoemaking workshops" were to be "assembled in these places, i.e., in Warsaw [or] Lublin, in concentration camps, by SS Obergruppenführer Krüger and SS Obergruppenführer Pohl. . . . The Wehrmacht is to pass their merchandise orders to us, and we will guarantee the continuance of deliveries of the clothing items they desire." This was a guarantee without guarantors. His fury at the interference in his business burst through when he went on, saying he "had given orders to proceed mercilessly against all those who believe they have to oppose this with alleged armaments interests, but in reality only wish to support the Jews and their businesses." This threat was also quite doubtlessly intended to intimidate the staff of the Armaments Inspection.

As though one could order factories to move to and fro like military units, Himmler directed that "the Jews who are in real armaments factories, i.e., weapons plants, auto plants, etc., [are to be] removed stage by stage. As a first phase, they are to be concentrated in separate rooms in the factories. As a second phase of this development, the employees of these rooms are to be exchanged and assembled in closed factories wherever feasible, so that we will then have just a few closed concentration camp factories in the Generalgouvernement," which naturally were to be annexed by the SS industrial concern.

The goal of utterly exterminating the Polish Jews was merely postponed. "We will then strive to replace this Jewish manpower with Poles and to concentrate the greater number of these Jewish concentration camp factories in a very few large Jewish concentration camp factories, wherever feasible, in the east of the Generalgouvernement. However, in accordance with *the Führer's wish*,[27] the Jews should disappear from there too."[28] This wording is evidence that Hitler not only approved but even ordered the murder of all Jews. In the hierarchy, a "wish" of Hitler's was generally viewed as an order in friendly guise.

One day earlier, on October 8, 1942, in Berlin, General Schindler had told me about his utter helplessness in regard to this situation. He spoke to me "about the tolerated position of the Armaments Inspector in the Generalgouvernement." He had been unable to prevent Himmler's evacuation order, even though he was the general in command. "The minister," the chronicle of my ministry goes on, "wanted an energetic representation of his interests with the government of the Generalgouvernement."[29] But this was an unfair demand, which was bound to remain sheer theory given the power situation. An internal struggle between Himmler and Frank had long since led to Himmler's having sole control of the Jewish question even in the Generalgouvernement.[30]

A few days later, on October 4, 1942, General Gienanth was replaced. Hitler's change of mind had meant nothing. On October 10 Gienanth's successor, General Haenicke of the Wehrmacht Command Staff, was informed from Keitel's immediate command area: "The Supreme Command of the Wehrmacht, in agreement with the SS Reichsführer, is firmly abiding by the principle that the Jews employed by the Wehrmacht for military auxiliary service and in the armaments industry are to be replaced instantly by Aryan workers."[31] This letter was accompanied by Himmler's most recent order (quoted above), which merely gave the Jews a period of grace to work for the German war effort. However, Keitel superfluously decided once again that his original armaments order was valid. The discussion with Hitler seemed not to have taken place. So Keitel could accurately estimate that under Himmler's influence, Hitler would not maintain his decision of September 12 for long. Keitel thought as little about the impact of his order on armaments as about the losses of thousands of soldiers due to his military orders, whereby he transmitted Hitler's senseless orders.

Gienanth's dismissal, Himmler's order, and Keitel's new letter must have had a depressing effect on Lieutenant General Schindler. In his activities report on the third quarter of 1942, he assumed that before long the 50,000 Jews still employed in factories of Armaments Inspection would be replaced by Poles.[32] Likewise, at the Armaments Commission meeting of October 24, 1942, Schindler was convinced that these 50,000 Jews "are to be removed from the factories" by early 1943, "i.e., replaced by a different manpower."[33] But, as we will see, this did not happen.

On December 4, 1942, Generalgovernor Frank had complained in his temperamental way about the absurd measures of the SS: "It is not unimportant manpower that has been taken from us in our time-tested Jewries. It is clear that the work process will be more difficult if, in the middle of this work process, the order comes to submit all Jews to annihilation. The responsibility for this is not that of the administration of the General-gouvernement. The directive for the annihilation of the Jews comes from a higher level."[34] Here too, there is an indication of the fundamental character of the decision on the "annihilation of the Jews," as Frank writes, conspicuously ignoring the usual prescription of language.

As Reichsleiter, Himmler was basically on the same level as Frank in the Party hierarchy. Frank could point out that in the early years of struggle, he had been Hitler's lawyer and had done more for the Party than Himmler with his initially subordinate security assignment. In the government domain, Frank, as governor general, had a higher rank than Himmler because he actually performed the functions of a head of state. Thus, when Frank said "higher level," he could only have meant Hitler himself. Frank never disputed the authenticity of his diary, which he surrendered to the Americans after his arrest. The morally annihilating and legally incriminating entries in this journal stunned us as defendants at the Nuremberg Trial. Criticism was limited to the stupidity of handing over this incriminating evidence to the enemy.

Despite his victory, Himmler viewed the officers of General Schindler's Armaments Inspection almost as saboteurs thwarting his orders. Four months later, in Warsaw, as Himmler informed Krüger, the SS commander in the Generalgouvernement, he summoned "the local man of the Army Armaments Inspection, a certain Colonel Freter." He made it clear to Freter that there were "still some 40,000 Jews in [Warsaw]. Some 24,110 of them are in textile and fur factories. I have ordered Colonel Freter to notify Armaments Inspector Schindler that I am astonished that my directives pertaining to Jews are not being obeyed. I have now set a deadline, February 14, 1943, by which time the following are to be carried out:

1. Immediate exclusion of the private firms. I consider it absolutely necessary that we see to it that these owners, who have been placed in a reserved occupation, are to be conscripted wherever feasible and sent to the front.
2. I order the Reich Security Headquarters to closely scrutinize the business dealings and profits of the firm of Walter C. Többens, Warsaw, with the help of auditors. If I am not mistaken, a once penniless man has developed, within the space of three years, into a prosperous owner—if not a millionaire—and he has done so because we, the State, have handed him cheap Jewish manpower.
3. The instant removal of all 16,000 Jews[35] to a concentration camp, preferably Lublin. A guarantee to the Armaments Inspection to perform and supply the same as was previously performed in regard to number and deadlines. I believe that it can also be done at lower prices."

Himmler obviously wanted to pass this manufacturing on to Pohl.[36]

A report on the implementation of the order was not long in coming. On February 2, 1943, the SS Oberführer in charge of Warsaw reported: "The preparations for the transfer of all textile-processing plants that employ Jews are in full swing. . . . A total of eight factories with some 20,000 Jewish workers are being moved to the concentration camp at Lublin."[37]

The Oberführer seems to have been too hasty in reporting his success. For two weeks later, according to the war diary of Armaments Inspection in the Generalgouvernement, only the "firm of Schultz and Co., Warsaw," was beginning "to transfer the factory and moving to Trawnika with the first 350 Jewish workers and with a portion of the furrier factory on Pavia Street."[38]

One and a half years later, when Warsaw had to be evacuated because of the approaching Soviet armies, a court established by SS Commander Stoph, Battle Commander for Warsaw, initiated a court-martial proceeding against Colonel Freter. It accused him of leaving Warsaw and directing all the necessary evacuation measures from outside. On September 15 I protested against a condemnation of Freter. We were, on the contrary, greatly indebted to him because he had transported 2,000 freight cars full of machines and matériel from Warsaw, which had to be evacuated; also, he had gone to Warsaw every day. The trial was halted in December 1944.[39]

Today we can no longer determine whether Himmler's preparations to ship the Jews from the Warsaw Ghetto led to the outbreak of the uprising of the Warsaw Ghetto. In any event, the smashing of the uprising brutally advanced Himmler's demand for the transfer of the ghetto factories. On April 21, 1943, the war diary of Armaments Inspection tersely remarks: "Because of increasing uncertainty in Warsaw Ghetto, transfer of all Jewish manpower of the ghetto's clothing and repair works."[40] A few days later, the "Armaments Command, Warsaw," reported "with radio message of April 26, 1943, that the situation in the Warsaw Ghetto is getting worse, and that, in a short time, there will be an all-out fight against the resistance nests located there."[41] On May 2, 1942: "The Jews are being taken from the ghetto factories of the Transavia and Döring firms in Warsaw."[42] Two days later: "Departure of the rest of the Jews from the Wehrmacht factories" (in contrast to armaments factories) "in the night of May 3–4, 1943."[43] The next day, May 5, 1943: "All equipment must be removed from the ghetto factories in three days since they are being blown up."[44]

The reports of the Armaments Inspection on the second quarter of 1943 summed up the situation: "The evacuation of the Warsaw Ghetto at the start of the period in question led to considerable production losses, especially for the factories located in the ghetto. Detailed reports on the situation were constantly submitted to the Herr Reich Minister for Armaments and Munitions. The same reports were submitted to the Herr Governor General."[45]

At the same time, the SS resorted to radical measures in other parts of the Generalgouvernement. On April 30, 1943, the "Armaments Command of Lvov" reported "that, according to a letter from the SS Police Commander of April 27, 1943, the firm of Schwarz and Co., Lvov, because of various irregularities that have occurred there, is having all its Jewish workers, as well as the machines deriving from Jewish ownership, removed. The entire factory, together with all ongoing and new orders, is being taken over by the German Armaments Works, Lvov" (an enterprise of Pohl's).[46] As always in such cases, the booty of machines and human potential was pocketed by the SS factories.

One month later, on May 31, 1943, Frank, in a work session of the administration of his Generalgouvernement, declared that "he had recently again received the order to carry out the *Ent judung* [= de-Jewification] in a very short time. We were forced to remove the Jews from the armaments industry and the war-industry factories as well if they were not used exclusively for war-crucial interests. The Jews, he said, were then assembled in large camps and handed over from there for daily work in in these armaments plants. However, the SS Reichsführer wishes an end to even the employment of these Jews. He [Frank] said he had discussed this question in detail with Lieutenant Schindler and he believes that in the final analysis, this wish of the SS Reichsführer cannot be carried out. Among the Jewish workers, there are special workers, precision mechanics, and other qualified artisans, who cannot easily be replaced by Poles. He therefore asks SS Obergruppenführer Dr. Kaltenbrunner" (who was present) "to describe this situation to the SS Reichsführer and to ask him to desist from the removal of these Jewish workers (i.e., into SS camps).[47]

Frank's tendency, visible in his speech, to protect his factories was not new, as the files now reveal. I was poorly informed at the time and saw him as my enemy. I did not realize that the governor general was actually my ally in the struggle for the undisturbed employment of Jews in our armaments factories.

But even Frank was ultimately powerless. Despite Frank's request to Kaltenbrunner, Himmler's order was carried out. We were all helpless in the face of this development. But even if Hitler had once again agreed to make an exception, the Warsaw Uprising would have put an end to the ghetto factories. After all, in this situation, there was a greater danger that fleeing Jews would join the partisan movement, which had long since brought catastrophic confusion to the supply line for the German army.

However, the Wehrmacht officers still would not give up. On July 31, 1943, Lieutenant Colonel Mathes of Armaments Inspection went to see Krüger, SS and Police Commander for the East, to obtain "measures against the disturbing removal of Jews from armaments and petroleum plants." He had success only in connection with the petroleum plants; for on August 27, 1943, the war diary says: "Start of removal of Jewish manpower from the war-crucial factories, except for the mineral oil factories in the district of Galicia."[48] In late August 1943, the Armaments Command of Lvov reported: "The Jewish workers were removed very suddenly from the defense plants of the Armaments Inspection in August; likewise from all factories of the war-crucial industry and the factories working for the needs of troops or for the commander in chief of the military district." (See Appendix 20.) "Only the Metrawatt firm kept 12 Jewish watchmakers, who cannot possibly be replaced by Aryan manpower. Their further employment in the plant is inadmissible. A solution is now being striven for in conjunction with the SS and Police Commander of Galicia, so that the productivity of Metrawatt will not be too greatly impaired."[49] These workers seem to have been so important that from

September 16 to 18, 1943, discussion took place in Berlin with the Armaments Office of my ministry and SD Headquarters.[50] The topic was "leaving Jewish specialized workers in the Metrawatt firm in Lvov."[51]

In general, however, no attention was paid to production losses. In those days, it was reported that from August 30 to September 5, 1943, "because of the removal of Jews by the SS from the Lamps and Metalware Factory of Emanuel Wachs and Co. in Krakow, the army order of 600,000 carbide burners was strongly impaired in its output for some time."[52] On September 4, 1943, "in the district of Krakow, all the Jewish women employed by clothing factories were transferred to closed SS camps. A few factories have thereby lost their skilled Jewish workers."[53] This was sheer self-destruction for an armaments industry that had been severely damaged for some time through aerial warfare.

Ultimately, the armaments authorities had to put up with the new situation. The activities report of July 1943 by the Defense Economy Officer in the Generalgouvernement stated: "In order to better utilize the Jewish manpower housed in the large work camps of Szebnie for the armaments industry, the Defense Economy Officer is negotiating with the camp leadership about transferring part of the Daimler-Benz production into the Jewish camp. The discussions have not yet ended since certain technical difficulties of the transfer must be dealt with."[54]

From August 5 to 8, 1943, the war diary of Armaments Inspection of the Generalgouvernement says: "Negotiations of the head of the administration division with the SS and Police Commander for Lublin whether and to what extent the existing facilities and capacity of the Jewish forced labor camps in Poniatowa, Prawnike, and Blizyn can be made useful for the office."[55] Nothing is known about the outcome of these efforts. All that is certain is that in these SS camps, the Jews performed only a fraction of the labor that they had previously performed in independent factories.

Chapter 20

Of Three Million,
One Hundred Thousand Survived

HIMMLER HAD GIVEN two basic speeches about the liquidation of all Jews within reach of the Germans. He never spoke of murder! When talking to the SS squad commanders in Posen on October 4, he stated: "I want to be fully open with you about a very difficult matter. . . . I mean the evacuation of the Jews." This was the usual camouflage term, which, however, he exposed with his next words: "The extermination of the Jewish people!"[1] Two days later Himmler went into greater detail when speaking to the Reichsleiters and Gauleiters, who were likewise assembled in Posen. "Gentlemen, it is easy to speak the sentence 'The Jews must be exterminated' with its few words. But for the man who must carry out what it demands, it is the very highest and most difficult thing in the world. We were confronted with the question: What about the women and children? I made up my mind to find a very clear solution here, too. For I did not feel I had the right to exterminate the men—that is, kill or have them killed—and allow the vengeance seekers in the form of children and grandchildren to grow up. . . . The Jewish question in the countries occupied by us will be settled by the end of this year. There will only be remnants left, individual Jews who have slipped underground."[2] In these two speeches, Himmler was, of course, addressing Party functionaries. He thus remained within the circle of those who, he could assume, politically advocated the most radical form of anti-Semitism.

As of the beginning of 1944, however, he quite obviously felt obliged to

tell the generals openly what had happened. Thus, on January 28, 1944, he
informed the front-line generals, who had convened in Posen, that the
Jewish question was solved. They [the Jews] would not take vengeance on
our children.[3] In May 1944 Himmler once again told generals that the
extermination of the Jews had been solved "in Germany in general and in
the territories occupied by Germany."[4] Three weeks later Himmler enlightened another group of generals: "The Jewish question [has been] un-
compromisingly solved according to orders."[5] And once again to generals
gathering in Sonthofen in late June 1944: "It is good that we were tough
enough to exterminate the Jews in our realm."[6]

One cannot assume that Himmler could have given his two Posen
speeches on October 4 and 6, 1943, with their disclosures about the annihilation of the Jews, without Hitler's express approval. Nor can one believe
that the generals convening in Posen and Sonthofen between January and
June could have been allowed to learn these facts without Hitler's consent.
If I as minister of armaments planned to present just comparative figures
on armaments output at a Gauleiter meeting, then such information, which
went against all rules of secrecy, had to be approved by Hitler. Even Goebbels had to submit to these restrictions. Bormann supervised the adherence
to these guidelines in every Gau by way of his subordinates, for instance,
the Gau leaders and district leaders, or the Gau industrial councillors. He
would never have failed to make Hitler aware of unreported disclosures—
especially if they had been made by his greatest rival in the power struggle,
his intimate friend Himmler.

Hence, could Himmler have dared to tell this inner Party group, on
October 6, 1943, about measures unknown to Hitler? Was he not bound to
reckon that, say, Goebbels, Ley, or Hitler's intimate friends from the early
Party days, e.g., Reich leaders Franz Xaver Schwarz and Max Amann,
would have spoken about Himmler's indiscretions the very next day at
headquarters?

I would presume that Hitler had asked Himmler to come out with the
facts on the practical "Jewish policies" to make the top men realize how
helpless their own personal situation was. In a certain sense, Hitler wanted
to illustrate what he meant by "burned bridges."

In addition to the information about the murder of the Jews, Himmler,
when speaking in Posen, broached another topic that was important to him.
We already knew of it from his various utterances during the preceding
months. He told the Reich leaders and Gau leaders in Posen: "You will
believe me when I tell you that I had great difficulties with many industrial
facilities. The [Warsaw] Ghetto manufactures fur coats, dresses, and the

like. If someone wanted to get there in the past, we were told: 'Stop! You're interfering with war industry! Stop! Armaments factories!" Naturally, this has nothing to do with Party Comrade Speer. You can't do a thing. It is this portion of the alleged armaments factories that Party Comrade Speer and I wish to cleanse together in the next few weeks and months. We will do this just as unsentimentally as all things must be done unsentimentally but magnanimously for Germany in the fifth year of the war."[7]

Two days earlier, on October 4, 1943, in a speech to the SS squad commanders, Himmler had already spoken about the latent resistance of the German population: "In the past, whenever someone wanted to shut down some Jewish firm, throw out a Jew, some Herr Paymaster So-and-So would protest: 'What, are you trying to damage the military power of the German people? You are sabotaging the war industry.' In reality, the Jew had donated a little fur coat to the paymaster. Today, when you remove 800 Jewish women from a factory, another gentleman comes along; he's just had a pair of brand-new boots made in the factory, and he says: 'I must inform you that you have crucially interfered with war production.' "[8]

When Himmler referred to the manufacture of furs, he deliberately ignored the fact that these were sheepskins for the troops. Furthermore, it was the quartermaster-general of the army who determined the size, manner, and place of their production, and not the minister of armaments.

Alleged "joint resolutions on the cleansing of armaments factories" would certainly have been recorded in the completely extant journals of Armaments Inspection of the Generalgouvernement or in the documents of the SS Reichsführer. Moreover, such conferences are not even mentioned in my ministry's files. The excerpts from the SS files do not exactly indicate that Himmler required my assistance for his draconian measures. Himmler and his subordinates hardly shied away from paralyzing production by removing Jewish armaments workers to concentration camps with no previous announcement, much less previous negotiation with Armaments Inspection. This happened even against General Schindler's plans and against the will of the governor-general, as revealed by the minutes of Frank's governmental meetings.

Himmler's agitated polemics against the industrial leaders reflected the same attitude that was generally shown by the SS in this period. As early as October 4, 1941, Heydrich had already openly attacked the industrial leaders. Meanwhile, things had come to such a pass that the industrialists were depicted wholesale as unrealiable, corrupt, and even enemies of the people. In the course of the Russian campaign, the power of the SS grew from month to month.

Himmler had thus bluntly told the Gau leaders: "The Jewish question in the countries occupied by us will be settled by the end of this year." The previous statements made it absolutely clear that he meant the murder of the Jews.[9]

However, Himmler was deliberately deceiving the Party hierarchy. As the preserved documents reveal, he continued doing everything he could, even after December 31, 1943, to "reserve" Jews for his industrial plans, i.e., for building up his industrial empire. It is conceivable that Hitler's orders interfered with Himmler's industrial plans, and that Himmler therefore preferred keeping this part of his truth a secret from the Gau leaders and informing them only of the other aspect of his actions. I am again thinking of something that Höss said when he spoke of a different Reich authority working against Himmler's exploitation plans. Höss pointed out that on January 26, 1942, i.e., four days before the Wannsee Conference, Himmler still considered it desirable to employ 150,000 Jews in armaments.[10]

In any case, Himmler was not serious about exterminating all Polish Jews by the end of the war. In *Anatomy of the SS State*, Helmut Krausnick (in the chapter "Persecution of the Jews") documents the following: On September 7, 1943, i.e., one month before Himmler's Posen speech, "the some ten existing labor camps of the SS and Police Commander in the district of Lublin [were] taken over by SS Economic Administrative Headquarters." Subsequently, this was to happen with "all labor camps in the Generalgouvernement." As Martin Broszat reported on concentration camps in the same book, profusely documenting his statements, Pohl, as chief of these headquarters, successively strove to make this manpower useful for his industrial efforts by improving the living conditions.[11] Recently, right-wing extremists have been pointing out these efforts of Pohl and Himmler to improve the working and living conditions of Jewish and other prisoners. But it is wrong of these groups to play these facts up as their discoveries in order to assert the unrealiability of previous historians.

On November 4, 1943, Globocnik reported to Himmler on his assignment in the annihilation of the Jews. And even he says: "On the other hand, I tried to provide a description of the labor operation, revealing not only the amount of work, but also with how few Germans this major operation was made possible. Today, at any rate, it has increased so greatly that well-known industries are expressing an interest in it. Meanwhile, I have handed these labor camps over to SS Obergruppenführer Pohl." Furthermore, this letter shows that Globocnik, presumably at Himmler's instructions, had "completed the Reinhardt Action, which I led in the Generalgouvernement, and disbanded all [extermination] camps."[12] This took place on October 19, 1943, not even two weeks after Himmler's speeches in Posen.

On October 19, 1943, during a work conference, the governor-general told "General Schindler, head of Armaments Inspection, SS Oberführer Bierkamp, and Major General Grünwald to go through the lists of Jewish camps in the Generalgouvernement and see how many inmates can be used as manpower." Thus, in contrast to Himmler's speech in Posen, the preservation of the available labor supply was accepted. "The rest," Frank went on "are to be deported from the Generalgouvernement," i.e., killed. On the other hand, there was no mention at any time of a joint inspection of the armaments factories by Himmler and me (such as Himmler had announced in his Posen speech) or by our respective organizations.[13]

At that time, there must have been two contradictory tendencies of the SS, even in the Generalgouvernement.[14] One day before Globocnik signed his concluding report, other SS officers had decided on a counterstroke; it was certainly aimed at the principles that Globocnik had expounded in his letter and that they must have been familiar with. Typical of the situation was a letter that Schieber wrote to me on May 7, 1944. He spoke about the great friction among SS commanders while building concentration camp divisions in the armaments factories. The cause, in Schieber's opinion, was "essentially the jealousy of the lower SS commanders."[15] But this cannot explain what the SS did on November 3, 1943. During a period of eleven hours, from 6 A.M. until 5 P.M., they shot 17,000 Jews in groups of ten.[16] Involved were factories of the SS-owned "East Industry," in which the confiscated Jewish factories were assembled. The action was aimed against Pohl's plans, as Dr. Max Horn, the assistant manager, desperately explained, because the "construction and expansion work done so far" was rendered "totally worthless" by this action.

After this annihilation, the SS and Police Commander of Warsaw, who belonged to the other side, remarked scornfully to someone on Pohl's staff: "East Industry! When I hear the word *industry*, I get nauseated!"[17] It is horrifying to see how a decision was made over the lives of 17,000 Jews.

Actually, there were two trends struggling against one another in the top SS leadership. One group wanted to spare the prisoners in order to use them as manpower to advance Himmler's industrial goals. The other group wanted, at best, to let the prisoners be worked to death, but really to liquidate them for the sake of ideology. Höss formulated this difference of opinions as follows: "The Reich Security Headquarters saw in every new labor camp, in every new thousand able-bodied prisoners, the danger of liberation, survival by some circumstance or other. However, Pohl seemed stronger, for behind him stood the SS Reichsführer, who kept insisting on more and more prisoners for the armaments industry."[18] Camp Commandant Höss's statements are underscored by an order that Himmler issued on January 15, 1943, to Reich Security Headquarters, albeit for a different reason: "I have assumed great tasks in the concentration camps for the sake of the overall armaments industry. That is where the manpower belongs."[19] Thus, even Himmler felt it was necessary to defend himself and clarify his aims to Reich Security Headquarters.

Here we must once again recall Höss's comment about the top-level opposition to Himmler's and Pohl's policies. For Globocnik had written an unvarnished letter on January 18, 1944 to Himmler, saying that " 'East Industry' and Deutsche Ausrüstungswerke [German Armaments Works] were factories run by me . . . which functioned without complaint when I was gone." However, "on November 3, 1943, the workers were removed from the labor camps and the plants were shut down. The camp officers were not informed of this action, even though the responsibility was theirs. I was therefore hindered in my supervision task. . . . On the day before the camp evacuation, General Schindler of the Armaments Inspection in Krakow, on the basis of a promise from SS Obergruppenführer Krüger, arranged with the camp officers that in the future, armaments orders would [be sent] to the labor camps of 'East Industry.' "[20]

As though lightning had struck, this critical interference with the jurisdiction of a man as high as Globocnik was accepted without rebuke and without any demand for investigation. Furthermore, it would have been incomprehensible of Himmler to allow this destruction of an industrial enterprise if Bormann, and thus Hitler himself, had not been behind such an action.

The destructive action of November 3, 1943, had paralyzed "East Industry." This is also reflected in the reports of the armaments agencies. At the meeting of the Armaments Commission of November 10, 1943, Schindler reported that "great difficulties [have] emerged in the Jewish employment operation because of the recent great removals in the Lublin area. These sudden losses, without previous notification of the East Industry Company, are chiefly affecting the clothing and equipment sectors."[21] On November 11, the diary of the Central Division of the Armaments Inspection also mentioned the action, while cautiously circumscribing the extermination events, as did all the other reports from armaments agencies: "Unexpected and total removal of Jewish workers from the factories of Walter C. Többins in Poniatowa and Schultz & Co. in Trawniki."[22] That same day, the war diary of the Administration Division recorded a report from the Armaments Command of Warsaw, which said that "because of definitive loss of Jewish manpower, production is interrupted in both firms."[23] The Defense Economy Leader, under the Supreme Command of the Wehrmacht, was even blunter in his report: "Major supply delays at various textile plants in Lublin district because of loss of Jewish manpower due to police actions" that were "ordered by the SD."[24]

These annihilation actions affected not only the "East Industry Works," but also the German Armaments Works, which were likewise under Pohl's aegis. "Business trip of Division V to Lvov for negotiating the placement or cancellation of orders from the German Armaments Works," says the war diary of the Armaments Inspection on November 19–26, 1943.[25]

Summing up these events, Schindler reported at the meeting of the Armaments Commission on December 29, 1943: "The resettlements [*sic!*] of Jews from the district of Lublin have caused a number of plants to shut down. The shutdown of the East Industry Works has been agreed on with the Higher SS and Police Commander, while the German Armaments Works will continue operating."[26] However, there was absolutely no mention of these events when the armaments inspector sent the Berlin Armaments Office an official overview of the fourth quarter.[27] This showed the extent to which these events were kept secret. The same silence is maintained by the official monthly reports of the Defense Economy Office in October, November, and December 1943.[28]

This is not the only example of the infighting and arbitrary actions on the higher levels of the SS. SS Obersturmbannführer Maurer had been appointed by Pohl a long time before that to increase the employment of concentration camp inmates in the armaments industry. In his capacity as head of Office D II in the Bureau for Concentration Camps, he wrote a letter on September 4, 1943, showing how little he himself knew about the actual conditions. Two months before the removal of 17,000 workers in Poland, he asked SS Obersturmbannführer Höss, the commandant of the concentration camp at Auschwitz: "On August 24, 1943, I told SS Hauptsturmführer Schwarz that I have to know the number of fully able-bodied and employable Jews, since I intend to remove Jews from the Auschwitz concentration camp in order to employ them in armaments factories in the Reich. On August 26, 1943, I repeated this message in a telegram. According to the telegram from there of August 29, 1943, of the 25,000 Jews imprisoned there, only 3,581 are able-bodied. These, however, are all employed in armaments projects and can therefore not be supplied. What are the other 21,500 Jews doing? Something doesn't make sense here! I ask you to investigate the matter again and report to me."[29]

This is an astonishing document, which in a certain way complements the mortality figures from July to December 1942. Even an agency chief in the Bureau for Concentration Camps did not know what was going on.

The enigma surrounding the murder of 17,000 Jewish workers is underscored when we read the following. On November 4, 1943, that is, just one day after the action, SS Obergruppenführer Krüger, the top SS officer responsible for the Generalgouvernement, promised[30] he would make 5,000 Jews available to the armaments industry in the near future. Krüger repeated this promise to General Schindler on November 10, 1943, adding that "another 5,000 Jews are to follow in the course of the next six months. These are mainly Jews housed in the Plaszow camp. This would bring the armaments industry," Schindler stressed, "a total of some 33,000 Jews, which would be about 20 percent of all workers. But since there is a possibility of sudden departure for these Jews too, Chairman [Schindler] must request precautionary measures to cover this possible loss, and address his request today to the Main Division for Labor [in the administration of the Generalgouvernement]."[31] The preceding events made this preventive demand seem advisable.

The first part of the promise was quickly kept. According to a report of the Armaments Inspection of November 16, 1943, a "transport of 2,500 Jewish workers from the forced labor camp of Pleszew" reached Skarzysko-Kamienna and was put to work in the Hugo Schneider Co., Leipzig, which produced munitions.[32] On November 18, 1943, another "transport, totaling 1,500 Jewish workers from the forced labor camp of Pleszew was sent to armaments plants in Kielce, Czestochowa, Pionki, Ostrowiec, and Starachowice."[33]

At that time for form's sake, Krüger was taking care of business only transitionally. A few weeks earlier, around mid-October, that is, before the mass liquidation, SS Obergruppenführer Krüger was replaced as Himmler's deputy in the Generalgouvernement. His successor was SS Obergruppenführer Koppe, who had previously resided in Greiser's Gau, the so-called Warta Gau. On October 27, 1943, Frank reported to his close staffers: "He was assured that the SS Obergruppenführer, in total contrast to the previous conditions, has been provided with a precise march route and a path to appropriate cooperation is to be found."[34]

Schindler visited Berlin to discuss the new situation created by Koppe's appointment. For Frank had simply made the new SS commander one of his state secretaries, thus granting him political functions in his government. The chronicle of November 17, 1943, reported on Schindler's visit: "The high-handedness of the administration in the Generalgouvernement has confronted the local armaments inspector, General Schindler, with an especially difficult task. The minister is discussing a solution of these problems with General Schindler and Hauptdienstleiter Saur: namely by appointing the new SS commander, Obergruppenführer Koppe, as deputy [of the minister] for armaments affairs in the government, which he feels would strengthen the work of the armaments inspector. General Schindler has agreed to this solution."[35]

On December 8, returning from his trip to Berlin, Schindler told the Armaments Commission that he welcomed "this appointment since Obergruppenführer Koppe (aside from his executive power as Higher SS and Police Commander) as a state secretary in the administration of the Generalgouvernement is in a far better position to represent armaments interests than the chairman of the Armaments Commission. It would be wrong to view these organizational changes as, say, a slight aimed at the armaments agencies or other organizations dealing with armaments. This new order can thus allow us to expect an important furtherance of armaments interests. Considerable relief was provided by the allocation of 4,000 Jews, which will be followed by a further allocation of 500 in the current month. Beyond that, we are to expect further allocations of Jews in the next four months."[36]

The development of the production figures does not speak for an essential increase in the number of workers during the second half of 1943. First, the loss of 17,000 trained Jews had to be made up for. According to a report from Armaments Inspection, the average monthly output in the first six months of 1943 rose from 46 million marks to 58 million in October, to 59 million in November, and to 60 million in December.[37] Of course, these armaments achievements in the Generalgouvernement were minimal compared with the overall German production. In December 1943, all the territory under German rule manufactured a total worth 2.3 billion. Thus, the Generalgouvernement produced only .0025 percent of the entire German armaments output.

"Something must, of course, be done about feeding the Jews," says a report from the Armaments Commission on January 12, 1944.[38] However, on March 8, 1944, at the next meeting of the Armaments Commission, Koppe refused to use his authority to settle the food issue. "Taking care of the armaments workers," he said, "which always became a chief topic of discussion, is the business of the appropriate main division of the government."[39] Five days later Schindler therefore turned to the "Main Division for Food and Agriculture [to discuss] the feeding of the Jews in the armaments factories."[40] No result was recorded. Presumably for a further discussion of Schindler's, the files contain a note saying: "E.L. [Main Division for Food and Agriculture in the administration of the Generalgouvernement] previously allocated far higher rations to the concentration camp Jews than to the Jews working in the plants." This sentence too shows that, contrary to Himmler's directives, great numbers of Jews were still employed outside the camps. "The concentration camp Jews receive, by way of the SS manager, food rations somewhat corresponding to those in the Reich, as approved by the Reich Minister of Food.[41] E.L. wants to give the Jews in the plants only the rations of the Polish armaments workers. Such an allocation would not suffice, given the extremely deficient energy of the Jews in heavy industry, since the Jews, as internees, cannot procure additional food, in contrast to the Poles, nor can they share in additional factory food."[42]

It was not within the jurisdiction of the armaments agencies to do more than demandingly point out the food abuses. Nevertheless, the situation could not have been as desperate for the Jews in the Generalgouvernement as for those in Reich territory. Simon Wiesenthal writes in his book *The Sunflower* about his experiences as a concentration camp inmate in the Generalgouvernement: "With the East Railroad, we were relatively well off. We had contact with the outside world and we also received more food."

The only constant statistics about the working Jews are those supplied by the Defense Economy Officer in the Generalgouvernement. However, these figures referred only to those Jews who produced items for general army needs, e.g., clothing, furs, shoes, sleds, and other articles for the front. Nevertheless, the development of these figures is interesting, for it probably mirrors the overall trend. According to these statistics, the number of Jews employed within the jurisdiction of the Defense Economy Officer rose from 15,091 in January 1943 to 15,500 in April, and then to 21,600 in July 1943. By the end of October 1943, the number of Jews working in these plants had by no means declined. It had actually gone up to 22,444, i.e., 800 more than in July. The number kept mounting. By the end of January 1944, it had risen by 3,852, i.e., 17 percent, to 26,296; in April, another 8 percent, to 28,537. Then, for May 1944, the figures show a decline to 27,439. However, parallel to this decline, the total number of workers employed in this area had gone down from 179,000 to 172,000. The percentage of decline is roughly the same in both cases. It was linked to the shutdown of manufacturing, which moved to the front-line area in Galicia at the end of May 1944.[43]

But what did these figures mean in the light of the millions of Jews who had once lived in Poland?

In a situation report for April 1944, the Defense Economy Officer in the Generalgouvernement wrote about "high demands placed by the front-line troops on artisans, cleaning personnel, and unskilled manpower, especially for field hospitals and fortification works," for the front was approaching Polish territory. He added: "Attempts are being made to obtain Jewish manpower from Hungary."[44] During this time, these Hungarian Jews were being taken to Auschwitz at Hitler's orders. In the report for May 1944, the Defense Economy Officer had to record the shattering of his hopes of the previous month: "An expansion of Jewish employment in the armaments factories would be urgently necessary, but is impossible at the moment because of a prohibition to export [he must have meant import] Jews into the Generalgouvernement."[45]

Again, one month later, on June 7, 1944, the Armaments Commission was told at its meeting: "The demands for Jews are extraordinarily great, but the reservoir of Jews will soon be exhausted. For the moment, some 5,000 Jews are being requested."[46] On July 5, 1944, it was stated to the same organization: "The employment of Jews would be a great relief. Unfortunately, attempts in this direction to bring 2,000 Jews from Lodz to the Generalgouvernement are being resisted by the SS Reichsführer."[47]

According to these notes, it is certain that meanwhile, the vast Jewish manpower reservoir of the Generalgouvernement was practically snuffed out. Grotesquely enough, they were now proposing the import of Jewish manpower from Hungary or Lodz.

According to General Gienanth's report of September 18, 1942, to the Wehrmacht Command Staff, 300,000 Jews were working in the Generalgouvernement in the autumn of 1942 for armaments and troop supplies. They included 100,000 skilled workers.[48] On January 25, 1944, Governor General Frank stated that some 100,000 Jews were still present throughout the entire Generalgouvernement.[49] It could be assumed that this number corresponded to the number of survivors, especially since it agrees with the 10,000 skilled workers mentioned by Gienanth.

What was the total number of Jews available for labor in 1942, and how many then vanished in the concentration camps? According to the labor report of the Main Division for Labor in the Generalgouvernement for December 1943, 1,426,495 Jewish workers were put to work in the year 1942, whereby "to be sure, some 980,000 were employed for a short period."[50] Thus 450,000 Jews, no doubt including the 300,000 mentioned by Gienanth, were working full time in the industry of the Generalgouvernement and thus immediately for the German war effort. Almost one million were on reserve.

With this one sentence, the head of the Main Division for Labor documents the number of Jewish workers before they were murdered; whereby he tersely added at the end of 1943 that he could not make any further manpower available, since "one must also consider the loss constituted by the employment of Jews."[51]

Then some million and a half Jewish workers included women, children over 15 years of age, and adults under 65 years of age. According to the age pyramid, the total number of Jews living in the Generalgouvernement at that time was considerably higher. Children below the age of 15 constitute an average of 33 percent of the overall population, and adults over 65 another 5 percent. Hence, the number of 1,426,000 working Jews would imply an overall Jewish population of 2,300,000.[52]

The report of the Main Division for Labor does not reveal in which month of 1942 these Jewish workers were still alive. However, Korherr, the "Statistics Inspectors" of the SS,[53] established that by December 31, 1942, 1,274,166 Jews had been "evacuated," i.e., transported to the extermination camps, from the Generalgouvernement (including Lvov). Hence, one may justifiably assume that the report of the Main Division for Labor referred to a number at the beginning of the year 1942. This assumption is supported by a remark made by State Secretary Bühler, the staffer closest to Governor General Hans Frank. On January 22, 1942, at the Wannsee Conference, Bühler stated that there were still two and a half million Jews in the Generalgouvernement.[54] Hence, there are two almost identical records on the number of Jews registered in the Generalgouvernement in the spring of 1942. There can be no doubt as to what happened to these Jews. For in the documents of the Warsaw Armaments Inspection of the Generalgouvernement we have read that two years later, in the summer of 1944, all possibilities of mobilizing Jewish manpower in the Generalgouvernement were exhausted.

It is obvious that the Labor Division's figure for Jewish laborers and State Secretary Bühler's overall figure for Jews in the Generalgouvernement did not cover all Polish Jews. Missing were the Jews in the western portion of Poland, which was a separate Gau, Wartaland, under Greiser, as well as the Jews settled in Upper Silesia. Furthermore, we must take into account the presumably countless Jews who were not officially registered in the Generalgouvernement because of Polish disorganization; they certainly were not interested in being listed in the German registers. Gerald Reitlinger assumes that the number of murdered Polish Jews lay between 2,350,000 and 2,600,000; however, judging by this report from the Main Division for Labor and other figures, one may conclude that Reitlinger's figures are too low. The number given by Raoul Hilberg, 3,000,000, must be closer to the truth.

The files of the East European Armaments Inspections reveal nothing about the further fate of the Jews. As these areas were gradually lost to the advancing Soviet troops, the Inspection disbanded. Only scattered documents show that some of the Jews employed in Poland were brought to Germany. Simon Wiesenthal reports in his book that he and his group, who were employed on the Eastern Railroad, got to Mauthausen, Austria. According to Eugen Kogon, 5,745 Polish Jews arrived at Buchenwald in January 1945.[55]

Chapter 21

Jews in the Gaus of the Reich

IN REGARD TO POLICIES on the Jews, two Gaus annexed after the division of Poland in 1939 were evidently not counted as German Reich territory: the Warta Gau, with Posen as its capital, under Gauleiter Greiser; and the Gau of Upper Silesia under Bracht. Both Gaus had been separated from Poland as former Reich territory. Here, Jews could be employed in the armaments industry. Given the high percentage of Poles in the population, Goebbels did not seem offended by the presence of the Jews.

In Breslau, the Armaments Inspection for Upper Silesia reported on November 9, 1942, that "Jewish workers employed in the armaments factories will be evacuated in the near future."[1] "Great difficulties [are expected], since some 41,000 Jewish workers were employed in the armaments industry and in the construction sector, and the Labor Employment Offices cannot find replacements for them. Some 10,000 or 12,000 Jewish workers are employed in the textile industry alone, and their loss would cast doubts on the undisturbed continuation of production."[2] At the same time, Schindler was likewise convinced that in the Generalgouvernement, 50,000 Jews should be removed from the factories.

These fears, however, did not come true. For at the end of December 1942, the quarterly report of the Breslau Armaments Inspection said: "Since the last report [at the end of September], the number of Jewesses employed within the jurisdiction of the Inspection has risen slightly."[3] At the end of June 1943, the complaint was heard again that "because of the removal of Jewish manpower, the lack of construction workers is quite noticeable."[4] However, an entry in late December 1943 by the same Armaments Inspection (which had now moved its seat to Katowice points out that the extermination measures, just announced by Himmler to the Reich leaders and Gau leaders in Posen, either had been delayed here or were merely on paper: "The feared removal of the Jews has not yet come, since, on a higher level, contrary directives have been issued in time."[5]

However, in Upper Silesia too, the SS insisted that the Jews be taken to concentration camps, exactly as in the Generalgouvernement. The report therefore continues: "Taking over the Jewish camps into the administration of concentration camps will cause very great problems because of the demanded head count of some 1,000 Jewesses and more in these camps, since in most cases it is impossible to build such large camps for these firms and employ 1,000 and more Jewesses for the firms involved. If the Economic Administrative Headquarters, Labor Group D, continues to insist on its demand of constructing only camps for 1,000 and more Jewesses, then in certain firms, e.g., Gruschwitz Textile Works in Neusalz, Methner & Frahme in Landeshut, or Leinag in Landeshut, production will drop around 30 or 40 percent. This production cannot be moved."[6]

This change in the Jewish policy caused the Armaments Inspector of Katowice to ask me to intervene with Himmler. On December 15, 1943, I wrote to him: "Armaments Inspector VIIIb in Katowice has notified me that the 40,000 inmates of the Auschwitz concentration camp can be made available," whereby it could be assumed that a high percentage of these prisoners were Jews. "Armaments Inspector Colonel Hüter can install 10,000 men immediately in the factories at Blechhammer, Heydebreck, and Auschwitz. . . . I need not elaborate on what help 40,000 or, for now, just 10,000 workers can mean for the armaments industry."[7] The letter had no effect. It must be recalled that several months earlier, Maurer too had hoped he would be allocated 21,500 Jews from Auschwitz as manpower for the armaments industry.

Since nothing happened, I again wrote to Himmler on February 23, 1944; referring to my December letter, I asked him "to give greater help to armaments than before by sending concentration camp prisoners to places which I regard as particularly urgent." For, as I told Himmler in the same letter, "for some time now, the influx of [Sauckel's deported] workers has considerably waned." For that reason, "all possibilities that we still have in Germany of procuring workers [must] be exhausted. This means that all available and employable manpower in Germany must be made useful for armaments, especially in the focal programs of the armaments industry."[8] I evidently had no idea that during those very months, hundreds of thousands of Jewish workers were being liquidated in the concentration camps. Otherwise I would not have so timidly asked whether 40,000 or at least 10,000 prisoners could not be supplied.

In the Posen Armaments Inspection itself, the killing measures announced in Himmler's Posen speech on October 6, 1943, were not carried out. On October 22, 1943, the war diary of the Posen Armaments Inspection said: "Discussion by ghetto administration in Lodz and production manager in Wa J Rü (Mun 4/V) Berlin[9] on the monthly manufacture of 20 million steel cores for infantry munitions. There was also discussion of taking over the manufacture of 500,000 moldings for 2 cm explosive shells with tracer path. The Supreme Command of the Army is prepared to make the special machines[10] available to the ghetto for manufacturing both items, in order to use the exceptionally large manpower capacity there."[11]

One week later, Government Director Weissker, who represented the Supreme Directorate of the Warta Gau, was more skeptical in his comment: "Changes in the populace of the Lodz Ghetto are expected. However, the clearing of the ghetto seems momentarily to be postponed for the sake of armaments manufacturing. Government Director Weissker will put in a good word with the Gauleiter [Greiser] so that the Wehrmacht manufacturing in the ghetto will not be imperiled."[12]

This remark shows that there was still a danger of implementation for the extermination goals that Himmler had announced 24 days earlier. One month later, on November 30, 1943, the situation got worse. This, however, contrasted with the simultaneous development in the Generalgouvernement and in Upper Silesia where a certain relenting was perceptible. It must have been Gauleiter Greiser, an extreme anti-Semite, who pushed in a radical direction here: "The directive for clearing the Lodz Ghetto does not appear to be rescindable," goes the Armaments Commission's report of November 30, 1943. "The evacuation deadline is not yet set. New manufacturing orders are not longer being taken by the ghetto." However, the chairman of the Armaments Commission, who was in charge of this matter, parenthetically added: "A stoppage of Wehrmacht orders is not known in the army branch of the Wehrmacht [a division of the Posen Armaments Inspection] and the Administrative Division."[13]

He was right. The Generalgouvernement itself was assigning production orders to Lodz, which Hitler had renamed Litzmannstadt after the World War I general. On December 10, 1943, the war diary of the Armaments Inspection in the Generalgouvernement had the following entry: "Discussion with ghetto administration of Litzmannstadt about manufacturing pouches for infantry spades."[14] On February 13, 1944, while visiting Posen, Himmler stated that production must continue. Greiser wrote to Pohl the next day: "The ghetto of Lodz will be reduced to a minimum population and will keep only the number of Jews that must absolutely be preserved for the sake of the armaments industry." He added: "The ghetto will not be transformed into a concentration camp." To be sure, Himmler's measure was only temporary, to protect armaments interests. Without giving a specific date, Himmler unswervingly stuck to the ultimate solution; for Greiser's report continues: "After the removal of all Jews from the ghetto and the dissolution of the same, its entire property is to become the property of the city of Litzmannstadt."[15]

This decision probably smashed Pohl's plans for complete control of the flawlessly operating armament factories in Lodz. Obviously disappointed, he replied that after this decision of Himmler's against the transformation into a concentration camp, "the SS Economic Administrative Headquarters will have nothing more to do with the matter." The grotesque normality of this correspondence is shown in the appended sentence: "In the next few days, I will write you separately about a share in our French wine contingent."[16]

Himmler's granted tolerance of important armaments manufacturing in Lodz lasted only four months. Then my Berlin Central Office of the Armaments Inspector was informed of the imminent evacuation of the Lodz Ghetto. Evidently it had thereupon issued orders which induced Gauleiter Greiser to inform Himmler on June 9, 1944:

"Reichsführer: The Armaments Inspection has undertaken considerable counterthrusts against your order to clear the ghetto in Litzmannstadt. In the night of June 5, Reich Minister Speer requested, through the officer on duty in the Armaments Inspection, the number of people employed in the various manufactures in the ghetto, their weekly work time, as well as the weekly output in the various branches of production, allegedly in order to present these figures to the Führer. Since I have finished the preparations for clearing the ghetto and have undertaken the first evacuations of the same, I duly inform you of this thrust to thwart your orders. Heil Hitler, Geiser."[17]

Himmler replied the next day: "Dear Greiser. Many thanks for your telegram of 6/9. I ask you to carry the matter out as before."[18]

Greiser's intervention was an open denunciation. It may have been partly due to the old animosity of high-level Party functionaries, who always saw me as an upstart in their ranks, a man who had bewitched Hitler with his architecture and thereby sneaked illegitimately into the close circle. But Greiser knew that Germany was being increasingly damaged by bombs in these months; he saw that Germany was heading toward disaster. He was smart enough to see the advantages that our war effort had from the employment of the Jews. Even if the Lodz production was not considerable when compared with the overall capacity of the armaments industry, he must have realized that in our crisis, any fraction of production counted, especially since in this spring, it was still relatively safe from aerial attack in Poland. His telegram indicated that any demonstration of the considerable achievements of the Jews was undesirable; yet he had to warn Himmler that such reports were in the making. Ths points to a truly bizarre situation, utterly eccentric despite its tragedy. Greiser's fanatical anti-Semitism, his hatred and his obedience, outweighed any rational consideration. He accepted the execution of production together with the execution of the Jews.

On June 7, two days after this nocturnal call to the armaments inspector of Lodz, I had a long discussion with Hitler. Although the minutes do not mention the Lodz matter, there is nevertheless reason to assume that I made Hitler aware of the production losses that could be expected. At any rate, Himmler's order was not carried out. One week later, on June 17, 1944, the war diary of the Litzmannstadt Armaments Command records: "Visit by Engineers Mayer and Mielke of the Labor Staff for Gun Munitions [of the Armaments Ministry] at the ghetto administration. The order for 20 million projectile cores a month is to be doubled. . . . Since the preservation of manpower has been promised and space is available, the ghetto administration is also to take over the large-scale revamping of infantry munitions machines."[19]

In September 1944 the attacking Soviet armies were approaching Lodz. According to an SD report of September 20, 1944, the industrial evacuation from Lodz was already concluded.[20] Thus, until then, the Lodz Ghetto had continued working for the German armaments industry, despite Himmler's announcements.

The London architect Roman Halter dates his transport from the Lodz Ghetto in September 1944. Twenty-seven years later, he informed me:

In 1944 I was in [the] Lodz Ghetto and working at a metal factory. When the liquidation of [the] Lodz Ghetto took place, the group of men, women, and children who were employed in the metal factory received a letter handed to them by either Mr. Bibow or Mr. Schernula. This letter was taken by the leader of our group, Mr. Chimovitcz, and when we reached Auschwitz with [a] transport scheduled for gassing, he approached the SS selection leader, to whom he presented this letter. We then had to wait for about an hour by the sidings of the rails in Auschwitz until it was verified whether this letter was a forgery or genuine. After the hour, we were taken to the camp, not the gas chambers, and sent in due course through another concentration camp, Schtutholl, to Dresden, where we worked in a munition factory which was part of the Reemtsma cigarette factory. This letter, which saved the life of 500 of us, was purported to have been written by you. The date was September, 1944. I was fifteen years of age at that time.

It is scarcely conceivable that this kind could have been a personal letter of mine. Presumably, it was an accompanying letter from the Posen Armaments Inspection, which, in keeping with the linguistic practice of that time, could have come from the "Speer Ministry."[21]

The principles of Jewish policies, which Hitler's order to Sauckel on September 22, 1942, had established, were canceled in April 1944 by Hitler himself. Now, all Jews were no longer to be removed from Germany; instead, as many as possible were to be brought back into Reich territory. During the three months of my critical illness, Hitler (as Ministerial Director Xaver Dorsch, head of the Todt Organization Central Office, recorded in his minutes of April 6/7, 1944) "has decided that he [will] personally contact the SS Reichsführer and have him procure the necessary 100,000 workers from Hungary in order to form the appropriate contingents of Jews. The Führer expressng demands—and is emphasizing the failure of the Construction Organization [of my ministry][22]—that this work should be built exclusively by the Todt Organization, and the manpower must be supplied by the Reichsführer."[23] The project in question was the immediate construction of six large bunkers in Germany, each with a surface area of 100,000 square meters. One week later Hitler ordered the immediate start of work, and Dorsch promised to complete the project by November 1944.[24]

On May 1, 1944, I returned to my duties, And on May 9 Hitler ordered, in one of my first meetings with him, "that 10,000 German soldiers that have been brought back from the Crimea are to be made available for guarding Hungarian Jews, concentration camp inmates, etc., employed in labor. I have telegraphed the necessary instructions to Field Marshal Keitel. The SS Reichsführer requests that the guard divisions are to come to him so that he may duly implement the transport from Hungary, etc. I have informed Field Marshal Keitel of this too."[25]

Two weeks later, in a speech to generals in Sonthofen, Himmlei boasted: "At the moment we are indeed bringing 100,000, and later another 100,000 male Jews from Hungary to concentration camps to build underground factories. However, not one of them will come within sight of the German people."[26] In mid-June 1944, the "Reich Plenipotentiary for Hungary," Legation Councillor Edmund Veesemayer, sent a top-secret telegram: "Transport of Jews from Carpathian area and Transylvania (Zones I and II) to places of destination on June 7, with a total of 289,357 Jews in 92 trains, each with 45 cars [is] completed. Original estimate of ca. 310,000 not reached, according to Hungarians, because of conscriptions in the meantime to Jewish military [Honved] labor service." On June 17, Zone III was evacuated, with another 50,805 Jews shipped to Auschwitz, and on June 30, 1944, another 41,499.[27] Within 23 days the SS had thus brought 381,661 Jews to the extermination camp.

On June 7, 1944, the same day on which Veesemayer completed his first action, I wrote to Keitel that I had been told that "of the Jews brought to Germany, only 50,000 or 60,000 [are] fit for employment. The rest are unemployable old people, children, sick people, etc."[28] At this time, according to Veesemayer's figures, a major portion of the almost 290,000 Hungarian Jews must have arrived from Zones I and II. Had I known this figure, the number reported to me, i.e., 50,000 to 60,000 able-bodied Jews, would have seemed absolutely incredible. There was a similar lack of clarity in the correspondence between Maurer and Höss.

We had hoped for Jewish manpower for the armaments industry, but "the armaments industry has so far received none of these [Hungarian] Jews. [According to Hitler's order,] they will first be used for building the large bunker works."[29] This fact is confirmed by the "Reports on the employed in the Reich," which were issued by my Planning Office. In late May 1944 there were no more than a total of 8,938 Jews working in Reich territory: 6,319 men and 2,619 women.[30]

There were also political difficulties interfering with the employment of more Jews. According to Schieber's letter of May 7, 1944, "200 or 300 Jewesses [were working] in an electrical wiring plant inside a rockhewn factory that is flawlessly equipped with ventilation, heating, daylight, and a large community kitchen. In accordance with Pohl's directive, allegedly at the orders of Gauleiter Sauckel and Mutschmann, they were removed and allocated to an SS concentration camp factory."[31] However, these difficulties seemed to be solved a few months later in the Gau of Saxony. A record of the meeting of the Armaments Inspection IVa, Dresden, on July 18, 1944, says under item 7: "Employment of Jews and prisoners. Controlled by SS Reichsführer. German women and girls employed as leadership personnel. Still in the making. Only possible for certain camps."[32] Since women were slated as guards, this must have referred once again to Jewish women.

In contrast to my remark to Keitel on June 7, large numbers of Hungarian Jews must have been available. For on August 7, 1944, General

Wäger, the head of the Armaments Office, sent me a memorandum saying that "Gauleiter Sauckel [has] prohibited the employment of Hungarian Jews in the Gau of Thuringia. This prohibition must be rescinded immediately: otherwise, other Gauleiters will issue similar prohibitions. That would make the employment of Hungarian Jews in the Reich impossible. Housing the Hungarian Jews in concentration camps will assure that neither the sensibilities of the population are offended nor that any harm comes to the Jews."[33] (See Appendix 19.)

It can no longer be determined whether I brought this matter up orally with Dr. Goebbels or directed Mayor Willi Liebel, head of the Central Office, to discuss this matter with Werner Naumann, Goebbels's state secretary. During this period, the ministry chronicle reports no discussion with Goebbels; it merely tells of general conflicts between him and me. However, on September 6, 1944, Armaments Inspector of Kassel IX, recorded: "Employment of Jewesses. So far 2,000 Jewesses have come to the district, of whom, however, 850 could not yet be employed."[34] In the light of this document, it may be assumed that the conflict was decided in my favor.

There is no reliable statistic on the number of Jews employed in concentration camps within the Reich until the end of the war. In 1970, Tuvia Friedman stated that 200,000 Jews survived the torments of slavery.[35]

Robert Jackson rightly said in his cross-examination: "If I understand you, you were fighting [in regard to the Jews] to have enough manpower for the armaments industry in order to win the war for Germany. And this anti-Semitic action was so intensive that you were robbed of your trained technicians and deprived of the possibility of carrying out your duties. Your task of producing weapons so that Germany could win the war was made very difficult by this anti-Jewish action undertaken by several of your fellow defendants."

I answered Jackson: "It is certain that it would have been highly advantageous to me if the Jews who were evacuated could have continued working for me."[36]

Jackson was only too correct. Irreplaceable leaders, who could be found in a high percentage of the German Jews, were lost to the German war effort because of the radical anti-Semitism. I am thinking, for instance, of atomic physicists, who then built the atomic bomb in the United States. This was in contrast to the First World War, when a Walther Rathenau or a Hugo Ballin had an important position in the war industry. But aside from the intelligentsia, it was rationally quite absurd, given our manpower shortage, that several millions of workers were killed instead of being employed in production. The Jews in particular would have been easily trained because of their remarkable intelligence. This was shown in 1943, when Polish and Russian women had to replace the Berlin Jews. Increasingly extended periods of training and months of increased scrapping were the regular consequences of the loss of Jewish manpower. Indeed, the history of the Berlin Armaments Inspection states for late 1941: "The performance [of the Jews] was very good in various areas, e.g., chemistry and textiles, as well as, especially, the electrical industry, where Jewish women proved to be very skillful drummers, etc."[37] One year later, the war diary of the Berlin Armaments Inspection expressly states that "the Jews are described as excellent workers by all factory managers and are comparable to skilled workers. The managers fear that they will have to replace each Jew with two Poles in order to meet their quotas."[38] Likewise, the quarterly report of the Breslau Armaments Inspection stated at the end of December 1942: "The achievements of the Jewish women are still very good, so several firms that already employ Jewish workers are constantly trying to obtain further allocations."[39]

The entries of the Armaments Inspections in the Generalgouvernement, in Posen, in Katowice, and in Reich territory all maintain that the agencies of my ministry were trying to employ as many Jews as possible. At the same time, for whatever reasons, they were trying to improve the living conditions of these Jews. However, there are no indications of my immediate intercession. Minor steps of mine toward improving the working conditions of prisoners were acknowledged by the court in the Nuremberg verdict. But I cannot recall that I forwarded any basic arguments that did not have a technical character. Now and then I assigned General Wäger or Liebel, head of the Central Office, to contact Pohl or other SS officers. The reports of the Armaments Inspections even show that my agencies were often not unsuccessful. But the considerations were always those of expediency. Was there, beyond this technical level, also a human side of the Jewish tragedy for me? Would I have acted differently if I had realized what was concealed behind the "transport"? Would I have made my office available to Hitler? Until the fall of 1944 I was one of those who put all qualms aside when the needs of the war demanded it. Also, I was so deeply in Hitler's thrall that I would have suppressed any comments merely because of a look of disapproval on his face.

Yet: How often Hitler had threatened the Jews with annihilation. For me, the tens of thousands who disappeared into the ghettos were lost to the labor process. To be sure, one occasionally heard that they were manufacturing items in Poland for the general needs of the army. And from my activities, I knew that this was really the case here and there. But was that a reply to the question of where these people were?[40] Today, almost forty years later, I grow dizzy when I recall that the number of manufactured tanks seems to have been more important to me than the vanished victims of racism.

Epilogue

The Somber Final Victory

THIS SINGLE PHRASE, "final victory," summed up all our hopes. It expressed our boundless confidence in and devotion to Hitler's plans. Oddly enough, the magic of these words was not broken even in the winter of 1941–42, when it was obvious that the pejorative opinion about the Soviet forces was not simply false but had actually turned into concern and terror about the disciplined, well-armed Red Army.

For Himmler, too, as "Reich Commissioner for the Solidification of German Peoplehood," the term "final victory" was a key phrase in his considerations about peacetime after the victory. He had received this title from Hitler on October 7, 1939, when the Polish campaign was about to end. During the next few years, Himmler used this appointment to claim exclusive power in all issues concerning the evacuation and resettlement of the "Eastern territory." These were issues involving millions of people. Himmler felt responsible for the planning, the organization, and also the movements of these human masses; but he gave no thought to the vast consequences for the people themselves. Whereby I mean not only the fate of the conquered nations, but also that of, say, the South Tiroleans, who had asserted their German ethnicity despite all Italianization attempts by the Fascist government. Now, Hitler and Himmler wanted to resettle them in the Crimea.

Kammler, advancing more and more to the foreground, ultimately became Hitler's chief figure in the air armaments industry at the end of the war. In the autumn of 1941, after the initial battles in the East, he had left the Air Ministry for Himmler's staff. Now he ran the bureau in charge of all SS construction. In this new capacity, one of his first official acts was to draft a proposal for a "provisional peace program of the SS Reichs-führer." Pohl, who was still Kammler's superior, submitted this proposal to Himmler on December 14, 1941, a time when the catastrophic winter was decimating the fighting power of German units in Eastern Europe. Using general maps, Kammler set up a construction program that would cost some 13 billion marks. His suggestions were divided over two large terri-tories, the future area of the Reich and the new eastern area. The Reich area referred to an expanded Germany, which was to include several countries listed in the memorandum. The entire areas of Poland, Czecho-slovakia, Scandinavia (not just Norway), and the Netherlands were to be incorporated into the German Reich. However, Kammler did not mention Burgundy, Alsace, Lorraine, Belgium, or the French coal district near Lille, even though Hitler in conversation often spoke of annexing these territories later on. Most likely Kammler could assume that the existing construction in these highly developed regions would satisfy Himmler's demands if the authorities could ruthlessly confiscate anything they wished.

These "large-scale construction measures of the German Police, includ-ing the peacetime lodgings of the Waffen-SS in the Generalgouvernement, the Protectorate, Scandinavia, and the Netherlands, [will] require around 7 billion marks." Kammler had also reckoned that "some 6 billion marks" would be used "for construction for the Waffen-SS as well as the SS and police bases in the new East European territory." This eastern territory was to have a colonial character and reach all the way to the Urals, the Volga, and Baku on the Caspian Sea. Since "this overall construction would be [divided] over five years, the result would be a yearly volume of 1.4 billion marks for the Reich area and 1.2 billion marks for the eastern territory," the memorandum concluded.[1] It was necessary, Pohl added, "to achieve independent sovereignty for construction now, during the war." This sovereignty was granted to the SS by the minister of the interior in July 1943.

Thus, the SS carried out its preparations according to plan and over a long period of time. Just a few months earlier, on October 4, 1941, SS Obergruppenführer Heydrich had met with Gauleiter Meyer (Rosenberg's state secretary) to reach an agreement among the SS agencies involved. "Heydrich stated that there were three reasons for securing factories for the SS [in the occupied Soviet territories]:

1. the establishment of SS and police bases;
2. the manufacture of raw materials for setting up settlements;

3. Speer's special assignment, for which vast amounts of raw material must be put aside for the construction of large-scale buildings [in Berlin and Nuremberg].

"Gauleiter Meyer declared that, basically, he saw the necessity for securing such factories, but that the Industrial Division of the East Ministry was somewhat surprised at receiving a list of more than 60 such factories. . . . It was agreed that . . . a joint directive would be issued, stating that needs of the SS would be met on an extensive scale by the civilian industrial administration, and that, internally, the SS would operate as a special administration in regard to the industrial administration." But this promise, which was quite unusual within the administrative realm of the East Ministry, was to be covered up: "However, in regard to the outside world, especially the Wehrmacht, the individual factory manager or trustee should operate merely as a deputy of the civilian industrial administration."[2]

For Kammler, who during these months was busy constructing crematoriums and extermination camps and expanding the concentration camps, such gigantic plans must have been a challenge to his organizational capacities. If he performed this assignment satisfactorily, he was bound to become one of the most powerful figures in the postwar construction industry. What was my yearly budget of 550 million marks as inspector general of the capital city of the Reich next to those 2.6 billion!

However, Himmler was anything but satisfied. In his reply of January 31, 1942, he warned his new department chief: "The absolutely enormous construction projects that we are planning for the Waffen SS, the General SS, and the Police are not included" in Kammler's plan.[3] Himmler's letter was not precise, but his remark indicated a considerably higher annual sum than 2.6 billion marks.

The scope of such plans for the conquered or to-be-conquered Soviet territories can be evinced in a conversation that took place during August 1942 in the Führer's headquarters. The topic was the German settlements in Eastern Europe. Himmler and Gottlob Berger, his head of SS Headquarters, were present along with representatives of the Ministry of the Interior and the Ministry of the East. Hitler did not attend. In the Soviet area, they decided, the Baltic states would be settled "with consideration for the Germanification abilities of the Estonians. . . . SS Squad Commander Greifelt has been directed to plan the resettlement of ethnic Germans from Transnistria."[4] Likewise, the fruitful Ukraine was to be "Germanized."

The first measures were to be carried out immediately: "There are 45,000 ethnic Germans in the Ukraine. . . . They are to be consolidated in some 100 villages. Some 10,000 ethnic Germans are to be settled in the Zhitomir area after the harvest is brought in." A rapid realization of this goal was obstructed by the indolence of German authorities. For "an inquiry to the commissioner general in Zhitomir revealed that there were neither maps of the condition of the soil, nor any statistics on the professions, economic situation, or family situation of ethnic Germans. The plans for distribution of land," Greifelt admonished, were "to be carried out immediately; the necessary artisans needed for this settlement were to be found immediately. . . . Consistent with the Führer's order, parts of the Ukraine are to be settled purely with Germans in the course of the next 20 years."[5]

Hitler had established this goal one year earlier. For he, not Himmler, was the driving force behind this staggering project. "The area," he said to us in the inner circle one evening, "must lose the character of the Asiatic steppe; it must be Europeanized! . . . The 'Reich peasant' is to live in outstandingly beautiful settlements. The German agencies and authorities are to have wonderful buildings, the governors' palaces. Around the agencies, they will cultivate whatever serves the maintenance of life. And around the city, a ring of lovely villages will be placed to within 30 or 40 kilometers. . . . That is why we are now building the large traffic arteries on the southern tip of the Crimea, out to the Caucasus mountains. Around these traffic strands, the German cities will be placed, as though pearls on a string, and around the cities, the German settlements will lie. For we will not open up Lebensraum for ourselves by entering the old godforsaken Russian holes. In terms of settlements, the Germans must stand on a higher level."[6]

However, Himmler's experts felt that the project should not commence immediately. "The start of the settlement is directed toward the main west-east and north-south transportation routes, according to the planned highways and the large railroad lines to be constructed. . . . The baselike settlement is planned in such a way that towns of 15,000 to 20,000 inhabitants are to rise at the cross points, and a completely German rustic population is to be settled around these towns."[7] A town of 20,000 people would have eaten up something like 2 billion marks in construction costs.[8]

While visiting the Ukrainian headquarters near Vinnitsa, Hitler had seen a considerable percentage of blond, blue-eyed people in the surrounding population. He saw them as descendants of the Goths, who had lived there for centuries. It was in reference to this experience that he asked in August

1942: Aren't there still enormous Germanic splinters [in the Ukraine]? Where else could the blond, blue-eyed children come from? . . . Where did the remnants of the ancient Goths wind up anyway? Languages can be lost, but the blood must remain somewhere!"[9]

According to this interpretation of history, which was held not only by Hitler, the German successes in early medieval colonization east of the Elbe were a historical fact. All these areas had long since become an obvious part of Germany, even in the geographical sense.

"The two or three million people that we need [for settlement]," Hitler continued in these nocturnal contemplations, "—we will have them faster than we think. We'll take them from Germany, the Scandinavian countries, the West European countries, and America. I myself will probably not live to see it, but within 20 years the area will comprise 20 million people. In 300 years it will be a flourishing park landscape of extraordinary beauty."[10] Hitler did not come up with such figures at random. As in the armaments industry, he would use statistics to bear out such number games. When consulting the "life pyramid" in his home encyclopedia, he must have assumed that during these 20 years the population would increase by 44 percent, according to the natural rate. He likewise assumed that at least 11 million "Germanic people" would be pouring into the colonized East European territories from the countries he had enumerated.

Programs on this scale, as Himmler established, could not be carried out by the German construction industry. They were too expensive and they greatly exceeded its capacities. "The construction costs could be kept to a minimum . . . [only] by training prisoners as craftsmen, indeed specialists, for instance specialists for digging basements, specialists for installing concrete ceilings, for putting up the walls of a house, for building the attic, for putting in the window frames. . . . Eighty percent of a [residential] house or a government building has to be supplied by us with our own material and our own energy. If we do not succeed," Himmler went on, "then we will neither get decent barracks, schools, or administrative buildings nor have homes for our SS men in the Old Reich, nor will I, as Reich Commissioner for the Fortification of German Peoplehood, be able to establish the gigantic settlements with which we will make Eastern Europe German."[11]

Ten days later Himmler thus sketched the practical labor as being done by prisoners, Kammler worked out a plan for making Himmler's ideas come true. This "Proposal for the Establishment of SS Construction Brigades" was transmitted to Himmler by Pohl on March 5. Kammler had taken up the initiative for the development of a new SS organization in the area of construction. This new organization would have been a construction empire, an appendage of the industrial empire of the SS.

Every concentration camp brigade would encompass two regiments, and every regiment three construction battalions: one for civil engineering, one for surface engineering, and the third for expansion. A construction battalion was to be subdivided into four companies, each with 200 men, 20 of them for interior service. Thus, each construction brigade, having 24 companies, would have comprised 4,800 prisoners. Naturally, it was explicitly assumed that these military units would consist of cheap labor— prisoners and Jews from concentration camps. How else could it have been possible to meet Himmler's demands for greatly lowering the construction overhead? It was therefore necessary "to allocate the necessary inmates, Jews, etc., for these construction brigades." However, Kammler stated, in regard to prisoners, whether used as skilled workers or manual laborers, one could assume only 50 percent of the work performance of Germans.[12]

Kammler's first measure was to demand at least one construction brigade for every jurisdiction of a supreme SS and Police Commander. Since there were some 20 such districts, including the annexed territories, Kammler was thus requiring the allocation of 96,000 prisoners and Jews, of whom he wanted to employ 67,500 at the start. But this number would meet only the need for the territory of the Reich. Yet, according to a later specification of Himmler's, less than one-tenth of the overall construction budget for Eastern Europe was to be allocated for the Reich. Kammler also demanded 47,500 prisoners and Jews for the Generalgouvernement, 60,000 for the East Area (Russia), that is, a total of 175,000 prisoners. However, on December 15, 1941, as Kammler regretfully declared, only 2,037 prisoners were employed as skilled workers in the SS construction sites and only 6,763 as manual laborers.[13]

From his activities in the Air Ministry, Kammler probably knew from experience that government enterprises (which included the concentration camp factories) did not achieve flawless performance. Kammler therefore tried to explain to Himmler that his notions of a construction program with prisoners comprising 80 percent and the leadership only 20 percent was illusory. "The experiences with public factories during the World War of 1914–18 and after the war [were] supposedly so bad that, aside from minor exceptions, these government enterprises had to be disbanded within a very short time after running up very great losses. . . . Government companies," Kammler instructed Himmler, "actually have greater overhead than enterprises run by private industry, if the money-saving computations are based on the actual expenditures and not on budgetary miscalculations."[14] Hence, Kammler concluded, in contradiction to Himmler's wishes, "the inclusion of the private construction industry and building trade [is] indispensable. That is the only way to utilize the technological achievements and efficiency measures and to employ the technological advances on a broad foundation."

Kammler therefore suggested the following to Himmler: They should "work out preliminary contracts with the building-materials industry, including the prefabricated-wares industry in order [to assure] a certain minimum production" of the general building trade for the peacetime plans of the SS "alongside the production of the SS-owned factories." SS Economic Administrative Headquarters, "after determining the provisional peacetime building program, [had] already begun purchasing raw materials for construction and making sure of production as far as possible." It had also "ordered the large-scale purchase of construction machines, construction tools, and tractors in the occupied territories."[15] All this is, of course, an example of how peacetime planning caused blockages in the middle of the war and how supplies were hoarded despite the shortages of materials and machines in other areas.

Kammler still had no experience with Himmler's inability to be instructed. With the frank statements of a newcomer in Himmler's apparatus, he had pointed out the inefficiency of government enterprises, in which he also included the concentration camp factories. This contradicted Himmler's express demands to have units of prisoners carry out 80 percent of the peacetime program. Naturally, Himmler kept insisting on having more and more concentration camp factories. He protested vehemently against the assumed labor performance of the prisoners: "I am not satisfied with the simple calculation that labor prisoners can perform only 50 percent of what German skilled workers can perform. It is, of course, very easy and convenient to simply assume the double amount. However, pressure must be applied here. As a practical result, the imprisoned manual laborer must perform more than the free manual laborer. It is not clear why the imprisoned skilled worker cannot achieve the same performance as the skilled worker who lives in freedom. Here we have the greatest reserve of manpower. The possibilities of utilizing it are the responsibility of the head of the Economic and Administrative Headquarters through the transfer of the Inspection of Concentration Camps."

Himmler felt it was necessary "to supply the industrious prisoners with women in brothels in the freest form. Likewise, there has to be a certain small pay for piecework. If these two conditions are met, then the work performance will increase enormously. If one were to deny these two conditions, especially the first one, one would practically be alien to the world and to life."[16]

All these statements indicate a grotesque lack of realism and a total dilettantism. Himmler did not want to face the true labor conditions in the concentration camps. He ignored the weak constitution of the prisoners, who would have been stronger with better treatment and nourishment. However, the broken morale of the inmates was bound to obstruct any improvement.

In his report of December 14, 1941, on the implementation of a provisional peacetime construction program, Kammler, under item 2, stated the following position on the Reich territory as expanded by the inclusion of Poland: "Concentration camps Reich territory 550 million marks."[17] As already explained, every camp barrack, including the adjacent facilities for plumbing, etc., cost 45,600 marks. It was to house 333 inmates. Thus, 550 million marks could have paid for 12,061 barracks, with enough room for *4,016,000 prisoners*.[18] There was no error in this computation, as I initially assumed. This one figure, namely 4 million concentration camp prisoners just for the Reich territory, shows the enormous dimensions of the planned program of slavery—a program that was meant to serve the peace and was called "the Peacetime Program of the SS Reichsführer."

This one figure of 4,016,000 prisoners makes a cruel perspective clear. That was the peacetime program of the National Socialist government: the suffering and misery of millions of human beings as a foundation for the glory, brilliance, and wealth of the Third Reich.

We must bear in mind that the concentration camps, under Goering, were originally meant for the removal of political opponents. When the camps were handed over to the SS, they were then filled with all the domestic and foreign elements regarded as "harmful." Jews, political opponents of all persuasions, Gypsies, clergymen, members of religious sects, etc., multiplied the number of inmates, who were also supposed to contribute to balancing or surpassing the enemy's tremendous war machine. In a third phase, however, Hitler decided to have millions of Jews killed in the concentration camps that Himmler wanted to use for manufacturing.

Here, however, Himmler's plans revealed cool calculations for a fourth phase, which was meant for a Reich of profound peace. There would be no enemies whatsoever. Every few years, Hitler planned merely to lead a small campaign beyond the Urals in order to demonstrate the authority of the Reich and to keep the military preparedness of the German army on a high level. This vision of a "peacetime Reich" was thus based on the existence of millions of permanent slaves, who were neither political opponents nor so-called "racial enemies." Because of economic necessity, they would be kept in camps all their lives—with "women in brothels."

This empire of slaves, which was to stretch all the way to the Urals, would be basic energy source of a Europe that had to prepare to conquer the greatest enemy: the United States of America.

Himmler added a handwritten remark in the margin of Kammler's memorandum on these construction brigades: "Have him get this number for the German East European provinces from staff headquarters. I estimate 80 to 120 billion."[19]

Ten days later, on March 23, 1942, Himmler specified the construction volume in the future German Reich territory: "I personally estimate that the construction program in the new German Gaus, Southeast Prussia, West Prussia, Wartaland, and Upper Silesia, will cost some 88 billion marks alone." Whereby Himmler meant the expenditures "for the farming and urban settlements."[20] The colonial territories in Eastern Europe, which Himmler had called the "east provinces," and for which he estimated construction investments of 80 to 120 billion marks, must be carefully distinguished from this program for the new German Reich territories.

Hitler had repeatedly spoken to us about a period of 20 years. And the extant documents regard this space of time as realistic. At best, one can therefore assume that the program was slated for 20 years, despite the occasional intention to carry it out within 10 years. The 88 billion marks for construction in the Eastern Gaus of the Reich, if divided over 20 years, would have meant an annual sum of 4.4 billion marks. According to Himmler's estimate, the expenditures for the Russian colonial area would have reached 80 to 120 billion marks, i.e., from 4 to 6 billion marks a year. Hence, together, this would have totaled about 9.4 billion marks for the East of the new Germany and for the colonial Eastern Europe. To gain some sort of yardstick, one can compare these sums of money with the capacity of the German building trade in that same year, 1942. The total was 13.2 billion marks.[21] In other words, Himmler's goals were equal to 71 percent of the overall German performance in construction.

In his letter of March 23, 1942, Himmler left no doubt that he still intended to have prisoners carry out 80 percent of the construction, which, as he and his staff had jointly worked out, would cost a yearly total of 9.4 billion marks. Kammler's figure of 4,016,000 prisoners, however, referred to the implementation of the original construction program with its yearly budget of 2.6 billion marks. Hence, if Himmler's estimated sum of about 9.4 billion marks was to be the basis, then this would constitute thrice the amount in Kammler's figures.

From a purely arithmetical viewpoint, triple the construction budget would require triple the number of prisoners. In sober terms, this meant that 14,450,000 slaves were necessary for carrying out the 20-year program. Of these fourteen and a half million prisoners, according to the prevailing practice of the SS, 37 percent would be omitted either for internal service or because of illness. Hence, 9,140,000 would remain available for construction sites. However, they were reckoning with a work performance of only 50 percent. This means that the performance of 14,500,000 prisoners would be equal to that of 4,570,000 free workers. Furthermore, Himmler was demanding that 20 percent be made up of skilled German workers. Thus, the slated budget would correspond to a performance by 5,484,000 workers.

Comparing the annual performance of the German construction industry with Himmler's intention to build at a yearly budget of 9.4 billion marks, we see that his project was not really impossible.

In June 1939, the amount of manpower in the German construction industry, including Austria and the Sudetenland, totaled 10,056,000 workers.[22] Himmler's estimate required 71 percent of the German construction capacity, i.e., in comparison with the actual figures, 7,140,000 workers to be employed on Eastern European construction sites. Hence, if we are to think through these future fantasies of Himmler's, it would soon have turned out that Kammler's calculations of the number of prisoners to be employed would not have covered the demand.

Some 14.6 million slaves working to carry out Hitler's and Himmler's construction plans: a human lifetime later, this seems like a sheer pipe dream. But we must not forget that between 1942 and 1945, Sauckel managed to deport 7,652,000 people from the occupied territories to Germany in order to use them in German industry.[23] The deportees mostly lived in German barrack camps. The documents do not reveal the estimates of mortality. Even assuming that the sanitary conditions, the food, and the medical attention were on the level of the Central Works, we can scarcely reckon that the mortality rate would have been lower than in that large-scale enterprise. The very hopelessness of seeing an end to such a slave existence in peacetime would have devoured any resistance and destroyed the will to live. The mortality rate at the Central Works was 0.8 percent a month. Every year, 10 percent of the workers perished. This means that in the course of 20 years all 14,450,000 prisoners would have had to be replaced after the first half of the labor period. By the end of 20 years, the same number would again have died. To work out these somber calculations all the way: Double the number of the slave army originally computed would not have been sufficient to implement the 20-year plan (not to mention the loss of manpower due to old age). Therefore, 29 million dead prisoners; 20 million Germans to resettle these areas. Such figures show what peace would have meant for the defeated nations: depopulation on one side, settlement on the other.

As with the extermination of the Jews, however, Himmler would have been the organizer of this slave realm in Eastern Europe. The program itself was not his; it was Hitler's. As early as October 1941 Hitler had said that there was only one mission for the Russian territories: "A Germanization by taking in Germans and regarding the native inhabitants as Indians." This meant having no consideration of their existence, not even hesitation in exterminating them. For Hitler often cited the fate of the Indians in the United States as a quite practicable solution when taking over a territory. "We need not feel any pangs of conscience," he said that same night. "We are not going to enter the Russian cities; they have to die completely" and "it makes absolutely no difference to me what posterity will say about the methods I had to use."[24]

There was no doubt about his resolution. On one of those nights, he cried out: "I am ice-cold in this matter. If the German people are not ready to commit themselves to their self-preservation, then fine: let them disappear!"[25] Can one still doubt the megalomania of murder, given his assurance? "I can imagine that some people will hold their heads today, wondering: How can the Führer possibly destroy a city like St. Petersburg [Leningrad]! When I realize that the species is in danger, then ice-cold reason takes the place of feeling: I see only the sacrifices demanded by the future if a sacrifice is not made today. Petersburg will vanish. Here we must resort to ancient principles; the city must be razed to the ground. Moscow [too], as the seat of the [Communist] doctrine must vanish from the face of the earth. . . . I will feel nothing when razing Kiev, Moscow, and St. Petersburg to the ground." In contrast to those remarks, he sounded almost human when he asserted: "I was happy that we did not have to destroy Paris. The destruction of Paris would have filled me with a pain as vast as my equanimity when I set out to destroy St. Petersburg and Moscow." Elsewhere he assured us: "We can win something only by means of a steadfast stubborn hardness."[26] This hardness was also obvious in the merciless elimination of millions of Russians, as posited in Himmler's program. Pity, he said, was inappropriate: the only suitable frame of mind was icy coldness. For, said Hitler, "we will absorb or drive away a ridiculous hundred million Slavs. If anyone speaks of taking care of them, he'll have to be put in a concentration camp right away."[27]

When Hitler and Himmler discussed these plans and settled on their ruthless implementation, they had presumably not yet gone into detail about the consequence of the program—the annihilation of millions of Slavs. But the goal was irrefutable. It represented a program that Hitler viewed as the historic documentation of his life's work for coming generations.

During those months and weeks, when Hitler and Himmler thrashed out the plans for this postwar Reich, we listened to Hitler's cheerful stories in his headquarters. I can still hear him saying: "I love people so much! . . . I find it insufferable when a car drives through puddles, splashing people along the road. It is especially mean when it splashes peasants in their Sunday best! When I catch up with bicyclists, I drive at high speed only when I see that the wind has blown away the dust [on the roads, which were often untarred in those days]. I wouldn't want to see anyone suffering or to hurt anyone. . . . Beauty should have power over people. We want . . . to avoid as far as humanly possible anything that harms our fellow-men. . . . I never enjoyed maltreating others, even though I realize that it is impossible to assert oneself without violence. . . . I feel fine in the historic society I find myself in, if there is an Olympus. In the Olympus that I shall enter, there will be the most illuminated spirits of all time."[28]

Imagine a man who could say all those things on one and the same day! We did not see the perversion of the murderous sentimentalist. We made things easy on ourselves. In Hitler's presence, we felt we were the lords of the imaginary world that we had created. We actually believed in Hitler's mission. My own monumental buildings, with the aesthetics that were possible for me, seemed to me a worthy crowning for that mission. From these edifices he would rule the world.

He saw himself as the benefactor of the Germans—without any self-irony, by the way. And we believed that this was the course of world history. We did not even find it absurd when he quite seriously and self-pityingly said about himself: *"I don't know, I'm colossally human."*[29]

Appendices

Appendix 1: On Hitler's Edict of September 1942

The situation of the people directly employed in armaments factories developed more favorably than that of the prisoners in SS concentration camps. The well-known psychotherapist Victor E. Frankl writes about his many years in a concentration camp: "How we envied those of us who had the chance to get into a factory and work in a protected room. Everyone wished for such a life-saving good fortune."[1] Bruno Bettelheim, likewise a distinguished psychologist, reports about his experiences: "Finding and keeping a good labor unit was always an opportunity of life and death."[2] And in his book *Die Sonnenblume,* Simon Wiesenthal writes: "For the Jews, it was advantageous that so many German firms thronged into the hinterlands [Poland]. The work in the outside units of the concentration camps was not especially hard." Elsewhere, Wiesenthal confirms this judgment: "Things went relatively well for us. We had contact with the outside world and we also received more food."[3]

Eugen Kogon reports: "Anyone who knew what was what volunteered, even if he knew almost nothing about a craft. . . . Skilled workers came into the workshops, which in any case was tantamount to something like initial life insurance."[4]

Elena Skrjabin, who was forced to work in a Rhineland factory, noted in her diary on March 11, 1943: "We whispered" to the Jews "that they had to cite some kind of special training or artisan ability as much as possible. What could save them now, we said, was some work to make themselves useful to the Germans."[5]

"Jews, deportees, and political prisoners in the death camps generally had death before their eyes," Leonhard Schwarz, a prisoner for many years, wrote me. "However, they had a chance to survive as soon as they were allocated to an armaments factory."[6]

According to Benjamin B. Ferencz, "it is true that many of the prisoners strove to get out of the concentration camps by working in wartime production. But this was not because they wished to support Hitler's war efforts or to enjoy the advantages of such an occupation. It happened because their only alternative was the gas chamber." Ferencz goes on: "It cannot be denied that the lives of many prisoners were saved indirectly by the fact that they were employed in crucial defense work. But this can hardly serve to morally justify a society whose motivation for using prisoners was not to save their lives, but to let them serve the society's or the nation's purposes. If Germany had won the war, then the fate of the Jews would have been sealed. Thus, the prisoners were employed in labor, not to save them, but to save Germany. Germany's victory spelled defeat for the prisoners and death for the Jews."[7] While many factory managers, for instance Heinkel, found satisfaction in buying and exchanging goods for additional food for deportees and prisoners, one must nevertheless acknowledge that Ferencz's statement is basically correct.

This process is summed up by Martin Broszat in *Anatomie des SS-Staates*: "The circumstance that since 1941–42, the concentration camp inmates were conscripted in increasing numbers for important work in the war industry contributed generally to loosening the earlier rules of the internal camp factories, which had been geared to terror, suppression, and discrimination."[8]

Needless to say, I was urgently interested in healthy workers. A worker required a training period of six to twelve weeks; and even after this period, for the next six months a high percentage of his output was unsatisfactory. It was only then that quality performance could be expected of a trained worker. This alone would have invalidated the frequently mentioned accusation of the prosecutor at Nuremberg in regard to "annihilation through labor" at the factories under my aegis.

Hermann Langbein, who spent long years at Auschwitz, writes in his book: "The most brutal terror, extremely harsh punishments, and a network of informers may produce full-capacity labor in outdoor work that can easily be surveyed. But such methods are useless when it comes to qualified work." He continues: "If prisoners were employed as skilled workers, then the management was interested in preserving their ability to work. For, unlike unskilled workers, they could not be replaced so easily."[9]

To avoid long transportation and travel time, special camps were set up in the proximity of the factories. However, these camps were not controlled by the factory managers or by my agencies; they were run exclusively by the the SS. Durng working hours, however, the prisoners received their instructions from the masters and foremen. "The firms have filled the workrooms with civilian workers, foremen, and masters in such a way," goes an anonymous report to Himmler's Personal Staff, "that in assembly-line work, a performance equal to that of the civilians is extracted from the prisoners."[10] By and large, the workers from concentration camps constituted only a portion of the staff in private armaments plants. They had been installed into the manufacturing process for production reasons; hence, they could not be worked harder than the civilian employees. For practical reasons, their working time was likewise the same as that of the civilians.

Hans Marsalek, in *Der Widerstandskämpfer*, reports: "The Luxemburgian political prisoner Eugen Thomé, number 47,849, describes as follows the assembly-line work in Hall 6 of Gusen I, where the prisoners assembled tommy-guns for the firm of Steyr-Daimler-Puch, Inc.: 'The production method was that of the modern factory, a concatenation, as assembly-line work. The blanks came from the central magazine and, following the operation, were processed from machine to machine, so that finished items came out at the end. For processes taking a longer time, a prisoner would work several machines.' "[11]

In general, a performance factor of only 50 percent was expected of prisoners in concentration camp factories.[12] The performance factor in mechanized armaments production would have been far higher than 50 percent of the normal achievement, as Marsalek establishes in the same article.

The production of tanks and guns was often forced ahead before offensives or in desperate military situations. At such times the weekly work average in these factories reached 60 to 64 hours for two to four weeks. However, this did not correspond to the average performance. A letter of Himmler's to Goering on March 9, 1944, states that the average working time of all prisoners, whether in the army, navy, or air armaments industry, was 240 hours a month, i.e., 55.4 hours a week.[13] This datum is confirmed by Schieber's letter of May 7, 1944, which says that 32,000 concentration camp prisoners worked 8 million hours a month, i.e., an average of 57.6 hours a week. For self-serving reasons, the factories heeded the limit beyond which mistakes occur because of fatigue. An increase in working hours, experience taught us, could lead to lower production because of increased scrapping.

In the United States, too, workers worked hard. In important branches of industry, for instance turbine and engine manufacturing, the index was 49.1 hours per week.[14] Since, the armaments industries of both the United States and Germany, had factories with lower priorities, the weekly average for industry overall was 45.2 hours in the United States and (according to Wagenführ) 49.5 hours in Germany.[15]

Appendix 2: Ohlendorf on Himmler

When questioned by the Military Tribunal on October 8, 1947, Ohlendorf stated that Himmler "did not want orderly conditions; he was the representative of a dualism. He was thereby trying to imitate Hitler on a small scale. Hitler likewise had a policy, which became fateful for us, to hand assignments, not to institutions, but to individual people. Himmler, too, characteristically gave assignments, not to institutions, but to individuals, and, if possible, one and the same assignment to several people. Although Himmler had no reason to think that any of his functionaries was growing too powerful, he believed that by using this method, he could prevent any of them from becoming more powerful with his office than he himself. Himmler was an opportunist of the day, who loved to assign individuals a day at a time, pick them up and then drop them again. In my opinion, this was bound to destroy any order in a nation, even during peacetime, especially, however, in such a hard war as Germany had to wage. What separated me from Himmler was the arbitrary nature of individual decisions; not only in the concrete assignments he distributed, but also in the legitimation of people, some of whom were unfit, corrupt, or so stodgy that no true leadership impulse could come from them. Perhaps that was why he appointed them in the first place."[16]

Appendix 3: Eugen Kogon's Assumption of Sabotage

Not just sabotage, as Kogon feels, but also large amounts of illegal manufacturing were the reason for unsatisfactory performances in concentration camp factories such as Buchenwald, Neuengamme, and Auschwitz. In the workrooms for assembling carbines at Buchenwald, "as much as half the working time of prisoners was filled with so-called 'slipshod work,' i.e., illegal activity for private purposes. Large amounts of precious woods, copper and bronze, gold, silver, all kinds of wrought iron, and a wealth of war-crucial raw material were constantly siphoned off for the needs of the SS commander. . . . Entire living room sets, inlaid furniture, costly single pieces, wrought metal pieces, busts, and sculptures drifted not only to the garrison areas but to all sorts of friends throughout Germany and even in other European countries."[17]

One should not exaggerate the effects of this corruption. The corruption was far worse in the allocation of food even though the illegal manufacturing was one source of the failure of the SS armaments industry. If I had had any notion of the degree of corruption in the leadership corps of the SS, then the Security Service of the SS would not have been ordered, on October 5, 1943, to report to me about illegal manufacturing of desirable goods like radios or refrigerators. There was suspicion that armaments factories were using raw materials meant for weapons "to also produce a few hundred radios, some 50 or 100 iceboxes or similar products. Such manufacturing only serves bribery. They are not actually given to the VIPs. But an item that can no longer be gotten anywhere else serves for bribery, whether delivered against payment or not."[18]

Not a single report followed. My staffers soon felt they had an explanation for this conspicuous silence: the SS must have used the offical assignment to obtain illegal luxury products for themselves. To be sure, at that time I did not yet know why, for instance, "the representatives of the well-known German firm Linde's Ice Machines had received an assignment to build a refrigeration faciliity for the Hygiene Institute of the Waffen-SS, Division for Spotted Typhus and Virus Research in Block 5 in Buchenwald. The assignment had the highest defense-industry priority. The real reason was so that the SS and Police Commander could preserve the roebucks he had killed on his hunts. Rationale: production of vaccine materials for the combat troops!"[19]

Appendix 4: The Legal Situation

Even during the Hitler period, the German national adminstration functioned according to past experience. All responsibilities were correctly distributed down to the last detail. Thus, for instance, the Reich Food Ministry, with the individual food bureaus, was in charge of food ration scales; the agricultural agencies of the Ministry of Economy were responsible for the allocation of clothing and footwear. The minister of labor, not the minister of armaments, was in charge of labor conditions; through his local labor agencies he allocated the requested manpower to the factories. These areas of responsibility also correspond to administrative practice in Western countries. Hence, on May 7, 1942, Gauleiter Fritz Sauckel, the Plenipotentiary for Labor Employment, gave the German Labor Front (the

Party organization that replaced the unions) "the sole and exclusive assignment for taking care of all foreign manpower employed in Reich territory."[20] Through this special agreement between Ley, the head of the Labor Front, and Sauckel, the Labor Front assumed direct responsibility for the camps. It had thus taken on an assignment lying outside its work realm.

More than a year later, on June 2, 1943, Sauckel and Ley detailed this edict by setting up a joint "Central Inspection for Foreign Manpower." This Central Inspection had to supervise all measures relating to the care of foreign laborers. Sauckel's executive directive of September 30, 1943, says: "Complaints about poor lodgings, food . . . will henceforth be channeled from me to the Central Inspection for verification and cessation of any defects. . . . If, for example, it is established, during the implementation of labor employment measures, that an unsatisfactory performance of foreign manpower is due to defective care, then the appropriate agencies of the German Labor Front are to be notified without delay, so that the latter can put an end to the deficiencies."[21]

During the Third Reich, this responsibility was, of course, theoretical in regard to concentration camp prisoners. Given Himmler's authority and his sole responsibility for the concentration camps, neither Sauckel nor Ley could do anything. It was actually the SS, more specifically its Economic Administrative Headquarters, that was in charge of the concentration camp inmates: "The Economic Administrative Headquarters was the top authority for the administration of the concentration camps, and its task was comprehensive. It was responsible not only for the details of pay, production, and employment of prisoners, but also for supplying food and clothing for the prisoners; and this latter obligation reached all the way down to the lowest level of distribution—the actual responsibility for seeing to it that the prisoners received the necessary rations. Clothing that is ordered or requested but not handed out will not protect people from freezing."[22]

In regard to this legal responsibility for the working conditons in the concentration camp at Auschwitz, the court ruled against Karl Krauch (I. G. Farben trial) on July 29, 1948: "The construction workers made available by the Auschwitz concentration camp were prisoners of the SS. They were lodged, fed, and guarded by the SS and also supervised in other respects. In the summer of 1942 a fence was put around the factory grounds. SS guards were not permitted within this area after this date, but they were still responsible at all times except when the prisoners were inside the enclosed area."[23]

Himmler had clarified who was responsible for constructing barracks. A letter of July 21, 1943, from the "SS Reichsführer and the German Police in the Reich Ministry of the Interior," in concordance with the Reich minister of finances and the Prussian minister of finances transferred "the implementation of the construction measures of the government police for all buildings and facilities exclusively or predominantly serving troop police purposes" to the "construction agencies of the SS Reichsführer and the head of the German Police." The list of structures that serve these troop police purposes encompasses "concentration camps including residential buildings and labor training camps. . . . If any technical inspection is done by the central authority, then the SS Reichsführer and Chief of the German Police—SS Economic Administrative Headquarters—is responsible."[24]

This took even the technical investigation of the concentration camps away from the Ministry of the Interior and its construction police agencies, which would have been legally responsible for the sanitary facilities and hygienic conditions. The verdict against Oswald Pohl therefore states that "Agency Group C was in charge of constructing and maintaining houses, buildings, and structures of the SS—the German Police—and the concentration camps and prisoner-of-war camps."[25]

So much for the responsibilities and jurisdictions of the SS authorities that I had to deal with. In regard to me, the International Military Tribunal stated in its verdict: "Speer had no immediate administrative responsibility for this [forced labor] program. Speer's position was such that he had nothing directly to do with the cruelties in the implementation of the forced labor program, even though he knew about them."[26]

Appendix 5: Mortality Statistics

I. Statistics from the jurisdiction of the Economic Administrative Headquarters, December 28, 1942 (Nuremberg Document 1469 PS)

ENTERING

Month	Arrivals	Transfers	Total
1942 July	25,716	6,254	31,970
August	25,407	2,742	28,149
September	16,763	6,438	23,201
October	13,873	5,345	19,218
November	17,780	4,565	22,345
Total	99,539	25,344	124,883

DEPARTING

Month	Releases	Transfers	Deaths	Executions	Total
July	907	4,340	8,536	477	14,260
August	581	2,950	12,733	99	16,363
September	652	6,805	22,598	144	30,199
October	1,089	6,333	11,858	5,945	25,235
November	809	5,515	10,805	2,359	19,478
Total	4,038	25,943	66,530	9,024	105,535

II. Statistics from Pohl's report on death cases in the concentration camps, September 30, 1943 (NO–1010)

Month	No. of Prisoners	Deaths	Percentage
1942 July	98,000	8,329	8.50
August	115,000	12,217	10.62
September	110,000	11,206	10.19
October	83,800	8,856	10.32
November	83,500	8,095	9.69
December	88,000	8,800	10.00
1943 January	123,000	8,839	8.00
February	143,100	11,650	8.14
March	154,200	12,112	7.85
April	171,000	8,358	4.71
May	203,000	5,700	2.80
June	199,500	5,650	2.83

Even a rough look at these figures reveals surprising differences. While Pohl, in his report to Himmler for July to November 1942, lists 48,703 deaths, the internal statistics of Economic Administrative Headquarters register 66,530. While the number of prisoners in Pohl's survey goes down by 10,000 from July to November 1942, it must have gone up, according to the internal survey of the SS Headquarters, by 19,348, given the arrival of 124,883 prisoners and the departure of 105,535 (based on the mortality figures in the same report).

Let us take the example of September 1942 to clarify the dfferences. If we once again look at the internal statistics of SS Headquarters for the explanation of the prisoners missing during September 1942, it turns out that in that month, 16,763 were brought in and 5,438 were transferred. In contrast with this overall increase, i.e., 23,201 new prisoners, the departure (not counting deaths) of 144 executed prisoners, 652 releases, and 6,805

III. Inconsistencies in Deaths Reported Between July and November 1942

	NUMBER OF PRISONERS*	NET NUMBER OF ARRIVALS WITHOUT DEATHS*,**	DEATHS REPORTED TO HIMMLER***	DIFFERENCE IN REGARD TO NEXT MONTH'S QUOTA PLUS	MINUS
July 1942	98,000	26,246	8,329		−917
Aug. 1942	115,000	24,519	12,217		−17,302
Sept. 1942	110,000	15,600	11,206		−28,594
Oct. 1942	85,800	5,841	8,856	+715	
Nov. 1942	83,500	13,672	8,095		−3,077
Dec. 1942	88,000				

* Figures from the order of the Economic Administrative Main Office, December 28, 1942 (Arolsen tracing service).

** Minus the transfers, executions, and releases, as indicated in the report of December 28, 1942.

*** Pohl's report to Himmler, September 30, 1943 (NO-1010).

Rücküberstellten transfers, i.e., a total of 7,601 people. So that in September 1942, one can assume the overall arrival of 15,600 people, not counting deaths. The deaths, however, did not add up to 11,206, as Pohl reported to Himmler, but 22,598![27] Yet this is far from explaining the macabre numerical acrobatics, for, ominously, the internal statistics reveal how many prisoners actually arrived during September 1942: 15,600. This number increases the unexplained difference of September 1942 to October 1942: 24,200 to 39,800, as opposed to the 11,206 deaths that Pohl reported to Himmler.

Appendix 6: Himmler's Deception

In June 1944 I did not suspect that Himmler had already advised Pohl two years earlier, when the concentration camps had been incorporated into the Economic Administrative Headquarters, to stress "in some way or other . . . that questions of prisoner inspection as well as the training purpose for trainable prisoners in concentration camps should remain unchanged . . . and independent of the industrial employment. . . . Someone might think that we are arresting people or, when they are arrested, keeping them inside in order to have workers."[28]

A few months later, however, ths seemingly just and legal argumentation yielded to a different plan, which established the contrary: "For reasons concerning the war effort and not to be gone into here," says an edict, "the SS Reichsführer and Chief of the German Police has ordered on December 14, 1942, that by the end of January 1943 at the latest, at least 35,000 able-bodied prisoners are to be sent to the concentration camps. To reach this number, the following is necessary: (1) As of now—initially by February 1, 1943—East European or other foreign workers who have escaped or are in breach of contract and do not belong to the allied, friendly, or neutral states . . . are to be committed to concentration camps as quickly as possible. Other agencies must, if necessary, be told that each single one of these measures is an indispensable measure by the Security Police, with appropriate concrete reasons in terms of each individual case, so that complaints can be avoided or at least cleared away."[29]

These two letters have one thing in common: Himmler's order to conceal the illegal measures from other agencies.

According to an agreement "with the Reich Minister for Justice and the Plenipotentiary for Labor Employment," as I wrote to Himmler on May 13, 1944, "if prisoners sentenced to several years are to continue being employed in the armaments industry after their release, this continuance is to be regulated by a service obligation in their previous place of work." In this matter, there was the directive of February 11, 1944, from Sauckel, the Plenipotentiary for Labor Employment, No. VIa 5131/32. But so far, I went on, "the prisoners designated as asocial are excluded from this regulation because of an earlier agreement between you and Party member Dr. Thierack. The workers, after completing their sentences, are handed over by the penitentiaries to the police," i.e., the concentration camps.[30] I argued (going beyond my jurisdiction) that "these prisoners too [have] been trained as skilled and specialized workers after years of employment in the manufacture of armaments. . . . Their removal from the factories of the armaments industry," i.e., to concentration camps, "would cause an enormous disturbance, given the steadily increasing labor shortage, and possibly interfere with the manufacture of the most important military equipment. This disturbance and the interference, especially long-lasting in regard to difficult manufacturing, will not be balanced out when the manpower that has been removed is reemployed, according to its technical abilities, in the new factories," i.e., concentration camps. "For the old factories will then have a gap, which can be closed only very gradually, while the transferred prisoners must first be trained in the new plant. Considering the aggravated aerial situation, everything in our power must be done to avoid any additional interference with manufacturing. May I therefore ask you, dear Party Comrade Himmler, to forego the removal of asocial and Polish prisoners to the extent that they can be designated as skilled and trained workers and are employed in the armaments industry."[31]

Appendix 7: Kranefuss and the Extension of a Contract

This dependency of SS Oberführer Kranefuss was also revealed when he encountered difficulties in his industrial activity. The files of the SS administration reveal that in July 1942 SS Oberführer Keppler, in his capacity as chairman of the board of Brabag, hesitated to renew Kranefuss's contract as head director of this company. Characteristically, when his contract ran out on April 30, 1942, Kranefuss did not complain to his top superior, Hermann Goering, the "Deputy for the Four-Year Plan." Instead, on May 14 he lamented to Himmler that Keppler had been evasive rather than giving in to his insistence. Keppler had said that his mother's death had greatly bereaved him and he wanted to put off the matter. He would first go on vacation for a few weeks.

Himmler's reaction was prompt. He ordered SS Obergruppenführer Karl Wolff to resolutely make it clear to SS Oberführer Keppler in his (Himmler's) name: He, the Reichsführer, was willing, in case there was no interest in renewing the contract, to consider an appropriate activity under his own aegis.[32] Himmler was thus trying to get people from industry for the construction of his industrial empire.

Apparently this intervention helped Kranefuss to overcome his difficulties with Keppler. For in his letter of September 4, 1942, to Dr. Brandt on Himmler's Personal Staff, he was again acting on behalf of Brabag.[33]

Appendix 8: Power Strivings of the SS in the Ministry for the East

Reichsleiter Rosenberg, Minister for the Occupied Eastern Territories, was, like Funk, a weakened man, whose actual power was no longer consistent with his position. Like Funk, too, Rosenberg tried to flee by dashing forward. His three insubordinate Reich commissioners for North, Central, and South Russia were systematically supported by Martin Bormann in their independent actions. Especially, however, the "Reich Commissioner for the Solidification of German Peoplehood," who was responsible to Himmler, had dared to exert power in the occupied portions of Russia that were under Rosenberg's jurisdiction.

Lately, "major difficulties" had emerged between the Reich minister and this Reich commissioner, according to a report that the latter's chief of staff sent to Himmler's Personal Staff on January 19, 1943. For instance, he said, Rosenberg's agencies were permitting Germans to resettle definitively in the "Eastland" and to open a factory. Marriages between Germans and members of other ethnic groups were supposedly possible with the permission of Rosenberg's commissioner-generals for the individual districts.[34] But this was not in any way to be viewed as his responsibility, said the report. On the contrary, it had to be demanded that such decisions were to be made by the SS agencies. Finally, they had to fight a directive that was to reconstrue the concept of "Jew" for the occupied Eastern territories. For here too, according to the report, they were planning to have the commissioner-general decide in cases of doubt. The "Reich Commissioner for the Solidification of German Peoplehood" had to insist that "the handling of the Jewish question remain within the jurisdiction of the police [i.e., the SS]."[35]

Rosenberg tried to resolve his problems by making SS Squad Commander Gottlob Berger, who was close to Himmler, the state secretary of his ministry. Rosenberg's effort to strengthen his position by bringing in the SS hierarchy was parallel in many respects to the events in the Ministry of Economy during the fall of 1942. However, Himmler apparently did not consider it advantageous to prop up Rosenberg's weakened ministry with one of his own most important staffers. Especially since this ministry was already indirectly under his sphere of power anyway. Not bothering to conceal the true power dynamics, a note by the "liaison officer of the SS in the Reich Ministry for the Occupied Eastern Territories" said that Rosenberg, i.e., the Reich Minister, "is willing to fulfill the conditions made by SS Squad Commander Berger or the SS Reichsführer." The fact of surrender could not be circumscribed more openly.

Ministerial Director Runte, one of Rosenberg's top staffers, realized (according to the "liaison officer" in his report of January 23, 1943) that even if Rosenberg's intention to appoint Berger state secretary "were to turn out negatively, this could alter nothing in the future development of the ministry." Runte also felt that "the powerful influence of the SS on the Reich Ministry for the East could be put off only for a time. This struggle would always end with the victory of the SS Reichsführer." The nascent movement to make Berger state secretary "was taking place at least outwardly in a still-dignified form for the Reich Ministry for the Occupied Eastern Territories."[36]

The head of the personnel division of Rosenberg's ministry, Ministerial Director Jennes, had stated, according to this SS report, that if Berger were appointed and thereby put in charge not only of the political division but also of the administration and the personal data, then he (Jennes) could foresee an instant launching of SS politics; i.e., all important positions would be filled by SS functionaries.[37]

On April 16, 1943, in a letter to Himmler, Berger had turned down the position offered him, unless Himmler himself were to order him to accept.[38] Himmler did not do so, and thus Berger did not become state secretary. Nevertheless, Himmler found a less conspicuous solution. In the summer of 1943 Berger became head of the "Command Staff for Politics" in Rosenberg's ministry, a position of the same importance as the one originally intended for him.

Thus things were running in Himmler's direction. Eighteen months later Gauleiter Lohse, Reich Commissioner for the Eastland,[39] stated that at the Reich Ministry for the Occupied Eastern Territories things had reached the point at which practically only the "blacks" (i.e., the SS, so called because of their black uniforms) "had any say." He had also declared "that the Führer was not at all agreeable to such a development and did not wish the SS 'to swallow everything' in the East."[40]

Appendix 9: State Socialism versus Capitalism

Several weeks after my speech at Essen on June 26, 1944, I induced Hitler to support me in this struggle of economic ideology. With a dubious result. Prior to his speech, I had given Hitler a few slogans such as "Free Economy after the War" and "Fundamental Rejection of Nationalization of Industry."[41] Hitler made clear his negative attitude toward a state economy, such as had to result from state socialism. He said: "The sole prerequisite for every true higher development, nay, for the further development of all mankind" is "in the furtherance of private initiative. When this war is decided with our victory, then the private initiative of German industry will experience its greatest era! The things that must then be created! Don't think that I am just going to build a couple of state construction bureaus or a couple of state industry bureaus."[42]

This was anything but the declaration I desired. Nevertheless, it directly contrasted with Himmler's and Bormann's rejection of the capitalistic structure of our economy.

Despite several contacts with Himmler, I was unfamiliar with his position—a sign of how little the leaders took their bearings from one another. Thus, during the first few months of captivity, in July 1945, I was still so ignorant of Himmler's attitude that I stated: "Himmler was the opposite of state socialism."[43] It was only Himmler's files that made me realize that Himmler was not so far from Goebbels, who noted in his diary on September 10, 1943: "National Socialism must go through a renewal. We must attach ourselves to the people more socialistically than before. . . . The National Socialist leadership must not form any ties to the aristocracy or the so-called society."[44]

Appendix 10: Further Statements of Ohlendorf

In an article entitled "Economic Balance Sheet," Ohlendorf again documents his embitterment at the methods necessitated by the war industry: "This trend toward serial and mass production, this trend toward further efficiency, toward the best possible worker, the best possible commerce, the best possible agriculture, the best possible industry [might] again wipe out three-quarters of the now independent entrepreneurs" if the peacetime problems were to be solved by way of mass production. "If we keep these problems in mind, then the issue of further social development is probably one of the most essential questions of destiny confronting us in peacetime."[45]

There would be "very serious questions about the insights that this war has brought us and the ultimate value of the economic methods forced upon us by the war," Ohlendorf had Hayler say at the end of January 1945. He again pointed out that the work method of the "self-responsibility of industry," i.e., the basis of an efficient manufacture (on which basis today's German Federal Republic has been attaining its economic successes), must not be given a fundamental importance: "The most urgent of these questions is whether the security of the Reich will in the future be contingent on the height of our production."[46]

It was *"a fundamental error to assume that the experiences of the war could just simply be transferred to peacetime conditions.* What may be correct in wartime, so far as methods and goals are concerned, need not be correct by a long shot for normal times."[47]

Ohlendorf then even comes to a positive verdict on the achievement of our organization, which, as we recall, he had vehemently fought two years earlier with Himmler: "One of the new phenomena in German industry is the introduction of the *self-responsibility of industry*. This self-responsibility may be necessary in such strenuous times as today and has certainly also led to great successes. But we must realize that this is a wartime institution which cannot be taken over into normal times if we adhere to the separation between state and industry and if we wish the sovereignty of the state to continue to be clearly emphasized." Now, in wartime, the point was "to achieve the ultimate from industry with all means," said Ohlendorf a few minutes later, meaning that during this emergency it might be necessary to ally oneself even with the devil![48] Unflinchingly, Ohlendorf continued his disparagement of the principles of self-responsibility when he further emphasized there must be no change in "the basic National Socialist law" under which National Socialism assumed power and for which it had gone to war: "Namely, to let one's people come to its highest and best development."[49] One and a half years earlier, Himmler had given an ultimatum, demanding the defamation of the self-responsibility of industry. But now, the alleged abuses were no longer worth mentioning, even though nothing had changed in the system of "self-responsibility."

The postponement of settling accounts with our "Americanized mammoth industry" for peacetime should not hide the fact that the basic attitude of the SS had not changed even in wartime. In May 1944 Schieber wrote: "The marked opposition of the SS against the notion of the self-reponsibility of industry plays a not inessential part here."[50]

At his trial, Ohlendorf had still not overcome his resentment when he declared: "The competition was no longer ready to reveal its real achievement to competitors. And broad portions of the people were no longer facing an objective state, they were dealing with individual industrial hyenas and monopolists; this was bound to make the conflicts between industry and the state larger and larger."[51]

Appendix 11: Restriction of Development

In my edict of October 9, 1943, on "The Concentration of Development," I had stated that "the length and technological risk of development [should] be in a sensible proportion to the foreseeable military or armaments value. An exception from these principles can be made only if one can expect new knowledge for the war effort or armaments industry from the processing of the development project. Developments that do not meet with these requirements are to be halted or dropped upon directions by the chairman of the appropriate commission."[52]

This edict was meant to concentrate technological talents on the development bureaus of those companies that could demonstrate the approved projects. It is a mistake to assume that orders of this kind were carried out strictly. There was too great a temptation to tacitly tolerate new developments in order to keep the technicians in a firm.

Hence, on December 21, 1943, I reminded the chairmen of the Armaments Commission that they "are fully and exclusively responsible for employing all talents and capacities available for development in their work areas in such a way as to achieve the greatest effect for the armaments industry and wartime production. . . . In case of difficulties, they have the right and the obligation to report to me personally and apply for requisite decisions."[53]

But this does not seem to have been effective either. I finally appealed to Hitler's authority. On June 19, 1944, at my wishes, he signed an edict that I had prepared on "The Concentration of the Armaments Industry and Wartime Production." This edict demanded that "current developments be restricted to the urgently necessary number, so that those projects that are capable, because of new, revolutionary features, of offering important advantages against the developments of the enemy can be carried out in a concentrated manner."[54]

Appendix 12: Fromm and Jüttner

Jüttner thus carried out the same activity that he had performed previously, though on a smaller scale, for the SS. In this SS capacity, he worked closely with Fromm before the putsch of July 20, 1944. In the course of time he had managed to achieve a good relationship with Fromm, who was suspicious of all Party and SS functionaries. When Fromm was arrested, Jüttner at first interceded for him, but then retreated when Fromm's case was viewed by Himmler and Goebbels as particularly critical.

Soon after July 20, there was an estrangement between my agencies and the Army Ordnance Office, which, as a part of army armaments under Fromm, had worked very closely with me: "Fromm's position is now assumed by Obergruppenführer Jüttner on behalf of the SS Reichsführer. Fromm is under arrest, that's all we know," the chronicle reported on August 24, 1944. It goes on: "Jüttner is making sure that nothing is lost in the transferal. He is therefore less open to making concessions than his predecessor. The peculiar double subordination of the Army Ordnance Office to the head of Army Armaments and to the Reich Minister for Armaments and Wartime Production was possible so far only because of the personal agreements between Colonel General Fromm and the minister. A clear handwritten settlement of the limits of powers and responsibilities was always refused by the minister until now. Both agencies felt fully responsible for the joint task. The minister's wishes were fully respected by the 'Head of Army Armaments' and by the 'Army Ordnance Office.' Jüttner has his head for now and support from the SS Reichsführer, which the former staffers did not have."[55]

The SS was so powerful that it could have afforded a fight with me, while I had to avoid it. Jüttner wanted to push back the influence of industry. Like all leading SS functionaries, he opposed the autonomy of industrial committees, as provided for by the self-responsibility of industry. In this way, he was no different from Ohlendorf, Berger, or Himmler. I was especially dependent on the Army Ordnance Office's keeping up its close contact with the main committees (for manufacturing) and with the development commissions of the industrial representatives. My system was built on this cooperation and would have collapsed without it.

Appendix 13: Der Grosswindkanal

In late January 1945, SS Obergruppenführer Rösener reported that Herbert Luckow, the business manager of air research, had come to him and expressed "his concern about the construction of the Grosswindkanal in the Otz Valley." Rösener asked the head of Himmler's Personal Staff "to inform the Reichsführer of this matter so that the Reichsführer too can induce the speediest termination of this project."[56]

Luckow had added a report, saying that the Grosswindkanal was "indispensable in the area of high-speed aircraft. In the opinion of prominent German scientists, the small German lead in the area of high-speed aircraft can be maintained in the future only with the help of such facilities. . . . The canal can be completed in the late fall of 1945 if (1) another 1,000 workers, if necessary prisoners (housing is available), can be added; (2) 1,100 tons of steel sheets are supplied; and (3) 10,000 tons of cement are made available for completing the concrete dam."[57] Even these minimal orders could not be filled at this point in the war. On February 10, 1945, Brand telegraphed SS Obergruppenführer Wolff, the Supreme SS and Police Commander of Italy, that he "would be grateful for information about whether Herr Herbert Luckow has talked to you about construction of Grosswindkanal in the Otz Valley and what orders you have given."[58] But meanwhile, Herbert Luckow could no longer be located.

Appendix 14: Armaments Dictate in Hungary

In 1944, in the light of air warfare against industry in the Reich territory, the industries of other countries, like Hungary, Czechoslovakia, and Poland, had become interesting. Since February 19, 1944, we had been maintaining a "German Industrial Commission for Hungary," abbreviated as Diko. Its purpose was to represent "German interests in the area of armaments and wartime production, with its seat in Budapest." But for the moment, we could only recommend, suggest, and express wishes; the decisions were made by the Hungarians themselves.[59]

On March 19, 1944, the situation changed. Hungary was occupied by German troops; and from then on, a shadow government under Prime Minister Stoyja ruled on behalf of the German government.

On March 29 Kehrl told the staffers of the Planning Office and the Raw Materials Office: "The altered political situation in Hungary gives us the possibility of fully mobilizing the local industrial strength for the war effort. Measures have accordingly been initiated."[60]

The negotiations about the use of Hungarian weapon capacities (carried on by the German Weapons Commission at the Honved Ministry on August 7–8, 1944) reveal that Hungarian armaments production was minimal in proportion to German armaments production. It amounted to 718 7.5 antitank guns, which were to be manufactured in the course of one year. By March 1947 they were to complete replacement barrels for the 8.8 antiaircraft guns and also an order of 580 10.5 cm. howitzers and 78 15 cm howitzers. The German commission also wanted the construction of all of six complete 21 cm no. 18 mortars. The production of the Hungarian "Turan" tank and the "Zrinyi" assault guns was to cease by early 1945 in favor of a production switch to German vehicles.[61]

Hitler, as stated in the Führer Protocol of April 6–7, 1944, was agreeable to having Hungarian industry made directly subordinate to the Diko and to exploiting Hungarian reserve capacity for Germany. Furthermore, he agreed that German industrial enterprises were to advise Hungarian factories or assume sponsorship for them. Also, orders from German industry could be transmitted directly to Hungarian companies. At the same time, they were to begin adapting the weapons program of the Hungarian army to that of the German weapons program. Hitler regarded notification of the Reich Foreign Minister as indispensable; but he stressed that he had now expressed his agreement with this proposal. Any objections from the Foreign Minister were not to be heeded.[62]

When Himmler concluded his transfer contract with the owners of the Weiss concern without our approval, our efforts to take active charge in Hungarian industry failed.

Appendix 15: Generator Problems

On November 3, 1944, during the meeting in Kleinbergen, Himmler promised Gauleiter Meyer the testing of the Ruehl generator. On November 10 I replied to Himmler that the tests were not up to expectations.[63] Despite this discouraging information, Meyer insisted two months later: "Two firms in my Gau are ready to construct the [Ruehl] generator and can be readapted instantly. Both companies already have the necessary experience in building generators. The factories are capable of building 600 generators a month. Also, nearly all subsidiary devices and replacement parts can be manufactured in my Gau. I ask you, most honored Reichsführer, to inform me as soon as possible when I can count on the supplying of the quotas."[64] Quotas, as Gauleiter Meyer knew, were allocated by me; but he most likely regarded Himmler as powerful enough to be able to give me orders.

I had already informed Himmler on November 10, 1944, of my decision to put my staffer Saur (rendered unassailable by Hitler's favor) "in charge of the production of generators in order to make sure that this generator program is carried out as briskly as possible. We are quite clear about its importance." According to Saur's plans, "the overall number of generators to be built is to be increased to 40,000 a month by the end of the year. [But] unfortunately two major generator factories have been badly damaged by aerial attacks, so we have gotten somewhat behind in carrying out this program."[65]

Neither Jüttner's nor Saur's efforts were successful. In July 10,400 generators had been built; in August, when production was still under Schieber, 11,700. In September Saur increased the number to 14,000 generators, but that was probably still due to Schieber's preparations. After that, the output slid down inexorably, at a faster rate than the index of the overall armaments industry. The latter actually rose from 297 in August to 301 in September, only 6 percent below the highest index ever: 322 in July

1944. However, Saur's generator production dropped from 14,000 in September to 6,900 in October, i.e., by 43 percent; and it never caught up again. As of December the armaments industry had collapsed for good.[66] There was no conceivable chance of resuming production, as Meyer foresaw it in January 1945. We were satisfied if we could still assemble a limited number of armament items from the component parts still available.

Appendix 16: Further Powers for Kammler

Thus, Himmler's edict of December 31 granted Kammler "power of decision in fundamental questions of the A-4 program. . . . Full responsibility for the acquisition of all remote rocket weapons, instruments, vehicles, and fuels is borne by the Ordnance Office" (which had been under Himmler since July 20, 1944) "on the basis of Kammler's demands."[67]

On February 6, 1945, Kammler extended his jurisdiction by means of an edict: "On the basis of the powers invested in me by the Reich Marshal of the Greater German Reich on January 26, 1945, the SS Reichsführer on December 31, 1944, and the Reich Minister of Armaments and Wartime Production on November 13, 1944, I hereby determine as part of the sector run by me" all remote-combat and air-defense rockets as well as "remote-control bodies for ground bombardment." Kammler's directive specified which instruments were to be developed further and which were to be "halted instantly." He determined that "the development and manufacturing employees freed by the stoppage of development or manufacturing projects are to be transferred within the rest of the program. The control of all development and testing measures of the overall program is under the Dornberger staff at the Reich Ministry for Armaments and Wartime Production, which is also his staff for carrying out the task assigned to me. The control of the production of all developments released for manufacturing or already in the manufacture of current instruments is under Special Committee zV of the Reich Minister for Armaments and Wartime Production, which will set up the program in cooperation with me."[68]

One day after Himmler's edict of February 6, 1945, Kammler added that he was "responsible to the SS Reichsführer for the development, testing, and manufacturing of all remote-combat weapons and aerial-defense instruments for all military and civilian affairs within the sector of central contruction." Kammler "as Special Committee 2 for implementing his assignments [would] stay in close contact with the plenipotentiaries of the Reich Ministry of Armaments and Wartime Production in regard to development, testing, and manufacturing." To reemphasize his responsibility, Kammler appointed as his representative "for all civilian administrative tasks the head of the Billeting Office of Central Construction, SS Standard Commander and Ministerial Director Dr. Wagner [and for] construction matters the head of SS Special Inspection II, SS Sturmbannführer Feissen."[69]

These latter edicts paid formal heed to the existence of an Armaments Ministry. But once again, Kammler's directive designated Dornberger's staff in the Supreme Command of the Army as his staff. The word *Abstimmung* ("cooperation," "agreement") established that the Special Committee for A-4 in my ministry could not implement any measure without Kammler's permission, with the well-considered proviso of not stripping this institution of my ministry, and hence me, of further responsibility.

Appendix 17: An Overzealous Kammler

This frivolous comment waved off an incident that I described in October 1952, when it was still relatively fresh in my mind: "Kammler and Saur reported to me in strong tones about the delay in transferring the Bavarian Motor Works to underground workshops in Alsace. Kammler stated that because of his slackness, Zipprich, the responsible director of the Works, had been sent to a concentration camp two days ago. The two men most likely expected my applause. Instead, I had one of my rare outbursts of rage. I yelled at Kammler, informing him that such delays were none of his business and that the man had to be released instantly.[70]

After this meeting, my chief secretary, Frau Annemarie Kempf, advised me either to destroy the stenographed protocol or at least not file it away, for my remarks to Kammler were not suitable for being made known to larger circles.

There was another time when I earnestly had to admonish Kammler: "Herr Geilenberg and Dr. Ganzemüller have informed me that in regard to the eight factories that we have appointed for manufacturing the 'Walter' [national gun], you also wish to try to create the conditions necessary for the operation of these plants. The Reichsführer was supposedly agreeable to your suggestion that you intercede in these matters. Much as I esteem your activity, as you know, I absolutely cannot allow you—even if it should happen in concordance with Herr Geilenberg or Dr. Ganzenmüller—to concern yourself with things that can only be steered and determined by my Central Office.

"The transports to the individual plants as well as the maintenance and operating of the plants are exclusively the business of my deputies. We have a sufficient number of them. I do not wish new agencies and jurisdictions created here. I therefore ask you to revoke all measures that you have

undertaken." In an addendum to this letter to Kammler, I asked Dorsch
and Geilenberg "to report within three days from the task force as to when
Kammler's task staffs have vanished from the construction sites."[71] Such
protests could not be very useful.

Appendix 18: Data on Jews Employed

There were three different categories of factories, whose given figures
were not attuned to one another. Because of these fragmentary reports, it
is impossible to work out clear-cut data on the number of Jews working
in the armaments production of the Generalgouvernement.

On the one hand, the Generalgouvernement was part of the "back area
of the Eastern Army." The commercial industry of the Generalgouvernement could be committed for orders by the front-line troops for immediate
military needs without intercession by other agencies. Furthermore, the
Armaments Inspection was in charge of the factories that worked directly
in the armaments industry as well as the connected supply firms. There
were also army factories, which were not under the Armaments Inspection.

These organizational differences also explain the contradictory figures on
the number of Jews employed in production. The data depended on which
areas were covered. Thus, on September 18, 1942, General Gienanth listed
a total of 300,000 Jews working for the commercial industry of the Generalgouvernement; whereas in the armaments area, General Schindler
listed 50,000 Jews on October 24, 1942. A report to Himmler at the end
of 1942 explained that there were 200,000 Jews in forced labor, i.e., in
the concentration camps.[72] But this report did not even include the Jewish
workers remaining in the still existing armaments factories.

On the other hand, a Defense Economy officer, responsible purely for
factories producing army supplies, listed 15,001 Jews among 105,000
workers in January 1943. On January 9, 1943, Himmler determined that
Warsaw alone still had 32,000 Jews in so-called armaments plants, 24,000
of them in textile and fur factories (which were not exactly armaments
plants; they produced items directly needed by the troops). Presumably,
Himmler's figures are extremely exaggerated. They are contradicted by a
monthly report on August 21, 1942, by the Supreme Field Command for
Warsaw. According to this report, in the month of July 1942, "a total of
about 9,950 Jews were employed in Warsaw by Wehrmacht agencies, aside
from armaments plants: (a) about 8,100 Jews in six factories and one
camp inside the ghetto; (b) 1,850 in eighty factories and three camps
outside the ghetto." Thus, while Himmler listed 24,000 Jews as employed

in the textile and fur plants in Warsaw, the local military office listed only 9,950. This figure is even more confusing, because on almost the same day, the Field Economy Office at the Supreme Field Command in Warsaw reported 6,000 Jewish workers "under the protection of the Wehrmacht on August 18–19, 1942."[73]

Incidently, during this phase of the Russian campaign, the army could still dare to speak quite openly of protecting Jews.

Appendix 19: A Retort

Wäger's memorandum of August 7, 1944,[74] had a letter draft attached to it. The letter, addressed to Goebbels in his capacity as Reich Plenipotentiary for the Total War Effort, goes in part: "On the basis of a decision of the Führer, as we all know, a large number of Hungarian Jews as concentration camp prisoners have been installed in the German war industry during the past few weeks. Experiences so far are quite positive, so great store is set by rapidly adding the still-unemployed Hungarian Jews to the armaments industry. Given the serious situation at the present, we must simply exhaust all possibilities to ease the problems of labor."

The following is substantially a repeat of the memorandum addressed to me: "Now, I have learned that Gauleiter Sauckel has totally prohibited the employment of Hungarian Jews in Thuringia as his Gau. In my opinion, this prohibition must not be maintained under any circumstances. Otherwise, the other Gauleiters could easily issue a similar prohibition. That would invalidate the entire employment of the Hungarian Jews. Needless to say, the employment of these Hungarian Jews in German Gaus also offends my sensibilities. But at the moment, we cannot forego such an emergency measure under any circumstances. Incidentally, by housing the Jews in concentration camps we can make sure that the sensibilities of the German population are not offended and that no harm is done by the Jews."[75] The two pages of this letter draft also bear the number 60 and 61 of the microfilm register of the Americans, while Wäger's memorandum bears the number 62. The two files also have this sequence in the German Federal Archives, which likewise confirms that the draft stems from the head of the Armaments Office.

Normally a letter signed by me was then dated and numbered before being mailed. Yet both the date and the registry number are missing both on the copy and in the notarization of my signature by means of the stamp "Signed Speer." Also, the secretary of the Office Group for Labor Employment inadvertently put the wrong zip code in the sender's address on the draft. She then subsequently changed "Berlin NW 7" to "Berlin W 8." This likewise indicates that the draft was written in the Office Group for Labor Employment.

Hundreds of carbon copies of letters preserved at the Federal Archives show how a letter was properly set up. For instance, my letter to Dr. Goebbels of July 26, 1944, which bears the registry number M 2415/44g and the stamp "Signed Speer."[76]

Lucy S. Dawidowicz mistakenly assumes that this letter was sent by me to Hitler and not to Goebbels. She believes that she has thus proved me guilty of an anti-Semitic mentality even though any signs of this are missing in my speeches and letters.[77]

Verbal injuries against Jews were customary in any speech, any article. Respectable architects without Party connections, for instance Schulte-Frohlinde, the Nuremberg architectural counselor and later head of the Construction Division of the German Labor Front, considered it advisable to point out the corrupting influence of Jews even in articles on German architecture. However, one certainly had the possibility of refraining from anti-Semitic remarks, and this was the course I chose.

Notes

The notation "Ba NS" indicates that a document is available in the West German Federal Archives.

CHAPTER 1

1. These entries were not published in Albert Speer, *The Spandau Diaries* (New York, Macmillan, 1976).
2. See Morgenthau *Diaries*, vols. I and II, published by the Congress of the United States, 1967.
3. Hermann Langbein, *Menschen in Auschwitz* (Vienna, 1972).
4. Also see Fabian von Schlabrendorf, *Begegnungen in Fünf Jahrzehnten* (Tübingen, 1979).

CHAPTER 2

1. At that time, in late January 1942, the development of the situation in Russia was viewed pessimistically. There was no thought of grand successes such as commenced after the spring offensive of 1942.
2. Himmler's letter to the head of inspection of all concentration camps on January 26, 1942 (Ba Collection Schumacher/329).
3. Hitler's edict of January 10, 1942.
4. From Rudolf Höss, *Kommandant in Auschwitz*, edited by Martin Broszat (dtv Dokumente, Munich, 1963), p. 179.
5. Unpublished notes written by Rudolf Höss in Cracow; photocopies are available in the Institute for Contemporary History.
6. Ibid.
7. Directive of March 16, 1942, by the head of SS Headquarters (Ba Collection, Schumacher/329).
8. Verdict against Oswald Pohl et al., November 3, 1947 (Ba. All. Proz. 1 XLI W4, p. 37).

9. Verdict against Pohl, p. 83.

10. Verdict against Pohl, p. 36.

11. Verdict against Pohl, p. 57a.

12. Addendum to verdict against Pohl et al, August 11, 1948 (Ba All. Proz. 1 XLI W5, p. 28).

13. In *Politische Zusammenhänge*, notes made for the American authorities during the first few weeks of my capitivity, completed in Kransberg in July 1945. A II, p. 4.

14. Confidential letter of Schieber to Himmler, June 17, 1941 (Ba NS 19/new 755).

15. Schieber's letter of July 31, 1941, to Himmler, and letter from Brandt, Chief of Himmler's Personal Staff, to Heydrich, August 4, 1941 (Ba NS 19/new 755).

16. Kammler's letter to Pohl, October 8, 1941, and Pohl's letter to Wolff, October 9, 1941 (Ba NS 19/new 755).

17. Notes on a meeting in Saur's office, March 16, 1942 (Ba NS 19/new 755).

18. Schieber's memorandum of March 17, 1942 (Ba NS 19/new 755).

19. Himmler's note on meeting with the Führer, March 17, 1942 (Ba NS 19/new 1447).

20. Minutes of a meeting with Hitler on March 19, 1942, item 30 (Ba R 3/1503).

21. Wolff's telegram to Schieber, March 18, 1942 (Ba NS 19/new 755).

22. Gottlob Berger's handwritten letter to Himmler, April 22, 1942 (Ba NS 19/new 755, possibly a photocopy).

23. Brandt's letter to Berger of April 28, 1942, and notification of the head of the SS Personnel Headquarters, SS Obergruppenführer Schmidt, May 4, 1942 (Ba NS 19/new 755).

24. Letter from Head of SS Personnel Office to SS Economic Administrative Headquarters, June 23, 1942 (Ba NS 19/new 755).

25. Schieber's memorandum of March 17, 1942 (Ba NS 19/new 755).

26. Pohl's letter to Himmler, July 11, 1942 (Ba NS 19/old 290).

27. Himmler's letter to Sauckel, July 17, 1942 (Ba NS 19/old 290).

28. Himmler's letter to Pohl, July 7, 1942 (Ba NS 19/old 290).

29. Himmler's note for meeting with the Führer, May 11, 1942, 7:30 P.M. (Ba NS 19/new 1447).

30. Reichsführer's telephone conversations, May 13, 1942 (Ba NS 19/new 1440).

31. Führer Protocol, July 6–8, 1944, item 21 (Ba R 3/1510).

32. Speer's speech in Posen to the Reichsleiters and Gauleiters, August 3, 1944 (Ba R 3/1553).

33. "Telephone conversations of the SS Reichsführer on 9/9/42: 3:10 P.M. Reich Min[ister] Speer, Wehrwolf [Hitler's headquarters]": "Large armaments orders. Discussion with Pohl" (Ba NS 19/new 1440).

34. Pohl's report to Himmler on September 16, 1942 (Ba NS 19/new 14) constitutes the reply to "telegram Hegewald no. 93515 of September 9, 1942, personal letter of SS Reichsführer of September 9, 1942, and personal letter of SS Reichsführer of September 9, 1942."

35. Chronicle of September 15, 1942 (Ba R 3/1735).

36. Pohl's letter to Himmler, September 16, 1942 (Ba NS 19/new 14).

37. Saur's letter to Pohl, September 19, 1942 (Ba NS 19/new 1542).

38. According to the figures of the Economic Administrative Headquarters, December 28, 1942 (Nuremberg document 1469 PS) and Pohl's report to Himmler, September 30, 1943 (Nuremberg document NO–1010).

39. According to the chronicle, during these days I met with Hermann Röchling, the industrial lord on the Saar and also head of the Reich Association for Iron, with the head of the Main Committee for Munitions, with the one for tanks, and with the one for vehicles.

40. Speer's letter to Himmler, March 25, 1943 (Ba NS 19/old 290).
41. Chronicle of September 18, 1942, p. 72 (Ba R 3/1736).
42. Pohl's letter to Himmler, September 16, 1942 (Ba NS 19/new 14).
43. Also see minutes of a meeting with Hitler, September 20–22, 1942, item 39 (Ba R 3/1505).
44. See minutes of meeting with Hitler, September 20–22, 1942, item 44 (Ba R 3/1505).
45. Joseph Goebbels, *Diaries*, May 12, 1942.
46. Minutes of Speer's meeting with Hitler, September 20–22, 1942, item 36 (Ba R 3/1505).
47. For, as Kersten remarks, Himmler was trying to "get in good [with Hitler's favorites], no matter how much he may have disliked them." From Achim Besgen, *Der stille Befehl* (Munich, 1960), Kersten's diary, p. 398.

CHAPTER 3

1. SS Obersturmbannführer Maurer was head of Agency D—Concentration Camps in the SS Economic Administrative Headquarters.
2. Schieber's letter to Speer, May 7, 1944 (Ba R 3/1631).
3. Schieber's letter to Speer, May 7, 1944 (Ba R 3/1631).
4. These statements are based on notes I made for the American military authorities during the first few weeks of my captivity, under the title *Politische Zusammenhänge* (Kransberg, July 1945).
5. From Achim Besgen, *Der stille Befehl* (Munich, 1960), Kersten's diary, p. 72.
6. Himmler's letter to Speer, March 5, 1943 (Ba NS 19/old 290).
7. Speer's letter to Himmler, March 25, 1943 (Ba NS 19/old 290).
8. Himmler's letter to Speer, April 24, 1943 (Ba NS 19/old 290).
9. Sauckel's protest can be inferred from Himmler's telegram to Sauckel, April 2, 1943 (Ba NS 19/old 284).
10. Himmler's telegram to Pister and Sauckel, April 14, 1943 (Ba NS 19/old 284).
11. From Eugen Kogon, *Der SS-Staat* (Frankfurt/Main, 1946), p. 276.
12. Minutes of Speer's meeting with Hitler, March 6, 1943 (Ba R 3/1507).
13. Pister's telegram to Dr. Brandt, command post of SS Reichsführer, July 14, 1943 (Ba NS 19/old 290).
14. Pister's telegram to Brandt, July 17, 1943 (Ba NS 19/old 290).
15. Two telegrams from Pister to Dr. Brandt on the personal staff of the SS Reichsführer, August 16, 1943 (Ba NS 19/old 290).
16. Draft of a telegram from Himmler to Speer, August 17, 1943, sent to Pohl for an opinion and with a handwritten remark: "Telegram has not been sent" (Ba 19/old 290).
17. Himmler's telegram to Pohl, August 17, 1943 (Ba NS 19/old 290).
18. Eugen Kogon, *Der SS-Staat* (Frankfurt/Main, 1965), p. 327.
19. For details see pp. 367–70 of Albert Speer, *Inside the Third Reich*. Also see Führer Protocol of August 19–22, 1943, item 24 (Ba R 3/1508).
20. From the report by Armaments Inspection IX, Kassel, which was subordinate to me (Ba RW 20/9/19). The reported figures differ from those of the SS listed by Kogon on page 279 of his book *Der SS-Staat*: SS casualties: 80 dead, 65 missing, 238 wounded; prisoners: 384 dead, 1,462 lightly or serious wounded. Who submitted a false report?
21. Minutes of a meeting with Hitler on October 12, 1944, item 9 (Ba R 3/1510).
22. As of November 1944 under the designation K 43.
23. Pohl's letter to Schieber, February 26, 1944 (Ba NS 19/old 278).
24. Pohl's letter to Himmler, February 28, 1944 (Ba NS 19/old 278).

25. Himmler to Pohl on March 7, 1944 (Ba NS 19/old 278).
26. Brandt's memorandum to Suchanek, March 7, 1944 (Ba NS 19/old 278).
27. Brandt's telegram to Behr, March 16, 1944 (Ba NS 19/old 278).
28. Pohl's letter to Himmler, March 17, 1944 (Ba NS 19/old 278).
29. Himmler's telegram to Schieber, March 21, 1944 (Ba NS 19/old 278).
30. Schieber's telegram to Himmler, March 23, 1944 (Ba NS 19/old 278).
31. Pohl's letter to Brandt, July 18, 1944 (Ba NS 19/old 278).
32. Output survey of Technical Office (Ba R 3/1729).
33. Himmler notes, meeting with Führer, April 17, 1943 (Ba NS 19/new 1447).
34. Pohl's report to Himmler, September 30, 1943 (NO 1010).
35. This percentage is abnormally high. For instance, a survey undertaken in February 1944 in the 118 largest industrial plants in the Gau of Lower Silesia shows an average of 6.5 percent out sick. Of course, individual factories had as much as 17.8, 18, 21.5, and 22 percent. *Krankenstand in der Industrie Niederschlesiens*, February 1944 (Ba R 3/813).
36. Pohl's draft of June 9, 1943, for a letter from Himmler to Speer (Ba NS 19/new 542). ·
37. Himmler's speech to the Reichsleiters and Gauleiters in Posen on October 6, 1943 (Ba NS 19 H R 10).
38. Schieber's letter to Speer, May 7, 1944 (Ba R 3/1631). Schieber had established that 32,000 prisoners would do 8 million hours of work.
39. Himmler's speech of June 21, 1944, to generals in Sonthofen. Printed in Heinrich Himmler, *Geheimreden* (Berlin 1974), p. 191.
40. From the armaments statistics of the Technical Office, January 1945 (Ba R 3/1751).
41. Pohl's letter to Himmler, June 14, 1944 (Ba NS 19/old 281).
42. Speer's memorandum to Hitler, July 20, 1944 (Ba R 3/1522).
43. Index figures of German armaments manufacturing, January 1945, Planning Office, Main Division for Planning Statistics (Ba R 3/1732).
44. Hitler's decision referred to all prisoners working for the armaments industry.
45. Albrecht Wacker includes this memorandum of November 1942 (Ba RH 11–1/53) in his dissertation on the K 98 carbine. His dissertation will be published under the title *Das System Adalbert* in 1982 or so.
46. Data from the Verlag für Wehrwesen, Bernard & Graefe, March 20, 1978.
47. According to a manuscript by Rolf Wagenführ, *The Rise and Fall of German War Economy, 1938–1945*, published by the British Bombing Survey Unit in September 1945, the German monthly armaments production reached a value of one billion marks in early 1942. Taking into account the values reached by mounting output in the individual months, a production value can be computed according to the overall index of armaments production, as listed in the summary report of the Planning Office for February 1942 (Ba R 3/1732):

October 1942	1,540,000,000 marks
November 1942	1,650,000,000
December 1942	1,810,000,000
January 1943	1,820,000,000
February 1943	2,090,000,000
March 1943	2,160,000,000
April 1943	2,150,000,000
Total	13,220,000,000 marks

48. According to Enno Georg, *Die Wirtschaftlichen Unternehmen der SS* (Stuttgart, 1963), pp. 42, 44, 56, the armaments plants assembled within the "German Armaments Factories" achieved production worth 23,204,032 marks in the concentration camps for the year 1943. This figure allows us to calculate the share of prisoners employed in the private sector of the armaments industry. It must have been as high as the number employed in concentration camps.

49. See Hans Marsalek, *Geschichte des Konzentrationslagers Mauthausen* (Vienna, 1974), p. 102.

50. Six marks a day was paid to specialized workers, four marks a day to manual laborers. Assuming that two-thirds were manual laborers, the average pay would be 4.70 marks per day. These figures are taken from undated, anonymous statements (Ba NS 19/new 2,302). They correspond to the figures in Eugen Kogon, *Der SS-Staat,* p. 273.

51. From Pohl's letter draft, June 9, 1943 (Ba NS 19/new 1542).

CHAPTER 4

1. It could be argued that on September 14, 1942, in a conversation with Dr. Georg Thierack, Goebbels said: "The Jews and the Gypsies should be unconditionally snuffed out." For Poles and Czechs, as well as for Germans sentenced to long prison stretches, "the best idea would be to annihilate them through work." (PS 682, vol. 3, red page 496. Also see vol. 5, blue page 442; vol. 6, blue page 379; vol. 18, blue page 486; vol. 19, blue page 55, 497.) Four days later Thierack met with Himmler in Streckenbach's presence to establish verbally that "we will annihilate through work." (PS 654, vol. 3, green page 504; vol. 3, red page 468; vol. 26, blue page 201.) Here, too, as so often, there are two truths. I personally assume that it was in keeping with Himmler's ambitious industrial plans to safeguard the prisoners for his purposes, but that he did not wish to imperil his reputation as a relentless pursuer of all enemies of the state, especially when talking to Minister of Justice Thierack.

2. Himmler's letter to Pohl, March 23, 1942 (Ba NS 19/new 2065).

3. Pohl's order of April 30, 1942 (Ba NS 19/new 1542).

4. Himmler's letter to Pohl, December 15, 1942 (Ba NS 19/new 1542).

5. Pohl's edict of October 26, 1943 in *Nationalzeitung,* November 1977.

6. From Hans Marsalek, *Die Geschichte des Konzentrationslagers Mauthausen* (Vienna, 1974), p. 43. The same is reported by Hermann Langbein in his book *Menschen in Auschwitz* (Vienna, 1972), pp. 43, 160, 350, 351. Also Eugen Kogon, *Der SS-Staat* (Frankfurt/Main, 1965), pp. 116, 119, 128, 300, 301.

7. Circular sent out by Agency Chief V, Artur Nebe, to all offices of the Reich Criminal Investigation Department, July 4, 1944 (Ba R 58/240).

8. From Eugen Kogon, *Der SS-Staat* (Frankfurt/Main, 1965), pp. 358–59. According to Heinz Höhne, *Der Orden unter dem Totenkopf* (Gütersloh, 1967), pp. 354–55, Pohl's second-in-command vehemently resisted the interference of investigators.

9. From Himmler's speech to SS squad commanders in Posen on October 4, 1944 (Nuremberg document 1918 PS).

10. From Goebbels's *Diaries,* entry of March 28, 1945.

11. From order of SS Economic Administrative Headquarters, December 28, 1942, on "Medical Activity in the Concentration Camps," File no. 14 h (KL) 12.42 Lg/Wy (Nuremberg document 1469 PS).

12. This edict of Himmler's cannot be located. The text derives from the order of

the SS Economic Administrative Headquarters of December 28, 1942, on "Medical Activity in the Concentration Camps" (Nuremberg document 1469 PS).

13. Order of SS Economic Administrative Headquarters, December 28, 1942, on "Medical Activity in the Concentration Camps," signed by an SS brigade commander, name illegible (Nuremberg document 1469 PS).

14. The various camp physicians were subordinate to the garrison physician at Auschwitz.

15. Pohl's report to Himmler, September 30, 1943, on deaths in concentration camps (Nuremberg document NO–1010).

16. The chronicle of the Armaments Ministry (Ba R 3/1737) merely reports that on March 30, 1943, I inspected the Hermann Goering Reich Works in Linz. The visit to Mauthausen probably took place on the same day.

17. These statements follow my defense testimony of June 19, 1946, at the International Military Tribunal in Nuremberg as printed in Adalbert Reif, *Albert Speer* (Munich, 1978), p. 38. Pohl, head of SS Economic Administrative Headquarters, indirectly confirmed that I had not previously inspected any other concentration camps when he voiced his regret on June 9, 1943, "that you formed your opinion on our prisoner labor employment during one tour of *one* of the sixteen concentration camps." Unmailed draft by Pohl, June 9, 1943, for a reply from Himmler to Speer's letter to Himmler of April 5, 1943 (Ba NS 19/new 1542).

18. Blaha's testimony at the International Military Tribunal in Nuremberg, January 14, 1946.

19. Hans Marsalek, *Die Geschichte des Konzentrationslagers Mauthausen* (Vienna, 1974), p. 186.

20. Eugen Kogon, *Der SS-Staat* (Frankfurt/Main, 1965), pp. 137, 287.

21. Edmund Richard Stantke, *Mordhausen, Bericht eines Augenzeugen über Mauthausen* (Neubau-Verlag Adolf Gross, Munich, c. 1947), pp. 20, 21.

22. From Rudolf Höss, *Kommandant in Auschwitz* (Stuttgart, 1958), p. 174.

23. Speer's letter to Himmler, April 5, 1943 (Ba NS 19/new 1542). Pohl remarked in his letter to Himmler of April 19, 1943 (Ba NS 19/new 1542): "According to the dictation mark, the author of the letter is Inspector Schwefel. Comment superfluous."

24. Fried's assumption is also refuted by a sentence in my letter to Himmler of June 10, 1943 (Ba NS 19/new 1542). For I expressly acknowledge that "in general" in the concentration camps inspected, "my efforts to achieve the greatest usefulness in the building sector by the most primitive means [were] received with understanding." Pohl, in his draft for a letter from Himmler to Speer, June 9, 1943 (Ba NS 19/new 1542) described as a primitive construction method "especially the conditions of irrigation and drainage in the former prisoner-of-war camp at Auschwitz, which was built in the summer of 1941."

25. "The Regulation of the Building Trade. Published by the Plenipotentiary for the Regulation of the Building Trade. Edition of March 1943," pp. 12, 14, 15 (Ba RD 77/3). The Plenipotentiary for the Regulation of the Building Trade was an organ of my ministry.

26. Pohl's letter to Himmler, April 19, 1943 (Ba NS 19/new 1542).

27. The date of the inspection tour can be roughly determined. On May 14, Himmler, as he writes, wanted to wait "for the result of the tour taken by SS Brigade Commander Dr. Kammler with the deputy of Minister Speer." On May 30, as a consequence of this inspection, additional iron rations were allocated. The files of the Armaments Ministry do not contain any data on the result of this inspection tour. Nor does the ministry chronicle reveal that any meeting on this matter took place in my office.

28. The previous allocations were 335 tons a month.
29. Speer's letter to Himmler, May 30, 1943 (Ba NS 19/new 994).
30. Speer's letter to Himmler, May 30, 1943 (Ba NS 19/new 994).
31. Pohl's letter draft of June 9, 1943 (Ba NS 19/new 1542).
32. Himmler's letter to Speer, June 15, 1943 (Ba NS 19/new 994).
33. Pohl's letter to Himmler—to Himmler's Personal Staff—of June 30, 1943 (Ba NS 19/new 1542).
34. The monthly iron allocation for the SS and the police is not available for the third quarter of 1943. But the amount was always the same, and during the first and second quarters of 1944, each organization received 6,400 tons a month. The allocation quantities are specified in Ba R 3/1983.
35. Secret statistical abstract on war production (Ba R 3/1730).
36. Goering's letter to Speer, May 2, 1944, which recently surfaced at an American auction.
37. Pohl's letter to Himmler, September 30, 1943, with accompanying table on mortality in these concentration camps (Ba NS 19/new 1542).
38. Pohl's letter to Himmler, September 30, 1943, and Himmler's letter to Pohl, October 8, 1943 (Ba NS 19/new 1542).
39. Hermann Langbein, *Menschen in Auschwitz* (Vienna, 1972), pp. 74–77. The author views this decrease in the death rate as due to efforts of Liebehenschel, the new commandant of all Auschwitz camps; however, he did not replace Höss, the former commandant, until November 11, 1943.
40. Pohl's draft for Himmler's letter to Speer, June 9, 1943 (Ba NS 19/new 1542).
41. Pohl's secret report to Himmler on September 16, 1942 (Ba NS 19/new 14). John H. E. Fried, formerly with the Nuremberg prosecutor, claimed in the *New York Times* of October 4, 1970, that I had agreed to Himmler's demand. But this demand was not approved. If I had released an additional quadruple amount, Pohl would most certainly not have failed to inform his superior of my approval instantly. Yet any indication of this is missing from the files.
42. Accompanying material to Speer's letter to Himmler, April 5, 1943 (Ba NS 19/new 1542). In my capacity as Plenipotentiary for the Building Trade, I regulated all construction in Germany by decontrol, i.e., not personally, of course, but through the appropriate staffers according to my general guidelines.
43. According to Martin Broszat, "Concentration Camps," in *Anatomie der SS*, p. 118, 600 barracks were to house 200,000 prisoners, hence 333 people per barrack. Bruno Bettelheim in *The Informed Heart* (Glencoe, Illinois, 1963), p. 117, reports that in 1938 the barracks he slept in housed 200 or 300 inmates. Later, however, this number was increased to 400, as revealed by a letter from Pohl to Himmler on September 16, 1942 (Ba NS 19/new 14). According to this same report of Pohl's, 300 barracks, including the requisite accompanying facilities, could be built for 13.7 million marks. Hence, the construction of a barrack, together with the opening of the terrain, could be estimated at 45,600 marks.
44. Speer's letter to Himmler, April 5, 1943 (Ba NS 19/new 1542).
45. Speer's letter to Himmler, April 16, 1943 (Ba NS 19/new 1542). The unfortunate development of the situation in the wood industry is revealed in Professor Rolf Wagenführ's *Rise and Fall of German War Economy* (BBSU, London, 1945), p. 13. The net production of the wood industry was 1,050,000,000 marks in 1940, rising to 1,124,000,000 marks in 1941, but falling to 1,100,000,000 marks in 1942. A report by the Armaments Commission of the Warta Gau, October 30, 1943 (RW 20–21/7) illustrates a detail of this situation: "The lumberyards at sawmills and in wholesale commerce are empty. Only 25 percent of the supplies of 40,000 cubic meters needed for the armaments factories are

guaranteed for the next three months." In Corinthia, too, a firm that had produced 30 to 50 barracks monthly at the start of World War II had to decrease production to 15 as of the fall of 1943 because of the wood shortage. (From a dissertation by Stefan Karner: *Die Rüstungsindustrie in Kärnten 1938 bis 1945* [Graz, 1976].)

46. Nuremberg document no. 399.
47. Ba Collection Schumacher/329.
48. Hans Marsalek, in *Geschichte des Konzentrationslagers Mauthausen* (Vienna, 1974), p. 103, published an original list, which concludes with 643,290 prisoners.
49. Eugen Kogon, *Der SS-Staat* (Frankfurt/Main, 1965), pp. 191–92.
50. Hermann Langbein, *Menschen in Auschwitz* (Vienna, 1972), pp. 73–74.
51. Simon Wiesenthal, *Die Sonnenblume* (Hamburg, 1970), p. 66.
52. Pohl's report of September 30, 1943 (Nuremberg document NO–1010).
53. Ibid.
54. From Heinz Höhne, *Der Orden unter dem Totenkopf* (Gütersloh, 1967), p. 402.
55. Rudolf Höss, *Kommandant in Auschwitz*, p. 175 (Stuttgart, 1958).
56. Letter from Kranefuss to Brandt, January 21, 1944 (Ba NS 19/new 1677).
57. Schieber's letter to Speer, May 7, 1944 (Ba R 3/1631).
58. Führer Protocol of June 3–5, 1944, item 22 (Ba R 3/1510).
59. It was the obligation of the Plenipotentiary for Labor Employment, i.e., Sauckel, to deal with this matter. He alone with his subordinate agencies could control the implementation.
60. By way of Mr. Belson, a British guard at Spandau Prison, I learned around 1950 that a Herr Siebenhaar had information that some forty workers had been removed by me from the concentration camp. These were foreigners, and I allegedly helped them return to their homelands. Countless Berlin workers could confirm this. This may have been an immediate consequence of my measures with Himmler which I undertook by way of Hitler.

CHAPTER 5

1. This report cannot be located in the archives. It was regarded as important, for on August 31, 1942 (Ba NS 19/new 755) A. Meines asked SS Obersturmführer Waringhoff, on the Personal Staff of the SS Reichsführer, to add it "to the mail to be read by the SS Reichsführer, so that he can read it in the airplane en route here."
2. The Personal Staff of the SS Reichsführer was considered one of the chief offices of the SS organization. This shows the importance it was accorded.
3. One of the largest factories that Schieber had built up for producing spun rayon from wood. Today it is still a valuable component of Austrian industry.
4. Kaltenbrunner was mistaken; the appointment of a factory director did not require the Gauleiter's approval.
5. Kaltenbrunner's letter to Wolff, September 16, 1942 (Ba NS 19/new 2039). The Himmler files do not divulge any reaction to Kaltenbrunner's massive attacks.
6. Letter from the Personal Staff of the SS Reichsführer to SS Hauptsturmführer Fälschlein in the house, September 25, 1942 (Ba NS 19/new 2039).
7. Himmler's letter to Ohlendorf, October 5, 1942, as top government secret (Ba NS 19/2039).
8. Quoted from Willi A. Boelcke, *Deutschlands Rüstung im Zweiten Weltkrieg* (Frankfurt, 1969), p. 22.
9. On page 62 of the ministry's chronicle, there is a copy of this letter to Hitler (Ba R 3/1737).

10. Himmler's telegram to Schieber, September 21, 1943 (Ba NS 19/new 2039).
11. Urgently needed ball bearings were imported from both Switzerland and Sweden.
12. Letter of June 21, 1944, from Speer to Hanke (Ba R 3/1582).
13. Hermann Giessler, *Ein anderer Hitler* (Starnberg, 1977), p. 434.
14. Neither the letter nor the draft is extant. However, the contents can be gleaned from Bormann's letter to Himmler of March 7, 1944 (Ba NS 19/new 2058).
15. Bormann's letter to Himmler of March 7, 1944 (Ba NS 19/new 2058). It is typical of my unsuspicious nature that around the time that Hanke sent his report to Himmler, I suggested him to Hitler for heading the newly founded Fighter Plane Staff, and that in late April 1945 I sent an effusive telegram celebrating Hanke for his achievements on behalf of the defense of Breslau (Ba R 3/1582).
16. Also see *Inside the Third Reich*, pp. 328 and 340. It is characteristic that this cunning attack took place during my ten weeks' absence from the ministry due to a severe illness. The intrigue to strip me of power fits in with other efforts during these weeks, launched by Himmler, Bormann, Goering, and old members of Dr. Todt's staff.
17. Bormann's letter to Himmler, May 8, 1944 (Ba NS 19/new 755).
18. Schieber's letter to Speer, May 7, 1944 (Ba R 3/1631). Also: *Inside the Third Reich*, p. 374 and footnotes 14, 17 on page 555. Given the espionage system maintained everywhere by the SD, one can assume that the SS leaders soon learned about this confidential letter.
19. This memorandum is not contained in the files.
20. Speer's letter of May 26, 1944, to Gauleiter Albert Hoffmann, from which details of the no-longer extant memorandum are taken (Ba R 3/1599).
21. Schieber's letter to Himmler, July 6, 1944 (Ba R 3/1631).
22. Speer's letter to Kaltenbrunner, July 21, 1944 (Ba R 3/1585).
23. Memorandum 3 D 4–6 Kr./Ka, July 27, 1944, with the remark "Speer dossier" from the Reich Security Headquarters (Ba R 3/1631).
24. Speer's telegram to Himmler, October 3, 1944 (Ba NS 19/new 2058). The contents of the Kaltenbrunner report can be gleaned from this telegram to Himmler.
25. Liebel's memorandum to me of October 12, 1944 (Ba R 3/1631), which reveals that Hitler made this decision "after a report from Reichsleiter Bormann."
26. Speer's letter to Bormann, October 29, 1944 (Ba R 3/1573).
27. Speer's letter to Himmler, October 26, 1944 (Ba NS 19/new 2058). Both letters were no doubt dictated on the same day. But the letter to Himmler left my ministry on October 26, and the one to Bormann on October 29.
28. From the telegram from SS Obergruppenführer Berger, head of the SS Headquarters in Berlin, to Himmler, October 31, 1944, 9 P.M. (Ba NS 19/2058). The text of the telegram, repeating my discussion with Schieber, is vague in spots. In regard to the transmission to Schieber, I had to be content with the reasons that Bormann had given. My greater knowledge was a matter of top secrecy.
29. Handwritten letter from Schieber to Speer, October 31, 1944 (Ba R 3/1631).
30. Hettlage, often attacked by SS circles, remained in office; however, General Wäger had to leave.
31. Taken from Berger's wire to Himmler, October 31, 1944 (Ba NS 19/new 2058).
32. Himmler's wire to Berger, November 1, 1944 (Ba NS 19/new 2058).
33. Confidential report of press office, signed Lorch, December 8, 1944, to Ohlendorf (Ba R 7/2014).
34. Speer's edict of November 12, 1944, on "Change in the Reich Ministry for Armaments and Wartime Production" (Ba R 43 II/1157a).
35. My letter to Jüttner of August 10, 1944 (Ba R 3/1584), reveals that I had to

defend myself against SS General Jüttner because an edict on the "Concentration of Armaments and War Production," which Hitler signed on June 19, 1944, at my suggestion, was not published until July 22. There was suspicion that General Wäger knew about the planned assassination of July 20 and therefore did not consider the publication necessary.

36. Himmler's letter to Speer, November 8, 1944 (Ba NS 19/new 2058).
37. Speer's letter to Himmler, November 10, 1944 (Ba NS 19/new 2058).
38. Speer's letter to Schieber, November 10, 1944 (Ba NS 19/new 2058).
39. Speer's letter to Himmler of November 24, 1944 (Ba NS 19/new 2058).
40. Dr. Walter Schieber had managed to manufacture spun rayon from potato tops after many years of development. Despite the minor heat value of the product, it garnered him Hitler's respect.
41. Führer Protocol, November 28, 1944, item 20 (Ba R 3/1511).
42. Handwritten notes on Speer's letters to Himmler, November 10 and 24, 1944 (Ba NS 19/new 2058).
43. Letter from Standard Commander Brandt to Brigade Commander Kranefuss, December 22, 1944 (Ba NS 19/new 2058).

CHAPTER 6

1. Remark by Straube's personal assistant, July 7, 1944 (Ba NS/19/new 1704).
2. See Heinz Höhne, *Der Orden unter dem Totenkopf* (Gütersloh, 1967), p. 379. Correspondence between Himmler and Reeder, February 16, 1943 (SS Reichsführer film reel 56).
3. Letter to Fritz Kranefuss from Karl Wolff, July 24, 1942 (Ba NS 19/new 2220).
4. It was customary at this time to invite industry leaders into my ministry. They worked without salaries but retained their large salaries for their industrial positions.
5. Letter of June 21, 1942, from SS Oberführer Fritz Kranefuss to SS Obergruppenführer Karl Wolff, along with accompanying material of June 2, 1942 (Ba NS 19/new 2220).
6. Letter from Kranefuss to Wolff, July 24, 1942 (Ba NS 19/new 2220).
7. From the material accompanying a letter written by Kranefuss to Obergruppenführer Wolff on June 21, 1942. The accompanying material is dated June 2, 1942 (Ba NS 19/new 2220).
8. Kranefuss's letter to Wolff, September 18, 1942 (Ba NS 19/new 2220).
9. Ohlendorf's letter to Himmler, August 26, 1942 (Ba NS 19/new 2039).
10. From Ohlendorf's testimony during cross examination by his attorney Dr. Aschenauer, October 6, 1947, at the Nuremberg Military Court IIa, case IX (Ba Allg. Proz. 1, XXVII A/5, 6).
11. See *Inside the Third Reich*, pp. 208–210.
12. Himmler's letter to Ohlendorf, October 5, 1942 (Ba NS 19/new 2039).
13. Ohlendorf's letter to Himmler, October 16, 1942 (Ba NS 19/new 2039).
14. In H. A. Turner's report *Hitler aus nächster Nähe* (Ullstein Verlag, Berlin, 1978, p. 390), Otto Wagener, Hitler's confidant and economic adviser, says that in 1932 Funk, although already Hitler's economic deputy, got involved with two black women in a Munich bar one night, even hugging and kissing them despite all doctrines of racial awareness.
15. Index figures of German armaments manufacturing (Ba R 3/1732).
16. The price portion of munitions manufacturing as compared with the overall armaments production for the three branches of the military was 29 percent during this period. That was why the doubling stuck out so broadly in the overall armaments index.

17. Himmler's conversation of October 21, 1942, with "SS Brigade Commander Ohlendorf in Berlin. Prohibition re accepting position in the Reich Economy Ministry."
18. Himmler's memorandum of October 21, 1942 (Ba NS 19/new 2039).
19. Ibid.
20. Ibid.
21. Himmler's note on October 21, 1942, on a telephone conversation with Wolff (Ba NS 19/new 1439).
22. Kranefuss's letter to Himmler, October 30, 1942 (Ba NS 19/2220).
23. Himmler's calendar page, March 25–26, 1943 (Ba NS 19/new 1444).
24. Führer Protocol of November 7–8, 1942, item 33 (Ba R 3/1506).
25. Regarding these intrigues in detail, see *Inside the Third Reich*, pp. 274–276.
26. Himmler's calendar entry, August 20, 1943: "4:00 P.M. to 4:30 P.M., Reich Minister Funk; 4:30 P.M. to 5:00 P.M., State Secretary Landfried" (Ba NS 19/new 1444).
27. Himmler's calendar entry, August 21, 1943: "8 P.M., dinner with Lammers and Funk" (Ba NS 19/new 1444).
28. According to the Ministry Chronicle of September 19, 1943, Hayler was already state secretary (Ba R 3/1740).
29. See *Inside the Third Reich*, pp. 223–24.
30. Ibid., pp. 274–75.
31. Data taken from "Proposal for Appointing the Head of the Reich Group for Commerce as State Secretary" (no date) (Ba 43 II/1141 b).
32. Data taken from "Proposal for Appointing Major General of Police Otto Ohlendorf as Ministerial Director with title of Under State Secretary" (undated, Ba R 43 II/1141 b). Despite Himmler's support, Funk could not get Lammers to accede to his desire to grant Ohlendorf the title of under state secretary. Funk's letter to Lammers of January 15, 1944, and Lammers's memorandum of January 25, 1944 (Ba R 43 II/1141 b).
33. Chronicle of September 19, 1944, p. 257 (Ba R 3/1740).
34. Confidential report, December 8, 1944, by Press and Public Relations Officer Lorch in the Reich Ministry of Economy to Ohlendorf (Ba R 7/2014).
35. As Dr. Theo Hupfauer informed me on March 10, 1977, Hayler did not unconditionally accept Ohlendorf's conception. This is consistent with my impression that Ohlendorf and not Hayler was to be seen as the driving force.
36. Letter from Liebel, head of Central Office, to State Secretary Dr. Hayler, September 11, 1944 (Ba R 3/1582).
37. These plans stem partly from my notes in Kransberg, July 1945, the so-called *Politische Zusammenhänge*, A 9, pages 3 and 4.
38. Page 518 of the session of the Military Court, Nr. II–A, Case IX, October 8, 1947; questioning of Otto Ohlendorf by his defense attorney Dr. Aschenauer (Ba Allg. Proz. 1, XXVII A/5, 6).
39. A photocopy of this memorandum was kindly supplied to me by David Irving.

CHAPTER 7

1. *Hitler aus nächster Nähe*, edited by H. A. Turner (Berlin, 1978), pp. 267–68.
2. These Gau economic advisers were directly responsible to Martin Bormann, who thus documented his personal interest in exerting an influence on economic issues.
3. From Ohlendorf's speech of June 15, 1944, to the Gau economic advisers of the National Socialist party in the Party Chancellery (Ba R 7/2017).
4. Speer's speech to the armaments industrialists in Essen on June 9, 1944 (Ba R 3/1550).

5. From Ohlendorf's speech of June 15, 1944, to the Gau economic advisers of the National Socialist party in the Party Chancellery (Ba R 7/2017).
6. Ohlendorf's article "Wirtschafspolitische Bilanz von 28. Dezember 1944" (Ba R 7/2018).
7. From the documents assembled by Ohlendorf for State Secretary Hayler's speech in Feldafing, late January 1945 (Ba R 7/2006).
8. Underlining in original text.
9. Underlining in original text.
10. Underlining in original text.
11. From the documents assembled by Ohlendorf for State Secretary Hayler's speech in Feldafing, late January 1945 (Ba R 7/2006).
12. From Ohlendorf's speech on June 15, 1944, to the Gau economic advisers of the National Socialist party in the Party Chancellery (Ba R 7/2017).
13. SS Brigade Commander Ohlendorf's speech on "German Social Economy and its Problems" in the work discussion of the Reich Ministry of Economy on sociological problems, December 1, 1944 (Ba R 7/2024).
14. As a parallel case, one might mention Arthur Nebe, likewise a high-ranking SS officer. Nevertheless, Nebe tried to satisfy Himmler and the SS leadership by multiplying his figures on the murder victims. See also Fabian von Schlabrendorf, *Begegnungen in Fünf Jahrzehnten* (Tübingen, 1979), pp. 174, 180, 220.
15. Ohlendorf's draft for a speech of Hayler's on January 22, 1945 (Ba R 7/2006).
16. Quotations from Adolf Hitler, *Monologe im Führerhauptquartier, 1941–1944* (Hamburg, 1980). Quotation from November 21–22, 1941, pp. 101–2, and from November 26–27, 1941, p. 110. These constructions are published in the illustrated volume *Albert Speer: Architectur* (Berlin, 1978).
17. Underlining by the author.
18. From Ohlendorf's speech, June 15, 1944, to the Gau economic advisers of the National Socialist party in the Party Chancellery (Ba R 7/2017). In German usage at that time, the word *zivilisatorisch* ("civilizational") had a pejorative, decadent connotation.
19. This entry is not included in *The Spandau Diaries*.

CHAPTER 8

1. This is revealed in a letter from Director General Voss to Himmler, March 30, 1942 (Ba NS 19/new 1935).
2. Führer Protocol of March 16, 1942, item 4 (Ba R 3/1503).
3. Letter from Director General Voss to Himmler, March 30, 1942 (Ba NS 19/new 1935).
4. Himmler to SS Standard Commander Voss, May 8, 1942 (Ba NS 19/new 1935).
5. This was the liaison staff, directly responsible to Voss, at the Skoda Works and the Brno Weapons Works for the Waffen-SS.
6. Voss's letter to Himmler, May 11, 1942 (Ba NS 19/new 1935).
7. Voss's letter to Himmler, June 4, 1942 (Ba NS 19/new 1935).
8. Voss's letter to Himmler, June 10, 1942 (Ba NS 19/new 1935).
9. Führer Protocol of May 6–7, 1942, item 40 (Ba R 3/1504).
10. Führer Protocol of May 13, 1942, item 31 (Ba R 3/1504).
11. Führer Protocol of September 4–9, 1942, item 18 (Ba R 3/1505).
12. Führer Protocol of January 18, 1943, item 7 (Ba R 3/1507).
13. Führer Protocol of February 6–7, 1943, item 7 (Ba R 3/1507).
14. Führer Protocol of July 8, 1943, item 4 (Ba R 3/1508).
15. Speer's letter to Jüttner, April 12, 1943 (Ba NS 19/old 338).

16. Führer Protocol of November 13–15, 1943, item 8 (Ba R 3/1508).

17. Führer Protocol of May 22–25, 1944, item 11 (Ba R 3/1509). The T-38 was known back then as an "assault gun" or "tank destroyer," since it was manufactured with a solidly installed gun and no revolving turret.

18. Production figures from "Armaments Statistics" (Ba R 3/1731).

19. Albeit without success. This will be the subject of my projected book *Remarks on the Armaments Industry*.

20. Führer Protocol of April 6–7, 1944, item 13 (Ba R 3/1509). Cf. also Führer Protocol of January 25–28, 1944, item 5 (Ba R 3/1509).

21. Führer Protocol of November 1–4, 1944, item 31 (Ba R 3/1510).

22. Führer Protocol of November 1–4, 1944, item 35 (Ba R 3/1510).

23. Voss's letter to Himmler, March 30, 1942 (Ba NS 19/new 1935).

24. See *Inside the Third Reich*, pp. 483–86.

25. In France and Belgium, there were no problems because of the military administrations. They cooperated as smoothly with my agencies as Colonel General Fromm (head of army armaments and commander in chief of the reserve army) or the General Staff of the army.

26. Chronicle of October 8, 1943, (Ba R 3/1738).

27. Speer's letter to Frank, March 2, 1944 (Ba R 3/1578).

28. Draft for an edict, attached to letter to Frank, March 2, 1944 (Ba R 3/1578).

29. Kammler's letter to Dr. Brandt, Personal Staff of SS Reichsführer, June 13, 1944 (Ba NS 19/new 317).

30. Speer's letter to Lammers, June 19, 1944 (Ba R 3/1768).

31. Speer's letter to Lammers, August 15, 1944 (Ba R 43 II 610).

32. Ohlendorf's testimony, October 8, 1946, at the Nuremberg Military Tribunal II, Case IX, p. 499. (Ba Allg. Prozess, 1, XXVII A5, 6).

33. Letter from Security Service of the SS, SD Head Department Prague, to Reich Security Headquarters III D, attention: SS Standard Commander Seibert. With copy for II Germany–East. Early June 1944 (R 58/1003).

34. Letter from Otto Saur, head of Technical Office, to SS Obergruppenführer Frank in Prague, August 28, 1944 (Ba R 3/1578). Naturally, the programs assigned to the factories by the Central Office required extreme efforts. Ultimate resources could be tapped only by means of this policy of extreme demands. Saur wrote in the same letter: "For educational reasons, all tank factories are making sure that the goal is absolutely achieved even if the vehicles are not ultimately quite complete and are not to be delivered. If a backlog is acknowledged, then one lacks the pressure to supply the backlog vehicles as quickly as possible."

35. Report by III Germany–East, November 6, 1944 (Ba R 58/1003).

36. Speer's letter to Frank, June 7, 1944 (Ba R 3/1578).

37. Report by III Germany–East, November 6, 1944 (Ba R 58/1003).

38. Report by III Germany–East, November 6, 1944 (Ba R 58/1003).

39. Report by the department head of III Germany–East of the Security Service, November 6, 1944, on trip to the Protectorate (Ba R 58/1003).

40. Report by the department head of III Germany–East of the Security Service, November 6, 1944, on trip to the Protectorate (Ba R 58/1003).

41. Report by III Germany–East, November 6, 1944 (Ba R 58/1003).

42. Führer Protocol of November 1–4, 1944, item 13 (Ba R 3/1510) and letter from Speer to Bertsch, November 11, 1944 (Ba R 3/1572). Dr. Walter Bertsch was a career official. He became an *Oberregierungsrat* (senior executive officer) in 1936 and then minister of labor and economy in Czechoslovakia in 1942. After the war he was sentenced to life imprisonment, and eventually died in prison. Presumably a position in my ministry would have spared him this fate.

43. Since I was carried by the influence of the industrialists who had maintained their sense of reality, I was relatively free of such effects, as revealed in chapters 28–32.
44. According to oral information from Herr Fremerey, July 3, 1977.
45. Speer's letter to Dr. Bertsch in Prague, January 6, 1945 (Ba R 3/1572).
46. See *Inside the Third Reich*, pp. 396–97; and Chronicle of August 10 and 31, 1944 (Ba R 3/1740).
47. Two letters from the Security Service, Head Department Prague, February 19, 1945, to Reich Security Headquarters, Berlin (Ba R 58/1033).
48. Joseph Goebbels, *Diaries*, entry of March 18, 1945.

CHAPTER 9

1. Memorandum by III German–West, September 20, 1944 (Ba R 58/976). Evidently the SD official had been transferred to this division after the disbanding of the SD office in Litzmannstadt.
2. Report by the SD Head Office Düsseldorf to the Reich Security Headquarters, Berlin, October 11, 1944 (Ba R 58/976).
3. SD Head Office Düsseldorf to Reich Security Headquarters, Berlin, November 23, 1944 (Ba R 58/976).
4. Report by SD Head Office Düsseldorf to Reich Security Headquarters, Berlin, October 11, 1944 (Ba R 58/976).
5. Report of November 6, 1944, on an "Office Trip by Office Head of III Germany–East to the Protectorate, October 24–31, 1944" (Ba R 58/1003).
6. Personal letter from Martin Bormann to the chief of the Reich Security Headquarters, SS Obergruppenführer Dr. Kaltenbrunner, April 4, 1945 (Ba R 58/976).
7. See *Inside the Third Reich*, p. 486.
8. Ohlendorf's memorandum to the head minister of the caretaker government, Count Schwerin von Krosigk, Flensburg, undated, but probably written between May 6 and 22, 1945 (Ba R 62/7).
9. On the other hand, there were heavy penalties if any staffer abused my system of trust. For instance, if they hoarded important raw materials by means of false figures, thereby keeping weapons from the front lines.
10. Ministry Chronicle, May 26, 1944 (Ba R 3/1739).
11. Speer's wire to Kaltenbrunner, June 28, 1944 (Ba R 3/1585).
12. Joseph Goebbels, *Diaries*, entries of March 28 and 31, 1945.
13. "Ne. metals" referred to shortage metals like chromium, molybdenum, nickel, etc.
14. Telegram from SS Squad Commander Müller to Himmler, June 25, 1942 (Ba NS 19/old 415).
15. Telegram from SS Squad Commander Müller to Himmler, July 14, 1942 (Ba NS 19/old 415).
16. Letter from Fritz Kranefuss to Dr. Rudolf Brandt, December 5, 1942 (Ba NS 19/new 2224).
17. Letter from Reich Security Headquarters to the adjutancy of the SS Reichsführer, January 11, 1943 (Ba NS 19/new 2224).
18. Goebbels's diary, from February 28 to April 10, 1945, offers a vivid insight into the bizarre possibilities of human self-delusion in desperate situations.
19. Cf. Kaltenbrunner's report of October 12, 1944, to Bormann in Karl Heinrich Peter, *Spiegelbild einer Verschwörung: Die Kaltenbrunner-Berichte an Bormann und Hitler über das Attentat am 20. Juli 1944: Geheimdokumente aus dem ehemaligen Reichssicherheitshauptamt* (Stuttgart, 1961).

20. See *Inside the Third Reich*, pp. 391, 394, 396.

21. See memorandum to Hitler, November 11, 1944 (Ba R 3/1528) and *Inside the Third Reich*, p. 414.

22. Speer's letter to the head of intelligence service of the SS Reichsführer, December 29, 1944 (mailed on January 6, 1945), including a memorandum to Herr Stahl, January 3, 1945 (Ba R 3/1768).

23. The quotation is from p. 104 of Hitler's *Mein Kampf*, edition of 1935. More about Lüschen's role during the last few weeks of the war in *Inside the Third Reich*, pp. 429, 464, 469, 476, 477, 478, 484.

24. Speer's letter to Kaltenbrunner, December 4, 1944 (Ba R 3/1585). The memorandum mentioned in this letter is not extant. Its gist may be gleaned from the letter.

25. Letter from SS Obergruppenführer Gottlob Berger, head of SS Headquarters, to Himmler, October 27, 1944 (Ba NS 19/old 378).

26. Written information from Otto Merker, June 28, 1973.

27. From Johannes Steinhoff, *In letzter Stunde* (Munich, 1974), pp. 118–19.

CHAPTER 10

1. Cf. also *Inside the Third Reich*, pp. 328–29.

2. Seeberg's letter to Reich Security Headquarters, Reputation Information, December 10, 1943 (Ba R 3/1628).

3. Concerning the development, see also *Inside the Third Reich*, pp. 336–44.

4. From the Ministry Chronicle, August 16, 1944 (Ba R 3/1740).

5. Speer's letter to Pleiger, August 8, 1944 (Ba R 3/1632).

6. From the Ministry Chronicle, August 16, 1944 (Ba R 3/1740).

7. Letter from SS Sturmbannführer Backhaus, personal assistant of Backe, Reich food minister, to SS Standard Commander Brandt, personal assistant of Himmler, August 26, 1944 (Ba NS 19/new 830).

8. Brandt's letter to Backhaus, August 31, 1944 (Ba NS 19/new 830).

9. Meine's memorandum to Brandt, September 1, 1944 (Ba NS 19/new 830).

10. Letter of SS Squad Commander Meinberg to Himmler, November 2, 1944 (Ba NS 19/new 1693).

11. Meinberg's letter to Sohl, October 19, 1944 (Ba NS 19/new 1683).

12. Sohl's letter to Meinberg, October 25, 1944 (Ba NS 19/new 1693).

13. Himmler's letter to Meinberg, November 22, 1944 (Ba NS 19/new 1693).

14. Himmler's letter to Speer, September 5, 1944 (Ba NS 19/old 294).

15. Letter from SS Standard Commander Klumm, personal assistant of SS Headquarters, to SS Hauptsturmführer Meine on Personal Staff of SS Reichsführer, November 15, 1944 (Ba NS 19/old 294).

16. Memorandum of "Leadership Deficiencies in the Luftwaffe and the Air Industry," undated, accompanying Himmler's letter to Speer, September 5, 1944 (Ba NS 19/old 294).

17. Speer's power of attorney for Professor Dr. Gladenback, September 5, 1944 (Ba R 3/1583).

18. Memorandum on "Leadership Deficiencies in the Luftwaffe and Air Ministry," undated, accompanying Himmler's letter to Speer, September 5, 1944 (Ba NS 19/old 294).

19. Speer's letter to Himmler, September 16, 1944 (Ba R 3/1583).

20. The dictation sign was TA, i.e., *Technisches Amt* (Technical Office), which was headed by Saur. Naturally, Himmler and Kaltenbrunner knew what this dictation sign meant. At this point in time, they evidently valued Saur's opinion more highly than mine.

21. Speer's letter to Himmler, October 8, 1944 (Ba NS 19/old 294).
22. Letter from head of SS Headquarters to Dr. Brandt, October 18, 1944 (Ba NS 19/old 425). According to the dictation sign, the letter was written by SS Standard Commander Klumm.
23. Draft for letter from Obersturmführer Friedrich Klumm to chief of Personal Staff of SS Reichsführer, October 18, 1944 (Ba NS 19/old 425).
24. Dr. Brandt's letter to SS Obersturmführer Klumm, October 30, 1944 (Ba NS 19/old 425).
25. Joseph Goebbels, *Diaries*, entries for March 28 and 31, 1945.
26. Himmler's letter to von Axthelm, general of the antiaircraft forces, September 9, 1944 (Ba NS 19/new 1677).
27. Letter of Dr. Brandt, Himmler's chief of staff, to SS Squad Commander Gottlob Berger, April 30, 1942. From *Mein Reichsführer* (dtv, Munich, 1970), p. 146.
28. Letter from SS Standard Commander Klumm, personal assistant of SS Headquarters, to SS Haupsturmführer Meine on the Personal Staff of the SS Reichsführer, November 15, 1944 (Ba NS 19/old 294).
29. Results of meeting of Armaments Staff, October 3–4, 1944 (Ba R 3/1761).
30. Likewise in Speer, *Politische Zusammenhänge* (Kransberg, July 1945), A VII, pp. 6a–7.
31. Memorandum by Albert Speer to Hitler, September 20, 1944 (Ba R 3/1526).
32. See also *Inside the Third Reich*, pp. 396–98.
33. Speer's letter to Kaltenbrunner, December 14, 1944 (Ba R 3/1585).
34. For many years, and still in November 1944, Schaaf had been director of the Eisenach Works of the Bohemian Moravian Works. He had an honorary position in my ministry. On November 17, 1944, in a meeting of the Armaments Staff, Saur determined that "Schaaf will be leaving the Armaments Staff and the Armaments Supply Staff" as of November 17, 1944 (Ba R 3/1761).
35. The Bohemian Moravian Works were prominently involved in the manufacture of airplane engines and hence extremely important in the armaments industry.
36. The rank of Scharführer corresponded to that of Unterfeldwebel, just below the equivalent of an American sergeant.
37. Memorandum of December 26, 1944, from SS Scharführer Wolf (Ba NS 19/488).
38. Speer's letter to Hille, December 29, 1944 (Ba R 3/1583).
39. Brandt's letter to the head of the Security Police and of the SD, January 9, 1945 (Ba NS 19/488).
40. Bormann's letter to SS Reichsführer Himmler, February 5, 1945 (Ba NS 19/old 378).
41. Himmler's letter to Bormann, February 15, 1945 (Ba NS 19/old 378).

CHAPTER 11

1. Corresponds to the rank of lieutenant.
2. Report by SS Untersturmführer Helmut Zborowski to SS Squad Commander Pohl, February 5, 1942 (Ba NS 19/old 1335).
3. These rocket bombers were evidently mass-produced aircraft that were to be armed with 500-kilogram rocket bombs.
4. Report from SS Untersturmführer Helmut Zborowski to SS Squad Commander Pohl, February 5, 1942 (Ba NS 19/old 1335).
5. Zborowski's letter to Himmler, February 26, 1943 (Ba NS 19/old 338).
6. See *Inside the Third Reich*, p. 273.
7. Dr. Brandt's letter to Zborowski, March 5, 1943 (Ba NS 19/old 338).

8. In the letter of February 26, 1943, Thedsen is still a captain in the navy.

9. Zborowski's letter to Himmler, April 11, 1943 (Ba NS 19/old 338).

10. Himmler's notes on telephone conversations, January 4, 1943 (Ba NS 10/new 1439).

11. Himmler's report notices for meeting with Hitler on April 17, 1943 (Ba NS 19/new 1447).

12. Himmler's calendar entry of May 14, 1943 (Ba NS 19/new 1444).

13. Calendar leaf of January 27, 1943: "5:00 P.M. to 5:30 P.M. Dr. Flettner" (Ba NS 19/new 1444).

14. Führer Protocol of August 19–22, 1943, item 28 (Ba R 3/1508).

15. From the minutes of a conversation with the head of Army Armaments, January 21, 1944. Quoted from Willi A. Boelcke, *Deutschlands Rüstung im Zweiten Weltkrieg* (Frankfurt, 1969), p. 292.

16. Führer Protocol of January 3–5, 1943, item 44 (Ba R 3/1507).

17. Himmler's letter to SS Economic Administrative Headquarters and SS Command Office, no day indicated, but from June 1943 (NS 19/new 768).

18. Himmler's letter of June 12, 1943, to Jüttner (NS 19/new 768).

19. See *Inside the Third Reich*, p. 224.

20. Himmler's letter to Kammler, June 15, 1943 (NS 19/new 768).

21. Jüttner's letter to Himmler, June 25, 1943 (NS 19/new 768).

22. Report by SS Command Headquarters, Office X, signed by SS Untersturmführer Reichauer, June 18, 1943 (NS 19/new 768).

23. Kammler's letter to Himmler, June 1943 (NS 19/new 768).

24. State Councillor Dr. H. Pendl's letter to Himmler, January 7, 1944 (Ba NS 19/new 2057).

25. Himmler's telegram to Kloth, April 30, 1944 (Ba NS 19/old 294).

26. Himmler's letter to SS Standard Commander Frosch, April 30, 1944 (Ba NS 19/old 294).

27. Himmler's telegram of April 30, 1944, to Pohl (Ba NS 19/old 294).

28. Himmler's calendar leaf of May 6, 1944: "1:30 A.M. to 12:30 A.M. Wankel Factory" (Ba NS 19/new 1445).

29. Brandt's telegram to Frosch, June 19, 1944 (Ba NS 19/old 294).

30. Wilhelm Keppler's letter of June 19, 1944, to Himmler (Ba NS 19/old 461).

31. From Frosch's letter to Himmler, August 5, 1944 (Ba NS 19/old 294).

32. Frosch's letter of August 5, 1944.

33. This is revealed in a letter of August 3, 1944, informing the Wankel Experimental Workshops of this decision by the Office Group for Development (Colonel Geist) (Ba NS 19/old 294).

34. Himmler's memorandum of August 8, 1944 (NS 19/old 294).

35. Memorandum of a Sturmbannführer on Himmler's staff, March 12, 1945 (Ba NS 19/old 294).

36. Paper given by SS Oberführer Dr. Schwab in the Munitions Commission on November 24, 1942 (Ba NS 19/old 425).

37. Paper given by SS Brigade Commander Dr. Schwab in the Tank Commission on August 3, 1944 (Ba NS 19/old 425).

38. Speer's letter to SS Obergruppenführer Jüttner, August 10, 1944 (Ba R 3/1768).

39. "Focal Points in Development," second directive of July 21, 1944, signed by Speer, pertaining to the Führer's edict of June 19, 1944, on "The Concentration of Armaments and Wartime Production" (Ba R 3/1768).

40. Wasag was one of the leading German manufacturers of explosives.

41. Dr. von Holt's letter of September 25, 1944, to the head of the SS Reichsführer's Personal Staff (Ba NS 19/old 1530).

42. Ibid. This letter also repeats Himmler's statement.

348 *Notes*

43. Proposal by Elemag (Elektro-Mechanische Apparatebaugesellschaft) of October 28, 1944 (Ba NS 19/old 199).
44. Lauterbacher's letter of November 13, 1944, to Himmler (Ba NS 19/old 199).
45. Letter from Office VI of January 8, 1945, to Dr. R. Brandt (Ba NS 19/old 199).
46. Letter from Professor Dr. Werner Osenberg, February 7, 1945, to Dr. Brandt (Ba NS 19/old 199).
47. Dr. Badstein's report of February 6, 1945, on the Elemag proposal (Ba NS 19/old 199).
48. Professor Dr. A. Meissner's opinion of January 27, 1945, and addendum of February 1, 1945 (Ba NS 19/old 199).
49. When Dr. Robert Ley appealed to me during that same month for assistance for an alleged invention of death rays, I reacted more strongly. See *Inside the Third Reich*, pp. 464–65.
50. Himmler's letter to Pohl, May 13, 1942. From *Reichsführer!* (dtv, Munich), p. 147.
51. Himmler's letter to Pohl, October 17, 1942. From *Reichsführer!* (dtv, Munich), p. 147.
52. Grohmann's letter of April 1, 1943, to SS Sturmbannführer Dr. Joachim Caesar. Agricultural Division in Auschwitz Concentration Camp. From *Reichsführer!* (dtv, Munich), p. 263.
53. Transocean-Europapress-I-Service Tokyo Report of December 28, 1944 (Ba NS 19/new 758).
54. Dr. Brandt's letter to Wagner, January 9, 1945 (Ba NS 19/new 758).
55. Telegram from Dr. Brandt, head of Himmler's Personal Staff, January 5, 1945 (Ba NS 19/new 758).
56. Dr. Brandt's telegram to Pohl, January 18, 1945 (Ba NS 19/new 758).
57. Brandt's telegram to SS Command Headquarters, January 18, 1945 (Ba NS 19/new 758).
58. Pohl's letter to Brandt, January 23, 1945 (Ba NS 19/new 758).
59. Letter of "SS Reichsführer, Personal Staff," undated, no copy, text crossed out (Ba NS 19/new 758).
60. Lipinsky's letter to Dr. Brandt, February 1, 1945 (Ba NS 19/new 758).
61. Brandt's telegram to Lipinsky, January 28, 1945 (Ba NS 19/new 758).
62. Report by the Supreme SS and Police Commander for the Southwest to Gauleiter Wilhelm Murr, Stuttgart, and Gauleiter Robert Wagner, Strasbourg, about a meeting with Himmler on June 22, 1944, in Alsace (Ba NS 19/new 371).
63. See *Inside the Third Reich*, p. 241.
64. Speer's letter to Himmler, September 23, 1944 (Ba R 3/1583).
65. Speer's letter to Goering, September 12, 1944 (Ba R 3/1580).
66. Speer's letter to SS Squad Commander Ohlendorf, January 29, 1945 (Ba R 3/1593). Ohlendorf's letter is not extant.
67. Speer's letter to Professor Gerlach, December 19, 1944 (Ba R 3/1579).

CHAPTER 12

1. Pohl's letter to Himmler, November 28, 1942 (Ba NS 19/old 278). The Reich agencies were the state supervision organs. Schulze-Fielitz was state secretary in my ministry.
2. Letter from Personal Staff of SS Reichsführer to Pohl, December 6, 1942 (Ba NS 19/old 278).
3. The industrial groups in the Reich Association of Industry were, to be sure, often identical with the Reich units.
4. Pohl's letter to Funk, November 28, 1942 (Ba NS 19/old 278).

5. Pohl's presentation to Himmler, December 2, 1942, on "Organization of Forces in the Food Area" (Ba NS 19/old 278). Underlining in original.

6. Pohl's letter to Himmler, January 8, 1943 (Ba NS 19/old 278).

7. Himmler's letter to Pohl, January 16, 1943 (Ba NS 19/old 278).

8. See *Inside the Third Reich*, pp. 252–264., especially about the powerlessness of this committee and Goebbels's efforts to introduce the Total War in his way.

9. Pohl's letter to Himmler, April 13, 1944 (Ba NS 19/new 1752).

10. From Frank's report of April 21, 1944 (Ba NS 19/new 1752).

11. Pohl's letter to Himmler, April 24, 1944 (Ba NS 19/new 1752).

12. Frank's report on the first meeting of the commission, which took place on Friday, April 21, 1944; the report accompanied Pohl's letter to Himmler, April 24, 1944 (Ba NS 19/new 1752).

13. Pohl's letter to Himmler, April 24, 1944 (Ba NS 19/new 1752).

14. Himmler was right to be worried. Korherr showed him that he "could instantly get three divisions with fighting strength from the main offices of the SS without the least detriment to administrative work." From Heinz Höhne, *Der Orden unter dem Totenkopf* (Gütersloh, 1967), p. 402.

15. Himmler's letter to Pohl, May 15, 1944 (Ba NS 19/new 1752).

16. From my ministry's Chronicle, August 23, 1944 (Ba R 3/1740).

17. Speer's letter to Himmler, June 9, 1943 (Ba NS 19/new 372).

18. Himmler's letter to Speer, June 19, 1943 (Ba NS 19/new 372).

19. Letter of SS Standard Commander With to SS Standard Commander Rhode, chief of Command Staff of SS Reichsführer, July 17, 1943 (Ba NS 19/new 372).

20. Berger's letter to Dr. Brandt, August 6, 1943 (Ba NS 19/new 372).

21. Brandt's letter to Berger, October 13, 1943 (Ba NS 19/new 372).

22. Berger's letter to Dr. Brandt (Personal Staff of SS Reichsführer), December 4, 1943 (Ba NS 19/new 372).

23. Dr. Brandt's letter to Berger, February 26, 1944 (Ba NS 19/new 372).

24. Speer's memorandum for Hitler, July 20, 1944 (Ba R 3/1522).

25. See also *Inside the Third Reich*, p. 270–271.

26. Heinz Höhne's *Der Orden unter dem Totenkopf* (Gütersloh, 1967) informed me that this was a well-considered plan to deprive Hitler of power with the help of Himmler and his SS.

27. See *Inside the Third Reich*, pp. 391, 392.

28. Berger's letter to Naumann, head of ministerial office in the Propaganda Ministry, August 16, 1944 (Ba NS 19/old 284).

29. Brandt's letter to Berger, August 21, 1944 (Ba NS 19/old 284).

30. See *Inside the Third Reich*, pp. 396, 397, 558.

31. Berger's letter to Naumann, head of Ministry Office in the Propaganda Ministry, August 16, 1944 (Ba NS 19/old 284).

32. From Statistical Abstract on War Production (Ba R 3/1730).

33. From index figures on German armaments output (Ba R 3/1732).

34. See *Inside the Third Reich*, pp. 208–210.

35. Berger's letter to State Secretary Naumann, head of Ministry Office in the Propaganda Ministry, August 16, 1944 (Ba NS 19/old 284).

36. Speer's circular to all agency heads in his ministry, March 13, 1944 (Ba R 43 II/668 b).

37. The text of Hitler's no longer extant directive is taken from Himmler's implementation edict of August 5, 1944.

38. Himmler's edict of August 5, 1944 (Ba NS 19/new 1707).

39. Pohl's draft of a letter dated January 29, 1945, which Himmler was supposed to send to me (Ba NS 19/new 1707).

40. Speer's telegram to Himmler, January 8, 1945 (Ba R 3/1768).

41. After the assassination attempt of July 20, 1944, Himmler was appointed to replace Fromm in all his duties. Naturally, he filled the most important positions of this office with high-ranking SS officers on his staff. One of them was SS Obergruppenführer Frank.
42. Himmler's telegram to Speer, January 12, 1945 (Ba R 3/1768).
43. Speer's letter to Himmler, January 17, 1945 (Ba R 3/1768).
44. Buhle reported on the new output of weapons and munitions, and Hitler instantly distributed these available armaments instruments to divisions that were to be set up. No experts were called upon, even though they alone could have seen to an expedient distribution.
45. From my elaboration on this issue in *Politische Zusammenhänge*, A II (Kransberg, July 2, 1945).

CHAPTER 13

1. Führer Protocol, June 3–5, 1944, item 21 (Ba R 3/1509).
2. Pohl's letter to Himmler, December 2, 1943 (Ba NS 19/old 778).
3. From the protocols of the Military Tribunal, No. II-A, case IX: Trial of Ohlendorf (Ba Allg. Proz., I, XXVII, A/5, 6).
4. Chronicle of April 4, 1944 (Ba R 3/1739).
5. "Re Individual Matters in Himmler Office," undated (Ba NS 19/old 184).
6. Hitler's edict of January 11, 1942 (Ba NS 19/old 281).
7. Speer's letter to Volkswagen Works, March 23, 1942 (Ba NS 19/new 1955).
8. Pohl's letter to Himmler, April 8, 1942 (Ba NS 19/new 1955).
9. Pohl's letter to Himmler, April 28, 1942 (Ba NS 19/new 1955).
10. Pohl's report to Himmler, September 16, 1942 (Ba NS 19/new 14).
11. Pohl's letter to Himmler, July 7, 1942 (Ba NS 19/old 415).
12. Memorandum of Personal Staff of SS Reichsführer, July 18, 1942 (Ba NS 19/old 415).
13. Himmler's letter to SS Obergruppenführer Jüttner, head of SS Command Headquarters, February 8, 1944 (Ba NS 19/new 1542).
14. Himmler's letter to Pohl, September 9, 1942 (Ba NS 19/new 14).
15. Urgent telephone call from Himmler to Pohl, May 4, 1944 (EAP-161-6-12/330; Ba NS 19/new 768).
16. Kammler's letter to Dr. Brandt, June 19, 1944 (Ba NS 19/new 768).
17. According to I. Bentley and F. Porsche, *Porsche* (Düsseldorf/Vienna, 1978), pp. 223–24, Porsche was assigned in 1944 to develop a new and faster type of V-1 flying bomb with a larger range. But "before we could complete our designs, the war was over," says the author.
18. Himmler's letter to Jüttner, August 1, 1944 (Ba NS 19/new 296).
19. In July 1944, a total of 95,700 generators were in operation. That month, 10,400 were manufactured. Statistical Abstract on War Production (Ba R 3/1730).
20. Himmler's letter to Pohl, August 12, 1944 (Ba NS 19/new 296).
21. Pohl's letter to Himmler, October 14, 1944 (Ba NS 19/new 296).
22. Brandt's letter to Pohl, October 7, 1944 (Ba NS 19/new 296).
23. Speer's memorandum to Hitler, November 11, 1944 (Ba R 3/1528).
24. Speer's memorandum to Bormann, November 6, 1944 (Ba R c/1573).
25. Himmler's telegram to Speer, November 3, 1944, 3:15 A.M. (Ba NS 19/new 296).
26. Himmler's telegram to Speer, November 3, 1944, 4:30 P.M. (Ba NS 19/new 296).
27. Berger's telegram to Himmler, November 6, 1944 (Ba NS 19/new 296).
28. Brandt's telegram to Berger, November 8, 1944 (Ba NS 19/new 296).

29. Himmler's telegram to Speer, November 3, 1944, 4:30 P.M. (Ba NS 19/new 296).
30. Speer's letter to Himmler, November 10, 1944 (Ba R 3/1583).
31. Letter to Gauleiter Hoffmann, Bochum, and same wording to Gauleiter Schless-mann, Essen, Gauleiter Dr. Meyer, Münster, Gauleiter Florian, Düsseldorf, and Gauleiter Grohe, Cologne, December 10, 1944 (Ba R 3/1583). This adminis-trative splintering of the Rhenish/Westphalian industrial area kept causing major bottlenecks, because I could not get these egocentric Party members to cooperate in economic matters.
32. Speer's letter to Himmler, November 10, 1944 (Ba R 3/1583).
33. Himmler's letter to Speer, November 21, 1944 (Ba NS 19/new 296).
34. Gauleiter Meyer's telegram to Himmler, November 4, 1944 (Ba NS 19/new 296). The telegram took two days to get from Warendorf to Berlin, a sign of the incipient disruption of the German communications network by air raids.
35. Brandt's letter to Kloth, November 25, 1944 (Ba NS 19/new 296).
36. Kloth's letter to Brandt, December 27, 1944 (Ba NS 19/new 296).

Chapter 14

1. Letter from Technical Office of Air Ministry to Milch, April 2, 1942 (Ba NS 19/old 1532).
2. Speer's letter to Himmler, April 20, 1942 (Ba NS 19/old 1532).
3. Pohl's letter to Himmler, June 9, 1942 (Ba NS 19/old 1532).
4. Brandt's letter from Himmler's Personal Staff to SS Gruppenführer Sachs, July 1, 1942 (Ba NS 19/old 1532).
5. Discussion with Reich marshal, June 29, 1942, item 6 (Ba R 3/1504).
6. Pohl's letter to Himmler, July 14, 1942 (Ba NS 19/old 1532).
7. Himmler's letter to Speer, July 15, 1942 (Ba NS 19/old 1532).
8. Brandt's telegram to Pohl, July 25, 1942 (Ba NS 19/old 1532).
9. Himmler's letter to Pohl, August 25, 1942 (Ba NS 19/old 1532).
10. Himmler's letter to Erich Koch, August 26, 1942. From *Reichsführer!*, dtv, p. 177.
11. Pohl's letter to Himmler, September 5, 1942 (Ba NS 19/old 1532).
12. Telegram from Supreme Command of Wehrmacht to SS Reichsführer's Com-mand Staff, March 18, 1943 (Ba NS 19/new 1706).
13. Letter from SS Squad Commander Paul Hennicke to SS Obergruppenführer Karl Wolff, July 2, 1940 (Ba NS 19/new 755).
14. Himmler's letter to SS Sturmbannführer Vogel, March 29, 1941. From *Reichs-führer!*, dtv, Munich, p. 104.
15. Führer Protocol, June 23, 1942, item 22 (Ba R3 1504).
16. Pohl's report to Himmler, February 12, 1943 (Ba NS 19/old 415a). On October 13, 1941, Hitler spoke of a surface area of 40,000 hectares. Adolf Hitler, *Monologe im Führerhauptquartier* (Hamburg, 1980), p. 78.
17. See also W. Treue, "Gummi in Deutschland zwischen 1933 und 1945," in *Wehrwirtschaftlice Rundschau,* 1955, pp. 184–85; and Heiber, *Hitlers Lagebe-sprechungen,* p. 150.
18. Himmler's order to the Supreme SS and Police Commanders for the East, East-land, Vistula, Warta, Central Russia, and the Ukraine, July 23, 1943 (Ba 26 IV vorl. 33).
19. Himmler's calendar entries, April 15, June 24, and November 30, 1943, as well as April 20, 1944 (NS 19/new 1444 and 1445).
20. Kehrl's letter to SS Sturmbannführer Dr. Brandt, March 30, 1944, with accom-panying report from the Society for Plant Rubber and Gutta-percha, February 23, 1943 (Ba R 3/1901).

21. A worker's yearly salary was 1,800 marks.
22. Report of the Raw Materials Office of the Minister of Armaments and War Production, April 14, 1944 (Ba R 3/1901).
23. See *Inside the Third Reich*, p. 315.
24. Führer Protocol, December 16–17, 1943, item 1 (Ba R 3/1508).
25. Contained in the protocol of a meeting with Governor-General Frank, May 8, 1944 (Ba R 52 II/216).
26. Keppler's report to Himmler, June 29, 1944 (NS 19/old 461). Keppler, as he informed Himmler, wanted to present an oral report on manganese deposits in the southeastern tip of the Generalgouvernement. The report of the expedition, he said, had already come in.
27. Report on meeting between Himmler and Frank on May 18–19, 1944 (Ba R 52 II/217).
28. Report on meeting with Governor-General Frank, June 3, 1944 (Ba R 52 II/218).
29. Führer Protocol of March 29, 1943, item 13 (Ba R 3/1507).
30. Himmler's calendar page of March 29, 1943: "12 to 2 P.M. R. Min. [Reich Minister] Speer. 2 to 3 P.M., lunch with Speer" (Ba NS 19/new 1444).
31. Führer Protocol of May 30, 1943, item 30 (Ba R 3/1507).
32. In other Gaus as well, for instance Thuringia, which was Sauckel's Gau, major Party-owned factories were set up; their surplus was supposed to benefit the Gau treasury and hence the Gauleiter.
33. Greiser's letter to Himmler, October 6, 1944 (Ba NS 19/old 198).
34. Himmler's letter to Greiser, October 22, 1944 (NS 19/old 198).
35. Urgent telegram from Himmler to Pleiger, August 4, 1944 (Ba NS 19/old 198).
36. Pleiger's telegram of August 6, 1944, to Personal Staff of SS Reichsführer (Ba NS 19/old 198).
37. Memorandum of an SS Hauptsturmführer (name illegible), August 15, 1944 (Ba NS 19/old 198).
38. From *Die Tat,* December 4, 1971; article by Hans Marsalek, Vienna.
39. Urgent telegram from Himmler to Pleiger, August 13, 1944 (Ba NS 19/old 198).
40. Pleiger's telegram to Himmler, August 16, 1944 (Ba NS 19/old 198).
41. Pleiger's telegrams to Himmler, September 12, September 21, September 26, October 12, October 26, November 8, and November 15, 1944 (Ba NS 19/old 198).
42. Himmler's telegram to Pleiger, January 6, 1945 (Ba NS 19/old 198).
43. Pleiger's telegram to Himmler, January 13, 1945 (Ba NS 19/old 198).
44. The factory in Falkenhagen produced N-material in connection with the nerve gas sarin.
45. Sarin is still stored today by the United States Army as a combat gas.
46. Führer Protocol, June 3–5, 1944, item 5 (Ba R 3/1509).
47. Buhle's telegram to Saur, July 7, 1944 (Ba NS 19/old 425).
48. Speer's letter to Himmler, July 26, 1944 (Ba NS 19/old 425). In May 1944, Schieber, in a report on "The Situation in the Area of Gunpowder, Explosives, Warfare Agents, R-Materials, and Titanium Tetrachloride," had pointed out that "a unit of the N-material installation will be test-operated in the coming weeks in the sea works" (Ba R 3/1857).
49. Führer Protocol, November 1–4, 1944, item 10 (Ba R 3/1509).
50. Schieber's memorandum on discussion of W[arfare] agents, November 2, 1944 (Ba R 3/1894).
51. Speer's letter to Keitel, October 11, 1944 (Ba R 3/1586).

CHAPTER 15

1. Letter of head of SS Headquarters, Gottlob Berger, to Himmler, December 16, 1942 (Ba NS 19/old 335).
2. "Report to Führer on January 23, 1943, item 8" (Ba NS 19/new 1474).
3. Stegmaier's letter to Berger, January 26, 1943, with the salutation: "Dear Friend Berger" (Ba NS 19/old 415a).
4. Berger's letter of February 1, 1943, to Himmler (Ba NS 19/old 415).
5. "Report to Führer on February 10, 1943, item 18. Colonel Dornberger to Führer" (Ba NS 19/new 1474).
6. "Report to Führer on April 17, 1943, item 3, Peenemünde" (Ba NS 19/new 1474).
7. Himmler's letter to Berger, April 10, 1943 (Ba NS 19/old 415a).
8. Kaltenbrunner's letter to Himmler, July 12, 1943 (Ba NS 19/old 415a).
9. Führer Protocol of July 8, 1943, items 18, 19, 20 (Ba R 3/1507).
10. Dornberger had meanwhile been promoted.
11. Himmler's letter to Lieutenant Colonel Engel, July 14, 1943 (Ba NS 19/new 949).
12. Hitler's edict of July 25, 1943 (Ba RD 76/1).
13. In his calendar entry, Himmler noted: "August 19, 1943, 7:30 P.M. to the Wolf's lair. 8:30 P.M., dinner with Bormann. 9:30 P.M., situation at Führer's" (Ba NS 19/new 1447).
14. According to Himmler's calendar entry of August 20, 1943, Saur and I were at Himmler's from 3 to 4 P.M. (Ba NS 19/new 1444).
15. Gerhard Degenkolb succeeded in increasing the production of locomotives from 1,918 in 1941 to 5,243 in 1943. In early January 1943 I assigned Degenkolb to carry out the production of the A-4. He set up a program scheduling the manufacture of 3,180 A-4's (V-2's) in 1943.
16. See *Inside the Third Reich*, p. 200.
17. Führer Protocol of March 19, 1942, item 28 (Ba R 3/1506).
18. In my speech to the Reichsleiters and Gauleiters of the Party in Posen on October 6, 1943, I repeated this argument: "I would like to look over the attempts made in all areas [with the A-4] and compare them with the successful attempts made with a racing car. This racing car has been manufactured individually by top experts, and we must now produce it on a mass scale like a normal automobile, but with the performance of a racing car. This transition from top-quality work to mass production will presumably cause some problems" (Ba R 3/1548).
19. Führer Protocol of August 19–22, 1943, item 24 (Ba R 3/1507).
20. Himmler's calendar page of August 21, 1943 (Ba NS 19/new 1444).
21. Himmler's letter to Speer, August 21, 1943 (Ba R 3/1583).
22. Outline of Himmler's speech, October 4, 1943, in Posen to SS squad commanders (p. 13 Dok. Nuremberg 1919 PS 129).
23. Himmler's speech to the SS squad commanders in Posen on October 4, 1943 (Nuremberg document 1919 PS).
24. According to E. Georg, *Die wirtschaftlichen Unternehmungen der SS* (Stuttgart, 1963), p. 38.
25. David Irving writes in *The Mare's Nest* (Boston, 1965), pp. 121–122: "The second result of the disorganisation and uncertainty stemming from the first R.A.F. Bomber Command attack on secret-weapons research at Peenemünde was that S.S. Reichsführer Heinrich Himmler now had the opportunity he had been seek-

ing since April to penetrate this, the most crucial field of the German war effort, as part of his sustained attempt to secure control over the entire German armaments sector. His method was attractive for its simplicity: the *S.S.* intervened wherever there was a gap where it could either offer assistance or remedy a defect. Once in, it tightened its grip until its control was absolute.

For his subversion of the secret-weapons programme, Himmler selected an *S.S.* engineer, Major-General Hans Kammler, the forty-two-year old designer of concentration camps in general and the Auschwitz gas chambers in particular. Kammler's career was to be a remarkable one: initially charged, as we shall see, with directing minor construction projects associated with the *A 4* programme, he was to end up as supreme tactical commander of all German secret weapons, including the *Me. 262* jet-fighter formations. The progress of his career may stand as a textbook example of controlled infiltration.

At 11.30 a.m. on the 22nd Himmler arrived at the 'Wolf's Lair' to conclude the final arrangements for the *A 4* rocket programme; the joint meetings with Hitler and Speer lasted until the early evening. Himmler was intervening to offer 'assistance' to Speer:

> Arising from a suggestion [Speer recorded that night] the Führer orders that—jointly with the *S.S.* Reichsführer [Himmler], and utilising to the full the manpower which he has available in his concentration camps—every step must be taken to promote both the construction of *A 4* manufacturing plants, and the resumed production of the *A 4* rocket itself.
>
> At Hitler's behest, production at Peenemünde was to be considered a temporary expedient only, until production could be resumed in factories safe from air attack, making use as far as possible of caves and suitable 'bunkers'. The expansion of the Peenemünde pilot factor was to be checked."

26. Kammler's telegram to Dr. Brandt, October 16, 1943 (Ba NS 19/old 273).
27. Assignment by Supreme Command of Army, Head of Army Armaments and Commander in Chief of Reserve Army, October 19, 1943.
28. Kammler's telegram to Dr. Brandt to inform Himmler, October 20, 1943, 8:15 P.M. (Ba NS 19/old 273).
29. Written information from Dr. A. Poschmann, February 13, 1978, to the author.
30. Chronicle of December 10, 1943 (Ba R 3/1738).
31. Chronicle of January 13, 1944, p. 8 (Ba R 3/1739).
32. Chronicle of January 14, 1944, p. 11 (Ba R 3/1739).
33. From Jean Michel, *Dora* (Paris, 1975), p. 175.
34. This was a major action, meant to benefit Sauckel's forced laborers too.
35. Written information from Dr. A. Poschmann, February 13, 1978, to the author.
36. Speer's letter to Brandt, August 5, 1944 (Ba R 3/1574).
37. According to a report from the Economic Administrative Headquarters, Office D/III, September 22, 1943 (NO 1010), they had managed to reduce the average mortality rate of all concentration camps to 2.09 percent of the inmates in August 1944. Hence, 5.7 percent was an abnormally high rate.
38. According to a report by Professor Dr. Walter Bartel of Humbold University, East Berlin, in *Der Widerstandskämpfer*, Vienna, 1969.
39. According to production figures in David Irving, *The Secret Weapons of the Third Reich* (London, 1964).
40. From Führer Protocol, May 13, 1944 (Ba R 3/1509).
41. According to Willi A. Boelcke, *Deutschlands Rüstung im zweiten Weltkrieg* (Frankfurt, 1969), p. 291.
42. Himmler's letter to Kammler, August 6, 1944 (Ba NS 19/new 2055). Copies were received only by SS Obergruppenführer Jüttner, chief of staff in Himmler's new capacity, and an SS Obersturmbannführer Grothmann.

43. Speer's letter to Jüttner, August 11, 1944 (Ba R 3/1768).
44. Himmler's telegram to Speer, September 29, 1944 (Ba NS 19/new 949).
45. Speer's telegram to Himmler, November 11, 1944 (Ba R 3/1583).
46. David Irving, *The Secret Weapons of the Third Reich* (London, 1964), p. 354.
47. Jüttner's edict as Chief of Staff of Army Armaments, December 31, 1944, to the agencies in his jurisdiction (MGFA, Do 44/119: FE 3033).

CHAPTER 16

1. Führer Protocol, April 11, 1943, item 4 (Ba R 3/1507).
2. Goering's letter to Speer, October 10, 1943 (Ba R 3/1580).
3. Speer's letter to Hitler, April 19, 1944 (Ba R 3/1516).
4. Letter from Dr. Abrahamczik to Personal Assistant Dr. Brandt, August 25, 1943 (Ba NS 19/old 273).
5. Letter of Reich Manager of *Das Ahnenerbe* to Dr. R. Brandt, Personal Staff of the SS Reichsführer, November 9, 1943 (Ba NS 19/old 273).
6. Dr. Brandt's letter to Sievers, December 3, 1943 (Ba NS 19/old 273).
7. Speer's letter to Kammler, December 17, 1943 (Ba R 3/1585).
8. Speer's letter to Himmler, December 22, 1943 (Ba R 3/1583).
9. Führer Protocol of March 5, 1944, item 1: "The Führer . . . acknowledges . . . Goering's edict for Kammler's special construction" (Ba R 3/1509).
10. Himmler's telegram to Supreme SS and Police Commander Koppe in Krakow, December 12, 1943 (Ba NS 19/new 317).
11. Brandt's letter to Koppe, January 26, 1944 (Ba NS 19/new 317).
12. Memorandum for Pohl in letter (Ba NS 19/new 317).
13. Pohl's letter to Dr. Brandt, February 17, 1944 (Ba NS 19/new 317).
14. Himmler's letter to Kammler, May 8, 1944 (Ba NS 19/new 228).
15. Brandt's letter to SS Obersturmbannführer Schleif and to SS Squad Commander Kammler, September 18, 1944 (Ba NS 19/new 228).
16. Schleif's letter to Dr. Brandt, September 25, 1944 (Ba NS 19/new 228).
17. Brandt's letter to Schleif, October 4, 1944 (Ba NS 19/new 228).
18. Schleif's letter to Brandt, October 9, 1944 (Ba NS 19/new 228).
19. Dr. Brandt's letter to Schleif, October 23, 1944 (Ba NS 19/new 228).
20. Schleif's letter to Dr. Brandt, November 21, 1944 (Ba NS 19/new 228).
21. Himmler's letter to Pohl, December 17, 1943 (Ba NS 19/new 317).
22. Pohl's letter to Himmler, January 24, 1944 (Ba NS 19/new 317).
23. Krauch's letter to Himmler, December 18, 1943 (Ba NS 19/new 1677).
24. Dr. Brandt's letter from the Personal Staff to SS Oberführer Kranefuss, December 29, 1943 (Ba NS 19/new 1677).
25. Letter from SS Oberführer Fritz Kranefuss, chairman of the board at Brabag, to Himmler, November 3, 1944 (Ba NS 19/new 1677).
26. Dr. Brandt's letter to SS Oberführer Fritz Kranefuss, November 7, 1944 (Ba NS 19/new 1677).
27. According to Speer Report No. 6 (p. 3) drawn up by the United States Strategical Bombing Survey, Geilenberg estimated that in November 1945, 90,000 tons of airplane fuel and jet fuel could be produced underground every month. In April 1944, before the start of the attack series, 175,000 tons of airplane fuel were manufactured.
28. Hermann Giessler, *Ein anderer Hitler* (Starnberg, 1977), p. 434.
29. Gebhardt's patients included King Leopold of Belgium and the leading Belgian electro-industrialist Danny Heinemann, owner of Sofina. He let the physician treat him at his hospital even after 1933.

30. Dr. Heissmeier's report: "Internistischer Befund am 9. Februar 1944" (private archive).

31. Report by Professor Dr. Gebhardt (private archive).

32. Professor Koch's report of February 15, 1944 (private archive).

33. In his diary, Milch noted on May 26, 1947, i.e. during his captivity: "Professor Koch, who, under pressure from Dr. Brandt, also treated him [Speer] at Hohenlychen, supposedly said that Gebhardt had told him they would now have to burst Speer's lung. When Koch refused, Gebhardt claimed he had merely wanted to test him." From David Irving: Tragedy of the German Luftwaffe

34. Professor Dr. Friedrich Koch remained the leading internist at the University of Berlin (Charité) during and after the Soviet occupation period.

35. Dorsch's protocol of his meeting with Hitler on March 5, 1944, item 9 (Ba R 3/1509). See also *Inside the Third Reich*, pp. 336–37.

36. Calendar page, March 6, 1944 (Ba NS 19/new 1445).

37. Calendar page, March 9, 1944 (Ba NS 19/new 1445). During this critical period, Himmler too visited Hitler conspicuously often. His calendar pages say: "March 15, 1944, conference with Führer, 3 to 4:30 P.M. March 16, 1944, lunch with Führer, 2 P.M. to 4 P.M. at Führer's; 7:30 P.M. supper with Führer. March 17, 1944, 2 P.M., lunch with Führer; 4 to 5:30 P.M., meeting with Führer. March 20, 1944, 2 P.M., Bormann's office. April 3, 1944, 2 P.M., lunch with Führer, stroll, tea, newsreel; 7 P.M. back to Bergwald [Himmler's house near Berchtesgaden]" (Ba NS 19/new 1445).

38. Himmler's letter to Goering, March 9, 1944, and Pohl's accompanying letter (US document 1584-PS, Exhibit US 221).

39. Sworn statement by Professor Koch, May 12, 1947 (private archive).

40. Sworn statement by Professor Koch, May 12, 1947 (private archive).

41. See *Inside the Third Reich*, pp. 334–35.

42. Himmler's assignment to SS Squad Commander Prof. Dr. Gebhardt, March 20, 1944 (Microfilm T-175, roll 70 F: 7228).

43. Sworn statement by Professor Koch, May 12, 1947 (private archive).

44. Speer's letter to Hitler, April 19, 1944 (Ba R 3/1516).

45. Calendar page, April 19, 1944: "11 A.M., SS Squad Commander F. Kehrl: 11:30, Berghof; 2:00, lunch with Führer; 3:00 P.M., Bormann; 4:30 P.M., Berchtesgaden; 8:30, supper with Field Marshal Keitel; 11:30, Dr. Desch. Almost illegible, it could mean "Dorsch." On April 20, around 3 P.M., Himmler again had lunch with Hitler at the Berghof, returning at 5:30 (Ba NS 19/new 1445).

46. See entries in the Chronicle of April 20–22, 1944 (Ba R 3/1739).

47. Speer's letter to Himmler, May 17, 1944 (Ba R 3/1583).

48. The Chronicle reports that on April 24, 1944, "at 10 A.M., the minister flies to Obersalzberg with Liebel, Hettlage, and Fränk. At 11:30 A.M., a meeting takes place with SS Reichsführer, Bergwald" (Ba R 3/1739).

49. SD report of July 2, 1944. From Heinz Boberach, *Meldungen aus dem Reich* (Neuwied, 1965).

50. Chronicle of April 24, 1944: "At 5:30 P.M., the minister goes to meeting with Führer—first time since he fell ill. He is received by Führer with utmost cordiality on the steps of the house. In the subsequent lengthy discussion, a total clarification of the situation takes place. The Führer declares that he is agreeable in advance to all measures that Herr Speer regards as correct in the area of construction. The brief personal conversation sufficed to destroy the months of efforts by others to separate construction from armaments, and to strengthen the minister's authority even more" (Ba R 3/1739).

51. See *Inside the Third Reich*, pp. 341–42.

52. Chronicle of April 26, 1944: "This evening closes with the minister's attempt to provide a similarly self-responsible position for the building trade, as the armaments industries have. It is simultaneously the end of this long, more or less secret, and not always nicely waged struggle of the Todt Organization against the building trade and vice versa" (Ba R 3/1739).

53. Himmler's calendar on April 27, 1944: "12:30 to 13:00 Min[isterial] Dir[ektor] Dorsch" (Ba NS 19/new 1445).

54. Führer Protocol of May 13, 1944, item 8 (Ba R 3/1509).

55. Führer Protocol of May 13, 1944, item 8 (Ba R 3/1509). The term "ready to build" in these reports was applicable to "the state that allows setting up and operating machine tools, whereby the air-conditioning systems [have to] be capable of functioning."

CHAPTER 17

1. Initially, Field Marshal Milch was to run the Fighter Plane Staff. He was supplanted by Saur while I was still out sick.

2. Statements in the Pohl trial, etc. (Ba Allg. Proz. 1, XL 1). Printed in an elaboration by Professor Dr. Walter Bartel of the Humboldt University, Berlin, p. 70.

3. A postwar report from Professor Bartel's elaboration.

4. An article by Hans Marsalek, Vienna, in *Die Tat,* December 4, 1971.

5. Additional verdict against Pohl et al. (Ba. Allg. Proz. 1 XLI W 5, p. 72). Includes Hohberg's testimony that he provided the initiative for calling in the SS for Fighter Plane Staff Program.

6. From *Kommandant in Auschwitz*, autobiographical material by Rudolf Höss, ed. by Martin Broszat (Munich, 1963), p. 191.

7. Himmler's speech to generals in Sonthofen, June 21, 1944, from Himmler: *Geheimreden* (Berlin, 1974), p. 199.

8. Kammler's letter to Dr. Brandt on Himmler's Personal Staff with accompanying graphs, January 11, 1945 (Ba NS 19/old 378).

9. The difference in regard to Kammler's data, i.e., 425,000 completed square meters of underground factories, must have been due to the fact that several months pass between the completion of a factory building and the beginning of operations. When interrogated at the Nuremberg Trial, I testified that, toward the end of the war, "with 300,000 square meters, an insignificant number of underground factories had been put into operation, but we were planning 3 million square meters." Speer's testimony at the Nuremberg Military Tribunal, printed in Adelbert Reif, *Albert Speer* (Munich, 1978), p. 37.

10. Chronicle of May 26, 1944 (Ba R 3/1739).

11. Himmler's directive to the SS Reich Police Physician, early March 1945. This title indicated that Gebhardt was the supreme SS physician.

12. Reproduced in facsimile in Hans Marsalek, *Die Geschichte des Konzentrationslagers Mauthausen* (Vienna, 1974), p. 103. Separated according to camps. The number coincides roughly with Sommer's testimony at the Nuremberg Trial; he stated that at the end of 1944 "approximately 500,000 or 600,000 concentration camp inmates were supplied by the SS Economic Headquarters for labor." Sworn statement by Sommer. Additional verdict against Pohl, et al (Ba Allg. Proz. 1 XLI pp. 5, 51).

13. From "Proposal for Simplifying the Organizational and Administrative Foundations of the Todt Organization," January 29, 1945 (Ba NS 19/new 1707). A statistic of November 30, 1944, shows that the Todt Organization had 1,284,200

workers. This figure breaks down into 260,500 free Reich Germans; 752,200 free foreigners (mainly forced to work by Sauckel's administration); 21,800 imprisoned Reich Germans (these must have been chiefly concentration camp prisoners); 115,700 foreign prisoners, and 134,000 prisoners of war.

14. Eugen Kogon, *Der SS-Staat* (Munich, 1974), p. 45.
15. Albert Speer's memorandum to Hitler, July 20, 1944, lists this division strength (Ba R 3/1522).
16. From Felix Kersten, *Totenkopf und Treue*, undated, p. 343.
17. Speech manuscript, taped, April 16, 1945 (Ba R 3/1557). See also *Inside the Third Reich*, p. 475.
18. Joseph Goebbels always wrote down his impressions on the next day, this must have come from Hitler to Goebbels on March 27, 1945.
19. Speer's memorandum to Hitler, March 15, 1945 (Ba R 3/1535).
20. Joseph Goebbels, *Diaries*, entry of March 31, 1945.
21. Joseph Goebbels, *Diaries*, entry of April 4, 1945.
22. Telegram of April 3, 1945, from SS Obersturmbannführer H. Karl, head of the Construction Inspection, Reich-South, to Standard Commander Schleif on Kammler's Berlin staff (Ba NS 19/old 1278).
23. Radio message from SS Obersturmbannführer Glaser, Upper Bavarian Experimental Institute, Oberammergau, about Karl, to Kammler (Ba NS 19/old 1278).
24. Mataré's radio message, April 8, 1945, to Kammler staff for SS Obergruppenführer Dr. Kammler (Ba NS 19/old 1278).
25. Radio message from SS Obersturmbannführer Staeding, Plenipotentiary of the Führer for Jet Planes, April 14, 1945, to Professor Messerschmitt and Director Degenkolb (Ba NS 19/old 1278).
26. Kammler's radio message of April 17, 1945, to SS Command Headquarters, Office II, Organization Division I (Ba NS 19/old 1678).
27. Kammler's radio message on April 16, 1945 (Ba NS 19/old 1278). The unimportant radio message was transmitted simultaneously to "Reich Minister Professor Speer, Reich Marshal of the Greater German Reich, SS Reichsführer, Liaison Officer of the Luftwaffe to the Führer Colonel von Below, Liaison Officer of the SS Reichsführer to the Führer SS Squad Commander and Lieutenant General of the Waffen-SS Fegelein."
28. Kammler's wire to Frank, Messerschmitt Works, Regensburg, April 16, 1945 (Ba NS 19/old 1278).
29. Jean Michel (a prisoner in the Central Works), *Dora* (Paris, 1975), pp. 299, 301.

Chapter 18

1. Situation report of Armaments Inspection III, Berlin, August 15, 1941 (Ba RW 20–3/15).
2. According to Rudolf Jordan, *Erlebet und Erlitten* (Starnberg, 1971), p. 234, "this extreme demand was made in September 1941 during the daily ministerial discussion with Dr. Goebbels."
3. From "History of Armaments Inspection III, Berlin, from October 1, 1940, to December 31, 1941," pp. 315–16 (Ba RW 20–3/10).
4. From "Situation Report of Armaments Inspection III, Berlin, November 15, 1941" (Ba RW 20–3/16).
5. From Robert M. W. Kempner, *Die Ermordung von 35,000 Berliner Juden*, p. 180.

6. From "History of Armaments Inspection III, Berlin, from October 1, 1940, to December 31, 1941," pp. 315–16 (Ba RW 20–3/10).

7. From "History of Armaments Inspection III, Berlin, from October 1, 1940, to December 31, 1941," pp. 315–16 (Ba RW 20–3/10).

8. From *News of the Reich Ministry of Weapons and Munitions*, no. 1, March 31, 1942.

9. Joseph Goebbels, *Diaries*, entry of May 17, 1942.

10. Thus, according to this figure, some 120,000 Jews were still living in Germany in May 1942.

11. Joseph Goebbels, *Diaries*, entry of May 17, 1943.

12. From "Situation Report of Armaments Inspection XIII, Berlin, November 15, 1941 (Ba RW 20–3/16). A further indication that a job in the armaments industry also protected the lives of the families of the Jews employed. The list drawn up by Robert M. W. Kempner covers only some 14,000 Jews deported from October 18, 1941, to September 26, 1942, from Berlin. In reality, however, the number must have been 35,000.

13. Excerpt from an unpublished journal entry of Joseph Goebbels, September 30, 1942. Supplied by David Irving.

14. Circular no. 108/42 of the Armaments Command Berlin III of the Reichminister for Weapons and Munition, November 6, 1942 (Ba RW 21–3/2).

15. Himmler's speech to the SS Junkers, November 23, 1942. From Heinrich Himmler: *Geheimreden* (Berlin, 1974), p. 200.

16. Sauckel's circular to the chairmen of the National Labor Offices, November 26, 1942. From IMT Trial, vol. 37, pp. 495–96.

17. War diary of the Armament Command, Berlin, of Armaments Inspection III, Berlin, November 9, 1942 (Ba RW 21–3/2).

18. Letter of the Plenipotentiary for Labor, March 26, 1942, to his National Labor Offices (Nuremberg Document L–156, Exhibit RF 1522). In Adelbert Reif, *Albert Speer*, p. 105. On April 23, 1943, the Reich Security Office also reported: "After the Reich Minister for Armaments and Munitions released those Jews that were active in war-crucial labor and not in camps, they were removed from their work on February 27, 1943, after previous agreement with the plenipotentiary for labor." Report by the Reich Security Headquarters, April 27, 1943. Photocopy in Robert M. W. Kemper, *Eichmann und seine Komplizen*.

19. Entry of February 27, 1943, in the war diary of the Berlin Armaments Command (Ba RW 21–3/2).

20. In its verdict, the Nuremberg Court did not conclude from this that I was involved in the deportation of these Jews.

21. Joseph Goebbels, *Diaries*, pp. 251–52.

22. According to oral information from Dr. Ernst Ludwig Ehrlich, October 20, 1978.

23. From *Spandau Diaries*, entry of November 25, 1954. During the Frankfurt Book Fair in the fall of 1975, Gerald J. Gross, of Macmillan Publishers, asked me to check the authenticity of Goebbels's diary pages, which had been offered to him at that time by a middleman. I spent several hours of two days reading these pages, during which period I came upon an entry, likewise from around late 1941, which, with almost the same as my own words in Spandau, expressed the propaganda leader's annoyance at the unteachable Germans, who had resisted his National Socialist slogans.

24. Himmler's speech to the SS squad commanders, October 4, 1943, in Posen (Nuremberg document 1919 PS).

25. Himmler's speech to the Reichsleiters and Gauleiters in Posen, October 6, 1943

(Ba NS 19/HR/10). During a long conversation in my Heidelberg home in 1975, Professor Erich Fromm commented that the nation of poets and thinkers, the nation of Goethe and Schiller, had not gone under in the period of National Socialism. Goebbels and Himmler offer evidence for this rule.

26. Joseph Goebbels, *Diaries*, entries of March 9 and 15, 1943.

CHAPTER 19

1. "Transcript of a discussion between SS Obergruppenführer Heydrich and Gauleiter Meyer in the presence of Ministerial Director Schlotterer, Reichsamtsleiter Dr. Leibbrandt, as well as SS Obersturmbannführer Dr. Ehrlich, October 4, 1941, 11 A.M." (Ba NS 19/new 1734).
2. Goering's letter to Heydrich, July 31, 1941. State Archive, Nuremberg.
3. T 501, film 219, National Archives, Washington, D.C., Record Services, p. 346. (In war diary of QQu, May 8, 1942.)
4. Ibid., p. 380.
5. Ibid.
6. Himmler's order to Krüger, July 19, 1942 (Ba NS 19/new 1757).
7. War diary of Warsaw Armaments Command, July 1942 (Ba RW 23/19).
8. Memorandum of July 27, 1942, of SS Hauptsturmführer and Staff Commander Fellenz, also deputy of SS and Police Commander in Krakow (Ba NS 19/new 1765).
9. These quotations are from the report of SS Untersturmführer Benthin, head of the field office of the Security Police in Przemysl, July 27, 1942 (Ba NS 19/new 1765).
10. Ibid.
11. Ibid.
12. Report on a meeting between Paul, the district captain for Przemysl, and SS Obersturmbannführer With of the staff of General Unruh, August 24, 1942 (Ba NS 19/new 1765). General Unruh was supposed to implement a special assignment from Hitler to mobilize soldiers as a result of administrative reductions.
13. A Supreme Field Command is a higher military administrative post, roughly on the level of the Armaments Inspection, which can be gleaned from the fact that it was headed by a lieutenant general.
14. T 501, film 216, National Archives, Washington, D.C., Record Service, pp. 965 and 966, August 5, 1942.
15. Ibid., pp. 924 and 925.
16. From war diary of the Warsaw Armaments Command, August 1942 (Ba RW 23/19).
17. Due to Hitler's order, on May 7, 1942, the Armaments Office (previously under the Supreme Command of the Wehrmacht and hence Field Marshal General Keitel) together with the Armaments Inspections for the Reich and the occupied and autonomous areas, passed into my jurisdiction.
18. Keitel's order to General Gienanth, the military commander in chief of the Generalgouvernement (Ba NS 19/new 253).
19. Himmler's telephone conversation of September 9, 1942 (Ba NS 19/new 1439).
20. The military commander in chief in the occupied territories were subject to the Supreme Command of the Wehrmacht.
21. Letter from General Gienanth, military commander in chief of the Generalgouvernement, September 18, 1942, to the Wehrmacht Commands Staff (Ba NS 19/new 353).

22. T 501, film 216, National Archives, Washington, D.C., Record Service, pp. 1129–30. Report period August 16 to September 15, 1942.

23. From the report of the Labor Office, subbranch Przemysl, Government Supreme Inspector Neumann, July 20, 1942, repeated in the report of SS Untersturm-führer Benthin, head of the field office of the Security Police in Przemysl, July 27, 1942 (Ba NS 19/new 1765).

24. Letter from General Gienanth, military commander in chief in the General-gouvernement, September 18, 1942, to Wehrmacht Command Staff (Ba NS 19/new 353).

25. Protocol of Speer's meeting with Hitler, September 20–22, 1942, item 44 (Ba R 3/1505).

26. Himmler's telephone conversation, September 22, 1942 (Ba NS 19/new 1439).

27. Underlined by author.

28. Himmler's order of October 9, 1942 (Ba NS 19/new 352). This order was sent to Pohl, Krüger, and Globocnik, inter alios.

29. Chronicle of the Armaments Ministry, entry of October 8, 1942 (Ba R 3/1737).

30. According to Heinz Höhne, *Der Orden unter dem Totenkopf* (Gütersloh, 1967), p. 293, the SS and police administration had split away from the administration of the Generalgouvernement and was playing itself up as the actual ruler of Frank's domain.

31. T 501, film 225, National Archives, Washington, D.C., Record Service, p. 2; and film 175, pp. 2–527, 359.

32. Report on the third quarter of 1942 by the Armaments Inspection in the Generalgouvernement (Ba RW 23/1).

33. Report on the meeting of the Armaments Commission of the Generalgouverne-ment, October 24, 1942 (Ba RW 23/2). This was a mixed commission, in which the local representatives of all the offices of my ministry under the chairmanship of General Schindler met with the representatives of those agencies of other government domains, for instance Labor, Food, Railroads.

34. Frank's diary. Government meeting of December 9, 1942 (Ba R 51 II/243, p. 16).

35. Evidently, these 16,000 Jews were a portion of the above-mentioned 40,000 Jews. According to testimony given by Captain Hassler on August 20, 1964, in the Wolf trial (quoted in the *Süddeutsche Zeitung*, Aug. 27, 1964, Hassler asked Colonel Freter in July 1942 whether it was true that the Jews were being annihilated. Freter supposedly remained silent to this question and then stated that Hassler had three alternatives: he could state his opinion out loud, and then his life would be destroyed; he could report that he was ill; or he could remain in the Armaments Command and support him, Freter, in doing whatever was still possible for the Jews.

36. Himmler's letter to Krüger, January 9, 1943 (Ba NS 19/new 352).

37. Here, a different number is given. Perhaps the SS itself had no clear overview of the Jewish manpower employed.

38. War diary of the Armaments Inspection of the Generalgouvernement, February 15, 1943 (Ba RW–23/3).

39. Speer's letter to the head of the Luftwaffe Legal Office, General Supreme Staff Judge von Hammerstein, September 15, 1944 (Ba R 3/1578). According to this, Colonel Freter was in the officers' corps; and if he thereby was under the jurisdiction of the Luftwaffe, this did not exclude the possibility that the SS battle commander handed down verdicts and carried out sentences through the local court-martials. According to information from the West German Federal Archive (Military Archive, Freiberg), of July 22, 1980, this proceeding was halted in December 1944.

40. War diary of the Armaments Inspection of the Generalgouvernement (Ba RW–23/3).
41. Ibid.
42. Ibid.
43. Ibid.
44. Ibid.
45. Ibid.
46. Ibid.
47. Frank's diary, entry of May 31, 1943 (Ba R 52 II/203, pp. 45ff.).
48. War diary of the Armaments Inspection of the Generalgouvernement (Ba RW–23/3).
49. Report of the Armaments Inspection of Lvov, late August 1943 (Ba R 3/233).
50. Ibid. The Armaments Inspection, under General Wäger, summed up and evaluated the work of the Armaments Inspections.
51. War diary of the Armaments Inspection in the Generalgouvernement, Luftwaffe Division, for the third quarter of 1943 (Ba RW 23/13).
52. Ibid.
53. Ibid.
54. Report of the Defense Economy Officer (who was not under the Armaments Inspection, but subject to the military commander in chief) in the General-gouvernement, July 1943 (Ba WJI, DI/246).
55. From the war diary of the Armaments Inspection of the Generalgouvernement (Ba RW 23/3).

CHAPTER 20

1. Himmler's speech to the SS squad commanders in Posen, October 4, 1943 (Nuremberg document 1919 PS).
2. Himmler's speech to the Reichsleiters and Gauleiters in Posen, October 6, 1943 (Ba NS 19 HR/10).
3. Himmler's speech to the front-line generals in Posen, January 26, 1944. From Heinrich Himmler, *Geheimreden* (Berlin, 1974), p. 201.
4. Himmler's speech to the generals in Sonthofen, May 5, 1944. From Heinrich Himmler, *Geheimreden* (Berlin, 1974), p. 203.
5. Ibid.
6. Himmler's speech to the generals in Sonthofen, June 21, 1944. From Heinrich Himmler, *Geheimreden* (Berlin, 1974), p. 202.
7. Himmler's speech to the Reichsleiters and Gauleiters in Posen, October 6, 1943, pp. 17, 19, 24. The fact that I had already gone back to the Führer's head-quarters in Rastenburg on this afternoon, when Himmler gave his speech (according to his calendar entry, from 5:30 to 7:30 P.M. [Ba NS 19 new/1444]) is confirmed by Dr. Walter Rohland, who was then director of the board at the largest German steel company, Vereinigte Stahlwerke, as well as Harry Siegmund, the personal assistant of Gauleiter Greiser in Poland, as well as Field Marshal Milch, in an inquiry made by John Toland.
8. Himmler's speech at the SS squad commander congress in Posen, on October 4, 1943 (Nuremberg document 1919).
9. Himmler's speech to the Reichsleiters and Gauleiters in Posen, October 6, 1943 (Ba NS 19 HR/10).
10. Himmler's letter of January 26, 1942 (Nuremberg document NO–500).
11. From Helmut Krausnick, "Judenverfolgung" in *Anatomie des SS-Staates* and Broszat's statements in the same book Olten, 1965).

12. Letter from the Supreme SS and Police Commander in the Operational Zone of the Adriatic Coastal Region, November 4, 1943 (Nuremberg document NO–056). The annihilation action took place under the code name "Aktion Reinhardt."

13. From Frank's diary. Work session of October 19, 1943 (Ba R 52 II/207).

14. Heinz Höhne, in *Der Orden unter dem Totenkopf* (Gütersloh, 1967), makes it sound credible that the Reich Security Headquarters under Kaltenbrunner and the Economic Administrative Headquarters under Pohl fought about the policies concerning prisoners of concentration camps. The Reich Security Headquarters, for security reasons, wanted to put to death all the prisoners who, through their imprisonment in concentration camps, had become potent foes of the regime. But even without these differences of opinion, these were quite simply struggles for positions between two powerful SS leaders.

15. Schieber's letter to Speer, May 7, 1943 (Ba R 3/1631).

16. Majdanek trial in the Düsseldorf state court, day 319 of the trial, according to a story in *Die Welt*, February 21, 1979, p. 4.

17. See Heinz Höhne, *Der Orden unter dem Totenkopf* (Gütersloh, 1967), p. 358.

18. See diary of Rudolf Höss, *Kommandant in Auschwitz* (Stuttgart, 1958), pp. 138–39.

19. Himmler's directive of January 15, 1943, to the Reich Security Headquarters to be transmitted to all Supreme SS and Police Commanders and Commander in Chief of the Security Police (Ba NS 19/new 1542).

20. Report by SS Squad Commander Globocnik to Himmler, January 10, 1944 (Ba All. Proz. 2 NO 1–60).

21. Meeting of the Armaments Commission, November 10, 1943 (Ba RW 23/3).

22. Entry of November 11, 1943, in diary of Central Division of Armaments Inspection of Generalgouvernement (Ba RW 23/3).

23. Entry of November 11, 1943, in war diary of Administration Division (Ba RW 23/3).

24. Situation report of Defense Economy Commander in Generalgouvernement, November 1943 (Ba WiI D 1/246).

25. From the war diary of the administration of the Armaments Inspection in the Generalgouvernement, November 19–26, 1943 (Ba RW 23/3).

26. Meeting of Armaments Commission, December 29, 1943 (Ba RMFRUK 465 b). These two companies, incidentally, were not directly part of the armaments industry, nor were they subject to the Armaments Inspection.

27. Overview of the Armaments Inspector of the Generalgouvernement, October, November, December 1943 (Ba RW 23/3).

28. Monthly reports of Defense Economy Officer in Generalgouvernement, October, November, December, 1943 (Ba NS 4 Au 8).

29. Letter from Maurer, head of Office D II in Office Group D, Concentration Camps, September 4, 1943 (Ba NS 4 Au 8).

30. According to war diary of Armaments Inspection Cracow, November 4, 1943 (Ba RW 23/3).

31. Report of the session of the Armaments Commission, November 10, 1943 (Ba RMFRUK 465 b).

32. Report of meeting of Armaments Commission, November 15, 1943 (Ba RW 23/3).

33. Ibid., November 18, 1943. This referred to armaments plants of the districts of Radom and Krakow.

34. Frank's diary, entry of October 27, 1943 (Ba R 52 II/208, pp. 54ff.).

35. Chronicle of Ministry, entry of November 17, 1943 (Ba R 3/1738). Koppe,

incidentally, was not extradited to Poland and not sentenced to death or life imprisonment. He died in the meantime.

36. Report on the meeting of the Armaments Commission of December 8, 1943 (Ba RMFRUK 465 b).

37. Report on the fourth quarter of 1943 of the Armaments Inspection of the Generalgouvernement (Ba RW 23/3).

38. Report on the meeting of the Armaments Commission of the Generalgouvernement, January 12, 1944, pp. 5–6 (Ba RW 23/4).

39. Report on the meeting of the Armaments Commission of the Generalgouvernement, March 8, 1944, pp. 2, 13 (Ba RW 23/4).

40. Schlindler memorandum of March 13, 1944 (Ba RW 23/4).

41. As we recall, the exceedingly low rations determined by the Reich Food Minister did not benefit the working prisoners, since the supplies were decimated by corrupt SS men.

42. Note for a meeting with Schindler, March 28, 1944 (Ba RMFRUK 465).

43. Statistic of the Defense Economy Commander in the Generalgouvernement (Ba WID 1/7).

44. Situation report of the Defense Economy Officer in the Generalgouvernement for April 1944 (Ba W I D 1/246).

45. Situation report of the Defense Economy Officer in the Generalgouvernement for May 1944 (Ba W I D 1/246).

46. Minutes of the meeting of the Armaments Commission, June 7, 1944 (Ba RMFRUK 465 b).

47. Minutes of the meeting of the Armaments Commission, July 5, 1944 (Ba RMFRUK 465 b).

48. Report by General Gienanth, military commander in chief in the Generalgouvernement, September 18, 1942, to the Wehrmacht Command Staff (Ba NS 19/new 353).

49. From the diary of Governor-General Hans Frank, December 4, 1942 (Ba R 52 II/198).

50. Labor report from the Main Division for Labor in the government of the Generalgouvernement for the month of December 1943 (Ba R 52 IV/130).

51. Ibid.

52. From *Grosser Brockhaus* (Leipzig,, 1939), vol. 3, p. 214.

53. Report of Statistics Inspector Korherr to Dr. R. Brandt, April 19, 1943 (Ba NS 19/new 1570).

54. Nuremberg document NG 2586–G, vol. 13, green page 219.

55. From Eugen Kogon, *Der SS-Staat* (Frankfurt, 1948), p. 215.

CHAPTER 21

1. Armaments Inspection VIII with its seat in Breslau covered Upper and Lower Silesia, in the spring of 1943 it generated Armaments Inspection VIII b, which, with its seat in Katowice, was responsible for the Upper Silesia industrial area.

2. From the war diary of Armaments Inspection VIII, November 20, 1942 (Ba RW 20/8–13).

3. Quarterly report of Armaments Inspection VIII, Wroclau, end of December 1942 (Ba RW 20/8–13).

4. Second quarterly report in 1943 of Armaments Inspection VIII b, Katowice (Ba RW 20/8–13).

5. From fourth quarterly report, 1943, of Armaments Inspection VIII b, Katowice (Ba RW 20–8/32).

6. From fourth quarterly report, 1943, of Armaments Inspection VIII b, Katowice (Ba RW 20–8/32).
7. Speer's letter to Himmler, December 15, 1943 (Ba R 3/1583).
8. Speer's letter to Himmler, February 23, 1944 (Ba R 3/1583). Himmler's answer is not extant.
9. This was an agency of the Army Ordinance Office, whose orders could be transmitted only by way of the Armaments Inspection, which was under my aegis.
10. Machine tools presumably from army-owned factories, whose transferal was by way of a planning agency in my ministry.
11. From the war diary of the Armaments Inspection in Posen, October 22, 1943 (Ba RW 20/21–4).
12. Report of the meeting of the Armaments Commission, October 30, 1943 (Ba RW 20/21–7).
13. Report of the Armaments Commission, November 30, 1943 (Ba RW 20/21–7).
14. War diary of the Economy Division-East of the Armaments Inspector in the Generalgouvernement of December 10, 1943 (Ba RW 23/3).
15. Letter of Gauleiter Greiser to Pohl, February 14, 1944, reporting on Himmler's visit (Ba NS 19/new 82).
16. Pohl's letter to Greiser, February 16, 1944 (Ba NS 19/new 82).
17. Gauleiter Greiser's telegram to Himmler, June 9, 1944 (Ba NS 19/new 82).
18. Himmler's telegram to Greiser, June 10, 1944 (Ba NS 19/new 82).
19. Entry in war diary of Armaments Command, Litzmannstadt, June 17, 1944 (Ba RW 20/21–9).
20. Memorandum of III D-West, September 20, 1944 (Ba R 58/976).
21. Letter from Roman Halter to Albert Speer, April 23, 1971 (private archive). A similar incident must have been the transfer of 900 Jews from the armaments factory in Krakow-Pleszew (often mentioned in the reports of the Armaments Inspection of the Governor-General) to Brünnwitz, Czechoslovakia. "Three hundred women," according to the German-language New York newspaper *Aufbau,* January 14, 1972, "had been sent to Auschwitz for annihilation. Oskar Schindler went to Berlin. With the help of the army, he got the Reich Security Headquarters to send these doomed women from Auschwitz to Brünnwitz because they were supposedly crucial for the factory, which had been switched over to war production." This measure must have been due to the Armaments Inspection of the Generalgouvernement, which actually cited the Armaments Office of my ministry. The army was not responsible for such questions and repeatedly showed its lack of interest even after Gienanth's downfall.
22. It was only as of late April 1944 that construction within the German Reich territory was under the Todt Organization, which had previously been responsible only for all construction in the occupied territories.
23. Minutes of Dorsch's conversation with Hitler, April 6–7, 1944 (Ba R 3/1509). Further details of this incident are in *Inside the Third Reich,* pp. 336–42.
24. From Dorsch's transcript, April 17, 1944 (Ba R 3/1509).
25. Minutes of Speer's meeting with Hitler, May 19, 1944, item 3 (Ba R 3/1509).
26. Himmler's speech to the generals at Sonthofen, May 24, 1944. From Heinrich Himmler, *Geheimreden* (Berlin 1974), p. 203.
27. Telegram from the Reich Plenipotentiary for Hungary, Legation Councillor Veesemayer (Nuremberg document NS 5619).
28. Speer's telegram to Keitel, June 7, 1944 (Ba R 3/1586). The draft for this letter came from the Armaments Office, Office Group for Labor, as indicated by the letterhead. The Italian soldiers disarmed after the Badoglio overthrow were described as military internees.

29. Ibid.
30. Report of manpower employed in the Reich, May 1944 (Ba R3 / 1965). Presumably, the Jews employed in Upper and Lower Silesia and the Warta Gau are not included in these figures. These monthly "Reports on the Manpower Employed in the Reich" generally included the foreign workers and those from the concentration camps in one single figure. It was only in May 1944 that the precise figure of the Jews employed in the German armaments industry was given separately.
31. Schieber's letter to Speer, May 7, 1944 (Ba R 3/1631).
32. Transcript of the meeting of Armaments Commission IVa, Dresden, July 18, 1944 (Ba RW 20–4/20).
33. General Wäger's memorandum for Speer, August 7, 1944 (Ba R 3/1580).
34. Memorandum of Armaments Inspection IX, Kassel, September 6, 1944 (Ba RW 20–9/19).
35. Article by Tuvia Friedman, chairman of the Jewish World Organization of the Victims of the Nazi Regime, in the *Jerusalem Post*, May 19, 1970. (Quoted by Ferencz, p. 182.)
36. Cross-examination by Robert Jackson, June 21, 1946, at the International Military Tribunal, Nuremberg, printed in Adelbert Reif, *Albert Speer* (Munich, 1978), p. 106.
37. From "History of Armaments Inspection III, Berlin, from October 1, 1940, to December 31, 1941," pp. 315–16 (Ba RW 20–3/10).
38. From the diary of Armaments Inspection, Berlin, December 1942 (Ba RW 21–3/1).
39. Quarterly report of Armaments Inspection VIII, Wroclaw, end of December 1942 (Ba R 20–8/13).
40. The Führer Protocols likewise do not mention this reservoir of manpower, whether individually or in general.

Epilogue

1. Pohl's letter to Himmler, December 14, 1941, with an elaboration by Kammler (Ba NS 19/new 2065).
2. Transcript of discussion between SS Obergruppenführer Heydrich and Gauleiter Meyer in the presence of Ministerial Director Schlotterer, Reichsamtleiter Dr. Leibbrandt, as well as SS Obersturmbannführer Dr. Ehrlich, on October 4, 1941, 11 A.M. (Ba NS 19/new 1734).
3. Himmler's letter to Pohl, January 31, 1942.
4. "Transnistria" referred to an area of the Ukraine located between the Dniester and the southern Bug and partially inhabited by Rumanians. Under Rumanian administration from 1941 to 1944, it is Russian today. (Source: *Brockhaus*, 1957.)
5. Memorandum of the head of SS Headquarters, G. Berger, to Himmler, August 17, 1942 (Ba NS 19/new 1704).
6. Quoted from Adolf Hitler, *Monologe im Führerhauptquartier 1941–1944*. (Hamburg, 1980), August 8, (p. 54) and October 17, 1941 (p. 90), as well as August 6, 1942 (p. 331).
7. Memorandum of the head of SS headquarters, G. Berger, to Himmler, August 17, 1942 (Ba NS 19/new 1704.)
8. As a comparison, a construction project in Ryad, Saudi Arabia, in 1979 cost 6 million Saudi riyals, i.e., 300 million marks or 150,000 dollars, for 600 apartments to house 3,000 people; in other words, it would cost 2 billion marks

to build for 20,000 people. Thus, Himmler's assumption of many billions of marks to open up these territories was not farfetched.

9. Quoted from *Hitlers Monologe* (Hamburg, 1980), August 6 and 8, 1942 (pp. 331 and 334).

10. Ibid., October 17, 1941 (p. 90).

11. Himmler's letter to Pohl, January 31, 1942 (Ba NS 19/new 2065). On July 1, 1943, Kammler, in a letter to SS Standard Commander With on General von Unruh's staff, brought up this program again: "However, there is one thing I can tell you in confidence on the basis of a detailed discussion at the Reichsführer's: The Reichsführer considers it necessary to carry out a gigantic postwar construction program under his own aegis" (Ba NS 19/new 2065).

12. Hans Marsalek, *Geschichte des Konzentrationslagers Mauthausen* (Vienna, 1974), p. 69, says: "It can be assumed that the performance factor of a Mauthausen prisoner was at least an average of 50 percent of a civilian worker's."

13. Kammler's report of February 10, 1942, which was transmitted to Himmler through Pohl on March 5, 1942 (Ba NS 19/new 2065).

14. Kammler went on about this point: "One need only look at the wood-processing factories and sawmills of the Preussische Heimstätten during the postwar period. Ever since the growing shortage of raw-construction materials and construction manpower in 1938," the Luftwaffe, the navy, the army, and especially the German Labor Front had created government plants. "These efforts are rejected for reasons of national policy and taxation by the Reich Ministry of Economy, the Reich Ministry of Finances, and the responsible Party offices, like Reichleiter Bormann's office."

15. Kammler's report of February 10, 1942, accompanying Pohl's letter to Himmler of March 5, 1942 (Ba NS 19/new 2065).

16. Himmler's letter to Pohl, March 23, 1942 (Ba NS 19/new 2065).

17. Kammler's outline to Pohl's letter to Himmler, December 14, 1941 (Ba NS 19/new 2065).

18. Underlined by author.

19. Himmler's memorandum of March 12, 1942, to Pohl's letter to Himmler of March 5, 1942, with Kammler's accompanying material of February 10, 1942 (Ba NS 19/new 2065).

20. Himmler's letter to Pohl, March 23, 1942 (Ba NS 19/new 2065).

21. From *Die Deutsche Bauwirtschaft im Kriegseinsatz* (April 1943), published by the Plenipotentiary for Construction. With its construction plans, which would take an estimated 20 years to implement, the Party was way behind Himmler's figures. By 1941, 27 German cities were to be fairly revamped in their town-scapes by Hitler, as I wrote to Franz Xaver Schwarz, Reich Treasurer of the Nazi party, on February 19, 1941 (Ba R 3/1733). The construction budget for these Party and hall constructions, as well as the Party forums, would be 22–26 billion marks, according to my letter to Bormann on November 26, 1940 (Ba R 3/1733). From 1.1 to 1.3 billion marks a year would have been needed to carry out the work. To be sure, most of this construction was to be done by the German construction industry. The work would have claimed 9.1 percent of the entire German building capacity.

22. According to *Statistisches Jahrbuch 1939/40* (Berlin, 1940), pp. 32–33, the numbers of construction workers for 1933 are listed for the German borders of 1933, with the figures for Austria on p. 152 and for the Sudetenland on p. 154. On p. 383, the statistical figures from 1933 to June 1939 make it possible to compute the increased percentages of construction workers and adjacent trades

for mid-1939. The result is 10,056,000 workers, which includes not only the construction trade but also the extraction of raw materials (by the Group for Stones and Earth), as well as plumbing, locksmithing, carpentry, woodworking, etc.

23. In August 1944, German industry employed 5,722,000 foreigners, not all of whom were forced deportees, and 1,930,000 prisoners of war, a total of 7,652,000 workers. From *Statistische Schnellberichte zur Kriegsproduktion* (Ba R 3/1730).

24. Quoted from *Hitlers Monologe* (Hamburg, 1980), October 17, 1941 (pp. 90f.) and from the minutes of my meeting with Hitler on May 24, 1942 (Ba R 3/1504).

25. Quoted from *Hitlers Monologe* (Hamburg, 1980), January 27, 1942 (p. 239). Also see *Inside the Third Reich*, p. 440.

26. Quoted from *Hitlers Monologe* (Hamburg, 1980): September 25, 1941 (p. 71); August 8, 1942 (p. 334); July 5, 1941 (p. 39); October 17, 1941 (p. 93); October 29, 1941 (p. 116); August 3, 1942 (p. 324). One might fault such a compilation for possible distortion. But all these quotations, although separated in time, reflect Hitler's overall position.

27. Quoted from *Hitlers Monologe* (Hamburg, 1980), August 6, 1942 (p. 331).

28. Quoted from *Hitlers Monologe* (Hamburg, 1980), January 16, 1942 (p. 209); January 24, 1942 (p. 226); September 25, 1941 (p. 71); December 1, 1941 (p. 149); September 23, 1941 (p. 67); February 27, 1942 (p. 303).

29. Quoted from *Hitlers Monologe* (Hamburg, 1980), January 25, 1942 (p. 229).

APPENDICES

1. From Viktor E. Frank, *Man's Search for Meaning*, p. 72, paperback edition.
2. Bruno Bettelheim, *The Informed Heart*, 1943.
3. Simon Wiesenthal, *Die Sonnenblume*. Hoffmann and Campe, 1970.
4. Eugen Kogon, *Der SS-Staat* (Frankfurt/Main, 1965), p. 89.
5. Elena Skrjabin, *Leningrader Tagebuch* (Munich, 1942), p. 174.
6. Letter from the 1st State President of the Association of Democratic Resistance Fighters and Victims, State Association of Schleswig-Holstein, June 22, 1977, to the author.
7. Benjamin B. Ferencz, *Less than Slaves* (Cambridge, 1979), pp. 8, 190.
8. Martin Broszat, *Anatomie des SS-Staates* (Olten, 1965), vol. 2, p. 126.
9. Hermann Langbein, *Menschen in Auschwitz* (Vienna, 1972), pp. 3, 10.
10. Anonymous report, undated, to the Personal Staff of the SS Reichsführer (Ba NS 19/new 2302).
11. Article by Hans Marsalek in *Der Widerstandskämpfer*.
12. Himmler's letter to Pohl, March 23, 1942 (Ba NS 19/new 2065).
13. Himmler's letter to Goering, March 9, 1944 (Document 1584 PS, Exhibit US–221).
14. *Statistical Abstract of the United States, 1946*, published by the U.S. Department of Commerce, U.S. Government Printing Office, Washington, D.C., p. 211.
15. From Wagenführ: *Die deutsche Industrie im Kriege 1939–1945*, p. 47. The monthly performance was multiplied by 12 and then divided by 52 weeks. This figure coincides with a manpower report of December 31, 1944, which says that in November 1944, 5,981,000 employees in the armaments industry worked a total of 1,122,000,000 hours. Manpower Report, December 31, 1944 (Ba R 3/3009).
16. From the questioning of Otto Ohlendorf at the Military Tribunal, No. II–A, Case IX, p. 509 (Ba Allg. Proz. I, XXVII, A/5, 6).

17. Eugen Kogon, *Der SS-Staat* (Frankfurt, 1965), pp. 292f. Hermann Langbein says the same thing in *Menschen in Auschwitz* (Vienna, 1972), pp. 179, 514.

18. From my statements to the Gauleiters in Posen on October 6, 1943 (Ba R 3/1548). The Chronicle, pp. 152, 156, reports that on October 5, 1943, I signed an edict on this cooperation with the SD.

19. Eugen Kogon: *Der SS-Staat* (Frankfurt, 1965), p. 294.

20. Agreement between Fritz Sauckel and Robert Ley, May 7, 1942 (Nuremberg document 1913/PS).

21. From Sauckel's implementation order of September 30, 1943 (Nuremberg document 1913/PS).

22. From the verdict against Oswald Pohl et al, November 3, 1947 (Ba Allg. Proz. 1 X LI W 4, p. 83).

23. Verdict against Karl Krauch et al (I. G. Farben trial), July 29, 1948 (Ba Allg. Proz. 1 Rep. 501 IX ZCe no. 1).

24. Himmler's edict of June 21, 1943 (Ba R 43 II/1031 c).

25. Verdict against Oswald Pohl et al, p. 9 (Ba Allg. Proz. 1 X LI W 4).

26. The Communist-oriented Anti-Fascist Work Group, in its information service of June 23, 1969, even stated, by citing this point in the verdict: "Armaments Minister Speer . . . with his own directives, provided a handle for avoiding the death of concentration camp prisoners in Leau; Speer ordered that the forced laborers be fed adequately, and that endurable work conditions be created for them in order to achieve good work performance."

27. Order of the SS Economic Administrative Headquarters, December 28, 1942, on "Medical Activity in the Concentration Camps" (Nuremberg document 1469 PS), signed illegibly by an SS brigade commander.

28. Himmler's letter to Pohl, May 29, 1942, from *Der Reichsführer*, dtv, p. 150.

29. Printed in Hans Marsalek, *Die Geschichte des Konzentrationslagers Mauthausen* (Vienna, 1974), p. 86.

30. The report of the meeting of the Posen Armaments Commission of November 30, 1943, says: "Zeiss, Herbertow near Sollau. Polish convicts, after serving a sentence of more than six months (now one year) are handed over to a concentration camp in the Reich and are lost to industry. Further employment as protected prisoners in the institution's factories is, unfortunately, not possible" (Ba RW 20–21/7).

31. Speer's letter to Himmler, May 31, 1944 (Ba R 3/1583).

32. From Kranefuss's report to SS Obergruppenführer Karl Wolff, head of the Personal Staff of the SS Reichsführer, June 2, 1942, as draft for letter of June 21, 1942 (Ba NS 19/new 2220). In the same report, Kranefuss asked for the support of the SS leaders so that Brabag would be granted a larger number of "War Service Crosses" from the appropriate agencies. This matter, although trivial in itself, shows the influence that Himmler was thought to have. Kranefuss ought to have followed regulations and appealed to Goering's Four-Year Plan administration. The awarding of medals in industry was not within Himmler's jurisdiction.

33. Kranefuss's letter to Dr. Brandt, personal assistant to Himmler, September 4, 1942 (Ba NS 19/new 2220).

34. The territories of the Reich Commissioners were subdivided into General Commissariats.

35. Letter from head of Staff Headquarters of the Reich Commissioner for the Solidification of German Peoplehood, January 19, 1943, to the SS Reichsführer, Personal Staff (NS 19/new 1704).

36. Memorandum of the "liaison commander" (of the SS) "with the Reich Minister for the Occupied Eastern Territories, a Hauptsturmführer, to Gottlob Berger,

chief of SS Headquarters, January 23, 1943. This memorandum was transmitted to Himmler's Personal Staff (Ba NS 19/new 1704).

37. Ibid.

38. Berger's letter to Himmler, April 16, 1943 (Ba NS 19/new 1704).

39. The Reich Commissariat for the Eastland administered the northern occupied areas of the Soviet Union. The above-mentioned commissioner generals were under its jurisdiction.

40. Memorandum of Personal Assistant Straube of the "Chief of the Command Staff for Policies," Himmler's liaison office in Rosenberg's ministry, July 7, 1944, addressed to SS Obergruppenführer Berger (Ba NS 19/new 1704).

41. Speer's outline for Hitler's speech at Platterhof, Obersalzberg, June 26, 1944 (Ba R 3/1550). See also *Inside the Third Reich*, pp. 358–361.

42. Hitler's speech to industrial leaders at Platterhof, Obersalzberg, June 26, 1944. Printed in Hildegard von Kotze and Helmut Krausnick, *Es spricht der Führer* (Gütersloh, 1966).

43. From Albert Speer, *Politische Zusammenhänge* (Kransberg, July 1945), B III, p. 1. The writings of Otto Wagener, Hitler's economic adviser, indicated the radical strivings of the powerful socialistic faction inside the Party for a socialization of economy and industry. See H. A. Turner, ed., *Hitler aus nächster Nähe* (Berlin, 1978).

44. Joseph Goebbels, *Diaries*.

45. Ohlendorf's article "Wirtschaftliche Bilanz," December 28, 1944 (Ba R 7/2018). Note at how late a point Ohlendorf was still being tormented by such problems.

46. Draft for Hayler's speech of January 22, 1945 (Ba R 7/2006). The accompanying letter of the press office of the Reich Ministry of Economy, signed Lorch, to Ohlendorf, January 22, 1945, indicates indirectly that this speech was scheduled for late January. This letter also seems to say that the quoted last portion of the speech draft was done in cooperation with Ohlendorf and is derived from his ideas.

47. Draft for Hayler's speech, January 22, 1945 (Ba R 7/2006).

48. Otto Ohlendorf's article "Staat und Wirtschaft," in the special issue of the Organ of the Reich Chamber of Commerce for President Pletzsch's seventieth birthday, partially reprinted in *Deutsche Allgemeine Zeitung*, August 8, 1944.

49. Draft for a speech by Hayler, January 22, 1945 (Ba R 7/2006).

50. Schieber's letter to Speer, May 7, 1944 (Ba R 3/1631).

51. Ohlendorf's questioning by his defense attorney Dr. Aschenauer. Session of Military Tribunal, No. II–A, case IX, October 8, 1947 (Ba All. Proz. 1, XXVII a/5, 6).

52. Edict of October 9, 1943, on "The Concentration of Development to the Areas of Armaments and War Production," signed by Speer (Ba R D 76 1).

53. Edict on "Tasks of the Commission Chairmen," December 21, 1943, signed by Speer (Ba R D 76/1).

54. Hitler's edict of June 19, 1944 (Ba RD 76/1).

55. Chronicle of August 24, 1944 (Ba R 3/1740).

56. Letter of Supreme SS and Police Commander in defense district XVIII, January 28, 1945, to SS Standard Commander Brandt (Ba NS 19/new 767).

57. Report by Herbert Luckow, business manager of Air Research, Munich, to the Supreme SS and Police Commander in Defense District XVIII, undated (Ba NS 19/new 767).

58. Telegram of February 10, 1945, from Brandt to SS-Obergruppenführer Wolff (Ba NS 19/new 767).

59. Edict by Reich Minister for Armaments and War Production, February 19, 1944 (Ba R 43 II/11570).

60. Chronicle of March 29, 1944 (Ba R 3/1739).
61. From Willi A. Boelcke, *Deutschlands Rüstung im Zweiten Weltkrieg* (Frankfurt, 1969), p. 349.
62. Führer Protocol, April 6–7, 1944, item 23 (Ba R 3/1509).
63. Speer's letter to Himmler, November 10, 1944 (Ba NS 19/new 296).
64. Meyer's telegram to Himmler, January 4, 1945 (Ba NS 19/new 296).
65. Speer's letter to Himmler, November 10, 1944 (Ba R 3/1583).
66. See *Inside the Third Reich*, p. 419.
67. Jüttner's edict as chief of staff of Army Armaments, December 31, 1944, to agencies of his jurisdiction (MGFA, DO 44/119: FE 3033).
68. Edict of SS Reichsführer, special plenipotentiary Z, February 6, 1945 (Ba R 26 III/52).
69. Kammler's edict on jurisdictions in the Central Works. February 7, 1945 (Ba R 26 III/52).
70. From a Spandau note, October 3, 1952 (private archive).
71. Speer's telegram to Kammler, February 15, 1945 (Ba R 3/1768).
72. Document Center, Doc. Series 4070–4075.
73. T 501, film 219, pp. 422, 424, 426, 434.
74. At the head of this memorandum of August 7, 1944, the author is given as: "Office Group for Labor Rü.A.Arb [Armaments Office for Labor] E I, 2–121." The address is likewise given: Berlin NW 7 / Unter den Linden 36. Schmelter, the head of this group, came from the office of the Reich Labor Ministry that had been assigned to Gauleiter Sauckel for questions of labor employment.
75. Draft of a letter from Office Group for Labor Employment in the Armaments Office of my ministry, August 1944, as appended to General Wäger's memorandum to Speer, August 7, 1944 (Ba R 3/1580).
76. Letter from Speer to Goebbels, June 26, 1944 (Ba R 3/1580).
77. This refers to Lucy S. Dawidowicz's article in *Commentary*, November 1970. Reprinted in Adelbert Reif, *Albert Speer* (Munich, 1978). The documents do not contain anything like a letter to Hitler with a content such as Mrs. Dawidowicz maintains.

Index